Survival Spanish
Text/Workbook

Third Edition

Used to support a video course in beginning conversational Spanish

MIAMI-DADE
COMMUNITY COLLEGE
Number one in America.

KENDALL/HUNT PUBLISHING COMPANY
2460 Kerper Boulevard   P.O. Box 539   Dubuque, Iowa 52004-0539

SURVIVAL SPANISH TEXT/WORKBOOK

Prepared by:

Miami-Dade Community College
11011 S.W. 104 Street
Miami, Florida 33176

Copyright © 1984, 1986, 1989 by Miami-Dade Community College

ISBN 0–8403–5515–7

Printed in the United States of America
10 9 8 7 6 5 4 3 2

IN MEMORIUM

Dedicated to Enrique Rosa

1919-1986

Once in our lives, some of us have been fortunate to be touched
by the example and caring of a great teacher. The colleagues
and students who worked with Enrique Rosa will always remember him
this way. His love of the Spanish language, his dedication to
students and his support to his colleagues prevailed during his
many years as an educator. We dedicate this book to his memory,
recognizing the many hours and love he put forth in its creation.

Dr. Piedad Robertson

December 18, 1986

SURVIVAL SPANISH

is partially based on the materials of

"Individualizing Spanish for Speakers of English"

a project funded under Title IV-C of the Office of

Educational Innovation of the U.S. Office of Education

Miami-Dade Community College acknowledges the efforts of the following
faculty and administrative staff responsible for the SURVIVALS SPANISH project:

PROJECT ADMINISTRATOR:

Dr. Piedad Robertson
Vice President for Education
Miami-Dade Community College

Dr. J. Terence Kelly
Vice President
Miami-Dade Community College
North Campus

Neal Glenn
Director, Open College
Miami-Dade Community College

PROJECT CONSULTANT

Dr. Mirta Vega
I.S.S.E. Project Director
Dade County Board for Public
Instruction

Dr. Mercedes Calvera
I.S.S.E. Project Writer
Dade County Board for Public
Instruction

EDITOR

Dr. Enrique R. Rosa
Professor & Chairman
Department of Foreign Languages
Miami-Dade Community College

Marlene Negrin
Staff Associate
Miami-Dade Community College

FACULTY CONSULTANTS:

Edwin T. Frank
Associate Professor
Miami-Dade Community College

Alberto J. Herrera
Associate Dean of Arts & Humanities
Miami-Dade Community College

Benigno Larrea
Associate Professor
Miami-Dade Community College

Dr. Osvaldo Lopez
Assistant Professor
Miami-Dade Community College

Dr. Charlotte Parraga
Professor
Miami-Dade Community College

Dr. Robert A. Vitale
Professor
Miami-Dade Community College

EXECUTIVE PRODUCER:

Andrew Martin
Media Production
Miami-Dade Community College

PROGRAM DIRECTOR:

Howard "Pat" Weaver
Director of Media Production
Miami-Dade Community College

PROGRAM HOSTESS:

Vivian Ruiz
Actress

PROJECT STAFF:

Stephanie Schinoff
Assistant Professor
Miami-Dade Community College

Cindy Elliott
Manager
Product Development & Distribution
Miami-Dade Community College

SURVIVAL SPANISH

SURVIVAL SPANISH . . . a 36-program video and audio series which

used supporting print materials produced by Miami-Dade Community

College including:

> Text/Workbook - <u>The Text/Workbook</u> presents each
> video lesson's introductory
> conversation, a list of new
> vocabulary words, proper
> grammatical usage, and exercises
> to practice writing in Spanish.

> Audiotape Script Booklet - <u>The Audiotape Script</u>
> <u>Booklet</u> consists of the actual
> scripts of the audiotapes used
> for additional drill and rein-
> forcement.

Copies of these materials are available from:

> Miami-Dade Community College
> Product Development and Distribution
> 11011 S.W. 104 Street
> Miami, Florida 33176
> (305) 347-2158

PREFACE

This Text/Workbook is designed to teach beginning conversational Spanish using dialogs to introduce and reinforce grammatical concepts and key phrases. These conversations are divided into topics such as Retail Sales, Food Services, Health Services, Travel Services, and other situational conversations.

Accompanying this text are 36, half-hour videotapes that present the conversations and grammar and provide an opportunity for the student to hear clear pronunciation. The videotapes give the student a chance to repeat new sounds and words. In addition, audiotapes and audiotape scripts taken from the programs are available for practice and drill. These scripts are located in a separate booklet. Also, four audiotapes are available which correspond to the Pronunciation Lesson, Page 1 of the Text/Workbook.

This Text/Workbook can be used in conjunction with the videotapes or it can be used alone in a regular classroom situation with the assistance of a teacher. Because of the modular design of Survival Spanish, the series can be used in either the 36-program format or a lesser number of programs. This text can be used for college credit courses or for non-credit courses. The target population includes post-secondary students, high school students, vocational students, or any other student population wanting to learn basic conversational Spanish with emphasis on oral communication.

Lessons in the course are based in part on "Individualizing Spanish for Speakers of English", a project funded under Title IV-C of the Office of Educational Innovation of the U.S. Office of Education.

Organization of the Text/Workbook

The first chapter of the Text/Workbook is a preliminary lesson entitled Lección De Pronunciación. This lesson gives the student all the necessary rules for syllabication, word stress and sounds, and an explanation of the Spanish alphabet. An accompanying tape is available so that the student will hear proper diction and will be able to practice new sounds. This chapter provides the necessary foundation for proper Spanish pronunciation for the remainder of the text.

The subsequent lessons introduce conversations related to the major topic areas followed by grammatical explanations in an outline format. The Vocabulario comprises a list of new vocabulary words from the lesson and is organized by parts of speech, expressions, and numbers. After the Vocabulario, the workbook segment of the text provides space for students to complete the Ejercicios in order to practice writing Spanish words and sentences. An answer key for the Ejercicios and glossary are located at the end of the Text/Workbook. It is suggested that the student acquire a Spanish-English, English-Spanish dictionary.

TABLE OF CONTENTS

TOPIC: VOWELS, DIPHTHONGS, ALPHABET, SYLLABIFICATION AND RULES FOR ACCENTS.

This series of tapes includes all the different sounds of the vowels, consonants and alphabet in Spanish. The first part of the tape familiarizes you with the particular sound, and the second part provides space to repeat the sound.

I. **The spanish vowels are: a, e, i, o, u.**

Besides the five vowels, y sounds like the vowel i when it is the last letter of a word and when it stands alone, y means "and."

The student must give very special consideration to the sound of the Spanish vowel. They are sharp and clear-cut: there is not a glide sound in any of them as is frequently the case with the English vowels. Even when the Spanish vowels are unstressed they retain their essential value. Listen to the following table of approximations.

> a is like the a in ah!, father
> e is like the e in pet, get
> i is like the i in machine
> o is like the o in window
> u is like the oo in boot, moon

Let's practice the sound of the Spanish vowels. I will pronounce the word and you will repeat it when you hear the tone, then I will say the word once more.

For the vowel a		For the vowel e		For the vowel i		For the vowel o		For the vowel u	
cama	(bed)	ese	(that)	amigo	(friend)	boca	(mouth)	uno	(one)
blanca	(white)	leche	(milk)	dinero	(money)	foto	(photograph)	bufanda	(scarf)
casa	(house)	mesa	(table)	lila	(lilac)	malo	(bad)	universidad	(university)
para	(for)	tela	(cloth)	camisa	(shirt)	boleto	(ticket)	lunes	(Monday)
sala	(living room)	té	(tea)	libro	(book)	botones	(bellboy)	seguro	(insurance)
				italiano	(Italian)				

Spanish does not require that you memorize the pronunciation of each word. Once you have learned the sound of the vowels, diphthongs, consonants and a few combinations of vowels and consonants, plus the rules for stress, you will be able to pronounce any Spanish word correctly even if you have never seen it before. In order to stress a word correctly, you must first learn to divide words into syllables. Study the rules for division of words into syllables, page 9 of your textbook.

II. Diphthongs

In Spanish, the vowels a, e, and o are considered strong vowels, and the vowels i, u, and y are considered weak vowels. A combination of a strong and a weak vowel form a diphthong and it is pronounced as a single sound. The two weak vowels i and u together form a diphthong. Let's practice diphthongs. First I will give you the sound of the diphthong and then I will pronounce a word that contains the diphthong. You will then repeat the word when you hear the tone. I will pronounce the word once more after you. Notice that diphthongs are pronounced as one single sound.

O.K. Let's practice.

ia	yah	piano	piano	p'yah-no
ie	yeh	yet	fiesta	f yes-ta
io	yoh	yoke	indio	in-dyoh
iu	yoo	use	ciudad	cyoodad
ua	wah	wasp	cuando	cwahn-do
ue	weh	well	puente	pwehn-te
uo	woh	woe	cuota	kwoh-ta
ui	wee	weep	cuidado	kwee-da-do
uy	wee	weep	muy	mwee
ai	eye	eye	aire	eye-re
ay	eye	eye	hay	(like letter i)
au	ow	caw	gaucho	gow-cho
eu	eh-oo (no similar sound in English)		Europa	eh-ooh-ro-pa
ei	ay	bay	pleito	play-to
ey	ay	bay	ley	lay
ou	ow	owner	bou	bow
oi	oi	coin	oigo	oi-go
oy	oi	coin	hoy	oi

Words that stress the weak vowel (i, u) of a diphthong form two separate syllables and require an accent mark on the weak vowel. pe-lu-que-rí-a, tí-o, dí-a, Ra-úl.

III. Now the Spanish consonants

1) B and V

There is no difference in the pronunciation of these two letters in Spanish. Let's practice. This sound of b and v is similar to b in boy.

banco	(bank)	vestido	(dress)
vaso	(glass)	favor	(favor)
vino	(wine)	televisor	(television set)
boca	(mouth)	rubio	(blond)
boleto	(ticket)	beber	(to drink)

2) Now the letter C

C before the vowels e and i has an /s/ sound like century and city. In any other position it is pronounced like the English /k/.

canal	(channel, canal)	centro	(center)
color	(color)	cine	(movie)
calor	(heat)	cena	(dinner)
crédito	(credit)	acción	(action)
cliente	(customer)		

3) Now CH

CH is a letter of the Spanish alphabet. It is pronounced like the English ch in China. Notice that this letter is not in the English alphabet.

chico	(boy)	leche	(milk)
chaqueta	(jacket)	mucho	(much)
cuchara	(spoon)	noche	(night)
estrecho	(narrow)	ocho	(eight)
fecha	(date)		

4) The next one is D

At the beginning of a breath group and after n or l, the letter d in Spanish is pronounced like the English d in day. When it appears between vowels, it has a very distinct sound, similar to the th in mother, than.

día	(day)	todo	(all)
dos	(two)	Estados Unidos	(U.S.)
cuando	(when)	idea	(idea)
falda	(skirt)	recado	(message)
sueldo	(salary)	dedo	(finger)

5) **The letter F**

There is no appreciable difference between the sound of f in English and in Spanish. There is no ph in Spanish.

6) **Now G**

G before e or i is pronounced like the English "h" in "how" and "packhorse." G before a, o, or u and before a consonant is pronounced like "gap", "goat", "gun", "glue", "grow." The combination gue and gui are pronounced like the English words "guitar" and "guest" -- the u being silent.

imagen	(picture)	gato	(cat)	gris	(gray)	seguir	(to follow)
origen	(origin)	amigo	(friend)	grande	(big)	pague	(pay)
página	(page)	seguro	(insurance)	globo	(globe)	águila	(eagle)
gente	(people)	pregunta	(question)	regla	(rule)	alguien	(someone)

When the u in the combination gue and gui has a sound, a dieresis is needed above the vowel ü.

vergüenza	(shame)	pingüino	(penguin)
agüero	(omen)	nicaragüense	(Nicaraguan)

7) **The next one is H**

H is always silent in Spanish.

hora	(time)	hospital	(hospital)
hermano	(brother)	huevo	(egg)
ahora	(now)	hay	(there is, there are)
hola	(hello)	hoy	(today)

8) **The letter J**

J is always pronounced like h in "how" and "packhorse" (see g before e or i).

José	(Joe)	bajo	(short, low)
jueves	(Thursday)	caja	(box)
julio	(July)	Juan	(John)
dibujo	(drawing)	naranja	(orange)

9) O.K. Now <u>L</u>

The "l" sound in Spanish is sharper and shorter than in English. To obtain this sound in English, you curl your tongue. In Spanish you flatten your tongue.

leche	(milk)	delgado	(thin)
hola	(hello)	regalo	(present)
final	(final)	pelo	(hair)
falda	(skirt)	novela	(novel)

10) Very good. Now <u>LL</u>

The sound of <u>ll</u> in Spanish is similar to the sound of "j" in English but more relaxed. This sound lies between the "y" sound in "year" and the "j" sound in "jam." Notice that this letter is not in the English alphabet. This sound varies from country to country.

calle	(street)	pasillo	(hall)
pollo	(chicken)	silla	(chair)
ella	(she)	talla	(size)
pantalla	(screen)	toalla	(towel)

11) The next one is <u>M</u>

As in English but more relaxed – less explosive and shorter.

mesa	(table)	jamón	(ham)
camisa	(shirt)	domingo	(Sunday)
camarero	(waiter)	momento	(moment)
amigo	(friend)	número	(number)

12) Now <u>N</u>

As in English but more relaxed – less explosive and shorter.

Ana	(Anna)	nuevo	(new)
nada	(nothing)	sonido	(sound)
noche	(night)	ventana	(window)
nunca	(never)	lunes	(Monday)

13) Next we have Ñ

It sounds like the "ny" in canyon and the "ni" in onion. Notice that this letter is not in the English alphabet.

otoño	(autumn)	pañuelo	(handkerchief)
español	(Spanish)	señor	(gentleman, Mr.)
baño	(bathroom)	teñir	(to tint, dye)
compañero	(companion)	uñas	(fingernails, toenails)

Let's contrast N and Ñ

cana	caña	mono	moño
cuna	cuña	mano	maño
pena	peña	arana	araña
tina	tiña	panal	pañal

14) Fine, now the letter P

P is less explosive than in English. Do not blow your breath out when making this sound as you do in English.

pan	(bread)	padre	(father)
Pepe	(Joe)	mapa	(map)
popular	(popular)	papa	(potato)
pasajero	(passenger)	pescado	(fish)

15) Now Q

This letter occurs only in the combination que and qui; it is pronounced like the English k and the u is silent.

que	(what)	porque	(because)
quince	(fifteen)	aquellos	(those)
aquel	(that)	quinina	(quinine)
quien	(who)	quinto	(fifth)

16) The letter R

This Spanish r does not sound as all like the English "r." Students should avoid giving this letter the English sound. Listen carefully to the tape and you will see that this Spanish sound is very similar to the "dd" sound in ladder, caddy.

cara	(face)	diario	(daily)	comer	(to eat)
pero	(but)	firma	(signature)	hacer	(to do, to make)
miércoles	(Wednesday)	frase	(phrase)	hablar	(to speak)
nombre	(name)	libro	(book)	dar	(to give)
número	(number)	puerta	(door)	mirar	(to look at)

17) And now RR

This is a strongly trilled sound which the student must learn. Notice that this letter is not in the English alphabet. Listen very closely to the tape.

perro	(dog)	recado	(message)	(Notice that at the beginning
radio	(radio)	rojo	(red)	of words, the RR sound is
narración	(narrative)	rubio	(blond)	represented by a single R.)
rato	(while)			

Let's contrast R and RR:

pero	perro	ahora	ahorra	coro	corro	garita	garrita
caro	carro	toro	torre	moro	morro	quería	querría
curo	curro	poro	porro	foro	forro	perito	perrito
mira	mirra	para	parra	cero	cerro		

18) Next we have two different consonants S and Z. They both sound like the English s in initial position. There is no /z/ sound in the Spanish spoken in Spanish America.

semana	(week)	zapato	(shoe)	blusa	(blouse)
casa	(house)	rosado	(pink)	cosa	(thing)
José	(Joseph)	mesa	(table)	comenzar	(to begin)
vaso	(glass)	asiento	(seat)	diez	(ten)
beso	(kiss)	arroz	(rice)	hermoso	(beautiful)
azul	(blue)	almorzar	(to have lunch)	gasolina	(gasoline)
lápiz	(pencil)	camisa	(shirt)	nariz	(nose)

19) O.K. Now <u>T</u>

This Spanish <u>t</u> is less explosive than in English. Do not blow your breath out when making this sound as you do in English. Place the tip of your tongue behind your top front teeth to pronounce this letter.

té	(tea)	bonito	(pretty)	hotel	(hotel)
tú	(you)	consulta	(doctor's office)	puerta	(door)
tijeras	(scissors)	cuatro	(four)	toalla	(towel)
boleto	(ticket)	cuarto	(quart, room)	tono	(tone)
alto	(tall, high)	gato	(cat)	traje	(suit)

20) Let's do <u>X</u> now

Two different sounds correspond to this letter. If it is followed by a vowel or <u>c</u>, it has a sound /ks/ as you do in English word except. If it is followed by a consonant other than <u>c</u>, it sounds like the English <u>s</u> in initial position: some, same, set.

Followed by a vowel or <u>c</u>   Followed by consonant other than <u>c</u>

examen	(exam)	explicar	(to explain)
excelente	(excellent)	extraer	(to extract)
exagerar	(exaggerate)	exquisito	(exquisite)
exceso	(excess)	expansión	(expansion)
excepto	(except)	exterior	(exterior)

21) And the last one is <u>Y</u>

As a final consonant and by itself, <u>y</u> "and," it has the same sound as the Spanish vowel <u>i</u>. In all other positions it has the same sound as the Spanish <u>ll</u>. (See <u>ll</u>.)

y	(and)	yo	(I)
hoy	(today)	mayo	(May)
muy	(very)	desayuno	(breakfast)
ley	(law)	ayer	(yesterday)
rey	(king)	mayor	(older)

IV. The Next Item Is the Spanish Alphabet

The letters of the Spanish alphabet and their names are as follows:

a	a	j	jota	r	ere
b	be	k	ka	rr	erre
c	ce	l	ele	s	ese
ch	che	ll	elle	t	te
d	de	m	eme	u	u
e	e	n	ene	v	ve or uve
f	efe	ñ	eñe	w	v doble
g	ge	o	o	x	equis
h	hache	p	pe	y	i griega
i	i	q	cu	z	zeta

Notice that there are 4 letters (ch, ll, ñ, rr) in addition to the letters present in the English alphabet. Each represents a single sound. The letters k and w are only used in words of foreign origin.

One last suggestion: It is very important that you master the rules for accents, given on page 10 of your textbook.

END OF PRONUNCIATION TAPE

V. Syllabification (Division of Words into Syllables)

1. A single consonant goes with the vowel that follows it· le-che, pe-rro, co-lor, i-ma-gen. Notice that ll and rr are single letters of the Spanish alphabet.
2. Two consonants are divided except the consonants "bl", "br", "cl", "cr", "dl", "dr", "fl", "fr", "pl", "pr", "tl", "tr", es-pa-ñol, al-mor-zar, lec-tu-ra, li-bro, ca-ble. (These combinations of consonants are called liquid. Notice that they are pronounced together and form a single sound.)
3. In combinations of three or more consonants, the last one begins a syllable except when there are liquid combinations which are inseparable. ins-tan-te, cons-pi-ra-ción, in-glés, es-tre-cho.
4. Two contiguous strong vowels (a, e, o) form separate syllables. a-é-re-o, le-er, ma-es-tro.
5. A combination of a strong vowel (a, e, o, with a weak vowel (i, u, y, o, two weak vowels (y, u, i) form a diphthong or one single sound.

V Accent

1. Words that end in a vowel, or in _n_ or _s_, are stressed on the next to the last syllable: ca-ma, a-pa-ra-to, o-ri-gen, ins-tan-te, mo-de-lo.

2. Words that end in a consonant other than _n_ or _s_ are stressed on the last syllable: ca-pi-tal, ma-yor, doc-tor, ins-pec-tor, fa-vor, pro-fe-sor.

3. Words not pronounced according to the previous two rules require an accent mark to indicate that the word is not stressed where it normally should be: ca-fé, fran-cés, lá-piz, ma-má, di-fí-cil, tam-bién, te-lé-fo-no, sá-ba-do, a-llí, au-to-mó-vil.

In addition to the above rules, a written accent is required to distinguish between words spelled alike but with a different meaning.

sí, "yes"; si, "if"; el, "the"; él, "he"; como, "as"; ¿cómo?, "how?"; mi, "my"; mí, "me"; etc.

LECCIÓN UNO

TOPICS: QUESTION WORDS: ¿QUÉ?, ¿DÓNDE?, ¿CUÁNTOS?, ¿COMO?, ¿POR QUE?, NOUNS AND GENDERS (MASCULINE OR FEMININE), NOUNS AND NUMBERS (SINGULAR OR PLURAL), INDEFINITE ARTICLES, GENDER AGREEMENT OF ADJECTIVES, NUMBER AGREEMENT OF ADJECTIVES, NUMBERS 1 THROUGH 10.

PRESENTATION OF MATERIAL

The conversations that accompany the structural material in this text deal with real-life situations presented in everyday spoken Spanish. Correct grammar or structure makes these conversations and structural material intelligible and understandable. For each Spanish Conversation of this text, you will be presented with an orderly and logical explanation of the grammatical points included in that conversation. In the interest of clarity and brevity, not every single grammatical point can be explained immediately as it appears in the dialogue. Those points not covered in one lesson will be explained in succeeding lessons. Footnotes will indicate in which lesson(s) such points are represented in case you wish to pursue that point.

CONVERSATION I

COMPRANDO UNOS PANTALONES		BUYING SOME PANTS
1. Empleada: Buenos días.[1] ¿Qué desea?[2]	–	Saleslady: Good morning. What would you like?
2. Cliente: Quiero comprar unos pantalones.	–	Customer: I want to buy some pants.
3. Empleada: Bien, aquí están.	–	Saleslady: Fine, here they are.
4. Cliente: Los blancos son[3] muy bonitos.	–	Customer: The white ones are very nice.

I. Question Words

The question words that are presented in this lesson are: ¿qué? "what?"; ¿cuando? "when?"; ¿cómo? "how?"; ¿cuántos? (¿cuántas?)[4], "how many?", ¿por qué? "why?"

Question words are used to begin some interrogative sentences.

The following interrogative sentences refer to situations in the clothing store. It is suggested that you memorize them.

For further explanations of the grammatical points in these sentences, see footnotes.

What would you like?	Qué desea (Ud.)?
Where are the pants?	Dónde están los pantalones?
Where is the hat?	Dónde está el sombrero?
How many pairs of pants would you like?	Cuántos pantalones desea (Ud.)?

---

[1] There are many expressions in Spanish which cannot be translated word for word in English. The first expression in the conversation Buenos días "Good morning" is a good example. Other useful greetings are "Good afternoon" -- Buenas tardes and "Good evening and Good night" which are both expressed by Buenas noches.

[2] Spanish uses two question marks to indicate a question. Usted, you (Ud.abbreviation), is seldom used in direct questions. That is why Ud. is often shown in parentheses. For the form desea, a regular verb of the -ar conjugation, see Lección Cinco.

[3] Son is a form of the verb ser, to be. See Lección Nueve.

[4] The interrogative word ¿Cuántos? changes to ¿Cuántas? for a feminine item. See agreement of adjectives in Lección Seis.

Why do you speak English?	[5]¿Por qué habla (Ud.) inglés?		
How are you?	¿Cómo está (Ud.)?		

II. Nouns and Gender (Masculine and Feminine)

1. Nouns are words that name a person or a thing· "hat" sombrero, "shirt" camisa, "boy" chico, "saleslady" empleada, are nouns.

2. Gender (masculine or feminine). Spanish assigns a gender to every noun, not just to nouns that name persons or animals of one sex or the other.

3. Most nouns that end in -o are masculine, most nouns that end in -a are feminine.

Masculine		Feminine	
hat	- sombrero	shirt	- camisa
book	- libro	purse	- cartera

When nouns refer to persons or animals they have the same gender as the persons or animals they refer to·

Masculine		Feminine	
man	- hombre	woman	- mujer
professor	- profesor	professor-	profesora
father	- padre	mother	- madre

Many other nouns that don't end in -o or -a have genders that the students must learn when they study vocabulary.

Masculine		Feminine	
belt	- cinturón	part	- parte
paper	- papel	night	- noche
hotel	- hotel	class	- clase
cable	- cable	flower	- flor
color	- color	afternoon	- tarde
animal	- animal	salt	- sal

III. Nouns and Number (Singular or Plural)

A noun in the singular indicates reference to one person or one thing. In Spanish, like in English, most nouns are either singular or plural[6].

Most nouns that end in a vowel form their plural by adding -s.

Singular	Plural
sombrero	sombreros
camisa	camisas
hombre	hombres
empleado	empleados

---

[5]The auxiliary verb for "do" or "does", used when asking questions in English is not translated into Spanish.
[6]Collective nouns in Spanish as well as in English are considered singular, i.e. "a collection" - una colección, "a group" - un grupo, etc.

Most nouns that end in a consonant form their
plural by adding -es.

Singular	Plural
cinturón	cinturones
mujer	mujeres
profesor (male)	profesores
papel	papeles

IV. Agreement of Indefinite Article un, una, unas, unos With the Nouns They Precede.

The indefinite articles in English are "a", "an"
for the singular and "some" for the plural.

For the indefinite articles in English, "a", "an"
and "some", there are four indefinite articles in
Spanish· un, una, unos, and unas.

a (an)
- un (masc. singular)
- una (feminine singular)

some
- unos (masc. plural)
- unas (feminine plural)

a hat	— un sombrero
some hats	— unos sombreros
a shirt	— una camisa
some shirts	— unas camisas

Most masculine singular nouns are preceded by the
indefinite article un. Most masculine plural
nouns are preceded by the article unos.

a salesclerk (masc.)	— un empleado
a friend (masc.)	— un amigo
a pupil (masc.)	— un alumno
a book	— un libro
a boy	— un chico
a man	— un hombre
a hotel	— un hotel
some friends	— unos amigos
some boys	— unos chicos
some books	— unos libros
some pants	— unos pantalones
some hotels	— unos hoteles

Most feminine singular nouns are preceded by
indefinite article una. Most feminine plural
nouns are preceded by the indefinite article
unas.

a tie	— una corbata
a saleslady	— una empleada
a purse	— una cartera
a woman	— una mujer
a flower	— una flor

some ties	— unas corbatas
some salesladies	— unas empleadas
some purses	— unas carteras
some girls	— unas chicas
some stockings	— unas medias
some women	— unas mujeres
some flowers	— unas flores

Gender agreement of adjectives

Many adjectives (descriptive words) have a masculine form ending in -o and a feminine form ending in -a. These adjectives agree in gender with the noun they describe.

a white hat	-	un sombrero blanco
a white shirt	-	una camisa blanca
a black hat	-	un sombrero negro
a black shirt	-	una camisa negra

Adjectives that do not end in -a or -o use the same form for masculine and feminine.

a green hat	-	un sombrero verde
a green shirt	-	una camisa verde
a blue hat	-	un sombrero azul
a blue shirt	-	una camisa azul

V. Number Agreement of Adjectives (Singular or Plural)

All adjectives must also agree in number (singular and plural) with the noun they describe. Adjectives that end in a vowel add an -s to form the plural. Adjectives that end in a consonant add -es to form the plural.

a white hat	-	un sombrero blanco
some white hats	-	unos sombreros blancos
a white shirt	-	una camisa blanca
some white shirts	-	unas camisas blancas
a black hat	-	un sombrero negro
some black hats	-	unos sombreros negros

a black purse	- una cartera negra
some black purses	- unas carteras negras
a blue hat	- un sombrero azul
some blue hats	- unos sombreros azules
a blue shirt	- una camisa azul
some blue shirts	- unas camisas azules

VI. Numbers from 1 through 10

one	- uno
two	- dos
three	- tres
four	- cuatro
five	- cinco
six	- seis
seven	- siete
eight	- ocho
nine	- nueve
ten	- diez

VOCABULARIO

NOUNS

alumno (a)	-	pupil
amigo (a)	-	friend
animal (m)	-	animal
bufanda (f)	-	scarf
cable (m)	-	cable
camisa (f)	-	shirt
cartera (f)	-	purse, wallet
chico (a)	-	boy, girl
cinturón (m)	-	belt
clase (f)	-	class
colección (f)	-	collection
color (m)	-	color
corbata (f)	-	tie
día (m)	-	day
empleado (a)	-	salesclerk
	-	employee
español (a)	-	Spanish
	-	Spaniard
flor (f)	-	flower
grupo (m)	-	group
hombre (m)	-	man
hotel (m)	-	hotel
inglés (a)	-	English
libro (m)	-	book
madre (f)	-	mother
media (f)	-	stocking
	-	sock
medio (m)	-	middle, half
mujer (f)	-	woman
noche (f)	-	night
padre (m)	-	father
pantalón (m)	-	pants
pañuelo (m)	-	handkerchief
papel (m)	-	paper
parte (f)	-	part
profesor (a)	-	teacher, professor
sal (f)	-	salt
sombrero (m)	-	hat
tarde (f)	-	afternoon

PRONOUNS

él	-	he
ella	-	she

ADJECTIVES

azul	-	blue
blanco	-	white
bonito	-	beautiful
bueno	-	good
español(a)	-	Spanish
inglês(a)	-	English
	-	British
medio	-	middle, half
morado	-	purple
negro	-	black
rosado	-	pink

VERBS

comprar	-	to buy
desear	-	to wish
estar	-	to be
hablar	-	to talk
querer	-	to want, to love
ser	-	to be

ADVERBS

aquí	-	here
bien	-	well, fine
muy	-	very

NUMBERS

uno	-	one
cinco	-	five
cuatro	-	four
diez	-	ten
dos	-	two
nueve	-	nine
ocho	-	eight
siete	-	seven
tres	-	three
seis	-	six

EXPRESSIONS

Buenos días	-	good morning
Buenas noches	-	good night,
	-	good evening
Buenas tardes	-	good afternoon

INDEFINITE ARTICLES

un (m)	-	a, an
uno (a)(m,f)	-	a, an
unos(as)(m,f)	-	some

QUESTION WORDS

¿cómo?	-	how?
¿cuánto?	-	how much?
¿cuántos?	-	how many?
¿cuándo?	-	When?
¿dónde?	-	Where?
¿por qué?	-	Why?
¿qué?	-	What?

1. Read the expressions given below. Match the expressions in Column A with the appropriate ones in Column B.

F 1. Where is the hat?

a. ¿Cómo está (Ud.)?

E 2. What would you like?

b. ¿Cuántas camisas desea (Ud.)?

D 3. Where are the belts?

c. ¿Por qué habla español (Ud.)?

B 4. How many shirts would you like?

d. ¿Dónde están los cinturones?

A 5. How are you?

e. ¿Qué desea (Ud.)?

C 6. Why do you speak Spanish?

f. ¿Dónde está el sombrero?

a. bufanda una

b. empleado un   un

c. chico un   una

d. corbata una   unos

e. cinturón un   unas

f. corbata una

g. cartera una

h. chicas unas

2. Read the following nouns at the left and the indefinite articles at the right. Choose the appropriate article for each noun. Write out the complete expression.

3. Translate into Spanish.

a. a belt ____cinturón____

b. some boys ____unos chicos____

c. a tie ____la corbata____

d. a saleslady ____una empleada____

[7]Work with a Spanish-English dictionary in order to find the meaning of new words.

-16-

e. some friends (mixed group) _unos ellas_

f. some pants _unos pantolones_

g. some salesladies _unas empleadas_

h. a purse _la cartera_

i. some stockings _unas medias_

4. **Fill in the blanks with the correct form.**

a. Quiero unas camisas ___blancas___ .

white

b. ¿Cuántas carteras ___negroes___ desea?

black

c. ¿Dónde están las corbatas ___verdes___ .

green

d. Los sombreros _blancos_ son muy bonitos.

white

5. **Translate the following numbers.**

a. 5 ___cinco___

b. 8 ___ocho___

c. 4 ___cuatro___

d. 3 ___tres___

e. 7 ___siete___

f. 2 ___dos___

g. 6 ___seis___

h. 10 ___diez___

i. 9 ___nueve___

j. 1 ___uno___

6. **Organize each group of word into two questions. Use all of the words given. Do not use a word more than once. Remember that Spanish questions require two questions marks (¿?)**

a. desea - ella - español - qué - por - habla - qué

¿Que ella desea? ¿Porqué habla español?

b. él - desea - está - dónde - cuántos - pañuelos (handkerchiet)

¿Cuántos pañuelos el desea?

¿Dónde está?

TOPICS: DEFINITE ARTICLES AND NOUNS, QUESTION WORDS: ¿CUÁNTO? ¿QUIEN?, ¿QUIENES? THE SINGULAR SUBJECT PRONOUNS, THE VERB ESTAR IN THE SINGULAR, LIMITED USE OF THE SUBJECT PRONOUN, USES OF THE VERB ESTAR.

CONVERSATION II

¿CUÁNTO CUESTAN?		HOW MUCH DO THEY COST?

1. Cliente:	¿Cuánto cuestan[1] los pantalones?	-	Customer:	How much do the pants cost?
2. Empleada:	Son[2] muy baratos.	-	Saleslady:	They are very inexpensive.
3. Cliente:	¿Dónde está el precio?	-	Customer:	Where is the price?
4. Empleada:	Aquí está. Ocho dólares más el impuesto.	-	Saleslady:	Here it[3] is. Eight dollars plus the tax.

I. Definite Articles and Nouns

In this conversation, the articles el and los are used, both meaning "the" in English.

el precio	-	the price
el impuesto	-	the tax
los pantalones	-	the pants

For the one definite article in English, "the", there are four definite articles in Spanish· el, la, los, las.

el (masc. singular)	-	
la (fem. singular)	-	
		the
los (masc. plural)	-	
las (fem. plural)	-	

| el sombrero | - | the hat (masc. singular) |
| los sombreros | - | the hats (masc. plural) |

| la camisa | - | the shirt (fem. singular) |
| las camisas | - | the shirts (fem. plural) |

Masculine Singular

el empleado	-	the salesclerk
el precio	-	the price
el alumno	-	the pupil
el chico	-	the boy
el hombre	-	the man
el cinturón	-	the belt
el pañuelo	-	the handkerchief
el cliente	-	the customer
el dólar	-	the dollar

Most feminine singular nouns are preceded by the definite article la. All feminine plural nouns are preceded by the definite article las.

Feminine Singular

la corbata	-	the tie
la billetera	-	the wallet
la empleada	-	the saleslady

-18-

[1] For the form cuestan see Lección Diecinueve.
[2] For the form son see Lección Nueve.
[3] There is no equivalent for "it" as a subject pronoun in Spanish, therefore, the subject pronoun which corresponds to "it" is omitted. The reason for not having "it" as a subject pronoun in Spanish is obvious: every noun is either masculine or feminine. The verb form used is the one which corresponds to él or ella.

la mujer	– the woman
la cartera	– the purse
la bufanda	– the scarf
la flor	– the flower
la tienda	– the store
la camisa	– the shirt

Feminine Plural

las corbatas	– the ties
las billeteras	– the wallets
las empleadas	– the salesladies
las carteras	– the purses
las bufandas	– the scarves
las flores	– the flowers
las camisas	– the shirts

II. The Question Word ¿Cuánto?

In conversation 2, the following question appears:

¿Cuánto cuestan los pantalones? – How much do the pants cost?

a. This question ¿cuánto cuestan? is used to ask for the price of some articles.

¿Cuánto cuestan los pañuelos rojos? – How much do the red handkerchiefs cost?

¿Cuánto cuestan los guantes? – How much do the gloves cost?

b. To ask for the price of one item, the question is: ¿Cuánto cuesta?

¿Cuánto cuesta el traje de baño verde? – How much does the green bathing suit cost?

¿Cuánto cuesta la blusa azul? – How much does the blue blouse cost?

c. ¿Cuántos, ¿Cuántas? "how many", was used in the preceding lesson.

¿Cuántos pañuelos desea? – How many handkerchiefs would you like?

¿Cuántas blusas desea? – How many blouses would you like?

¿Cuántos trajes de baño desea? – How many bathing suits would you like?

III. Question Words ¿Quién? "Who?" "Whom?" and its Plural ¿Quiénes?

¿Quién es él? – Who is he?

¿Con quién estudia ella? – With whom does she study?

¿Para quién son estos libros? – For whom are these books?

¿Quién eres? – Who are you?

When we change the previous question to the plural, Spanish uses ¿quiénes?

¿Quiénes son ellos? – Who are they?

¿Con quiénes estudia ella? – With whom does she study?

¿Para quiénes son estos libros? – For whom are these books?

¿Quiénes son Uds.? – Who are you?

IV. The Singular Subject Pronouns

The singular subject pronouns in Spanish are:

Yo	-	I
tú	-	you (familiar)
Ud.	-	you (formal)
él	-	he
ella	-	she

Notice that tú and Ud. translate into English as "you". The reason for this is that Spanish uses a familiar form tú "you" to address members of the family, very close friends and peer groups. Otherwise the form Ud. (usted) "you" is generally used.

V. The Verb Estar[4] with the Singular Subject Pronouns

yo estoy	-	I am
tú estás	-	you are (familiar)
Ud. está	-	you are (formal)
él está	-	he is
ella está	-	she is

VI. The Limited Use of the Subject Pronouns

In all the examples given in this lesson, the answers to the questions do not carry the subject pronouns. Generally in Spanish, once the identity of the subject has been established, all references to that particular subject omit the use of the pronoun; this is not the case in English in which you must always state the pronouns in answering question refering to persons or things.

Singular forms of the verb estar:

¿Cómo está Ud.?	-	How are you?
Estoy bien, gracias.	-	I am fine, thanks.
¿Cómo está él?	-	How is he?
Está bien, gracias.	-	He is fine, thanks.
¿Cómo está ella?	-	How is she?
Está bien, gracias.	-	She is fine, thanks.

VII. Uses of the Verb Estar

The verb estar "to be" has three main uses: (a) to express location - where a person or thing may be found (b) in expressions which refer to how people are feeling and to inquire about their health (c) in expressions which refer to condition of things.

a. Location: in expressions which indicate where someone or something is located.

¿Dónde está la empleada?	-	Were is the saleslady?
Está aquí.	-	She is here.
¿Dónde estás?	-	Where are you (familiar)?
Estoy aquí.	-	I am here.
¿Dónde está el libro?	-	Where is the book?
Está aquí.	-	It is here.

---

[4]See page 39, 1. a + b.

b. **People's feelings and health:**

¿Cómo estás?   - How are you (familiar)?

Estoy bien, gracias.- I am fine, thank you.

¿Cómo está?   - How are you (formal)?

Estoy bien, gracias.- I am fine, thanks.

¿Cómo está él?   - How is he?

Está bien, gracias.- He is fine, thanks.

¿Cómo está ella?   - How is she?

Está bien, gracias.- She is fine, thanks.

c. **Condition of things·**

El café está frío. - The coffee is cold.

La leche está fría.- The milk is cold.

El postre está malo.- The dessert is spoiled (bad).

La leche no está buena.- The milk is spoiled (bad).

La camisa está sucia. - The shirt is dirty.

Los pantalones están - The pants are dirty.
sucios.

Note that in each case the noun being described has undergone a change: from hot to cold, from good to spoiled and from clean to dirty. These examples point out the condition of the subject.

Also note that frío, bueno, malo, y sucio are adjectives; therefore, they require agreement. In these cases they agree with the subject of the sentences café, leche, postre, camisa, and pantalones.

To indicate the condition of a thing, use the adjectives bueno and malo, but for people's feelings and health use bien and mal.

VOCABULARIO

NOUNS

Andrés (m)	-	Andrew
arroz (m)	-	rice
billetera (f)	-	wallet
blusa (f)	-	blouse
café	-	coffee
casa (f)	-	house
chaqueta (f)	-	jacket
China (f)	-	China
cliente (m,f)	-	customer
dólar (m)	-	dollar
frase (f)	-	phrase
gracias (f)	-	thanks
guante (m)	-	glove
hermano (a)	-	brother, sister
impuesto (m)	-	tax
leche (f)	-	milk
naranja (f)	-	orange
número (m)	-	number
persona (f)	-	person
perro (a)	-	dog
pollo (m)	-	chicken
postre (m)	-	dessert
precio (m)	-	price
radio (m)	-	radio (set)
radio (f)	-	radio (transmission)
rosa (f)	-	rose
señor (Sr.)	-	Sir, Mr.
señora (Sra.)	-	Madam, Mrs., Lady
suéter (m)	-	sweater
tienda (f)	-	store
traje de baño(m)	-	bathing suite
zapato (m)	-	shoe

PRONOUNS

tú	-	you (familiar)
usted (Ud.)	-	you (formal)
yo	-	I

ADJECTIVES

amarillo	-	yellow
barato	-	inexpensive
frío	-	cold
mal, malo	-	bad, mischievous
mi	-	my
naranja(m&f)	-	orange (the color)
rojo	-	red
sucio	-	dirty
verde	-	green

VERBS

costar	-	to cost

DEFINITE ARTICLES

el	-	the (masc., singular)
la	-	the (fem., singular)
las	-	the (fem., plural)
los	-	the (masc., plural)

ADVERBS

más	-	more, plus
no	-	no

1. Fill in each blank space with the appropriate definite article.

   a. *el* amigo   f. *la* corbata

   b. *el* sombrero   g. *los* suéteres

   c. *la* billetera   h. *el* empleado

   d. *la* chaqueta   i. *la* tienda

   e. *los* pantalones   j. *el* hermano

2. Give the Spanish for the English article written below the blank space.

   Aquí está *el* precio, *la* camisa cuesta
            a.(the)   b.(the)

   nueve dólares más *el* impuesto, y *los*
                 c.(the)   d.(the)

   dos pañuelos cuestan cuatro dólares. *Los*
                                  e.(the)

   precios son muy baratos.

3. Complete the appropriate questions for each of the answers given by the employee. Imagine that you are the customer.

   a. Cliente: ¿ *Donde están* pañuelos?

   Empleada: Aquí están.

   b. Cliente: ¿ *Cuando cuestan* bufanda blanca?

   Empleada: Tres dólares más el impuesto.

   c. Cliente: ¿ *Como está* David?

   Empleada: Está bien.

   d. Cliente: ¿ *Donde están* empleados?

   Empleada: Están en la tienda.

   e. Cliente: ¿ *Cuanto cuestan* chaquetas azules?

   Empleadas: Son Muy baratas.

4. Change the model sentence to substitute each of the cue words written below. Make any other necessary changes.

   Model: Los pañuelos blancos cuestan ocho dólares.

   a. *Las* blusas *azules cuestan dos dólares.*

   b. *Las camisas* verdes *cuestan dos dolares.*

   c. *Los puntalones blancos cuestan* siete *dolores*

   d. *Los* guantes *rosados cuestan siete dolores*

   e. *los sombreros* azules *cuestan un dolor.*

   f. *los zapatos amarillos cuestan* diez *dolores.*

   g. *Las* corbatas *verdes cuestan tredolares.*

   h. *Las faldas* amarillas *cuestan cuatro dolores.*

   i. *La corbata rosado cuesta* seis *cinco dolores.*

5. Organize the following groups of words into meaningful sentences.

a. por b. amigos c. en
   está   dónde   empleado
   la   los   tienda
   qué   están   el
   empleada ¿?   está
   aquí   la
   ¿?

d. días e. muy
   cómo   está
   él   gracias
   buenos   bien
   está
   ¿?

a. _¿Porque está la empleada aquí?_

b. _¿Donde están los amigos?_

c. _El empleado está en la tienda._

d. _Buenos Días ¿Como está el?_

e. _está muy bien, Gracias_

6. Give the correct Spanish sentence for each of the situations described.

a. Andrés arrives at the store in the afternoon and greets the saleslady.

   He says: _Hola_ ¿ _Como esta_ ?

b. Ask where the employee is.

   ¿ _Donde esta empleada_ ?

c. Ask who the employee is?

   ¿_____?

d. If somebody is looking for you, you help that person by saying:

   Estoy alli

e. You want to find out how Robert is feeling. You ask Andrés?

   ¿ _Como esta Roberto_ ?

f. To let your friends know that you are feeling fine, you tell them:

   Estoy bien, Gracias

7. Write the accent mark on the appropriate vowel.

a. Aquí esta él sombrero.

   _____

b. ¿Que desea él?

   _____

c. Estoy en la tienda.

   _____

d. Estas muy bien.

   _____

e. ¿Quien es él?

   _____

f. ¿Quienes son ellos?

   _____

TOPICS: THE VERB <u>ESTAR</u> WITH PLURAL SUBJECT PRONOUNS, QUESTIONS AND ANSWERS USING THE VERB <u>ESTAR</u>, NEGATIVE SENTENCES, REPLACING NOUNS BY SUBJECT PRONOUNS, COMBINING TWO SUBJECT PRONOUNS, NUMBERS 11 THROUGH 29.

CONVERSATION III

PROBANDOSE UNOS PANTALONES			TRYING ON SOME PANTS

1.	Cliente:	¿Puedo[1] probarme los pantalones?	-	Customer: May I try on the pants?
2.	Empleada:	¿Qué talla usa[2] Ud.?	-	Saleslady: What size do you wear?
3.	Cliente:	La diez.	-	Customer: Size ten.
4.	Empleada:	Aquí los[3] tiene[4].	-	Saleslady: Here they are.
5.	Cliente:	¿Dónde está el probador?	-	Customer: Where is the fitting room?
6.	Empleada:	Allí.	-	Saleslady: Over there.

I. **The Verb <u>Estar</u> with Plural Subject Pronouns**

Nosotros estamos	-	We are (masculine)
Nosotras estamos	-	We are (feminine)
Uds. están	-	You are (plural)
Ellos están	-	They are (masc. or mixed group)
Ellas están	-	They are (feminine)

_____

Carlos y María están aquí.	-	Carlos and Maria are here.
Tú y yo estamos listos.	-	You (fam.) and I are ready.
El y yo estamos bien.	-	He and I are well.

Uds. no están listos.	-	You are not ready.
Las camisas están sucias.	-	The shirts are dirty.
Los pantalones no están sucios.	-	The pants are not dirty.

Notice that the compound subject pronouns <u>tú y yo</u>, and <u>él y yo</u> require the verb form <u>estamos</u>; they are both equivalent to <u>nosotros</u>.

Now that you are familiar with the subject pronouns in Spanish (<u>yo</u>, <u>tú</u>, <u>Ud.</u>, <u>él</u>, <u>ella</u>, <u>nosotros</u>, <u>nosotras</u>, <u>Uds.</u>, <u>ellos</u>, <u>ellas</u>), from now on you will refer to them in their grammatical terms. The following chart is self explanatory·

---

[1]For the form <u>puedo</u> from the verb <u>poder</u> see <u>Lección Diecinueve</u>.
[2]For the form <u>usa</u> from the verb <u>usar</u> see <u>Lección Cinco</u>.
[3]For the form <u>los</u> see Lección Veintidós (object pronoun "them").
[4]For the form <u>tiene</u> from the verb <u>tener</u> see <u>Lección Diecisiete</u>.

Subject Pronoun		Grammatical Term		
Yo	-I	First person singular	¿Dónde estás?	Where are you? (familiar)
Tú	-you	Second person singular (fam.)	Estoy en la tienda.	I'm in the store.
Ud.	-you	Second person singular (formal)	¿Dónde está Ud.?	Where are you? (formal)
El	-He	Third person singular (masc.)	¿Cómo están Uds.?	How are all of you?
Ella	-She	Third person singular (fem.)	Estamos bien, gracias.	We are fine, thanks.
Nosotros	-We	First person plural (masc.)	¿Dónde está ella?	Where is she.
Nosotras	-We	First person plural (fem.)	Ella está allí.	She is there.
Uds.	-You	Second person plural (formal)[5]	¿Cómo están ellos?	How are they? (masc. or mixed group)
Ellos	-They	Third person plural (masc. or mixed)	Ellos están bien.	They are fine.
Ellas	-They	Third person plural (fem.)	¿Cómo están ellas?	How are they? (fem.)
			No están mal.	They aren't bad.

II. Questions and Answers Using the Verb Estar

¿Cómo estás?	How are you? (familiar)
Estoy bien, gracias.	I'm fine, thanks.
¿Cómo está Ud.?	How are you? (formal)
Estoy bien, gracias.	I'm fine, thanks.

Bien and mal do not change for gender and number (masculne and feminine). They are adverbs and always used to refer to how people are feeling and to inquire about their health.

When a question is asked in the third person singular or plural, the answer requires a different form of the verb to agree with the subject pronoun of the answer.

---

[5]The second person familiar plural (vosotros, -as) is not included because it is not used in the Spanish spoken in Spanish-American countries.

III. Negative Sentences

To make a negative statement or to ask a negative question the word <u>no</u> is placed directly before the verb.

A		B
No quiero comprar camisas hoy.	–	I don't want to buy shirts today.
María no está bien.	–	Mary is not well.
Él y yo no estamos listos	–	He and I are not ready.
Los zapatos no están sucios.	–	The shoes are not dirty.
El café no está frío.	–	The coffee is not cold.
¿Por qué no está aquí la empleada?	–	Why isn't the saleslady here?

IV. Replacing Subject Nouns by Subject Pronouns

The pronouns in column B correspond to the nouns in column A.

A	B
Juan	él
María	ella
María y yo	nosotros (nosotras if yo is feminine)
Carlos y yo	nosotros
Juan, Maria y yo	nosotros
Juan y Carlos	ellos
Carlos y María	ellos
María y Carmen	ellas
Los alumnos	ellos
Las alumnas	ellas
Juan está bien.	(El) está bien
María está bien.	(Ella) está bien
María y yo estamos aquí.	(Nosotras) estamos aquí. (if yo is feminine)
Carlos y yo estamos aquí.	(Nosotros) estamos aquí.
Juan y Carlos están allí.	(Ellos) están allí.
Carlos y María están allí.	(Ellos) están allí.
María y Carmen están bien.	(Ellas) están bien.
Los alumnos están bien.	(Ellos) están bien.
Las alumnas están bien.	(Ellas) están bien.

V. Combining Two Pronouns

Pronouns can be combined in Spanish.

Tú y yo	– Nosotros (nosotras if both pronouns refer to feminine persons)
Tú y él	– Uds.
Tú y ellos (ellas)	– Uds.

```
Ud. y yo          -     Nosotros (nosotras if both
                        pronouns refer to feminine persons

El (ella) y yo -        Nosotros (nosotras if all pronouns
                        refer to feminine persons)

Ellos (ellas)           Nosotros (nosotras if all pronouns
   y yo                 refer to feminine persons)
```

VI Numbers: 11 to 29

Notice that numbers 16 to 19 can be written two different
ways but the pronunciation is the same for both.

11	-	once	16 - diez y seis or dieciséis
12	-	doce	17 - diez y siete or diecisiete
13	-	trece	18 - diez y ocho or dieciocho
14	-	catorce	19 - diez y nueve or diecinueve
15	-	quince	20 - veinte

Again numbers from 21 through 29 can be written
two ways but both pronunciations are the same.

[6]21 -   veinte y uno or veintiuno

22 -   veinte y dos or veintidós

23 -   veinte y tres or veintitrés

24 -   veinte y cuatro or veinticuatro

25 -   veinte y cinco or veinticinco

26 -   veinte y seis or veintiséis

27 -   veinte y siete or veintisiete

28 -   veinte y ocho or veintiocho

29 -   veinte y nueve or veintinueve

---

[6]Veinte y uno(a) and veintiuno(a) require agreement for gender.

VOCABULARIO

NOUNS

abrigo (m)	-	overcoat
departamento (m)	-	department
falda (f)	-	skirt
Juan	-	John
probador (m)	-	fitting room
ropa (f)	-	clothes, clothing
saya (f)	-	skirt
talla (f)	-	size
traje (m)	-	suit
vestido (m)	-	dress

falda, (handwritten note next to saya)

PRONOUNS

ellos(as)	-	they
nosotros(as)	-	we
Ustedes (Uds.)	-	you (plural)

ADJECTIVES

gris	-	grey
listo	-	ready, smart

PREPOSITION

en	-	in, on
hasta	-	until

VERBS

poder	-	to be able
probar	-	to taste, to prove, to try on (clothes)

ADVERBS

ahora	-	now
allí	-	there
luego	-	later

NUMBERS

catorce	-	fourteen
diez y nueve (diecinueve)	-	nineteen
diez y ocho (dieciocho)	-	eighteen
diez y seis (dieciséis)	-	sixteen
diez y siete (diecisiete)	-	seventeen
doce	-	twelve
once	-	eleven
quince	-	fifteen
trece	-	thirteen
veinte	-	twenty

EXPRESSIONS

hasta luego	-	so long, I,ll see you later

1. Write two conversations between the customer and the employee. one starting from line **a**, and another one starting form line **b**.

   a. Cliente   Quiero comprar un abrigo.

      Empleado. _____

      Cliente. _____

   b. Cliente.   ¿Puedo probarme la chaqueta?

      Empleada. _____

      Cliente. _____

      Empleada. _____

      Cliente. _____

2. Use the correct form of **estar** to complete the following paragraph. (Imagine an employee giving the information.)

   Aquí _estan_ los abrigos y los sombreros
        a

   negros. El traje gris _está_ en el probador.
                  b

   Andrés no _está_ en el probador. Allí
          c

   estan la empleada y una cliente. Andrés
    d

   y yo _estamos_ aquí, no _está_ bien. La
        e   f

   cliente y la empleada _estar_ muy bien.
                          g

3. Fill in the blanks replacing the subject by a single pronoun and give the correct form of the verb **estar**.

   a. _Ellas_   _estan_   bien.
      (María y Carmen)   (estar)

   b. _Nosotros_   _estamos_   bien.
      (Tú y yo)   (estar)

   c. _Ellos_   no _estar_   bien.
      (Juan y Carlos)   (estar)

   d. _Ellas_   _estan_   aquí.
      (María y Carmen)   (estar)

   e. _Nosotros_   _estamos_   allí.
      (Roberto y Ana y yo)   (estar)

   f. _Ellos_   _estan_   allí.
      (Carlos y Ana)   (estar)

   g. _Nosotros_   _estamos_   aquí.
      (Ana y yo)   (estar)

   h. _Ellas_   _estan_   aquí.
      (las empleadas)   (estar)

   i. _Ellos_   _estan_   allí.
      (los clientes)   (estar)

   j. _Ellos_   _estan_   aquí.
      (los chicos y las chicas) (estar)

4. Answer the following questions in Spanish. (Do not use subject pronouns in your answers.)

a. ¿Dónde están Juan y tú ahora?

Estan en la playa.

b. ¿Cómo están Carlos y Roberto?

Estan bien.

c. ¿Dónde estás?

Estoy bien.

d. ¿Dónde está Ud.?

Ud está en la tienda.

e. ¿Dónde están Uds.?

Estan en el restaurante de China.

5. Change the following affirmative statements to negative ones.

a. Aquí está el precio. _No esta el precio._

b. Los trajes son muy baratos. _No son my baratos_

c. Quiero comprar una chaqueta. _No quiero comprar_

d. Puedo probarme los pantalones. _No puedo_

e. La cliente desea seis vestidos. _No desea_

f. Ud. usa la talla doce. _No usa_

g. Aquí están los zapatos. _No estan._

6. Write out the numbers to the following question:

Question: ¿Qué talla usa Ud.?

(size)

a. Uso la talla   16   _diez y seis_

b. Uso la talla   24   _viente y cuatro_

c. Uso la talla   12   _doce_

d. Uso la talla   21   _viente y uno_

e. Uso la talla   14   _catorce_

f. Uso la talla   27   _viente y siete_

g. Uso la talla   13   _trece_

h. Uso la talla   20   _viente_

i. Uso la talla   15   _diez y cinco_

j. Uso la talla   18   _diez y ocho_

7. Change the model sentence by substituting each of the words written below. Make any necessary changes.

Model: ¿Dónde está el probador?

a. ¿_Donde está_ la empleada?

b. ¿_Donde_ están _los chicos._?

c. ¿Cómo _está_ ?

d. ¿_Com está_ usted?

e. ¿_Ellos_ están _en la playa_ ?

f. ¿Dónde _estamos_ ?

g. ¿_Donde está_ el vestido?

h. ¿_Ellas_ están _en Nordstrom_ ?

8. **Name the article of clothing presented at the right to complete each of the expressions given by the customer(s).**

Cliente 1: Estamos en el departmento de ropa.

2: (Yo) deseo una ___Vestida___ .
     _a

Cliente 1: (Yo) quiero una

b ___blusa___ azul y unos

c ___camisa___ negros.

Cliente 1: Las ___camisas___ son baratas.
                      _d

Cliente 2: La ___falda___ blanca.
                  _e
           cuesta $25.00.

Cliente 1: No es barata. ¿Cuánto
           cuesta el ___traje___ ?

Cliente 2: Cuesta $18.25.

9. **Answer the following questions based on the content of exercise number 8. Do not give one word answers.**

   a. ¿Dónde están las clientes?

      Está alli.

   b. ¿La cliente no. 1 desea una cartera?

      Una cartera esta aquí.

   c. ¿Qué quiere comprar la cliente no. 2?

      Desea la vestida allí.

d. ¿Es barata la falda?

   Sí, desea barata la falda

e. ¿Qué cuesta $18.25?

   El·traje cuesta 18.25 dolores

10. **Translate into Spanish.**

    a. What would you like? _¿Que desea?_

    b. The red ones are pretty. _Los rojas estan bonitas_

    c. Over there. _allí_

    d. May I try on the pants? _¿Puedo probar el pantantores?_

    e. Here it is. _Está aquí_

    f. How many ties do you want? _¿Cuando cuesta desea?_

    g. How much does the wallet cost? _¿Cuando cuesta la cartera?_

11. **Write the accent mark on the appropriate vowel.**

    a. ¿Cuánto cuesta él sueter?

    b. Los zapatos están allí.

    c. Usa la talla ocho.

    d. Puedo comprar el cinturon.

    e. Estamos bien, ¿Cómo estas tú?

12. **Write out the numerical answers to the following problems.**

a. Siete y cuatro son   7+4 = 11

b. Nueve y cuatro son   9+4 = 13

c. Siete y cinco son   7+5 = 12

d. Diez y ocho son   10+8 = 18

e. Cinco y nueve son   5+9 = 14

f. Once y dos son   11+2 = 13

g. Doce y siete son   12+7 = 19

h. Nueve y ocho son   9+8 = 17

i. Once y nueve son   11+9 = 20

j. Catorce y dos son   14+2 = 16

TOPICS: THE USE OF THE FORM SE, CARDINAL NUMBERS 30 THROUGH 199, DAYS OF THE WEEK

CONVERSATION IV

¿DÓNDE SE PAGA?		WHERE DOES ONE PAY?
1. Cliente: ¿Dónde se paga? ¿Aquí?	–	Customer: Where does one pay? Here?
2. Empleada: No, en la caja.	–	Salesgirl: No, at the cash register.
3. Cliente: ¿Dónde está?	–	Customer: Where is it?[1]
4. Empleada: Allí, cerca de la puerta.	–	Salesgirl: Over there, near the door.

I. **Use of the Form se .**

Spanish uses the form se to express the meaning of the English one in expressions like the following.

Where does one pay (the bill)?

(Where do you pay?)

> ¿Dónde se paga (la cuenta)?

Where does one buy pants?

(Where do you buy pants?)

> ¿Dónde se compran pantalones?

Notice that the verb pagar agrees with the implied noun la cuenta – the bill; and comprar agrees with pantalones – pants.

Study the following examples which depict typical conversational situations·

¿Dónde se compran los libros?	– Where does one buy the books?
Los libros se compran en la librería.	– One buys the books in the bookstore.

¿Cuándo se paga?	– When does one pay?
Se paga ahora.	– One pays now.
Se está bien aquí.	– One feels fine here. (We're just fine here.)

II. **Numbers 21 through 199.**

Just by learning a vocabulary of only 8 new words, you can learn to count to 199; these words are·

30	treinta
40	cuarenta
50	cincuenta
60	sesenta
70	setenta
80	ochenta
90	noventa
100	ciento or cien

---

[1]Notice that it as a subject pronoun does not translate into Spanish.

Any number from 20 to 99 is formed like English except that the word y "and" is introduced before the digits.   Study the following examples:

21   -   veinte y uno[2]

32   -   treinta y dos

43   -   cuarenta y tres

54   -   cincuenta y cuatro

65   -   sesenta y cinco

76   -   setenta y seis

87   -   ochenta y siete

98   -   noventa y ocho

99   -   noventa y nueve

Spanish uses the word cien for "100" but when it is followed by another number it becomes ciento, e.g. ciento uno, "101", ciento cincuenta, "150."

All numbers from 100 through 199 are simple combinations of the 8 new ones presented in this lesson, plus the ones learned before.

Examples:

103	ciento tres	136	ciento treinta y seis
114	ciento catorce	147	ciento cuarenta y siete
119	ciento diez y nueve	158	ciento cincuenta y ocho
125	ciento veinte y cinco	169	ciento sesenta y nueve

III. Days of the week

The days of the week are masculine.   In context they are generally preceded by the article el or los.

on Monday	-	el lunes
on Tuesday	-	el martes
on Wednesday	-	el miércoles
on Thursday	-	el jueves
on Friday	-	el viernes
on Saturday	-	el sábado
on Sunday	-	el domingo

To make them plural from lunes thru viernes, change el to los, for sábado and domingo, besides changing el to los you add an s thus making them los sábados and los domingos.   Example·

on Mondays	-	los lunes
on Tuesdays	-	los martes
on Wednesdays	-	los miércoles
on Thursdays	-	los jueves
on Fridays	-	los viernes
on Saturdays	-	los sábados
on Sundays	-	los domingos

Notice that the days of the week are not capitalized in Spanish.

---

[2]Numbers from 21 through 29 can be written also as one word: veintiuno, veintidós, veintitrés, veinticuatro, veinticinco, veintiseis, veintisiete, veintiocho, veintinueve.

VOCABULARIO

NOUNS

automóvil (m)	–	automobile
caja (f)	–	box, cash register
cuenta (f)	–	account, bill, check
domingo (m)	–	Sunday
jueves (m)	–	Thursday
librería (f)	–	book store
lunes (m)	–	Monday
martes (m)	–	Tuesday
miércoles (m)	–	Wednesday
puerta (f)	–	door
sábado (m)	–	Saturday
viernes (m)	–	Friday

PREPOSITIONS

cerca de	–	near
de	–	of, from

ADVERBS

menos	–	less

VERBS

aprender	–	to learn
pagar	–	to pay
practicar	–	to practice
vender	–	to sell

NUMBERS

cien, ciento	–	one hundred
cincuenta	–	fifty
cuarenta	–	forty
noventa	–	ninety
ochenta	–	eighty
sesenta	–	sixty
setenta	–	seventy
treinta	–	thirty

EJERCICIOS

1. Translate into Spanish using the expression _se_.

   a. Where does one buy?

   ¿Donde se compra?

   b. Where does one buy the books?

   ¿Donde se compran los libros?

   c. One feels well here.

   ¿Se esta bien aguí?

   d. One pays at the cash register.

   Se paga en la caja.

   e. Where does one pay the tax?

   ¿Donde se paga el impuesto?

   f. How does one learn Spanish[3]?

   ¿Como se aprende español?

   g. How does one practice Spanish[4]

   ¿Como se practica español?

   h. House for sale.[5] (One sells a house)

   Se vende la casa.

   i. Spanish is spoken here (one speaks Spanish here).

   Se habla español aguí

2. In order to practice the numbers you have learned in this lesson, write out the words as in the model.

   Model: 14 + 7 = 21· Catorce más[6] siete son[7] viente y uno.

   a. 20 + 10 = _viente más diez son treinta_

   b. 10 + 8 = _diez más ocho son diez y ocho_

   c. 30 + 20 = _treinta más vienta son cincuenta_

   d. 40 + 50 = _cuarenta más cincuenta son noventa_

   e. 34 + 30 = _treinta y cuatro más trienta son sesenta y cuatro_

   f. 50 + 30 = _cincuenta más trenta son ochenta_

   g. 15 + 14 = _quince más catorce son diez y nueve._

   h. 60 + 10 = _sesenta más diez son setenta_

   i. 70 + 21 = _setenta más viente y uno son noventa y uno_

   j. 80 + 13 = _ochenta más catorce son noventa y tres._

3. Follow the model.

   Model: 30 − 9 = 21: Treinta menos[8] nueve son veinte y uno.

   a. 25 − 10 = _viente y cinco menos diez son quince_

   b. 50 − 8 = _cincuenta menos ocho son cincuenta y dos._

---

[3]To learn = _aprender_ (in this case, the verb form is _aprende_)
[4]To practice = _practicar_ (in this case _practica_)
[5]Sells - _vende_ from the verb _vender_, "to sell"
[6]Más in these expressions means "plus"
[7]Son here means "they are"
[8]Menos here means "minus"

c. 99 − 9 = _noventa y nueve menos nueve son noventa_

d. 15 − 10 = _quince menos diez son cinco_

e. 40 − 20 = _cuarenta menos viente son viente._

f. 81 − 1 = _ochenta y uno menos uno son ochenta._

g. 13 − 10 = _catorce menos diez son tres._

h. 9 − 3 = _nueve menos tres son seis_

i. 90 − 40 = _noventa menos cuarenta son cincuenta_

j. 98 − 63 = _noventa y ocho menos sesenta y tres son_
   $\frac{60}{35}$ _trenta y cinco._

4. **Translate into Spanish.**

a. 100 _cien_

b. 185 _ciento ochenta y cinco_

c. 123 _ciento viente y tres_

d. 105 _ciento cinco_

e. 109 _ciento nueve_

f. 137 _ciento trenta y siete_

g. 192 _ciento noventa y dos_

h. 101 _ciento uno_

i. 150 _ciento cincuenta_

j. 182 _ciento ochenta y dos_

5. **Read aloud all the numbers in exercises 2, 3, and 4.**

6. **Translate into Spanish and then change to the plural.**

a. on Monday _el lunes (los)_

b. on Tuesday _el martes (los)_

c. on Wednesday _el miércoles (los)_

d. on Thursday _el jueves (los)_

e. on Friday _el viernes (los)_

f. on Saturday _el sabado   los sabados_

g. on Sunday _el domingo   los domingos_

7. **Translate into Spanish.**

a. Where are you on Sundays?

   ¿Donde esta los domingos?

b. When are you in class?

   ¿Cuando esta en clase?

8. **Answer in complete Spanish sentences the questions you translated in exercise 7.**

a. _¿Esta en su casa?_

b. _¿Esta en clase todos dias?_

TOPICS: THE PRESENT TENSE OF REGULAR-AR VERBS

CONVERSATION V

PAGANDO DE CONTADO		PAYING CASH	
1. Cajera: ¿Cómo va[1] a pagar?	–	Cashier:	How are you going to pay?
2. Cliente: De contado. ¿Cuánto es?	–	Customer:	Cash. How much is it?
3. Cajera: Nueve dólares más el impuesto.	–	Cashier:	Nine dollars plus tax.
4. Cliente: Aquí tiene[2] un billete de diez.[3]	–	Customer:	Here's a ten dollar bill.
5. Cajera: Tome[4] el cambio. Muchas gracias.	–	Cashier:	Here's the change. Thank you very much.

I. The present tense of regular -ar verbs

1. A sentence consists of two main parts: the subject and the verb phrase, also called the predicate. Verbs in general tell what the subject is doing. In the sentence Carlos habla mucho "Charles talks a lot", Carlos is the subject. What does he do? The word habla gives the answer; it is a verb.

2. Verbs are normally given in the infinitive form; that is, they are found in dictionaries and vocabulary lists in the infinitive form. Spanish infinitives end in -ar, or -er, or -ir.

Examples of -ar infinitives:

comprar	–	to buy
pagar	–	to pay
hablar	–	to talk
estudiar	–	to study
llegar	–	to arrive

Examples of -er and -ir verbs:

comer	–	to eat
vivir	–	to live

In this lesson the conjugation of the regular -ar verbs in the present tense will be learned.[5]

---

[1]For the form va see conjugation of the verb ir, "to go", in Lección Catorce.

[2]Very often word for word translation does not occur; tiene is a form of the verb tener, "to have"; for its conjugation see Lección Diecisiete.

[3]The noun dólar, "dollar", is implied in Spanish. For the use of de see Lecciónes Nueve and Trece.

[4]As in number 2, word by word translation seldom occurs. For the form tome from the verb tomar, "to take", see Lección Dieciocho.

[5]For the conjugation of regular -er and -ir verbs, see Lección Quince.

3. A verb in the infinitive form has two parts, the stem and the ending. The stem of a verb **is the part of the infinitive that precedes the** -ar, -er, and -ir endings. In the verb comprar, "to buy", the stem is compr- and the ending is -ar. In order to conjugate[6] a verb, the different endings corresponding to the subject pronouns are added to the stems. The following chart gives the endings for -ar regular verbs that correspond to the different subject pronouns.

comprar "to buy"

(yo)	compr-o	-	I buy
(tú)	compr-as	-	you (familiar) buy
Ud., él, ella	compr-a	-	you (formal) he she buys
(nosotros) (nosotras)	compr-amos	-	we buy
Uds., ellos, ellas	compr-an	-	you (plural) they masc./fem. buy

Spanish speakers almost always omit the subject pronouns (especially yo, tú and nosotros) that are made clear by the verb endings -o, -as, -amos, respectively.

4. **Meanings of the present tense in Spanish.**

a. The present tense in Spanish is the equivalent of three structures in English.

Hablo
- I speak
- I do speak
- I am speaking

b. It can even be used to express future action:

Pago la cuenta mañana - I will pay the bill tomorrow.

Llegamos el lunes. - We will arrive on Monday.

---

[6]To conjugate a verb means to make it "agree" with different subject pronouns. Thus in English the verb "to be" would conjugate: "I am, you are, he is, etc."

VOCABULARIO

NOUNS

aguero (m)	–	omen
baño (m)	–	bathroom
billete (m)	–	bill (bank note), ticket (bus, theatre, etc.)
cajero (a)	–	cashier
cambio (m)	–	change
cocina (f)	–	kitchen
comedor (m)	–	dining room
cosa (f)	–	thing
cuarto (m)	–	room, bedroom
dinero (m)	–	money
dormitorio (m)	–	room, bedroom
escuela (f)	–	school
gato (a)	–	cat
gimnástica	–	gymnastics
ginebra (f)	–	gin
giro (m)	–	gyration, turn, money order
góndola (f)	–	gondola – *boat*
guerra (f)	–	war
guitarra (f)	–	guitar
identificación	–	identification
nicaraguense	–	Nicaraguan
origen (m)	–	origin
pasillo (m)	–	hall
pinguino (m)	–	penguin
sala (f)	–	living room
señorita (f)	–	Miss, young lady
teléfono (m)	–	telephone
terraza (f)	–	terrace

ADJECTIVES

francés	–	French
general	–	general
otro	–	another
todo	–	all

VERBS

comer	–	to eat
contestar	–	to answer
escuchar	–	to listen
estudiar	–	to study
llamar	–	to call
llegar	–	to arrive
necesitar	–	to need
tomar	–	to take, to drink
vivir	–	to live

ADVERBS

hoy	–	today
mañana	–	tomorrow
mucho	–	much
siempre	–	always

PREPOSITIONS

con	–	with

EXPRESSIONS

de contado	–	cash
todos los días	–	every day

EJERCICIOS

1. **Write the correct form of the verb that corresponds to the subject pronoun given.**

   a. Yo _hablo_ (hablar) español.

   b. El y ella _practican_ (practicar) con Maria.

   c. Nosotros _llegamos_ (llegar) tarde.

   d. Tú y yo _pagamos_ (pagar) más.

   e. Ud. y yo _necesitamos_ (necesitar) dos identificaciones.

   f. Carlos y María _llegan_ (llegar) temprano.

   g. Carlos, María y yo no _hablamos_ (hablar) francés.

   h. Yo _estudio_ (estudiar) español.

2. **Write the verb form for the appropriate missing tenses. (1-18). Notice the infinitives at the top of the frame.**

	Estudiar	Hablar	Practicar	Llamar
Yo	estudio	6. _hablo_	11. _practico_	llamo
Tú	1. _estudias_	hablas	12. _practicas_	15. _llamas_
Usted (Ud.)	2. _estudia_	7. _habla_	practica	16. _llama_
El	estudia	8. _habla_	13. _practica_	llama
María	3. _estudia_	9. _habla_	practica	17. _llama_
Nosotras	4. _estudiamos_	hablamos	14. _practicamos_	18. _llamos_
Miguel y yo	5. _estudiamos_	10. _hablamos_	practicamos	llamamos

Notice that usted is abbreviated <u>Ud</u>. and that ustedes becomes <u>Uds</u>.

3. **Write the Spanish for the following English verb forms and corresponding pronouns.**

a. She practices _Ella practica_

b. They (feminine) speak _Ellas hablan_

c. You (familiar) need _Tú necesitas_

d. Juan and I arrive _Nosotros llegamos_

e. María and Jose study _Ellos estudian_

f. I don't practice _No practico_

g. He and I speak _Nosotros hablamos_

h. They (masculine) don't answer

Ellos No contestan

4. **Answer the following questions. Observe that each group of exercises has a model to be followed.**

A. Model – ¿Necesitas uno? Sí, necesito uno.

1. ¿Llegas ahora? _Sí, llego ahora_

2. ¿Hablas con ellas?

Sí hablo con ellas.

3. ¿Estudias ahora? _Sí, estudio ahora_

4. ¿No pagas hoy? _No pago ahora_

5. ¿Practicas siempre aquí?

No practico aquí.

B. Model – ¿Necesitan Uds. uno? Sí, necesitamos uno.

1. ¿Llegan Uds. ahora? _Sí, llegamos_

2. ¿Hablan Uds. con ellas? _Sí hablamos_

3. ¿Estudian Uds. ahora? _Sí estudiamos_

4. ¿No pagan Uds. hoy? _Sí pagamos_

5. ¿Practican Uds. siempre aquí?

Sí practicamos.

5. **Rewrite each sentence to agree with the new subject.   A. Hablamos mucho.**

1. Yo _hablo_

2. Juan y Carlos _hablan_

3. Tú _hablas_

4. Uds. _habla_

5. Ella _habla_

6. Ud. y él _hablan_

6. **Write the correct form of the present tense of the verb in parenthesis.**

Todos los días cuando yo _llego_ a mi
a.(llegar)

casa de la escuela, _llamo_ por
b.(llamar)

teléfono y hablo con Marta.

Hoy Marta no está en casa y otra chica

contesta . Ella no _habla_ inglés.
c.(contestar)   d.(hablar)

Es una señorita española. En la escuela,

nosotros _practicamos_ español, yo _necesito_
e.(practicar)   f.(necesitar)

practicar mucho.

TOPICS: AGREEMENT OF ADJECTIVES ENDING IN -E, A <u>CONSONANT</u>, OR -<u>ISTA</u>, COLORS THAT DO NOT REQUIRE AGREEMENT, CARDINAL NUMBERS BEYOND 199

CONVERSATION VI

	PAGANDO CON UN CHEQUE		PAYING BY CHECK
1. Cajera:	¿Cómo va a pagar?	— Cashier:	How are you going to pay?
2. Cliente:	Con un cheque.	— Customer:	By check.
3. Cajera:	Necesita dos identificaciones.	— Cashier:	You need two "ID's."
4. Cliente:	Aquí están.	— Customer:	Here they are.
5. Cajera:	Tome[1] el recibo y gracias señorita.	— Cashier:	Here is the receipt and thank you, Miss.

I.   **Agreement of adjectives ending in -e, a <u>consonant</u> or -<u>ista</u>**

1. Some Spanish descriptive adjectives end in -e, in a <u>consonant</u>, or in -<u>ista</u>. These adjectives have <u>only one</u> form for both masculine and feminine.

   Examples:

   el sombrero verde - the green hat

   la billetera verde - the green wallet

   la chaqueta azul - the blue jacket

   el vestido azul - the blue dress

   el chico pianista - the boy pianist

   la chica pianista - the girl pianist

2. As discussed in <u>Lección I</u>, adjectives that end in a consonant form their plural by adding -<u>es</u>. All other adjectives end in a vowel; therefore, they form their plural by adding -<u>s</u>. Study the following examples as a review.

los sombreros verdes - the green hats

las billeteras verdes - the green wallets

los vestidos azules - the blue dresses

las chaquetas azules - the blue jackets

los grupos fascistas - the Fascist groups

las ideas comunistas - the Communist ideas

II· **Colors (adjectives) that do not require agreement**

The adjectives <u>lila</u> - "lilac", <u>café</u> - "brown"[2], <u>naranja</u>[3] - "orange", and <u>marrón</u> - "reddish brown" do not require agreement.

Examples:

el vestido lila   - the lilac dress

los vestidos lila   - the lilac dresses

la camisa lila   - the lilac shirt

---

[1]For <u>tome</u> from the verb <u>tomar</u>, "to take", see commands <u>Lección Diez y Ocho</u>
[2]The <u>words</u> <u>carmelita</u>, <u>castaño</u> and <u>pardo</u> are also used for brown in some Spanish speaking countries.
[3]<u>Anaranjado</u>, "orange-like color", requires agreement.

las camisas lila	–	the lilac shirts
el pantalón café	–	the brown pants
los pantalones café	–	the brown pants
la blusa café	–	the brown blouse
las blusas café	–	the brown blouses
el pañuelo naranja	–	the orange handkerchief
los pañuelos naranja	–	the orange handkerchiefs
la cartera naranja	–	the orange purse
las carteras naranja	–	the orange purses

III. Numbers beyond 199

1. The multiples of 100 are·

doscientos, -as	–	200
trescientos, -as	–	300
cuatrocientos, -as	–	400
quinientos, -as	–	500
seiscientos, -as	–	600
setecientos, -as	–	700
ochocientos, -as	–	800
novecientos, -as	–	900

2. Any number between 201 and 999 can be obtained by combining the multiple of a hundred desired with any of the numbers from 1 to 99.

doscientos setenta y ocho	– 278
quinientos nueve	– 509
setecientos quince	– 715
novecientos cuarenta y nueve	– 949
trescientos catorce	– 314
cuatrocientos ochenta y siete	– 487
ochocientos doce	– 812

3. Any number that involves a multiple of 100 except 100, requires agreement in Spanish.

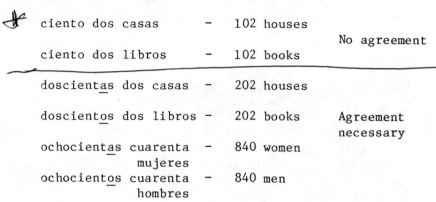

ciento dos casas	–	102 houses	No agreement
ciento dos libros	–	102 books	
doscientas dos casas	–	202 houses	
doscientos dos libros	–	202 books	Agreement necessary
ochocientas cuarenta mujeres	–	840 women	
ochocientos cuarenta hombres	–	840 men	

4. The multiples of 1,000 are·

mil	–	1,000
dos mil	–	2,000
tres mil	–	3,000
nueve mil	–	9,000
novecientos mil	–	900,000

5. To form any number beyond 1,000, the smaller number follows mil "one thousand."

mil cuatrocientos noventa y dos	–	1,492
mil doscientos doce	–	1,212
mil setecientos setenta y seis	–	1,776
setecientos mil doscientos cuatro	–	700,204

VOCABULARIO

NOUNS

auto (m)	–	car
baile (m)	–	dance
canción (f)	–	song
cara (f)	–	face
capítulo (m)	–	chapter
cheque (m)	–	check
examen (m)	–	exam, test
lección (f)	–	lesson
mesa (f)	–	table
pianista (m,f)	–	pianist
recibo (m)	–	receipt
restaurante (m)	–	restaurant
silla (f)	–	chair

ADJECTIVES

anaranjado	–	orange colored
café	–	brown
carmelita	–	brown
caro	–	expensive
castaño	–	brown
comunista	–	communist
difícil	–	difficult
elegante	–	elegant
fácil	–	easy
fascista	–	fascist
grande	–	big
inteligente	–	intelligent
lila	–	lilac
marrón	–	reddish brown, maroon
nuevo	–	new
pardo	–	brown
pequeño	–	small, little
popular	–	popular
simpático	–	nice, pleasant
socialista	–	socialist

NUMBERS

cuatrocientos	–	four hundred
doscientos	–	two hundred
mil	–	one thousand
novecientos	–	nine hundred
ochocientos	–	eight hundred
quinientos	–	five hundred
seiscientos	–	six hundred
setecientos	–	seven hundred
trescientos	–	three hundred

CONNECTORS

pero	–	but

1. Change the following expressions to the plural.

   a. el guante amarillo

   Los guantes amarillos

   b. la chaqueta verde

   Las chaquetas verdes

   c. un suéter rojo

   Unos súeteres rojos

   d. el traje azul

   Los trajes azules

   e. una bufanda rosada

   Unas bufanda rosadas

   f. la billetera negra

   las billeteras negras

2. **Supply the correct form of the adjectives.**

   a. Los vestidos _blancos_ no son _caros_ .
   white   expensive

   b. Quiero comprar unos zapatos _negros_
   black

   y unas medias _negras_ .
   black

   c. El libro es _fácil_ pero los capítulos
   easy

   3 y 4 son _difíciles_ .
   difficult

   d. Los automóviles _azules_ y el radio _grande_
   blue   big

   llegan hoy.

   e. Hablamos de las corbatas _elegantes_ y de
   elegant

   los trajes _caros_ .
   expensive

3. Read the following nouns at the left and the descriptive adjectives at the right. Choose the appropriate adjective for each noun. Write out the complete expression.

   a. ~~señora~~   verdes _autos verdes_

   b. ~~silla~~   fácil _canción fácil_

   c. ~~autos~~   nueva _silla nueva_

   d. canción (song)   inteligente _Señora inteligente_

4. Fill in each of the blanks with the appropriate form of the descriptive adjective **nuevo**.

   a. los bailes _nuevos_

   b. la lección _nueva_

   c. las frases _nuevas_

   d. las mesas _nuevas_

5. Write the plural of the following expressions.

   a. el examen fácil _los examenes faciles_

   b. la señora inteligente _las señoras inteligentes_

   c. el restaurante popular _los restaurantes populares_

d. el chico simpático _los chicos simpáticos_

d. la cartera naranja _las carteras naranjas_

6. Translate into Spanish.

a. the white telephone _el teléfono blanco_

b. the big woman _el mujer grande_

c. the easy lesson _el lección fácil_

d. the red cars _los automóviles rojos_

e. the difficult chapter _el capítulo difícil_

Read carefully

a. rojo	- red	f. azul	- blue
b. rosado	- pink	g. verde	- green
c. café (circled)	- brown	h. naranja	- orange
d. amarillo	- yellow	i. blanco	- white
e. negro	- black	j. lila	- lilac

plural (handwritten note pointing to café)

7. Use two of the adjectives listed above to modify each of the following nouns. Use these adjectives in the same order in which they are written. Make the necessary changes.

a. las mesas _rojas_ y _rosadas_

b. los teléfonos _café_ y _amarillos_

c. el auto _negro_ y _azul_

d. la silla _verde_ y _naranja_

e. la mesa _blanca_ y _lila_

8. Translate into Spanish; write out the numbers.

a. 281 houses _dosciento ochenta y uno casas_

b. 3983 books _tres mil novicientes ochenta tres libros_

c. $257,609 _dos cientos cincuenta siete mil seiscientos y nueve_

d. 3337 chickens _tres mil ~~trescientas~~ trenta y siete pollos_

e. 13649 telephones _trece mil seiscientos cuarenta nueve teléfonos._

TOPICS: THE ADJECTIVES <u>BUENO</u> AND <u>MALO</u>, USE OF <u>DE QUÉ</u> IN QUESTIONS, THE VERB <u>LLAMAR</u>, GREETINGS

CONVERSATION VII

USANDO LA TARJETA DE CRÉDITO		USING THE CREDIT CARD	
1. Cajera: ¿Cómo va a pagar?	–	Cashier:	How are you going to pay?
2. Clienta: Quiero ponerlo[1] en la cuenta.	–	Customer:	I want to charge it.
3. Cahera: Déme[2] su tarjeta de crédito.	–	Cashier:	Give me your credit card.
4. Cajera: Firme aquí[2], por favor, gracias.	–	Cashier:	Sign here, please, thank you.

I. The adjectives <u>bueno</u> and <u>malo</u>

The adjectives <u>bueno</u> and <u>malo</u> may precede the noun they modify. In this position the short forms <u>buen</u> and <u>mal</u> are used for the masculine singular.

un mal momento	–	a bad moment
un buen chico	–	a good boy
un buen trabajo	–	a good job
un buen día	–	a good day
un mal día	–	a bad day

If the adjectives <u>bueno</u> and <u>malo</u> are used in their plural or feminine forms, the long forms are used:

una buena chica	–	a good girl
unos buenos libros	–	some good books

II. Use of <u>de qué</u> in questions

When asking for colors of things, Spanish requires the use of <u>de</u>:

–De qué color es la camisa?	–	What color is the shirt?
Es verde.	–	It[3] is green.
¿De qué color es el vestido?	–	What color is the dress?
Es azul y rojo.	–	It's blue and red.

Notice that the answers to the questions do not require the use of <u>de</u>.

If the question is asked about color or colors of plural items, the verb form changes to <u>son</u> and the color or colors change to the plural·

¿De qué color son las camisas	–	What color are the shirts?
Son verdes.	–	They[4] are green.
¿De qué color son los zapatos?	–	What color are the shoes?
Son blancos y negros.	–	They are black and white.

---

[1]For <u>ponerlo</u> see <u>Lección Veintidós</u>.
[2]For <u>déme</u> and <u>firme</u> see <u>Lección Diez y Ocho</u>.
[3]Remember that "it" as a subject does not translate into Spanish, it is merely implied.
[4]Like "it" in footnote 3, "they" does not translate in this case.

III. Uses of the verb llamar

The verb llamar is usually translated as "to call."

(Yo) llamo	-	I call
(tú) llamas	-	You (fam.) call
Ud., él, ella llama	-	You (formal), he, she, calls
Nosotros/as llamamos	-	We call
Uds., ellos, ellas llaman	-	You (pl. formal), they call

The verb llamar is also used to ask for someone's name.

¿Cómo se llama Ud.? -   What is your name?

In this example, Spanish uses the equivalent of "How do you call yourself?" When asking "What is your name?" The word se, a pronoun, means "yourself.[5]" In order to work with this construction, the following pronouns are needed.

[6]me	-	myself
te	-	yourself (familiar)
se	-	yourself (formal)
nos	-	ourselves

Study the following questions - answer examples:

¿Cómo te llamas? - What's your name (familiar)?

Me llamo María. - My name is Maria.

¿Cómo se llama Ud.? - What's your name (formal).

Me llamo Carlos. - My name is Carlos.

¿Cómo se llama él?   -   What's his name?

Se llama Alberto.   -   His name is Alberto.

¿Cómo se llama ella? -   What's her name?

Se llama Alicia.   -   Her name is Alicia.

Notice that answers to questions asking for his or her name use the same form of the verb as in the questions.

IV. Greetings

Thus far, the adjective buenos has been used in its masculine plural form to modify the word días in the expression buenos días or "good morning", that means that días (or the singular form día) is masculine although it ends in a. It also means that bueno when used with a feminine noun will change to buena, and with a feminine plural noun it will change to buenas. What would the equivalent of "Hello" be in Spanish? Hola is roughly the form used, but there is one important difference in its use. It is a familiar form of greeting, to be used only if you address the person in the tú form.

For a more formal or polite greeting, Spanish uses buenas. It can be used any time of the day.

You are familiar with Buenos días, "good morning" as mentioned before. The afternoon greeting up to sundown is buenas tardes, after sundown is buenas noches[7] which translates to either "good evening" or "good night." It is important for you to notice that Spanish does not differentiate between "good evening" and "good night."

---

[5]In other cases se will have other meanings.
[6]Me, te, se, nos are reflexive pronouns. See Lección Treinta y dos.
[7]Notice that día is masculine and tarde and noche are feminine and that is why we say buenas tardes and buenas noches.

NOUNS

almuerzo (m)	–	lunch
centavo (m)	–	cent, penny
crédito (m)	–	credit
favor (m)	–	favor
momento (m)	–	moment
moneda (f)	–	coin
negocio (m)	–	business
tarjeta (f)	–	card
tiempo (m)	–	time, weather
trabajo (m)	–	work

ADJECTIVES

alto	–	tall
rubio	–	blond
vertical	–	vertical
viejo	–	old

VERBS

dar	–	to give
firmar	–	to sign

PRONOUNS

me	–	myself, me
nos	–	ourselves, us
se	–	himself, herself yourself (polite) themselves
te	–	yourself (familiar), you (familiar)

EXPRESSIONS

¡Hola!	–	Hello!
por favor	–	please
Buenas	–	a formal greeting

1. Answer the following questions in Spanish.

a. ¿Cómo te llamas?

Me llamo _____ Ernesto

(name)

b. ¿Cómo se llama ella?

Se llama _____ Angela

(name)

c. ¿Cómo se llama Ud?

Se llama _____ Juan

(name)

d. ¿Cómo se llama él?

Se llama _____ Pablo

(name)

2. Ask names in the following situations.

a. To a new boy in the neighborhood.

¿Cómo te llamas?

b. To a gentleman you just met.

¿Cómo se llama?

c. To a friend for his sister's name.

(Use pronoun ella for "his sister".)

¿Cómo se llama ella?

d. To a friend for his uncle's name.

(Use pronoun él for "his uncle".)

¿Cómo se llama él?

e. To a lady next door.

¿Cómo se llama señorita?

3. Give in Spanish the following phrases using the short forms of bueno and malo.

a. a good boy

el buen chico

b. a bad day.

el mal día

c. a bad business

el mal negocio

d. a good student

el buen estudiante

e. a good belt

el buen cinturón

4. Using the colors, answer the questions.

a. ¿De qué color son los guantes? (gray)

Los guantes son grises

b. ¿De qué color es la camisa? (blue and green)

La camisa es azul y verde

c. ¿De qué color son las blusas? (white)

Las blusas son blancas

d. ¿De qué color son los zapatos? (gray and black)

Los zapatos son grises y negros

e. ¿De qué color son los trajes? (brown)

Los trajes son cafés

f. ¿De qué color es el auto? (yellow)

El auto es amarillo

5. Translate into Spanish.

   a. What color is your new car?

      ¿De que color es su nuevo automovil?

   b. What color are the new shoes?

      ¿De que color son los zapatos nuevos?

   c. What do you want?

      ¿De que quieres?

   d. Give me your credit card.

      ¿Deme su tarjeta de crédito?

   e. What color is the house?

      ¿De que color es la casa?

6. Read the expressions given below. Complete the expressions in Column A with the appropriate ones from Column B according to the lines of the conversation.

A		B
a. Firme	B	ponerlo en la cuenta.
b. Quiero	A	aquí.
c. ¿Cómo	D	su tarjeta de crédito?
d. Déme	C	va a pagar.

7. Complete the following line of conversation with the appropriate words. Choose from the words below.

   ¿Va a __ponerlo__ en __la__ __cuenta__? Firme
                a   b   c
   __aquí__, gracias.
       d

   cuenta-cheque-ponerlo-la-aquí.

8. Organize the following groups of words into meaningful expressions.

a. pagar	b. tarjeta	c. gracias	d. cuenta
a	su	favor	en
cómo	crédito	aquí	quiero
va	déme	firme	la
¿?	de	por	ponerlo

9. Write a four-line conversation between a cashier and a customer. The customer wants to charge her purchase. Practice the exercise orally.

   Cajera: a. ¿Como va a pagar?

   Cliente: b. Deme su tarjeta de credito.

   Cajera: c. Firme aquí, por favor, gracias.

   Cliente: d. Quiero ponerlo en la cuenta.

10. Change the singular sentences to the plural and the plural sentences to the singular. Give the English meaning of the new sentence.

    a. Yo pago de contado. Pagamos de contado

    b. Ellos toman el cambio. Toma el cambio

    c. Necesitas un billete de cinco. Necesitamos un billete de cinco

    d. Usted necesita dos identificaciones.
       Necesitamos dos identificaciones

    e. Firmamos aquí.
       Firmo aquí

11. Match the subject pronoun written at the left with the correct verb form written at the right.

a. nosotros — estudia

b. ustedes — hablan

c. yo — practicamos

d. tú — llamas

e. usted — llego

12. Write the correct form of the present tense of the verb in parentheses.

a. Nosotros _tomamos_ el cambio.
   (tomar)

b. Ella _paga_ los pantalones rojos.
   (pagar)

c. Ellas _necesito_ el cheque.
   (necesitar)

d. Nosotros _compramos_ con la tarjeta de crédito.
   (comprar)

e. Yo no _pago_ de contado, quiero ponerlo
   (pagar)
   en la cuenta.

13. Write the appropriate form of the descriptive adjective in parentheses. Remember, each adjective has to agree with the noun it modifies.

a. El billete de veinte es _nuevo_ (new).

b. La moneda de un centavo es _vieja_ (old).

c. El cheque es _amarillo_ (yellow).

d. Las identificaciones son _buenas_ (good).

e. La tarjeta de crédito es _roja_ (red).

f. La cliente es _buena_ (nice) y _bonita_ (pretty).

g. La cajera es _alta_ (tall) y _rubia_ (blonde).

14. Write the plural of the following expressions.

a. Es un examen muy viejo. _Son unos exámenes muy viejos_

b. La cajera alta habla. _Las cajeras altas hablan_

c. La tienda popular está aquí. _Las tiendas populares están aquí._

d. El abrigo azul está aquí. _Los abrigos azules están aquí_

e. La cliente simpática compra. _Las clientes simpáticas compran_

15. From the following list, write beside each noun all the adjectives that agree with it.

bueno   ~~rubias~~   popular   nueva   ~~altos~~

a. departamento de ropa _bueno_

b. cajeras _rubias_

c. moneda _nueva_

d. billete _popular_

e. empleados _altos_

LECCIÓN OCHO

TOPICS: REVIEW LESSON 1 THROUGH 7, INTRODUCTION TO CONVERSATION IN A RESTAURANT

When learning a foreign language, a constant review of the material learned is a must. In this lesson you will attempt to use actively each of the points learned so far through two series of exercises. Each exercise in Section A will review only one grammatical point. Section B will review at random the points covered in Section A.

CONVERSATION VIII

	EN EL RESTAURANTE PIDIENDO UNA MESA		IN THE RESTAURANT ASKING FOR A TABLE
1.	Camarera: Buenos días. ¿Cuántos son?	–	Waitress: Good morning. How many are there?
2.	Cliente: Queremos una mesa para cuatro, por favor.	–	Customer: We want a table for four, please.
3.	Camarera: Está bien. Síganme.[1]	–	Waitress: All right. Follow me.
4.	Camarera: Aquí tienen una mesa para cuatro. ¿Les gusta?[2]	–	Waitress: Here is a table for four. Do yo like it?[3]
5.	Cliente: Sí, está muy bien.	–	Customer: Yes, it's fine.
6.	Camarera: Aquí tienen el menú.	–	Waitress: Here is the menu.
7.	Cliente: Muchas gracias. Tenemos mucha hambre.	–	Customer: Thank you very much. We are very hungry.

Section A

1. Fill in the blanks with the proper question words chosen from the list at the right, no question word should be used more than once.

   a. ¿_____ es él?

   b. ¿_____ practica ella?

   c. ¿_____ vive Juan?

   d. ¿_____ habla español María?

   e. ¿_____ estudia Pedro?

   f. ¿_____ se llama ella?

   g. ¿_____ años tiene Raúl?

   h. ¿_____ cuestan los pantalones?

   cuánto — How much
   cuántos — How many
   cuándo — When
   quién — Who
   cómo — How
   qué — what
   dónde — Where
   por qué — why / because

2. Choose the questions that match the answers.

   a. ¿Qué estudia?
      ¿Quién estudia? — Robert estudia.

   b. ¿Quién es?
      ¿Por qué es. — Es Alicia.

   c. ¿Cómo es?
      ¿Cómo se llama? — Ella se llama María.

   d. ¿Qué practica?
      ¿Dónde practica? — Practica español.

---

[1]For an explanation of síganme, form of the verb seguir, to follow, see Lección Veintidós.
[2]For the verb gustar see Lección Veintitrés, and also for the pronoun les see Lección Veintitrés.
[3]Notice that this sentence is not a literal translation.

3. Supply the indefinite article.

   a. Quiero comprar _las_ casas.

   b. Necesitas _la_ corbata azul.

   c. ¿Por qué no compras _el_ cinturón también?

   d. _Los_ empleados hablan español.

   e. Aquí están _los_ amigos de Alberto.

4. **Fill in the blanks with the proper form of the definite articles in Spanish.**

   Aquí _los_ precios son muy buenos, _los_
         a   b

   guantes cuestan tres dólares, _el_ traje
                                c

   de baño cuesta nueve dólares más _el_
                                        d

   impuesto, y _el_ cinturón azul cuesta
                   e

   cuatro dólares. _las_ medias son muy
                         f

   bonitas y _las_ camisas son de todos
                  g

   los colores.
     h

5. **Complete the sentences by writing the form of the verb <u>estar</u> according to the subject given for each one. Write the complete sentence.**

   Model: Roberto está en la clase.

   a. Elena y Ana _están_ .

   b. Elena _está_ .

   c. Yo _estoy_ .

   d. Uds. _están_ .

   e. Tú y yo _estamos_ .

   f. Ellos _están_ .

   g. Tú _estas_ .

   h. Tú y él _están_ .

6. **Replace the underlined nouns and pronouns by pronouns.**

   a. <u>Carlos y yo</u> estamos aquí.

   Nosotros .

   b. <u>El y María</u> están bien.

   Ellos .

   c. <u>José, Carlos y yo</u> trabajamos aquí.

   Nosotros .

   d. <u>Tú y ella</u> no estudian español.

   Ellas .

   e. <u>Irene y Lola</u> no necesitan zapatos.

   Ellas .

   f. <u>Ud. y él</u> están en la clase.

   Ellos .

   g. <u>María y Teresa</u> no están en la tienda.

   Ellas .

7. **Write out the following additions and subtractions.**

   a. 5 + 6 son 11

      cinco más seis son ~~son~~ once

   b. 9 + 3 son 12

      nueve más tres son doce

   c. 9 + 4 son 13

      nueve mas cuatro son trece

   d. 11 + 8 son 19

      doce más ocho son diez y nueve

   e. 15 + 9 son 24

      quince más nueve son viente y cuatro

   f. 10 + 4 son 14

      diez más cuatro son catorce

   g. 20 - 4 son 16

      viento menos cuatro son dieziseis

   h. 29 - 4 son 25

      viente nueve menos son vienticinco

   i. 28 - 8 son 20

      viente ocho menos son viente

   j. 23 - 6 son 17

      viente tres menos son dizisiete.

8. **Complete the answers for the following questions.**

   a. ¿Dónde está Elena?

      Está en la cocina.

   b. ¿Están ellos en el portal o en la sala?

      Estan en la sala.

   c. ¿Cómo está María?

      María esta muy bien.

   d. ¿Estás en el comedor?

      No, _estoy_ en la cocina.

   e. ¿Están Uds. en el portal?

      Sí, _Estan_ aquí.

9. **Translate into Spanish.**

   a. on Monday   en el lunes

   b. on Sundays   en los domingos

   c. on Wednesdays   en los miercoles

   d. on Saturday   en el sabado

   e. on Tuesdays   en los martes

10. **Translate into Spanish.**

   a. some pupils

   b. the sisters   los hermanas

   c. a friend   a amigo

   d. the companion

e. a pupil _____

f. a sister ___a hermana___

g. the friends ___los amigos___

h. a companion _____

11. **Answer affirmatively in Spanish.**

    a. ¿Llegas tarde los lunes?

    ___Llego tarde los lunes___

    b. ¿Habla Ud. español?

    ___Sí, habla español.___

    c. ¿Necesitan Uds. dos identificaciones?

    ___Sí, necesitan dos identificaciones___

    d. ¿Estudian María y tú aquí?

    ___Estudian aquí___

    e. ¿Pagan ellos las compras de contado?

    ___Sí, pagan las compras de contado.___

12. **Change the following expressions to the plural.**

    a. la camisa azul.

    ___las camisas azules___

b. el traje gris

___los trajes grises___

c. la chaqueta café

___las chaquetas cafés___

d. la blusa blanca

___las blusas blancas___

e. el libro naranja

___los libros naranja___

f. el cinturón negro

___los cinturones negros___

Section B

1. **Make up one question for each statement. Use the appropriate question words and verb forms.**

   a. ¿___Quién él es___?

   Es Roberto Pérez.

   b. ¿___Cómo se llama___?

   Se llama Roberto Pérez.

   c. ¿___Cómo estas (familiar)___?

   Estoy bien, gracias.

   d. ¿___Dónde estamos___?

   Estamos en la escuela.

   e. ¿___Dónde ella vive___?

   María vive en Miami.

2. **Organize the following groups of words into meaningful expressions based on the conversations.**

   a. están - bien - aquí

   Aquí, están bien.

   b. días - desea - buenos - qué ¿ ?

   Buenos días. ¿Qué desea?

   c. muy - son - blancos - bonitos - los

   Los blancos son muy bonitos

   d. pantalones - quiero - unos - comprar

   Quiero comprar unos pantalones.

3. **Translate into Spanish.**

   a. Where is the white shirt?

   ¿Dónde esta la camisa blanca?

   b. Why don't you speak Spanish?

   ¿Porque no hablas español?

   c. How much are the black belts?

   ¿Cuantos esta los cinturones negros?

   d. What would you like?

   ¿Que desea?

4. **Organize the following groups of words into meaningful expressions.**

   a. los - cuánto - pantalones - cuestan - ¿?

   ¿Cuanto cuestan los pantalones?

   b. precio - el - está - dónde - ¿ ?

   ¿Dónde está el precio?

   c. baratos - son - muy

   Son muy baratos.

   d. el - está - ocho - aquí - más - dólares - impuesto

   Aquí Esta ocho dólares más el impuesto

   e. probador - el - está - dónde - ¿ ?

   ¿Dónde está el probador?

   f. usted - talla - qué - usa - ¿ ?

   ¿Que usted usa talla?

   g. pantalones - probarme - los - puedo - ¿ ?

   ¿Puedo probarme los pantalones?

5. **Write the correct Spanish sentence for each of the following situations.**

   a. You arrive at the store at 2 P.M. and the saleslady greets you. She says:

   Hola ¿ *Como esta Ud.* ?

   b. To find out the price of a pair of black shoes, you ask:

   ¿ *Cuantos cuestan los zapatos negros* ?

   c. To learn how Roberto is feeling, you ask him (familiar):

   ¿ *Core estas Roberto* ?

d. To learn how Roberto is feeling, you ask a mutual friend.

¿ _Cómo esta Roberto_ ?

e. While at the store around 8 P.M. you run into a friend from school and her father. You greet them by saying·

Hola ¿ _Como esta_ Carmen?

¿ _Como esta_ Sr. Martínez?

6. Translate into Spanish.

a. Why aren't you in class?

Translation: _¿Porque no esta en Clase?_

b. Where is he on Thursday?

Translation: _¿Donde esta el en Jueves_

c. Where does one pay?

Translation: _¿Donde se pagar?_

d. How much do they cost?

Translation: _¿Cuantos westan?_

7. Organize the following group of words into meaningful expressions.

a. puerta - de - allí - cerca - la - ,

Allí, cerca de la puerta.

b. la - en - caja - no - ,

No, en la caja

c. paga' - se - dónde - ¿ ? - aquí - ¿ ?

¿Donde se paga? ¿aqui?

d. cambio - gracias - el - muchas - tome

Tome el cambio, mucho gracias

e. pagar - a - cómo - va - ¿ ?

¿Como va a pagar?

f. diez - aquí - billete - un - tiene - de

Aqui Tiene un billete de diez

8. Supply the correct forms based on the model sentence.

Model: Las chicas compran las camisas azules.

a. _La_ chica _compra la camisa_ azul.

b. Yo _compro los_ pañuelos _azules_

c. Juan y yo _compramos los pañuelos_ verdes.

d. Carmen y María _Compran los_ vestidos _azules_

e. Ella _compra los_ ~~sotos~~ baratos.
   Sombreros

9. Answer in Spanish using the color given.

    a. ¿De qué color es la blusa.

       La blusa es blanca (white)

    b. ¿De qué color son los pantalones?

       Los pantalones son azules (blue)

    c. ¿De qué color es el traje?

       El trajes es gris (gray)

    d. ¿De qué color es la casa?

       La casa es verde (green)

10. Organize the following groups of words into meaningful expressions.

    a. recibo - señorita - el - y - tome - gracias -,

       Tome el recibo señorita, gracias

    b. las - aquí - tiene

       Aquí las tiene

    c. identificaciones - necesita - dos

       Necesita dos identificaciones

    d. cheque - un - con

       Con un cheque

    e. pagar - a - cómo - va - ¿ ?

       ¿Cómo va a pagar?

    f. tarjeta - su - crédito - déme - de

       Deme su tarjeta su crédito

    g. gracias - favor - aquí - firme - por - ,

       Firme aquí, por favor, gracias

    h. cuenta - en - quiero - la - ponerlo

       Quiero ponerlo en la cuenta

11. Change the following sentences to agree with the new subject given.

    a. Ella es una buena chica.

       El *es unbueno chico*

    b. Yo estoy bien aquí.

       Nosotros *estamos bien aquí*

    c. ¿Cuándo estás tú en la clase?

       ¿ *Esta* él *en la clase* ?

    d. El teléfono es blanco y amarillo.

       La camisa *es blanca y amarilla*

    e. Tú eres francés.

       Nosotros *somos franres* .

    f. Yo estoy en la tienda.

       ¿Quién *estas en la tienda* ?

12. Translate into Spanish.

    a. How are you going to pay?

       ¿Cómo va a pagar?

    b. Cash. How much is it?

       Dinero. ¿Cuántos es?

c. By check.

pena cheque

d. I want to charge it.

Quiero

e. Sign here, please, Thank you.

Firme aqui, por favor, gracias

f. What color is the car?

¿De que color de Automovil?

g. What colors are the shirts?

¿De que color Son las camisas?

h. The shirts are white and orange.

Las camisa son blanco y naranja.

i. Here is a ten dollar bill.

aqui es un billete de diez

j. May I try on the pants?

Puedo probarme los pantalones

k. Where is the fitting room?

Donde esta el probaros

l. It is very inexpensive.

Esta muy caro.

m. I want to buy a white handkerchief.

Quiero comprar a pañuela blanca

n. I want to buy a black belt size thirty six.

Quiero comprar a el cinturon negro talla trenta y sies.

VOCABULARIO

NOUNS

año (m)	- year
compañero (a)	- companion
desayuno (m)	- breakfast
Elena	- Helen
hambre (f)	- hunger
harina (f)	- flour
menú (m)	- menu
papa (f)	- potato
portal (m)	- porch
té (m)	- tea

VERBS

gustar	-	to like, to please
seguir	-	to follow

ADVERBS

sí	-	yes
tarde	-	late

EXPRESSIONS

buen provecho -   enjoy your meal

TOPICS: THE VERB SER, "TO BE", TELLING TIME, THE PREPOSITION DE TO EXPRESS POSSESSION

I. The Verb Ser, "to be."

Ser is one of the two main verbs which means "to be" in English. The other one is estar which is studied in Lección 3. Both ser and estar appear in the preceding conversation. Notice that their meaning is not the same.

A. Conjugation of ser:

(Yo)	soy	–	I am
(tú)	eres	–	You (familiar) are
Ud.	es	–	you (formal) are
El, ella	es	–	He, she is
Nosotros/as	somos	–	We are
Uds.	son	–	You (plural) are
Ellos, ellas	son	–	They are

1. Uses of ser:

Ser is used to link the subject with a noun. In these cases it always tells what the subject is.

Somos mecánicos.	–	We are mechanics.
Soy el cliente.	–	I am the customer.
Ella es la empleada.	–	She is the clerk.
El es el profesor.	–	He is the professor.
Juan y Carlos son alumnos.	–	John and Charles are students.

2. Ser is used to link the subject with an adjective when the adjective describes an intrinsic characteristic of the subject. An adjective describes an intrinsic quality when it points to an inherent quality of the subject. For adjectives that describe a state, conditions, or feelings, see Lección 2, page 21.

María es inteligente.	–	Mary is intelligent.
Las mesas son verdes.	–	The tables are green.
El chico es muy alto.	–	The boy is very tall.
Anita y Alicia son rubias.	–	Anita and Alicia are blondes.

Notice that inteligente, verdes, alto and rubias represent characteristics inherent to the subject.

3. Ser is used to express origin of persons or things.

Víctor es de Francia.	–	Victor is from France.
El café es de Colombia.	–	The coffee is from Colombia.
Somos de Buenos Aires.	–	We are from Buenos Aires.
Ellos son de España.	–	They are from Spain.
¿Eres de Costa Rica?	–	Are you from Costa Rica?
No, soy de Guatemala.	–	No, I am from Guatemala.

4. Ser is used to express possession.

Es la blusa de María.	–	It is Mary's blouse.
La casa es de Juan.	–	The house is John's.
Los pantalones son de Juan.	–	The pants are John's.
La señora es la madre de Berta.	–	The lady is Bertha's mother.

The use of apostrophes to express possession is a feature of the English language. In Spanish, the **verb** <u>ser</u> plus <u>de</u> is used.

5. Ser is used for asking and telling time, and to indicate the time of day.

¿Qué hora es?	–	What time is it?
Es tarde.	–	It is late.
Es mediodía.	–	It is noon.
Es medianoche.	–	It is midnight.
Es temprano.	–	It is early.
Es hora.	–	It is time.
Es la una.	–	It is one o'clock.[4]
Son las dos.	–	It is two o'clock.

II. Telling Time.

Two different forms of <u>ser</u> have to be used when telling time in Spansh. The singular form <u>es</u> with one o'clock – <u>Es la una</u>, and the plural form <u>son</u> with all the other hours from 2 to 12.

Son las dos.

Son las tres, etc.

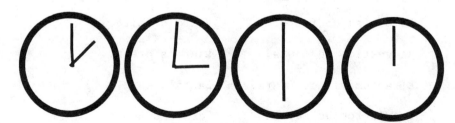

Es la una.   Son las tres.   Son las Seis.   Son las doce.

Hour + y + minutes, cuarto or <u>media</u>

Son las tres   Son las cuatro   Son las once   Son las dos
y cinco   y cuarto.   y veinticinco   y media.

Notice that when the minute hand passes the half hour on the clock, you start subtracting from the next hour. With this in mind, study the following examples of time:

Hour + <u>menos</u> + minutes or <u>cuarto</u>:

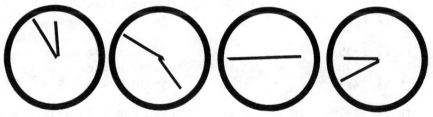

Son las doce   Son las cinco   Son las tres   Son las nueve
menos cinco.   menos diez.   menos cuarto.   menos veinte.

Es la una menos   Es la una menos   Es la una menos
veinte y nueve.   veinte.   cuarto.

---

[4]There is no translation for "o'clock" in Spanish.

Son las dos menos
veinte y nueve.

Son las dos
menos cuarto.

Son las dos
menos cinco.

These examples are chosen to serve as reminders
of the changes from <u>son las ...</u> to <u>es la ...</u> and
vice versa. When the minute hand passes the half
hour, or 12:30, the correct expression is <u>Es la una</u>
<u>menos</u> the number of minutes.

For further illustration study the following examples:

It is 12:35	-	Es la una menos veinticinco.
It is 1:30	-	Es la una y media.
It is 1:35	-	Son las dos menos veinticinco.
It is 12:40	-	Es la una menos veinte
It is 12:29	-	Son las doce y veinte y nueve.
It is 3:45	-	Son las cuatro menos cuarto.
It is 7:55	-	Son las ocho menos cinco
It is 6:15	-	Son las seis y cuarto.

Some useful time expressions:

en punto	-	exactly, sharp
a eso de	-	at about
como a	-	at about

de la mañana	-	A.M.
de la tarde	-	afternoon
de la noche	-	P.M. (after sundown, and midnight)
¿A qué hora?	-	At what time?
Son las doce en punto.	-	It is exactly twelve o'clock It is twelve o'clock sharp.
A eso de las dos termino.	-	At about 2 o'clock I'll finish.
Como a las dos termino.	-	At about 2 o'clock I'll finish.
Son las nueve y media de la mañana.	-	It is 9:30 A.M.
Es la una y doce de la tarde.	-	It is 1:12 P.M.
Son las ocho y media de la noche.	-	It is 8:30 P.M.
¿A qué hora llegan ellas?	-	At what time are they arriving?

III **The Preposition <u>de</u> to Express Possession:**

La camisa de Pedro.	-	Pedro's shirt.
El vestido de Laura.	-	Laura's dress.
El automóvil de Laura.	-	Laura's car.
Los libros de Carmen	-	Carmen's books.
Los lápices de los alumnos.	-	The students' pencils.
Es de Carlos.	-	It is Carlos'.
Son de María.	-	They are Mary's.

VOCABULARIO

NOUNS

biblioteca (f)	-	library
boda (f)	-	wedding
Buenos Aires	-	capital city of Argentina
camarero (a)	-	waiter, waitress
Costa Rica	-	country in Central America
España	-	Spain
Francia	-	France
hora (f)	-	hour, time
lápiz (m)	-	pencil
Londres	-	London
llamada (f)	-	call
Madrid	-	capital of Spain
mantequilla (f)	-	butter
mecánico (m)	-	mechanic
medianoche (f)	-	noon, midday
menudo (m)	-	small change
París	-	capital of France
punto (m)	-	point, dot
tren (m)	-	train

ADJECTIVES

Americano (a)   -   American

VERBS

terminar - to finish

EXPRESSIONS

a ...	-	at about ...
a eso de ...	-	at about ...
como a ...	-	at about ...
de la mañana	-	a.m. (in the morning)
de la noche	-	p.m. (after sundown, but before midnight)
de la tarde	-	p.m. (in the afternoon)
en punto	-	on the dot, exactly, sharp

1. Use the proper form of the verb **ser**.

   a.   Yo _soy_ de Miami.

   b.   Tú _eres_ de Atlanta.

   c.   Ellos _son_ alumnos.

   d.   El libro _es_ viejo.

   e.   Ud. _es_ alto.

   f.   Ellas _son_ rubias.

   g.   Nosotros _somos_ americanos

   h.   Ella _es_ profesora.

   i.   La casa _es_ de Juan.

   j.   Los pantalones _son_ blancos.

2. Read the time indicated on each of the following clocks. Write the time expression in Spanish using words, not numbers.

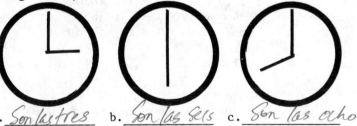

   a. _Son las tres_   b. _Son las seis_   c. _Son las ocho_

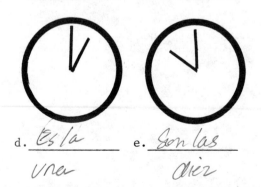

   d. _Es la una_   e. _Son las diez_

3. Write a Spanish sentence to give the time expressed in figures. Use only words in your answers.

   a.   5:00   _Son las cinco_

   b.   11:00   _Son las doce_

   c.   4:00   _Son las cuatro_

   d.   7:00   _Son las siete_

   e.   12:00   _Son las doce_

4. Write out in Spanish the following times.

   a.   It is 1:23   _Es la una mas veinte y tres_

   b.   It is 1:30   _Es la una y media_   OR

   c.   It is 12:45   _Es la una menos quince_

   d.   It is 12:29   _Son Es la doce y veinte y nueve_

   e.   It is 11:55   _Son las doce menos cinco_

   f.   It is 12:05   _Son las doce y cinco_

   g.   It is 9:15   _Son las nueve y cuarto_

5. Using the cue, answer the following questions.

   a.   ¿A qué hora es la boda? (12:45 P.M.)

   Es la una menos cuarto.

   b.   ¿A qué hora llega el tren de París?
        (6:35 A.M.)

   Son las seis y treinta y cinco.

c. ¿A qué hora estudias en la biblioteca
    (1:45 P.M.)
    Son las dos menos cuarto.

d. ¿A qué hora hablan Uds. con él en Londres?
    (5:00 P.M.)
    Son las cinco

e. ¿Por qué a las cinco?
    (either: the call costs less)
    La llamada cuesta menos

    (or: the calls are inexpensive)
    Las llamadas son baratas

f. ¿Cuándo llega Ud.? (On Monday at 8·50 P.M.)
    El lunes son a las nueve menos diez.

g. ¿Cuánto cuesta la llamada a Madrid? ($4.95)
    Cuesta cuatro y noventa y cinco dólares.

6. Organize the following groups of words into
    meaningful sentences.

    a. López   b. rubia   c. Arturo
        el   María   son
        es   es   y
        señor   alumnos
        Miami   María
        de

    a. _El señor López es de Miami_
    b. _María es rubia_
    c. _Arturo y María son alumnos._

d. Sr. _Es el Sr. López_
    el
    López
    es

7. Complete each of the following sentences
    with a present tense form of the verb _ser_
    according to the subject given.

    Ella _es_ rubia.

    a. Ellos _son_ americanos.

    b. Nosotros _somos_ americanos.

    c. Tú _eres_ María.

    d. Usted _es_ el profesor.

    e. Yo _soy_ alto.

8. Write the correct Spanish sentence for each
    of the following situations.

    a. The teacher does not know one of the
        girls in his class. He asks Arturo:

        ¿ _Quién es ella_ ?

    b. You are writing information on a card.
        It is important to know what country you
        are from. You will find the following
        question:

        ¿ _De dónde es Ud._ ?

-69-

9. **Write the Spanish for the following English sentences.**

a. It is twelve o'clock.

Son las doce

b. It is early.

Eres temprano.

c. I am French.

Soy frances

d. You are intelligent. (familiar)

Eres inteligente

e. Ana is the pianist.

Ana es la pianista

10. **Organize the following groups of words into meaningful expressions (to show possession).**

a. unos	b. Rosa	c. del
camisas	de	camisa
de	la	la
chicos	blusa	chico
las		

a. Las camisas de unos chicos

b. La blusa de Rosa

c. La camisa del chico.

---

d. Las camisas de Arturo

d. las	e. el
Arturo	de
de	chica
camisas	vestido

e. El vestido de una chica.

11. **Replace each underlined expression using the word in parentheses. Make any other necessary changes. Write the new expression.**

a. La camisa de los chicos. (amigo)

La camisa del amigo

b. La blusa de Rosa. (señora)

La blusa de la señora

c. Las blusas de unas chicas. (chica)

Las blusas de la chica.

d. La camisa de un chico. (señor)

La camisa del un señor

e. La blusa de la profesora. (Ana)

La blusa de Ana

f. Las camisas de unos chicos. (tíos)

Las camisas de unos tíos

g. La camisa de Arturo. (alumno)

La camisa del alumno

-70-

TOPICS: SYLLABIFICATION, WORD STRESS AND WRITTEN ACCENTS, IDIOMATIC EXPRESSIONS WITH THE VERB ESTAR, SER AND ESTAR CONTRASTED

CONVERSATION IX

ORDENANDO EL DESAYUNO		ORDERING BREAKFAST
1. Cliente: Señorita, queremos desayunar.	–	Customer: Miss, we want to have breakfast.
2. Camarera: Muy bien. ¿Qué desean?	–	Waitress: Very well. What would you like?
3. Cliente: Jugo de naranja y después jamón y huevos.	–	Customer: Orange juice and then ham and eggs.
4. Camarera: ¿Desean huevos revueltos o fritos?	–	Waitress: Would you like scrambled or fried eggs?
5. Cliente: Fritos. También queremos pan y mantequilla.	–	Customer: Fried. We also want bread and butter.
6. Camarera: ¿Desean café con leche o chocolate?	–	Waitress: Would you like coffee with milk or cocoa?
7. Cliente: Café con leche, por favor.	–	Customer: Coffee with milk, please.
8. Camarera: Está bien. En seguida lo[1] traigo[2] todo.	–	Waitress: All right. I'll bring it all right away.

I. Syllabificaton, word stress and written accents

Spanish does not require that you memorize the pronunciation of each word. Once you have learned the sounds of vowels, consonants and a few combinations of vowels and consonants, plus the rules of stress, you will be able to pronounce any Spanish word correctly even if you have never seen it before. It is imperative – and this is extremely important, that the syllabic nature of the Spanish language be understood. The Pronunciation Lesson (p. 1) presents what is needed for the correct pronunciation of Spanish. The first section is the division of words into syllables which is a must for understanding rules for stress. It is not possible to learn sounds from a written explanation, so this part of Lesson 10 should be studied (after you have listened to) or while listening to the Pronunciation Lesson tapes.

II. Idiomatic expression with the verb estar

The following expressions are commonly used in Spanish.

1. To express any date.

Estamos a cinco.	–	It is the fifth.
Estamos a veinte y uno	–	It is the twenty first.

2. To express seasons and months of the year

Estamos en mayo.	–	It is May.
Estamos en otoño.	–	It is autumn.

Notice that these idiomatic expressions do not comply with the rules for the use of estar, nor are they literal translations of the English expressions.

III. Ser and Estar contrasted.

When the uses of the verb estar were presented in Lección 2, p. 20, its three main uses were studied. They are as follows:

a. to express location

---

[1] For lo, a direct object, see Lección Veintidós.

[2] Traigo, present tense of the verb traer, "to bring". Spanish often uses present tense when English uses future, "will bring".

b. to express feelings and health

c. to express the condition of persons or things

Obviously, if you know the uses of <u>estar</u>, any
situation that does not fall in any of these three
categories calls for <u>ser</u>. This is an easy and
sure way to handle the two verbs <u>ser</u> and <u>estar</u>
until you do it naturally as they become part
of your speech habit.

NOUNS

aparato (m)	-	appliance, machine
azucarera (f)	-	sugar bowl
calle (f)	-	street
cama (f)	-	bed
capital (f)	-	capital (city)
capital (m)	-	capital (wealth)
carpintero (m)	-	carpenter
cereal (m)	-	cereal
copa (f)	-	glass with a stem
crema (f)	-	cream
chocolate (m)	-	chocolate, cocoa
dúo (m)	-	duet
Europa	-	Europe
farmacia (f)	-	drug store
fiesta (f)	-	party
fruta (f)	-	fruit
huevos (m)	-	egg
imagen (f)	-	picture, image
inspector (m)	-	inspector
instante (m)	-	instant
jamón (m)	-	ham
jugo (m)	-	juice
mamá (f)	-	mother
mayo (m)	-	May
modelo (m)	-	model
otoño (m)	-	autumn
pan (m)	-	bread
pastel (m)	-	pie, pastry
peluquería (f)	-	beauty parlor
pimentero (m)	-	pepper shaker
provecho (m)	-	benefit, advantage
salchicha (f)	-	sausage
salero (m)	-	salt shaker
salud (f)	-	health
servilleta (f)	-	napkin
sopa (f)	-	soup
taza (f)	-	cup
tío (a)	-	uncle, aunt
tocino (m)	-	bacon
tomate (m)	-	tomato
toronja (f)	-	grapefruit
torre (f)	-	tower
tostada (f)	-	toast (bread)
uva (f)	-	grape

ADJECTIVES

caliente	-	hot
delgado	-	thin
enfermo	-	sick
especial	-	special
frito	-	fried
mayor	-	greater, older
revuelto	-	scrambled
solo	-	alone
tostado	-	toast
triste	-	sad

VERBS

desayunar	-	to have breakfast
leer	-	to read
traer	-	to bring

ADVERBS

después	-	after, then
también	-	also
en seguida	-	right away

PREPOSITIONS

para	-	for

1. **Divide the following words into syllables.**

buenos	bue-nos	China	chi-na
comprar	com-prar	chico	chi-co
unos	u-nos	ocho	o-cho
bien	bien	amarillo	a-ma-ri-llo
desea	de-se-a	pollo	po-llo
que	que	perro	pe-rro
días	di as	arroz	a-rroz
quiero	quie-ro	torre	to-rre
aquí	a-quí	Ricardo	Ri-car-do
los	los	español	es-par-ñol
blancos	blan-cos	señor	se-ñor
muy	muy	baño	ba-ño
son	son	cuanto	uan-to
bonitos	bo-ni-tos	pantalones	pan-ta-lo-nes
número	nú-mer-o	cuestan	ues-tan
frase	fra-se	dónde	dón-de
cara	ca-ra	precio	pre-cio
José	Jo-sé	dólares	dó-la-res
Julio	Ju-lio	impuesto	im-pues-to
naranja	na-ran-ja	sombrero	som-bre-ro
		camisas	ca-mi-sas

negro	ne-gro
morado	mo-ra-do
rosado	ro-sa-do
rojo	ro-jo
verde	ver-de
azul	a-zul
zapatos	za-pa-tos
guantes	guan-tes
billetera	bi-lle-te-ra
suéter	své-ter
pañuelo	pa-ñue-lo
traje	tra-je
(usted)	us-ted
él	él
ella	e-lla
biblioteca	bi-blio-te-ca
gracias	gra-cias
empleado	em-ple-a-do
tienda	tien-da
cliente	clien-te
cuántos	cuan-tos
síganme	sí-gan-me

tienen	tie-nen
una	un-a
mesa	me-sa
cuatro	cua-tro
para	pa-ra
gusta	gu-sta
menú	me-nú
mucha	mu-cha
hambre	ham-bre
tenemos	te-ne-mos
desayuno	de-sa-yu-no
especial	es-spe-cial
huevos	hue-vos
jamón	ja-món
salchichas	sal-chi-chas
papas	pa-pas
harina	ha-ri-na
tostada	to-sta-da
mantequilla	man-te-qui-lla

2. **Use the correct form of ser or estar in the present tense.**

a. Tú ___estás___ triste.

b. ___estamos___ a cinco.

c. El dúo ___es___ francés.

d. Nosotros ___somos___ mecánicos.

e. Usted ___está___ en la biblioteca.

f. Yo ___estoy~~soy~~___ enfermo.

g. ___Estamos___ en otoño.

h. El ___es___ el profesor.

i. Ellas ___son___ de Francia.

j. Tú ___estás___ en los Estados Unidos.

k. Las servilletas ___están~~son~~___ en la mesa.

l. Pedro ___es___ de Caracas.

m. Usted ___es___ francés.

n. Usted ___está___ en Francia.

o. El ___está___ aquí.

p. Elena y María ___son___ de España.

q. Rosa ___es___ española.

r. Tú ___eres___ de Miami.

s. Tú ___estás___ en Miami.

t. El café ___está___ caliente.

u. Los pantalones ___son___ muy bonitos.

v. ¿Dónde ___está___ el precio?

w. ¿Dónde ___está___ el probador?

x. ¿Dónde ___está___ la caja?

y. ¿Cuánto ___es___ ?

3. **Answer these questions.**

a. ¿Quién eres? ___Soy Ernesto___

b. ¿De dónde eres? ___Soy de Sunnyvale___

c. ¿Qué eres? ___Soy estudiante___

d. ¿Dónde estás ahora? ___Estoy en Miami___

e. ¿Cómo estás? ___Estoy bien___

4. **The following words have the stress on the underlined vowel. Study them and decide whether they should have written accents.**

a. est**a**

b. s**i**ganme

c. cu**a**tro

d. g**u**sta

e. ti**e**nen

f. men**u**

g. desay**u**no

h. h**a**mbre

i. espec**i**al

j. hu**e**vos

k. jam**o**n

l. salch**i**chas

m. p**a**pas

n. har**i**na

o. tost**a**da

p. caf**e**

q. mantequ**i**lla

r. compr**a**r

s. cam**i**sa

t. ch**e**que

5. **Write the Spanish for the following English sentences.**

a. We are ready. _____Estamos_____

b. She is very pretty. _Ella es muy bonita_

c. They are smart. (feminine) _Ellas son listas_

d. You are not sick. (formal) _No estás_
   enfermo.

6. **Organize the following groups of words into meaning-ful sentences.**

a. en   b. choferes   c. la

   estamos   son   estás

   otoño   ellas   escuela

                             en

d. Francia   e. es

   estoy   el

   en   simpático

a) Estamos en otoño   _b) Ellas son choferes_   _c) Estás en la escuela._

a) Estoy en Francia   _e) El es simpático_

7. **Read each question and the two answers which follow, then underline the answer which is the logical and correct response to the question.**

a. ¿Quién eres?

   Soy francés.
   (Soy Pedrito.)

b. ¿Cómo estás?

   (Estoy enferma.)
   Soy delgada.

c. ¿Dónde estás?

   Soy francés.
   (Estoy en la biblioteca.)

d. ¿Qué eres?

   (Soy mecánico)
   Estoy triste.

e. ¿De dónde eres?

   Estoy en Francia.
   (Soy de Francia.)

Read the following question and answer.

What day is today?   –   ¿Qué día es hoy?

Today is Monday.   –   Hoy es lunes.

8. **Give six answers to this question using a different day of the week in each one, from Tuesday to Sunday.**

¿Qué día es hoy?

a. _Hoy es martes_   d. _Hoy es viernes_

b. _Hoy es miércoles_   e. _Hoy es sábado_

c. _Hoy es jueves_   f. _Hoy es domingo_

9. **Write a description of yourself. Be sure that with the information given you can answer the following questions.**

¿Quién eres?   ¿De dónde eres?

¿Qué eres?   ¿Dónde estás ahora?

¿Cómo estás?

Soy Pablo; Estoy bien; Estoy
en la escuela; Soy boxeo
Soy de China.

-77-

TOPICS: PREDICATE NOUNS AND PREDICATE ADJECTIVES, THE VERBS <u>DESAYUNAR</u>, AND <u>CENAR</u>, THE EXPRESSON <u>ES HORA DE</u> PLUS INFINITIVE, THE EXPRESSIONS <u>DE LA MAÑANA</u>, <u>DE LA TARDE</u> AND <u>DE LA NOCHE</u>

CONVERSATION X

ORDENANDO EL ALMUERZO		ORDERING LUNCH	
1. Camarera: ¿Qué desean almorzar?	–	Waitress:	What would you like to have for lunch?
2. Cliente: Queremos arroz con pollo.	–	Customer:	We want chicken and yellow rice.
3. Camarera: ¿Qué desean tomar?[1]	–	Waitress:	What would you like to drink?
4. Cliente: Solamente agua.	–	Customer:	Just water.
5. Camarera: ¿Qué desean de postre?	–	Waitress:	What would you like for dessert?
6. Cliente: Flan y después café.	–	Customer:	Flan and coffee later.
7. Camarera: ¿Café con crema o café solo?	–	Waitress:	Coffee with cream or black?
8 Cliente: Café solo, por favor.	–	Customer:	Black, please.

Special custard (handwritten note)

I. Predicate nouns and predicate adjectives

Both verbs <u>ser</u> and <u>estar</u> are commonly used as linking verbs. <u>Ser</u> links the subject with nouns or adjectives, while <u>estar</u> can only link the subject with an adjective. These nouns and adjectives are called predicate nouns and predicate adjectives respectively; they tell who, what or how the subject is.

El es el profesor. – He is the professor.

El camarero es alto. – The waiter is tall.

El camarero está listo. – The waiter is ready.

Predicate nouns and predicate adjectives must agree with the subject of the sentence.

Examples of predicate nouns:

El es el profesor.	–	He is the professor.
Ella es la profesora.	–	She is the professor.
Ellos son los pianistas.	–	They are the pianists.
Ellas son las camareras.	–	They are the waitresses.

Examples of predicate adjectives with <u>ser</u>:

El camarero es alto.	–	The waiter is tall.
La camarera es rubia.	–	The waitress is blonde.
Los estudiantes son inteligentes.	–	The students are intelligent.

---

[1]It is common to use interchangeably <u>tomar</u> or <u>beber</u> meaning "to drink".

Las camareras son altas. - The waitresses are tall.

Examples of predicate adjectives with estar.

El camarero está listo. - The waiter is ready.

La camarera está enferma. - The waitress is sick.

Los vestidos están sucios. - The dresses are dirty.

Las camisas están limpias. - The shirts are clean.

II. The verbs desayunar, and cenar

The verbs desayunar "to have breakfast" and cenar "to have dinner" are regular -ar verbs.

(Yo)	desayun-o
(Tú)	desayun-as
Ud., él, ella	desayun-a
(Nosotros, -as)	desayun-amos
Uds., ellos, ellas	desayun-an

(Yo)	cen-o
(Tú)	cen-as
Ud, él, ella	cen-a
(Nosotros, -as)	cen-amos
Uds., ellos, ellas	cen-an

Examples of desayunar and cenar:

Los lunes desayunamos temprano. - On Mondays we have breakfast early.

A veces ceno con Alberto. - At times I have dinner with Alberto.

No cenamos en casa los sábados. - We do not have dinner home on Saturdays.

Ella cena temprano los domingos. - She has dinner early on Sundays.

Ellos desayunan huevos con jamón. - They have ham and eggs for breakfast.

A menudo cenamos paella. - Often we have paella for dinner.

Notice that in the last two examples, the verbs desayunar and cenar are followed by the name of the foods while English uses a different form.

These verb forms can also be expressed as nouns:

el desayuno - breakfast

la cena - dinner

III. The expression es hora de plus infinitive

The expression in Spanish es hora de plus a verb in the infinitive means "it is time" plus an infinitive in English.

Examples:

Es hora de pagar. - It is time to pay.

Es hora de desayunar. - It is time to have breakfast.

Es hora de cenar.   -   It is time to have
                                      dinner.

Es hora de almorzar.   -   It is time to have
                                      lunch.

IV. The expressions de la mañana, de la tarde and de la noche.[2]

For A.M. or "in the morning", Spanish uses de la mañana;
from noon to sundown or "in the afternoon", de la tarde,
and from sundown to midnight or "in the evening", de la
noche.

Examples:

El tren llega a las ocho   -   The train arrives at
de la mañana.   8 A.M.

Hoy llamamos a Madrid a   -   Today we called Madrid
las dos de la tarde.   at 2 P.M.

La tienda tiene una   -   The store has a special
venta especial hoy a las   sale today at 7 P.M.
siete de la noche.

Note that these expressions are used after an indicated
hour. To say "in the morning", "in the afternoon", and
"in the evening", or "at night" in general, use por la
mañana, etc.

Elena va a la tienda por   -   Elena goes to the store in
la mañana.   the morning.

(Yo) estudio por la tarde. -   I study in the afternoon.

---

[2]These expressions were mentioned on page 66.

Son las ocho de la noche - It is 8 o'clock pm

Es la una menos viente - 1 minus 20

or 12:40 pm

Coctel de frutas - fruit cocktail
Jugo de tomate - tomato juice
Sopa de cebolla - Onion Soup
Sopa de fideos - noodle Soup
Sopa de arroz - rice Soup

Biftek empanizado - breaded steak
Costillas de puerco - pork chops
pollo frito - fried chicken
Huevos hervidos - boiled eggs
Tortilla de jamón - ham omelette

Pargo al horno - broiled red snapper
Cangrejo relleno - stuffed crabs
Langosta - lobster
Camarones rebozados - breaded shrimp

VOCABULARIO

NOUNS

agua[3] (f)	- water	Jorge	- George	
bandeja (f)	- tray	juego (m)	- game	
biftek (m)	- steak	langosta (f)	- lobster	
camarón (m)	- shrimp	lechuga (f)	- lettuce	
cangrejo (m)	- crab	manzana (f)	- apple	
caña (f)	- cane	marisco (m)	- seafood	
cebolla (f)	- onion	nariz (f)	- nose	
coctel (m)	- cocktail (drink)	narración (f)	- narrative	
costilla (f)	- rib	natilla (f)	- pudding, custard	
cuchara (f)	- spoon	paella (f)	- dish of yellow	
ensalada (f)	- salad		rice, chicken and	
espárrago (m)	- asparagus		seafood	
estación (f)	- station,	pantalla (f)	- screen	
	season of year	pargo (m)	- red snapper	
Estados Unidos	- United States	parque (m)	- park	
fideo (m)	- noodles	pescado (m0	- fish	
	(vermicelli)	plato (m)	- plate	
flan (m)	- custard	puerco (m)	- pork	
fresa (f)	- strawberry	puré (m)	- purée	
habichuela (f)	- string bean	puré de papas(m)	- mashed potatoes	
helado (m)	- ice cream	televisor (m)	- TV set	
horno (m)	- oven	tijeras (f)	- scissors	
idea (f)	- idea	tortilla (f)	- omelette	
invierno (m)	- winter	vaso (m)	- glass	
jarra (f)	- pitcher	ventana (f)	- window	
		vez (f)	- turn, time	

VERBS

ahorrar - to save
almorzar - to have lunch
cenar   - to have dinner

ADVERBS

solamente   - only

PREPOSITIONS

después de   - after

EXPRESSIONS

a menudo	- often
a veces	- at times
al horno	- baked
arroz con leche	- rice pudding
ensalada mixta	- tossed salad
es hora de	- it is time

PRONOUNS

alguien   - someone

ADJECTIVES

aquel	- that,
aquella	- that
empanizado	- breaded
excelente	- excellent
hervido	- boiled
limpio	- clean
rebozado	- breaded, basted
relleno	- stuffed

---

[3]Agua, "water" is feminine, but use the masculine definite article _el_, because it begins with stessed _a_.

EJERCICIOS

1. **Translate the following sentences into Spanish.**

    a. We are intelligent. _Somos inteligentes_

    b. We are students. _Somos estudiantes_

    c. The girls are blonde. _~~Ellas~~ Las chicas son rubias_

    d. They are Americans. _Ellos son Americanos_

    e. Ann is sad. (today) _Ana está triste_

    f. You are tall. _Eres alto (Ud es alto)_

    g. John is the professor. _Juan es el profesor._

    h. Mary is sick. _Mary está enferma_

    i. The dish is ready. _El plato está listo_

    j. The waiter is smart. _El camarero es listo_

2. **Translate into Spanish.**

    a. We often have dinner early.

    A menudo cenamos temprano.

    b. It's time to have breakfast.

    Es hora de desayunar.

    c. We have lunch at eleven thirty.

    Almorzamos a las once y media

    d. On Sundays we have dinner after 6 P.M.

    Los sábados cenamos después a las seis de la tarde.

    e. The game is at 10:15 A.M.

    El juego es a las diez y cuarto de la mañana.

    f. I always study at 6:30 A.M.

    Yo siempre estudio a las seis y media de la mañana

    g. Peter always has ham and eggs for breakfast.

    Pedro siempre desayuna jamón y huevos.

    h. It is time to study.

    Es hora de estudiar.

    i. The train arrives at 10:00 P.M.

    El tren llega a las diez de la noche.

    j. It is 10:45 A.M.

    Es hora de diez y cincuenta y cinco de la mañana.

3. **Organize the following group of words into a meaningful expression:**

a. solo	b. pollo	c. hora	d. noche
con	con	es	cenamos
crema	queremos	desayunar	de
o	arroz	de	
café	no	no	viernes
café	hoy		después

    a. Café con crema o café solo.

    b. No queremos arroz con pollo hoy.

    c. No es hora de desayunar.

    d. Los viernes cenamos después de las ocho de la noche

    las

    los

    la

    ocho

    de

1. Rewrite the following words and use accents, if needed. The main emphasis is marked by the underlined stressed vowel.

   a. televis_o_r

   b. cr_é_dito

   c. cuch_a_ra

   d. id_e_a

   e. _a_lguien

   f. ag_ü_ero

   g. v_a_so

   h. delg_a_do

   i. pant_a_lla

   j. vent_a_na

   k. ot_o_ño

   l. c_a_ña

   m. popul_a_r

   n. l_á_piz

   o. mi_é_rcoles

   p. narrac_i_ón

   q. ah_o_rra

   r. nar_i_z

   s. tij_e_ras

   t. excel_e_nte

   u. desay_u_no

(handwritten notes):
Ensaldas – Legumbres vegetables
lettuce salad — Ensalda de lechuga
esparagus — " espárragos
tossed salad — " mixta
mashed potatoes — Pure de papas
String beans — Habichuelas
rice pudding Natilla — Arroz con leche / Natilla
ice cream — Helados / Flan
Flan — Pastel de manzana
apple pie
Strawberries with Crema — Fresas con crema

2. Write the proper form of either **ser** or **estar**.

   a. Yo ___soy___ americano.

   b. Tú ___estás___ en los Estados Unidos.

   c. Ellas ___son___ de Francia.

   d. Nosotros ___estamos___ en Miami.

   e. Usted ___es___ francés.

   f. Ella ___es___ española.

   g. Ella ___está___ en España.

   h. El ___está___ aquí.

   i. Yo ___~~es~~ estoy___ en el parque.

   j. El desayuno ___está___ frío.

   k. El otoño ___está___ una estación.

   l. ___Está___ a cinco de mayo.

   m. Pablo y Jorge ___~~es~~ son___ los camareros hoy.

-83-

LECCIÓN DOCE

TOPICS: CONTRACTIONS <u>AL</u> AND <u>DEL</u>

CONVERSATION XI

	ORDENANDO LA CENA			ORDERING SUPPER
1.	Camarera:	¿Están listos para ordenar?	– Waitress:	Are you ready to order?
2.	Cliente:	Sí, queremos paella.	– Customer:	Yes, we want paella.
3.	Camarera:	¿Qué desean tomar?	– Waitress:	What would you like to drink?
4.	Cliente:	Coca-Cola.	– Customer:	Coca-Cola.
5.	Camarera:	¿Desean postre?	– Waitress:	Would you like dessert?
6.	Cliente:	Sí, por favor.	– Customer:	Yes, please.
7.	Cliente:	Queremos tocino del cielo y después café.	– Customer:	We want <u>tocino del cielo</u> and coffee later.

I.   **Contractions <u>al</u> and <u>del</u>.**

In Spanish, when the article <u>el</u> follows the preposition <u>a</u> or <u>de</u> two contractions occur:

$$a + el \longrightarrow al$$

$$de + el \longrightarrow del$$

They are the only contractions in the Spanish language.

Examples:

Camino <u>al</u> restaurante.   –   I walk to the restaurant.

Camino a los restaurantes.   –   I walk to the restaurants.

Camino a la mesa.   –   I walk to the table.

Camino a las mesas.   –   I walk to the tables.

Escuchamos <u>al</u> cocinero.   –   We listen to the cook (masc.)

Escuchamos a los cocineros.   –   We listen to the cooks.

Escuchamos a la cocinera.   –   We listen to the cook. (fem.)

Escuchamos a las cocineras.   –   We listen to the cooks. (fem.)

Ellos llegan del cine.   –   They arrive from the movies.

Ellos llegan de la ciudad.   –   They arrive from the city.

Ellos llegan de las montañas.   –   They arrive from the mountains.

Hablan de los postres.   –   They talk about the desserts.

Hablan de la paella.   –   They talk about the paella.

Hablan de las carnes.   –   They talk about the meats.

Notice that only the article <u>el</u> forms contractions when it follows the prepositions <u>a</u> or <u>de</u>.

A word of caution: Remember, that the apostrophe plus <u>s</u> ('s) to express possession is a feature of the English language. In Spanish, use the preposition <u>de</u> to express possession in all cases in which English uses ('s).

Examples:

El menú del restaurante.   - The restaurant's menu.

La servilleta del   - The customer's napkin.
cliente.

La sopa del chico.   - The boy's soup.

La sopa de la chica.   - The girl's soup.

La ensalada de la chica.   - The girl's salad.

La mesa de los señores.   - The gentlemen's table.

Tortilla de jamon - ham omlette

VOCABULARIO

NOUNS

apellido (m)	-	last name, surname
la carne (f)	-	meat
cielo (m)	-	sky
cine (m)	-	movie house
la ciudad (f)	-	city
cocinero (a)	-	cook
comida (f)	-	meal
cubiertos (m)	-	flatware
ensalada (f)	-	salad
ensalada mixta (f)	-	tossed salad
la legumbre (f)	-	vegetable
maíz (m)	-	corn
montaña (f)	-	mountain
pavo (m)	-	turkey
teatro (m)	-	theatre

ADJECTIVES

asado	-	baked, roasted
cansado	-	tired

pavo asado - baked turkey

natilla - custard

VERBS

caminar	-	to walk
llevar	-	to take, to carry
ordenar	-	to order

EXPRESSIONS

de día	-	daytime, during the day
de noche	-	nighttime, during the night
tocino del cielo	-	a Spanish custard dessert

CONTRACTIONS

al (a + el)	-	to the
del (de + el)	-	of the, from the

de — of, from

EJERCICIOS

1. **Change the following sentences to agree with the nouns given.**

   a. La ensalada de los chicos necesita sal.

      La ensalda *del* chico necista saul .

   b. Las mesas de las señoras están listas.

      La mesa de señor está listas .

   c. Quiero llevar los postres al comedor.

      Quiero llevar el pavo al comedor .

   d. Queremos llevar los cubiertos a las mesas.

      Queremos llevar los cubiertos a la mesa.

   e. Estoy muy cansado de la comida de los restaurantes.

      Estoy muy cansado de la comida del restaurante.

2. **Supply the correct form.**

   a. Queremos Cangrejo *relleno* y sopa de *cebolla* .
      _____stuffed crab_____ _____onion soup____

   b. Los chicos quieren ensalda mixta
      _____tossed salad_____

   c. La langosta es muy cara, voy a ordenar
      The lobster

      pargo asado .
      baked red snapper

   d. Ordenan √ *arroón* Camprizado y langosta los
      _____breaded shrimp_____ ____lobster____

   sábados. *de la*

   e. La ensalday lechuga y las habichwela están.
      ____lettuce salad____ ____string beans____

   aquí.

   f. El maiz y el puré de papas no son platos
      ___corn___ ___mashed potatoes___

   populares.

   g. Los postres más caros son las fresa con crema
      _____strawberries with cream

   y el flan.
      ____custard____

   h. Tomamos[1] helado , pero no queremos pastel de manzana.
      ___ice cream___ ___apple pie___

3. **Organize the following groups of words into meaningful expressions.**

   a. y - flan - después - café

      Flan y després café

   b. con - pollo - llevamos - arroz

      Llevamos arroz con pollo

   c. de - postre - desean - que - ¿ ?

      ¿ Qe desean de postre?

---

[1]In Spanish one drinks ice cream.

4. **Write the appropriate answer for each question.**

   a. ¿Qué desean almorzar?

   Queremos arroz con pollo.

   b. ¿Qué desean tomar?

   Solamente agua

   c. ¿Qué desean de postre?

   Queremos flan y café

5. **Complete the following sentences using the appropriate prepositions and definite articles or contractions.**

   a. Camino _a la_ casa.
           to the

   b. Llego _del_ parque.
           from the

   c. Camino _a los_ parques.
           to the

   d. Llego _de las_ casas.
           from the

   e. Camino _al_ cuarto.
           to the

   f. Camino _al_ teatro.
           to the

   g. Llego _del_ cuarto.
           from the

   h. Llego _de los_ cuartos.
           from the

   i. Camino _al_ baile.
           to the

   j. Llego _del_ baile.
           from the

   k. Camino _al_ automóvil.
           to the

   l. Camino _a la_ biblioteca.
           to the

6. **Translate the following into Spanish.**

   a. the pupil's (masc.) car

   El automóvil del alumno

   b. the teacher's (masc.) coat

   La chaqueta del profesor

   c. the pupil's (masc.) friend

   El amigo del alumno.

   d. the teacher's (fem.) blouse

   la blusa de la profesora.

   e. the boy's shirts

   Las camisas del chico.

TOPICS: NOUNS USED TO MODIFY OTHER NOUNS (NOUNS USED AS ADJECTIVES), SUMMARY OF THE USES OF THE PREPOSITION DE

CONVERSATION XII

ORDENANDO LA MERIENDA		ORDERING A SNACK	
1. Cliente: Señorita, queremos merendar.	-	Customer:	Miss, we want to have a snack.
2. Camarera: Bien, ¿qué desean?	-	Waitress:	Well, what would you like?
3. Cliente: Queremos batidos y medianoches.	-	Customer:	We want shakes and medianoches[1]
4. Camarera: ¿Batidos de fruta o de chocolate?	-	Waitress:	Fruit shakes or chocolate shakes?
5. Cliente: Dos de chocolate y dos de mamey.	-	Customer:	Two chocolate and two mamey.[2]
6. Camarera: ¿Cuántas medianoches?	-	Waitress:	How many medianoches?
7. Cliente: Cuatro, por favor.	-	Customer:	Four, please.

I. Nouns used to modify other nouns

In English, nouns can be used as adjectives, e.g. "dining room table", "butter knife", "tomato salad", "apple pie". "Dining room", "butter", "tomato", and "apple" are nouns that function as adjectives mofifying the nouns "table", "knife", "salad" and "pie" respectively. In Spanish, a noun cannot function as an adjective; therefore, when a noun is modifying another noun, the preposition de is used to link the two nouns.

Mesa de comedor	-	dining room table
Cuchillo de mantequilla	-	butter knife
Sopa de tomate	-	tomato soup
Pastel de manzana	-	apple pie
Sopa de pollo	-	chicken soup
Programa de televisión	-	television program

Note that the word order of the Spanish expressions is reversed as compared to English. This follows the principle that in Spanish the word or descriptive phrase goes after the noun that is being modified.

II. Summary of the uses of preposition de

In Lesson 7, the expression de qué color is used to ask what color something is.

¿De qué color es la casa?	-	What color is the house?
¿De qué color son las camisas?	-	What color are the shirts?
¿De qué color quieres los lápices?	-	What color pencils do you want?

---

[1]Medianoches: plural form of medianoche, a small sandwich, oval in shape, made with a special Cuban bread that is slightly sweet. The bread is spread with butter (sometimes with mustard) and is filled with sliced ham, roast pork, cheese and pickles.

[2]Mamey: The fruit from the American mammee tree.

Origin of a person or thing which uses the preposition de was also presented in Leccion Nueve.

Los alumnos son de Caracas.	-	The students are from Caracas.
El pan es de Francia.	-	The bread is from France.
Soy de París.	-	I am from Paris.

Also in lesson nine, possessions using the preposition de were studied.

La camisa de Arturo es verde.	-	Arturo's shirt is green.
La casa de Marta es grande.	-	Marta's house is big.
Las sillas de Carlos son azules.	-	Carlos' chairs are blue.
El sombrero de Víctor no está aquí.	-	Victor's hat is not here.

Remember that the use of apostrophe plus s to express possession is a feature of the English language, therefore, everytime an apostrophe plus "s" is used in English, you must use the preposition de in Spanish. Even in cases in which the thing possessed is implied in English, the preposition de is required in Spanish. Study the following examples·

Voy[3] a la casa de María.	-	I'm going to Mary's.
Es de Aurora.	-	It is Aurora's.

The question phrases ¿de quién? and ¿de quiénes?

When the possessor of something is to be identified, ask the following questions:

Whose shirt is it?	-	¿De quién es la camisa?
Whose house is it?	-	¿De quiénes es la casa?

In Spanish, there are two forms for "whose": de quién, to ask about one possessor and de quiénes to ask about two or more possessors.

¿De quién es el teléfono?	- Whose telephone is it?
¿De quién es el auto?	- Whose car is it?
¿De quiénes son las camisas?	- Whose shirts are they?
¿De quiénes son las carteras?	- Whose purses are they?
¿De quién son los zapatos?	- Whose shoes are they?

---

[3]For the conjugation of the verb -ir, "to go" see Lección Catorce.

VOCABULARIO

NOUNS

agencia (f)	-	agency
álbum (m)	-	album
arreglo (m)	-	repair
avión (m)	-	airplane
batido (m)	-	shake
boleto (m)	-	ticket
cena (f)	-	dinner
cerveza (f)	-	beer
consulta (f)	-	doctor's office
cuchillo (m)	-	knife
disco (m)	-	record
ejercicio (m)	-	exercise
fotografía (f)	-	photo, picture
gente (f)	-	people
hijo (a)	-	son, daughter, child
mamey (m)	-	mammee
medianoche (f)	-	type of sandwich
merienda (f)	-	afternoon snack
milla (f)	-	mile
mínimo	-	minimum
niño (a)	-	boy, girl, baby
ómnibus (m)	-	bus
pasaje (m)	-	transportation ticket, passage, fare
playa (f)	-	beach
programa (m)	-	program
refresco (m)	-	refreshment
tierra (f)	-	earth, land, soil, *ground*
tenedor (m)	-	fork
turista (f,m)	-	turist, *tourist*
vainilla (f)	-	vanilla
Venezuela	-	country in South America
viaje (m)	-	trip, journey
vino (m)	-	wine

joven - young man

ADJECTIVES

joven	-	young (adult)
mínimo	-	minimum
rápido	-	quick
tinto	-	red (wine)
venezolano	-	native of Venezuela

VERBS

arreglar	-	to arrange, to fix
merendar	-	to have a snack

ADVERBS

generalmente	-	generally

QUESTION WORDS

¿de quién(es)?	-	whose?

¿de quienes? - whose (plural)

De (uses of)

1) express origin or pt. of departure
2) link two nouns when one describes the other
3)

-91-

1. Replace each underlined noun using the word in parentheses. Make any other necessary change and write the new expressions.

   a. La camisa de los <u>chicos</u>. (amigo)

   La camisa del amigo.

   b. La blusa de Rosa. (señora)

   La blusa de la señora

   c. Las blusas de unas <u>chicas</u>. (chica)

   Las blusas de la chica.

   d. La camisa de la <u>chica</u>. (señor)

   La camisa del señor.

   e. La blusa de Ana. (chico)

   La blusa del chico.

   f. Las camisas de unos <u>chicos</u>. (tíos)

   Las camisa de unos tíos.

   g. La camisa de <u>Arturo</u>. (alumno)

   La camisa del alumno.

2. Complete the answer to each of the following questions.

   ¿De quién es el teléfono?

   a. *Es de la* niña.

   ¿De quién es el auto?

   b. *Es de la* chica.

   ¿De quién es la casa?

   c. *Es del* señor.

   ¿De quiénes son las camisas?

   d. *Son de* los alumnos.

   ¿De quién es el sombrero?

   e. *Es del* profesor.

   ¿De quién son las blusas?

   f. *Son de* María?

3. Fill in the blanks to complete the sentence using only the prepositions <u>a</u>, <u>de</u>, and the definite articles.

   La casa es *del* Sr. Pérez y el auto es
         a

   de la señora. El teléfono *de*
     b   c

   ellos[4] es 648-9031. Ahora llamo a la casa

   del tío *de* los Pérez. La
    d   e

   casa es blanca y el auto *de* él[4] es
                     f

   "beige".

---

[4]The Spanish possessive formed with <u>de</u> is also used with the pronouns, but no contraction takes place when <u>de</u> is followed by the pronoun él -- "he."

4. **For each numbered space chose the appropriate expression from the list at the right.**

El arreglo ___*del*___ auto.
        a
          ~~de la~~

La orden ___*de los*___ clientes.
        b
          ~~del~~

Un plato y ___*el*___ tenedor.
        c
          ~~el~~

La cliente ___*de la*___ farmacia.
        d
          ~~de los~~

5. **Read the model expression, then construct a new expression by substituting the words written below each model. Make any other necessary changes.**

a. Un amigo del chico.

/pasaje/avión *Un pasaje de avión.*

b. Los alumnos hablan bien.

/turista/inglés *La turista habla inglés.*

c. El profesor de la chica es el señor.

/viaje/chico/martes *El viaje del chico es el martes.*

d. ¿Está el alumno en la biblioteca de la escuela?

/señora/cuarto/hotel ¿? *Está la señora en el cuarto del hotel.*

e. La casa de los hermanos.

/boleto/ómnibus *El boleto del ómnibus.*

6. **Organize the following groups of words into meaningful expressions.**

a. unos   b. Rosa   c. del

~~camisas~~   ~~de~~   ~~camisa~~

~~de~~   ~~la~~   ~~la~~

~~chicos~~   ~~blusa~~   ~~chico~~

~~las~~

d. las   e. el

Arturo   de

de   chica

camisas   pañuelo

una

a. *Las camisas de unos chicos.*

b. *La blusa de Rosa.*

c. *La camisa del chico.*

d. *Las camisas de Arturo.*

e. *El pañuelo de una chica.*

1. Translate into Spanish

   a. They are from the United States.

   Ellos son de los Estados Unidos.

   b. It is daytime.

   Es de día

   c. What color is the car?

   ¿De que color es el automovil?

   d. We are in Miami.

   Somos en Miami.

   e. I arrived at the dance at 10.

   Llego al baile a las diez.

   f. It is nighttime.

   Es de noche

   g. The pupil's car is green.

   El automovil del alumno es verde

   h. The photo album is grey.

   El álbum de photo es gris.

   i. We arrive (are arriving) from the park.

   Llegamos del parque

   j. The professor's jacket is nice.

   La chaqueta del profesor es buena.

   k. Rosa's blouse is pink.

   La blusa de Rosa es rosada.

   l. Juan is from Florida.

   Juan es de Florida

   m. The English class is at 2:30.

   La clase de ingles es a las dos y media.

   n. I walk from the theatre to the house.

   Camino del theatro a la casa.

   o. We are from Miami.

   Somos de Miami.

2. Fill in the blanks with the preposition de if necessary.

   a. Los discos son ___de___ Portugal.

   b. Unas camisas ___de___ los chicos.

   c. El vestido ___de___ fiesta es azul.

   d. Rosa es ___de___ Venezuela.

   e. Juan es _____ inteligente.

   f. Las camisas ___de___ Arturo son blancas.

   g. Veo _____ el libro.

   h. Pedro es _____ Venezolano.

   i. ¿ ___De___ quién es el sombrero?

   j. Desayunamos ___de___ huevos.

k. El profesor _de_ la chica es el Sr. López.

l. El está en la biblioteca _de_ la escuela.

m. La casa es _de_ los hermanos Peréz.

n. Estoy en la consulta _de_ Pedro.

o. Yo vivo _____ aquí.

3. Translate into Spanish.

a. I want to have a snack.

   Quiero merendar

b. Are all of you ready to order?

   ¿ Estan listos para ordenar ?

c. Peter wants a strawberry shake.

   Pedro quiere un batido de fresa.

d. She wants to have breakfast.

   Ella quiere desayunar

e. Well, what do you want.

   Bien, ¿que desea ?

f. Mary wants apple pie.

   Maria quiere pastel de manzana.

g. What is today's special?

   ¿ Cual es el especial de hoy ?

h. We want to have dinner.

   Queremos cenar.

i. John and Mary want refreshments.

   Juan y Maria quieren refrescos

J. George, wants tomato juice.

   Jorge, quiere jugo de tomate

k. I want pork chops and rice.

   Quiero costilla de puero y arroz.

l. How many madianoches?

   Cuantos medianoches .

m. Four, please.

   Cuatro, por favor

n. Do all of you want dessert?

   Quieren Uds. postre .

o. Yes, four rice puddings, please.

   Si, cuatro arroz con leche, por favor

4. Answer the following questions in Spanish.

a. ¿Qué día es hoy? (Monday)

   Hoy es el lunes.

b. ¿Cuándo está Ud. en la playa? (Sundays)

   Ud estoy en la playa   los domingos.

c. ¿Qué días habla con ella? (Mondays, Wednesdays, and Fridays)

   Habla con ella en los lunes, los miercoles, y los viernes.

d. ¿Cuándo visitas a María? (on Thursday)

Visito a María en los jueves.

e. ¿Desayuna Ud. en el restaurante? (on Sundays)

Desayuno en el restaurante en los domingos.

f. En el restaurante, ¿cuál es el especial del domingo? (fruit cocktail, chicken with rice, lettuce salad and ice cream)

El especial es coctel de fruta, pollo con arroz, ensalda de lechuga y helado

5. **Translate into Spanish.**

a. Fruit juice   _jugo de fruta_

b. Tomato salad   _ensalda de tomate_

c. Roast turkey   _pavo asado_

d. Chocolate ice cream _helado de chocolate_

e. Apple pie   _pastel de manzana_

f. French fries   _papas de fritas_
   (fried potatoes)

g. Ice water   _agua fría_

h. Red wine   _vino tinto_   _descripcion_

i. Cold beer   _cerveza fría_

j. White wine   _vino blanco_

6. **Use the proper form of <u>ser</u> or <u>estar</u>.**

a. ¿Dónde _está_ el restaurante nuevo?

b. Allí _está_ .

c. ¿Cuánto _es_ la cena allí?

d. _es_ ocho dólares mínimo.

e. ¿Quiénes _estan_ en el restaurante?

f. El Sr. y la Sra. Fernández _estan_ allí.

g. ¿Cómo _estan_ ellos?

h. ¿De qué color _es_ el traje de él?

i. ¿De quién _es_ el abrigo negro?

j. _es_ de la señora.

k. ¿Qué hora _es_ ?

l. _Es_ la una y media.

m. _Son_ las ocho y cuarto.

n. La camisa de él _es_ verde.

o. Los zapatos de ella _Son_ azules.

7. **Choose the word that agrees.**

a. restaurantes — (1.) nuevos

   2. bonito

b. mesas — 1 pequeña

   (2.) bonitas

8. Give a "yes" and "no" answer to each of the questions. Write a complete sentence.

    a. ¿Habla español Ud?

        1. _Sí, hablo español_ (yes)

        2. _No hablo español_ (no)

    b. ¿Es bueno el libro de español?

        1. _Sí, es bueno_ (yes)

        2. _No es bueno_ . (no)

9. Write the appropriate definite articles to complete each of the expressions.

    _El_ impuesto de _la_ ropa.
      a   b

    _El_ empleado y _el / la_ cliente.
      c   d

    _La_ falda de María y _los_
      e   f

    pantalones de _____ Arturo.
                g

    Veo _la_ talla diez en _el_
           h   i

    probador de _la_ tienda.
             j

TOPICS: THE VERB IR, "TO GO", USES OF THE PREPOSITION A WITH THE VERB IR. REVIEW CONVERSATIONS LECCIONES 1 THROUGH 13

I. In Spanish, as well as English, the verb "to go",
    ir is used constantly in conversation. It is an
    irregular verb and its conjuction should be
    learned as one of a kind.

(Yo)	voy	-	I go
(Tú)	vas	-	you go (fam.)
Ud.	va	-	you go (formal)
Él, ella	va	-	He, she goes
(Nosotros(as))	vamos	-	We go
Uds.	van	-	You go (plural)
Ellos, ellas	van	-	They go

II. **Uses of the preposition a with the verb ir**

1. **The preposition a is required after the verb
    ir when it is followed by a destination.**

(Yo) Voy a la tienda.	-	I go (am going) to the store.
(Tú) Vas a la farmacia.	-	You go (are going) to the drug store. (fam.)
(Ud.) Va al cine.	-	You go (are going) to the movies. (formal)
Él (ella) va a la oficina.	-	He (she) goes (is going) to the office.

Nosotros (as) vamos al restaurante.	-	We go (are going) to the restaurant.
Uds. van a París.	-	All of you go (are going) to Paris.
Ellos (ellas) van a Londres.	-	They go (are going) to London.

2. **The preposition a is required after the verb ir
    when it is followed by a verb in the infinitive
    which expresses what the person is going to do.**

(Yo) Voy a estudiar.	-	I'm going to study.
(Tú) Vas a desayunar.	-	You are going to have breakfast.
Ud. va a comprar leche.	-	You are going to buy milk.
Él (ella) va a pagar de contado.	-	He (she) is going to pay cash.
Nosotros (as) vamos a hablar con Carlos.	-	We are going to talk with Carlos.
Uds. van a estar aquí hoy.	-	All of you are going to be here today.
Ellos (ellas) van a ir ahora.	-	They are going to go now.

Notice that the preposition a has no translation
in English in the previous examples given. It is
not a translation of the preposition "to" used in
English to express the infinitive form of the
verb i.e., "to study", estudiar, "to buy",
comprar, etc.

3. A third use of the preposition <u>a</u> with the verb <u>ir</u> is to translate the preposition "at" when expressing the time at which a person is going.

    Voy a las cuatro. -   I'm going at four.

Observation: The prepostiion "at" usually translate into Spanish as <u>en</u> (Espero en la biblioteca; El está <u>en</u> la oficina.) This use of <u>a</u> for "at" is one of the few exceptions.

4. In most other cases the verb <u>ir</u> does not require the preposition <u>a</u>.

    Voy temprano.   -   I'm going early.

    Vamos en seguida   -   We are going right away.

    El va hoy.   -   He is going today.

    ¿Vas con ellos?   -   Are you going with them?

-99-

VOCABULARIO

NOUNS

centro (m)   - center, downtown
cereza (f)   - cherry
croqueta (f)   - croquette, fritter
galleta (f)   - cracker
el limón (m)   - lemon
el melocotón (m) - peach
oficina (f)   - office
regalo (m)   - present, gift

ADJECTIVES

mejor   - better

VERBS

buscar   - to look for
ir   - to go
reservar - to reserve

CONNECTORS

o   -   or

EXPRESSIONS

más o menos - more or less
adiós   - goodbye

QUESTION WORDS

¿adónde? (a dónde?) - where (to)?

EJERCICIOS

In the exercise below, the forms of the present tense of the verb **ir** combined with a varied vocabulary are used.

1. **Read the following conversation in order to answer in complete sentences the questions related to it.**

Juan: ¿A dónde vas, Pilar?

Pilar: Ana y yo vamos a las tiendas.

Juan: ¿Necesitan muchas cosas?

Pilar: Ana quiere comprar un regalo.

Juan: Voy con ustedes.

reference back of the book

A. ¿A donde va Pilar? *Va a las tiendas*

B. ¿Quiénes van con Pilar? *Juan y ana*

C. ¿Qué quiere comprar Ana? *Un regalo*

D. ¿Quién quiere ir con Ana y Pilar? *Juan*

E. ¿Cuántas personas van a las tiendas? *Tres personas*

2. **Complete each of the sentences by using forms of the verb ir. Write each sentence.**

A. María y Pilar __*Van*__ a la casa de Juan.

B. María __*Va*__ a la tienda.

C. ¿A dónde __*Vamos*__ tú y yo?

D. Luego (yo) __*Voy*__ con Juan.

E. (Nosotros) no __*Vamos*__ a la oficina.

F. ¿(Tú) __*Vas*__ a la escuela ahora?

G. Ustedes __*Van*__ al cine.

3. **Organize into meaningful sentences the following group of words.**

a. ~~a~~ b. ~~centro~~ c. ~~no~~
~~escuela~~ ~~con~~ ~~tienda~~
~~van~~ ~~Juan~~ ~~voy~~
~~ellas~~ ~~al~~ ~~la~~
~~la~~ ~~va~~ ~~a~~
~~ahora~~ ~~las~~

a. *Ellas van a la escuela ahora.* ~~chicas~~

b. *Juan va al centro con las chicas.*

d. ~~casa~~ e. ~~tienda~~

c. *No voy a la tienda.*

~~a~~ ~~vas~~

d. *Tú y yo vamos a la casa*

~~yo~~ ~~la~~

~~vamos~~ ~~cuándo~~

e. ¿*Cuándo vas a la tienda?* ~~tú~~ ~~a~~

~~y~~ ¿ ?

~~la~~

4. **Complete the answers to the following questions using the verb ir.**

a. ¿Vas a la escuela?

Sí, __*Voy a la escuela*__

b. ¿Cuándo van las chicas a la casa?

__*Las chicas van a la casa*__ ahora.

-101-

c. ¿Van ustedes al cine?

Sí, _Vamos al cine_

d. ¿A dónde va ella?

Ella va a la tienda.

e. ¿No van ellos?

No, _ellos van no van_

5. **Read the following conversation, then answer the related questions using complete sentences.**

Cliente: ¿Cuánto es un almuerzo para un grupo?
Camarero: ¿Cuántos son en el grupo?
Cliente: Somos diez. 10
Camarero: El almuerzo para diez es treinta dólares. 10→30
Camarero: ¿A qué hora van a almorzar?
Cliente: A las doce y media más o menos. 12:30 pm
Camarero: Bien, voy a reservar una mesa para diez.

a. ¿A dónde va el grupo?

Va a un restaurante

b. ¿Qué quieren?

Quieren almuzar

c. ¿Cuánto es la cuenta?

Treinta dólares

d. ¿Cuántos son?

Son diez personas.

e. ¿A qué hora van?

A las doce y media, más o menos

6. **Complete the expression Es hora de..., "It is time to"... with the words for breakfast, lunch, snack and dinner considering the time given.**

a. Son las cuatro menos cuarto de la tarde.

Es ahora de merendar.

b. Son las siete y media de la mañana.

Es ahora de desayunar.

c. Es la una menos veinte y cinco de la tarde.

Es ahora de almorzar.

d. Son las ocho de la noche.

Es ahora de cenar

1. **Complete the sentences by translating the words in parentheses.**

   a. Quiero comprar (a belt) _un cinturón_ .

   b. Quiero comprar (a handkerchief) _un pañuelo_ .

   c. Quiero comprar (a tie) _la corbata_ .

   d. Quiero comprar (a shirt) _la camisa_ .

   e. Quiero comprar (a scarf) _la bufanda_ .

   f. Quiero comprar (a purse) _la cartera_ .

   g. Quiero comprar (some stockings) _las medias_ .

2. **Match the expression in column A with the appropriate ones in column b.**

	A		B
a.	Buenos _días_ .		son muy bonitos
b.	Quiero comprar _unos pantalones_ .		desea
c.	¿Qué _desea_ ?		unos pantalones
d.	Los blancos _son muy bonitos_ .		días

3. **Organize the following groups of words into meaningful expressins.**

   a. están – bien – aquí

   Bien, están aquí.

   b. días – desea – buenos – qué – ¿ ? –,

   Buenos días ¿Qué desea?

   c. muy – son – blancos – bonitos – los

   Los blancos son muy bonitos

   d. pantalones – quiero – unos – comprar

   Quiero comprar unos pantalones.

4. **Complete the sentences by translating the words in parentheses.**

   a. ¿Cuánto cuestan (the pants)?

   los pantalones

   b. ¿Cuánto cuestan (the gloves)?

   los guantes

   c. ¿Cuánto cuestan (the shoes)?

   los zapatos

   d. ¿Cuánto cuesta (the sweater)?

   el sombrero.

   e. ¿Cuánto cuesta (the hat)?

   el sombrero

   f. ¿Cuánto cuesta (the bathing suit)?

   traje de baño

   g. ¿Cuánto cuesta (the wallet)?

   la billetera

5. Complete the following sentences from the list of words below.

Los _puntalones_ son muy _baratos_. Ocho
dolares más el _impuesto_.

~~baratos~~ - impuesto - dólares - ~~pantalones~~

6. Organize the following groups of words into meaningful expressions.

a. el - está - ocho - aquí - más - dólares -

impuesto -,

Aquí está ocho dólares más el impuesto.

b. pantalones - probarme - los - puedo - ¿ ?

¿ Puedo probarme los puntalones?

c. probador - dónde - está - el - ¿ ?

¿ Dónde está el probador?

7. Complete the sentences by translating the words in parentheses.

a. Puedo probarme (the overcoat)?

el abrigo

b. ¿Puedo probarme (the dress)?

el vestido

c. ¿Puedo probarme (the suit)?

el traje

d. ¿Puedo probarme (the skirt)?

la falda

e. ¿Puedo probarme (the jacket)?

la chaqueta.

f. ¿Puedo probarme (the blouse)?

la blusa

8. Translate into Spanish.

a. Who? _Quienes_   e. How many? _Cuantos_

b. How? _Como_   f. How much? _Cuanto_

c. Where? _Donde_   g. What? _Que_

d. When? _Cuando_   h. Why? _por que_

9. Complete the following sentences using the proper form of estar.

a. ¿Dónde _estan_ las medias?

b. ¿Dónde _estamos_ la empleada y yo?

c. ¿Por qué _estas_ tú aquí?

d. Nosotros _estamos_ muy bien.

e. Yo _estoy_ mejor hoy.

f. ¿Allí _esta_ la chaqueta barata?

10. **Translate into Spanish.**

a. Where do you pay? Here?

¿Dónde ~~se~~ paga? Aquí

b. No, at the cash register.

No en la caja.

c. Where is it?

¿Dónde está?

d. Over there, near the door.

Allí, cerca de puerta

11. **Match the expressions in Column A with the appropriate one from Column B.**

A		B
a. De	Contado	más el impuesto
b. Nueve dólares	Más el impuesto	pagar
c. ¿Cómo va a	pagar ?	contado
d. Tome	el cambio	billete de diez
e. Aquí tiene un	billete de diez	el cambio

12. **Translate into Spanish.**

a. How are you going to pay?

¿Cómo va a pagar?

b. By check.

Con un cheque.

c. You need two "ID's."

Necesitas dos identificaciones

d. Here they are.

Aquí las tiene.

e. Here is the receipt, and thank you, Miss.

Aquí tiene el recibio y gracias señorita.

f. I want to charge it.

Quiero ponerlo en mi cuenta

g. Give me your credit card.

Deme su tarjeta de credito.

h. Sign here, please. Thank you.

Firme aquí por favor, gracias.

13. **Match the expressions in Column A with the appropriate ones in Column B.**

A		B
a. Gracias	señorita	dos identificaciones
b. Tome	el recibo	un cheque
c. Necesita	dos identificaciones	el recibo
d. Con	un cheque	señorita

14. **Organize the following words into meaningful expressions.**

a. pagar - a - cómo - va ¿ ?

   ¿Cómo va a pagar?

b. tarjeta - su - crédito - déme - de

   Déme su tarjeta de crédito.

c. gracias - favor - aquí - firme - por - ,

   Firme aquí por favor — gracias.

d. cuenta - en - quiero - la - ponerlo

   Quiero ponerlo en la cuenta

15. **Change the singular sentences to the plural, and the plural sentences to the singular.**

a. Pago de contado.

   Pagamos de contado

b. Toman el cambio.

   Toma el cambio.

c. Necesitas un billete de cinco.

   Necesitan un billeta de cino

d. Usted necesita un libro.

   Ustedes necesitan un libro

e. Firmamos aquí.

   Firmo aquí.

16. **Write the plural of the following expressions.**

a. Un examen muy fácil.

   Unos examenes muy fáciles

b. La cajera alta habla.

   Las cajeras altas hablan

c. La tienda popular.

   La tiendas populares

d. El abrigo azul está allí.

   Los abrijos azules están allí

e. La cliente simpática compra.

   Las clientes simpáticas compran.

17. **Translate into Spanish.**

a. Good monring. How many are there?

   Buenos Días ¿Cuántos son?

b. We want a table for four, please.

   Queremos una mesa para cuatro, por favor.

c. All right. Follow me.

   Muy bien. Síganme.

d. Here is a table for four.

   aquí tiene una mesa para cuatro.

e. Do you all like it?

¿Les gusta?

f. Yes, it's fine.

Sí, está muy bien.

g. Here is the menu.

Aquí tienen el menú.

h. Thank you very much.

Muchas gracias.

i. We are very hungry.

Tenemos mucho hambre.

18. Complete the expressions by choosing the appropriate word from the list below.

a. Señorita, queremos _desayunar_.

b. ¿Qué _desean_?

c. Jugo de _naranja_ y después _jamón_ y _huevos_.

d. También queremos _pan_ y _mantequilla_.

e. ¿Desean huevos _revueltos_ o _fritos_?

f. ¿Desean café con _leche_ o chocolate?

g. _En seguida_ lo traigo todo.

fritos	jamón	revueltos	en seguida
desean	desayunar	pan	mantequilla
naranja	huevos	leche	

19. Translate into Spanish.

a. Do you want to have lunch? (you, singular, formal)

¿Desea (quiere) almorzar?

b. We want chicken and yellow rice.

Queremos arroz con pollo.

c. What would you like to drink?

¿Qué desean tomar?

d. Just water.

Solamente agua.

e. What would you like for dessert?

¿Qué desean de postre?

f. Custard and coffee later.

Flan y después café.

g. Coffee with cream or black?

¿Café con crema o solo?

h. Black, please.

Café solo por favor.

20. Complete the sentences by choosing the appropriate words from the list below.

a. Señorita, queremos ___*merendar*___ .

b. Bien, ¿Qué ___*desean*___ .

c. Queremos _*batidos*_ y _*media noches*_

d. ¿Batidos de _*chocolate*_ o de _*frutas*_ .

e. Dos batidos de chocolate y dos de

___*mamey*___ .

mamey   chocolate

batidos   frutas

desean   medianoches

merendar

-108-

TOPICS: THE PRESENT TENSE OF REGULAR -ER AND -IR VERBS, THE QUESTIONS ¿CÓMO SE LLAMA? AND ¿CUÁL ES SU NOMBRE?

CONVERSATION XIII

	PIDIENDO UN TURNO[1]		ASKING FOR AN APPOINTMENT
1.	Recepcionista: Consulta del doctor Pérez	–	Receptionist: Doctor Pérez' office.
2.	Paciente: Señorita, quisiera[2] un turno.	–	Patient: Miss, I would like an appointment.
3.	Recepcionista: ¿Qué día lo[3] quiere?	–	Receptionist: What day do you want it?
4.	Paciente: El lunes.	–	Patient: On Monday.
5.	Recepcionista: ¿A qué hora?	–	Receptionist: At what time?
6.	Paciente: A las tres.	–	Patient: At three o'clock.
7.	Recepcionista: ¿Cuál es su nombre?	–	Receptionist: What is your name?
8.	Paciente: Ana López.	–	Patient: Ana López.
9.	Recepcionista: Muy bien, adiós.	–	Receptionist: Very Well, goodbye.

I. The Present Tense of Regular -er and -ir Verbs

The conjugation of -er verbs and -ir verbs are almost identical. Only the first person plural (nosotros/as) is different.

Notice that the ending for the first person plural, nosotros is -emos for the -er verbs and -imos is for the -ir verbs.

	comer - to eat	vivir - to live
(Yo)	com-o	viv-o
(Tú)	com-es	viv-es
Ud., él, ella	com-e	viv-e
(Nosotros/as)	com-emos	viv-imos
Uds., ellos, ellas	com-en	viv-en

-er and -ir verbs·

comer	–	to eat	conversar	- to chat
ver	–	to see	entrar	- to come in, to enter
leer	–	to read	contestar	- to answer
beber	–	to drink	preguntar	- to ask
aprender	–	to learn	buscar	- to look for
vender	–	to sell		
deber	–	to owe, must		
creer	–	to believe		
vivir	–	to live		
abrir	–	to open		
escribir	–	to write		

[1]Cita is the strict Spanish translation for appointment, but pedir un turno is more widely used.

[2]Quisiera roughly translates "I would like". It is a more polite form for a request. You may, nevertheless, use quiero which means "I want".

[3]for lo see Lección Veintidós.

Como costillas de puerco. — I eat pork chops.

Lees el menú. — You read the menu.

Ellos no comen en el comedor. — They don't eat in the dining room.

No vendemos huevos aquí. — We don't sell eggs here.

¿Por qué no come ella? — Why doesn't she eat?

¿Dónde viven Uds.? — Where do all of you live?

Vivimos en una casa grande en París. — We live in a big house in Paris.

Ellos escriben la hora del turno. — They write down the time for the appointment.

Leemos y escribimos español. — We read and write Spanish.

II. In another lesson, you learned that the Spanish for "What is your name?" is ¿Cómo se llama Ud.? or ¿Cómo te llamas? depending upon whether you address the person in a formal way, ¿Cómo se llama Ud.? or in a familiar way ¿Cómo te llamas? In this lesson's conversation, ¿Cuál es su nombre? also translates "what is your name?" Cuál usually means "which", but in Spanish you use cuál when asking a name of a person. Remember, that languages often can't be literally translated.

When asking the name of someone else you can use the following forms:

¿Cuál es el nombre de él? — What is his name?

¿Cuál es el nombre de ella? — What is her name

Following the same form, when trying to find out the name of the person you are talking to, you ask:

¿Cuál es el nombre de Ud.? — What is your name?

In Spanish, you may also use the word su in a question to find out "his", "her" or "your" name because su means "his", "her" or "your", therefore, the question ¿Cuál es su nombre? carries three meanings:

What is his name?

What is her name? ¿Cuál es su nombre?

What is your name?

However, this form, ¿Cuál es su nombre? is only used when the meaning of su is clearly indicated in the conversation. It is, of course, more precise to use ¿Cuál es el nombre de él?, ¿Cuál es el nombre de ella?, ¿Cuál es el nombre de Ud.? This usage avoids any possible confusion.

NOUNS

carta (f)	–	letter
enfermero (a)	–	nurse
médico (a)	–	medical doctor
nombre (m)	–	name
turno (m)	–	appointment, turn

VERBS

abrir	–	to open
beber	–	to drink
conversar	–	to talk
creer	–	to believe
deber	–	to owe, must
entrar	–	to enter
escribir	–	to write
pedir	–	to request
preguntar	–	to ask
trabajar	–	to work
ver	–	to see

ADJECTIVES

su	–	your (formal), his, her, their

1. **Read the following sentences. Write C, if the sentence is correct, and I, if the sentence is incorrect.**

    I   a. Nosotros bebes agua.

    C   b. El abre la caja.

    I   c. Tú come ahora.

    C   d. Yo vivo aquí.

    C   e. Nosotros abrimos la caja.

    I   f. Ellas come ahora.

    C   g. Usted bebe agua.

2. **Match the subject pronouns in Group A with the correct verb forms in Group B.**

A	B
a. Tú	come
b. Ellos	vivimos
c. Yo	bebes
d. Nosotros	abren
e. Ella	vivo

3. **Translate into Spanish.**

    a. I eat now. *Como ahora*

    b. We drink water. *Bebemos agua.*

    c. They (feminine) open the box.

    Ellas abren la caja.

    d. He lives here. *El viva aquí.*

    e. You (familiar) open the box.
    Tú abres la caja.

4. **Write the following verb forms in the plural.**

    a. bebo *Bebemos*

    b. abre *abren*

    c. comes *comen*

    d. vivo *vivimos*

5. **Read carefully.**

    Ana vive cerca de Rosa. Ana abre la puerta de la casa y Rosa entra. Las chicas meriendan y luego conversan.

    Answer in complete sentences the questions related to the preceding narrative.

    a. ¿Dónde vive Rosa? *Cerca de Ana.*

    b. ¿Quién abre la puerta? *Ana abre la puerta.*

    c. ¿Quién entra en la casa?
    Rosa entra en la casa

    d. ¿Dónde meriendan las chicas?
    meriendan en la casa de Ana.

6. **Rewrite each of the following expressions, changing the infinitive in parentheses to the correct verb form of the present tense.**

    a. Ana y yo *conversamos* en la casa.
    (conversar)

    b. Las chicas no *deben* mucho.
    (deber)

c. Ellas _escriben_ una carta.
    (escribir)

d. Ana y Rosa _leen_ el libro de la tía.
    (leer)

e. ¿Usted _cree_ ?
    (creer)

f. Nosotras _vemos_ a Roberto.
    (ver)

7. **Organize the following group of words into meaningful sentences.**

a. carta   b. chicas   c. la

de   en   yo

tío   viven   Ana

el   casa   casa

escribe   la   en

una   las   conversamos

Juan   y

a. El tío de Juan escribe una carta.

b. Las chicas viven en la casa.

c. Ana y yo conversamos en la casa

d. lees   e. meriendan

los   Juan

ahora   y

libros   conversan

¿ ?   Ana

          y

¿Lees los libros ahora?

Ana y Juan meriendan y conversan

8. **Answer in complete sentences.**

a. ¿Viven Ana y Juan en la casa de Rosa?

No, _ellos no viven en la casa de Rosa_

b. ¿Debes mucho?

No, _debo mucho._

c. ¿Qué escribe Juan?

Juan escribe una carta

d. ¿Conversan Uds. mucho?

Sí, _conversamos mucho_

9. **Translate the following sentences into Spanish. (Use se, te, me)**

a. What is your name (fam.)?

¿Cómo te llamas

b. What is your name (formal)?

¿Cómo se llama?

c. My name is John.

Mi nombre es Juan; Me llamo Juan

d. Her name is Mary.

Se llama María.

LECCIÓN DIECISÉIS

TOPICS: ORDINAL NUMBERS, STEM-CHANGING VERBS (E > IE), DIRECTIONAL POINTS

CONVERSATION XIV

LA PRIMERA VISITA AL DOCTOR		THE FIRST VISIT TO THE DOCTOR
NOMBRE, DIRECCIÓN Y TELÉFONO		NAME, ADDRESS AND PHONE NUMBER

1.	Recepcionista:	Buenas tardes. ¿Viene[1] por primera vez?	— Receptionist:	Good afternoon. Are you here for the first time?
2.	Paciente:	Sí, señorita.	— Patient:	Yes, Miss.
3.	Recepcionista:	¿Cuál es su nombre?	— Receptionist:	What is your name?
4.	Paciente:	Mi nombre es Ana López.	— Patient:	My name is Ana López.
5.	Recepcionista:	¿Cuál es su dirección?	— Receptionist:	What is your address?
6.	Paciente:	Mi dirección es calle Flores número diez y ocho.	— Patient:	My address is No. 18 Flores Street.
7.	Recepcionista:	¿Cuál es su teléfono?	— Receptionist:	What is your phone number?
8.	Paciente:	Mi teléfono es 435-0102.	— Patient:	My phone number is 435-0102.

I. Ordinal Numbers

Ordinal numbers function as adjectives therefore, if they are used in conjuction with a noun; they must agree with the gender and the number of the noun being modified.

Primero and tercero drop the -O before masculine singular nouns. Ordinal numbers are seldom used beyond décimo, "tenth".

primero	(a, os, as)	first
segundo	(a, os, as)	second
tercero	(a, os, as)	third
cuarto	(a, os, as)	fourth
quinto	(a, os, as)	fifth
sexto	(a, os, as)	sixth
séptimo	(a, os, as)	seventh
octavo	(a, os, as)	eigth
noveno	(a, os, as)	ninth
décimo	(a, os, as)	tenth

Examples:

El primer grupo.

La primera parte.

El segundo plato.

La segunda visita al médico.

El tercer hijo.

La tercera hija.

El noveno empleado.

La décima empleada.

Los primeros lugares.

Las primeras lecciones.

---

[1]For the conjugation of the verb venir see Lección Dieciocho.

II. Stem-changing Verbs (e ie)

As we explained in Lección 5, the stem of a verb is the part of the infinitive that precedes the -ar, -er and -ir. In the verb querer the stem is quer and the ending is -er.

In some Spanish verbs, the vowel e of the stem changes to ie in all the forms of the present tense, except in those corresponding to nosotros/as. Since these do not follow the regular pattern of conjugated verbs, they are termed "stem-changing."

In this lesson, the following three -ar stem-changing verbs will be presented: pensar, "to think" or "to intend", merendar, "to have a snack", and cerrar, "to close", two -er verbs: querer, "to want", and entender, "to understand", and two -ir verbs: sentir, "to feel" and preferir, "to prefer."

Examples :

	Pensar	Querer	Preferir
Yo	pienso	quiero	prefiero
Tú	piensas	quieres	prefieres
Ud., él, ella	piensa	quiere	prefiere
Nosotros/as	pensamos	queremos	preferimos
Uds., ellos, ellas	piensan	quieren	prefieren

III. Directional points

The four basic directional points are norte, "North", sur, "South", este, "East", and oeste, "West." The following come from the four basic directional points: noreste, "Northeast", noroeste, "Northwest", sureste, "Southeast", suroeste, "Southwest."

(Notice that directional points are not capitalized in Spanish.)

Study the following question-answer examples which involve addresses:

¿Dónde vives? — Where do you live?
Vivo en la calle 42 noroeste, número 18. — I live at 18 NW 42nd Street.

¿Dónde viven ellos? — Where do they live?
Viven en la calle 12 suroeste, número 82. — They live at 82 SW 12th Street.

¿Dónde vive Ud.? — Where do you live?
Vivo en la calle 82 noroeste, número 182. — I live at 182 NW 82nd Street.

VOCABULARIO

NOUNS

avenida (f)	-	avenue
cafetería (f)	-	coffee shop
dirección (f)	-	address, direction
este	-	East
noreste (m)	-	Northeast
noroeste	-	Northwest
oeste (m)	-	West
segundo (m)	-	second (part of a minute)
sur (m)	-	South
sureste (m)	-	Southeast
suroeste	-	Southwest

norte - north (handwritten)

ADJECTIVE

ligero	-	light, not heavy

VERBS

cerrar	-	to close
entender	-	to understand
pensar	-	to think
preferir	-	to prefer
sentir	-	to feel
venir	-	to come

ADVERBS

nada	-	nothing

NUMBERS

cuarto	-	fourth
décimo	-	tenth
noveno	-	ninth
octavo	-	eight
primero	-	first
quinto	-	fifth
segundo	-	second
séptimo	-	seventh
sexto	-	sixth
tercero	-	third

CONNECTORS

porque	-	because

EXPRESSIONS

al mediodía	-	at noon time

1. Write a new sentence using the subject pronouns in parentheses. Make all necessary changes.

   a. El merienda con ella. (ustedes)

      Uds. meriendan con ella

   b. El y yo pensamos en la fiesta. (tú)

      Tú piensas en la fiesta

   c. Yo cierro la puerta. (nosotros)

      Nosotros cerramos la puerta

   d. ¿Sienten ellos el frío? (usted)

      ¿Siente vd. el frío?

   e. El no quiere pescado. (yo)

      Yo no quiero pescado

2. For each of the following verb forms, write S if it is singular, and P if it is plural.

   a. Meriendas   *S*

   b. Pienso   *S*

   c. Sentimos   *P*

   d. Quieren   *P*

   e. Cierra   *S*

3. Translate into Spanish the word(s) written in parentheses.

   Nosotras *queremos* ¿Y tú?
   (want)

   Yo *cierro* la puerta y *meriendo* .
   (close)   (have a snack)

   Usted *prefiere* agua fría.
   (prefer)

   Ella no *quiere* merendar.
   (want)

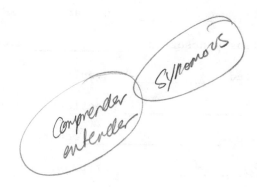

-117-

4. Fill in the blanks with the appropriate tenses.

Infinitive	(Yo)	(Tú)	(Usted, él, ella)	(Nosotros/as)	(Ustedes, ellos ellas)
Pensar	1. pienso	piensas	2. piensa	pensamos	3. piensan
Cerrar	cierro	4. cierras	cierra	5. cerramos	6. cierran
Sentir	7. siento	8. sientes	9. siente	10. sentimos	sienten
Entender	entiendo	11. entiendes	12. entiende	13. entendemos	14. entienden
Merendar	15. meriendo	meriendas	16. merienda	17. merendamos	18. mrerienden
Preferir	19. prefiero	20. prefieres	21. prefiere	preferimos	22. prefieren

5. Complete the following sentences with the correct form of **querer**.

a. (El) _quiere_ hablar.

b. (Ellos y nosotros) _queremos_ comer.

c. (Usted) _quiere_ venir.

d. (Yo) _quiero_ practicar.

e. (Ellas) _quieren_ cenar.

f. (Yo) _quiero_ arroz blanco.

g. ¿Qué (tú) _quieres_ ?

h. El _quiere_ pescado.

i. Ella _quiere_ ensalada de pollo.

j. (Nosotros or nosotras) no _queremos_ pan.

k. ¿Ustedes _quieren_ agua fría?

l. ¿Qué _quieren_ ellos?

6. Translate into Spanish.

a. I close the door.

Cierro la puerta

b. Do you think about the party (familiar)?   _Tú_

¿ Piensas en la fiesto ?

c. You have a snack with her (formal).

Ud. merienda con ella.

d. He understands Spanish.

Él entiende el espanal.

e. She wants soup.

Ella quiere soupa.

f. Do all of you feel the cold?

¿ Sienten Uds. el frío ?

g. They prefer coffee (masc).

Ellos prefieren café.

h. We close the door.

Nosotros cerramos la puerta.

i. We have a snack with her.

Nosotros merendamos con ella.

j. We understand Spanish.

Nosotros entendemos el español.

a. ¿A dónde va María?

María va a la cafetería

b. ¿Por qué no va al restaurante?

Porque solamente merienda al mediodía

c. ¿Quiénes van al restaurante?

Van Pedro, Carlos, y Carmen

d. ¿Por qué María prefiere ir a la cafetería?

Ella quiere algo ligero.

e. ¿Quién siente frío? Who feels cold?

Carmen siente frío.

7. **Read the conversation below and answer the questions in complete sentences.**

Pedro: Pensamos ir al restaurante hoy.

Carlos: Yo pienso comer bien.

Pedro: ¿Piensas ir también, María?

María: No, Uds. piensan almorzar. Yo solamente meriendo al mediodía. Prefiero ir a la cafetería porque quiero algo ligero.

Something light.

Carlos: Cierran la cafetería a las dos.

María: Voy a salir en seguida; no quiero llegar tarde.

Pedro: ¿No sientes frío hoy, Carmen?

Carmen: Sí, siento frío pero prefiero el invierno. ¿Por qué no caminamos al restaurante?

8. **Translate into English the conversation of Exercise 7.**

Pedro: We are planning to go to the restaurant today.

Carlos: I am planning to eat well.

Pedro: Are you planning to go María?

María: No, you are planning to have lunch. I only have a snack in the afternoon. I prefer to go to the cafeteria because I want something light.

Carlos: The cafeteria closes at 2 pm.

María: I'm leaving right away. I don't want to arrive late.

Pedro: Don't you feel cold today Carmen?

Carmen: Yes I feel cold but I prefer the winter. Why don't we walk to the restaurant?

9. Translate the following addresses into Spanish and write out the numbers. (Use cardinal numbers)

a. 211 SW 79th Avenue

Avenida setenta y nueve del suroeste, número doscientos y once

b. 19 NE 121st Street

Calle ciento viente y uno del noreste, número diez y nueve.

c. 15 NW 70th Street

Calle setenta del noroeste, número quince.

d. 19 SE 102nd Avenue

Avenida ciento y dos del sureste, número diez y nueve.

TOPICS: THE VERB TENER, ITS CONJUGATION AND USES, THE PERSONAL A, THE EXPRESSIONS "ME DUELE" ... AND ME DUELEN..."
PARTS OF THE BODY, THE HEAD AND THE NECK

CONVERSATION XV

EDAD, OCUPACIÓN Y ESTADO CIVIL		AGE, OCCUPATION AND MARITAL STATUS	
1. Recepcionista:	¿Cuántos años tiene?	–Receptionist:	How old are you?
2. Paciente:	Tengo veintitrés años.	–Patient:	I am 23 years old.
3. Recepcionista:	¿Es soltera, casada, divorciada o viuda?	–Receptionist:	Are you single, married, divorced or widow?
4. Paciente:	Soy casada.	–Patient:	I am married.
5. Recepcionista:	¿Cuál es su ocupación?	–Receptionist:	What is your occupation?
6. Paciente:	soy[1] recepcionista.	–Patient:	I am a receptionist.
7. Recepcionista:	¿Quién le[2] recomendó[3] al doctor?	–Receptionist:	Who recommended the doctor to you?
8. Paciente:	La señora de Martínez.	–Patient:	Mrs. Martínez.

I. The verb tener

Tener is another verb where the vowel e of the stem changes to ie in all forms of the present tense except for the ones corresponding to yo and nosotros/as. The form for yo adds a g to the stem and no ie.

Tener		To have
(Yo)	tengo	I have
(Tú)	tienes	You have (familiar)
Ud., él, ella	tiene	You, he, she has
(Nosotros/as)	tenemos	We have
Uds., ellos, ellas	tienen	All of you, they have

When you studied the conversations that took place at the restaurant, there were three lines using the verb tener:

Aquí tiene una mesa para cuatro.	– Here is a table for four.
Aquí tiene el menú.	– Here is the menu.
Tenemos mucha hambre.	– We are very hungry.

In this lesson's conversation, "Age, Occupation and Marital Status", the verb tener appears twice.

¿Cuántos años tiene?	– How old are you?
Tengo 23 años. ⟶	– I am 23 years old.

In all previous examples, common English usage demands the use of the verb "to be". In the same situations, common Spanish usage demands the usage of the verb tener, "to have."

---

[1]Spanish does not use the indefinite article when stating a profession, religion or political affiliation.
[2]For the use of le (indirect object pronoun) see Lección Veintitrés.
[3]Recomendó is a form of the past tense, see Lección Veintisiete.

The verb tener is used in a number of important idioms in Spanish. The following list includes the most common·

tener hambre	to be hungry
tener sed	to be thirsty
tener prisa	to be in a hurry
tener razón	to be right
no tener razón	to be wrong
tener suerte	to be lucky
tener frío	to be cold
tener calor	to be hot
tener sueño	to be sleepy
tener miedo	to be afraid
tener éxito	to be successful
tener ... años	to be "year" old

One important feature of the verb tener is that when followed by an infinitive, it requires the word que before that infinitive. In this case, tener que always means "to have to".

(Yo) tengo que ir.	I have to go.
(Tú) tienes que estudiar.	You have to study.
Ella tiene que hablar más.	She has to speak more.
Ud. tiene que llegar más. temprano.	You have to arrive early.
Ellos tienen que comprar los libros.	They have to buy the books.

II. The Personal a

A. The preposition a is required before the direct object when it refers to a definite person, or personified animal or thing. Personified animals are pets such as dogs, cats, and even horses when they are considered part of the family. Personified things are cities and countries because they are made up of people.

(Yo) Veo a la chica.

Veo el libro.

Llamo a los empleados.

Llevo los platos de postre.

Llevo a mi perro al veterinario.

Llamo a Madrid los sábados.

Llamo la atención a los alumnos.

III. The expressions: me duele ... and me duelen ...

When you want to express that a certain part of your body hurts, you use the forms me duele or me duelen plus that part of parts of your body that hurt. If the part hurting is singular you use me duele, if it is plural you use me duelen.

Me duele la cabeza.	- I have a headache.
Me duelen los ojos.	- My eyes hurt.
Me duele el cuello.	- My neck hurts.
Me duelen los labios.	- My lips hurt.
Me duele la garganta.	- I have a sore throat.

IV. LAS PARTES DEL CUERPO
VOCABULARIO BÁSICO
LA CABEZA Y EL CUELLO

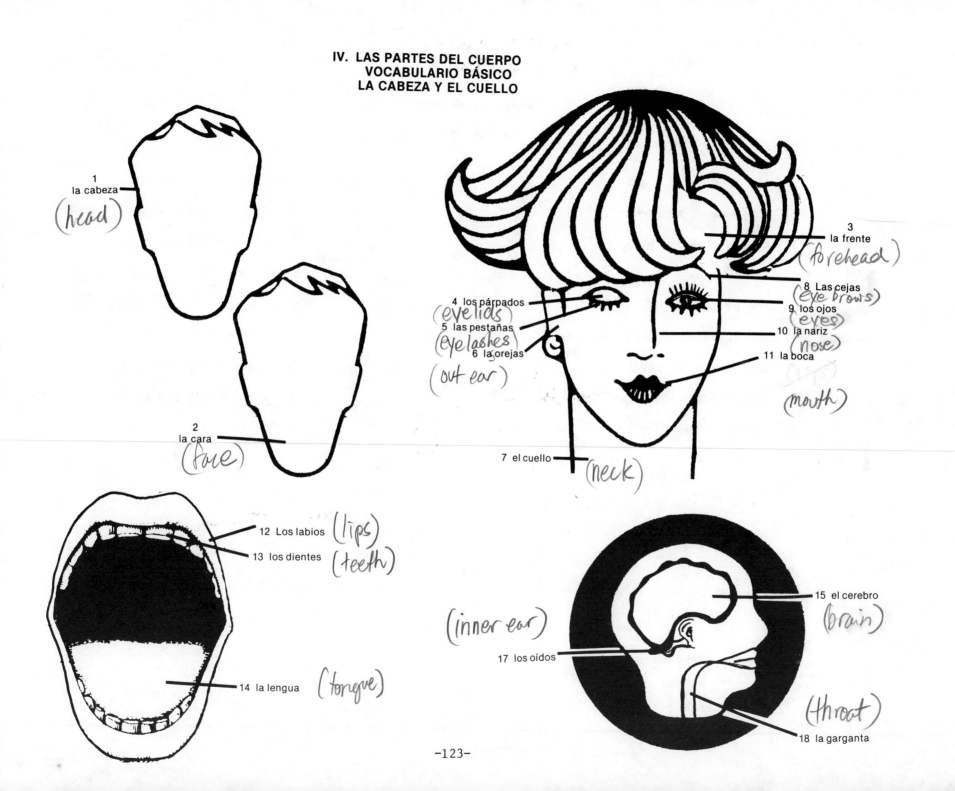

1 la cabeza (head)

2 la cara (face)

3 la frente (forehead)

4 los párpados (eyelids)

5 las pestañas (eyelashes)

6 la orejas (out ear)

7 el cuello (neck)

8 Las cejas (eyebrows)

9 los ojos (eyes)

10 la nariz (nose)

11 la boca (mouth)

12 Los labios (lips)

13 los dientes (teeth)

14 la lengua (tongue)

15 el cerebro (brain)

17 los oídos (inner ear)

18 la garganta (throat)

-123-

THE PARTS OF THE BODY

BASIC VOCABULARY

THE HEAD AND THE NECK

1) the head   la cabeza

2) the face   la cara

3) the forehead   la frente

4) the eyelids   los párpados

5) the eyelashes   las pestañas

6) the outer ear   las orejas

7) the neck   el cuello

8) the eyebrows   las cejas

9) the eyes   los ojos

la nariz   10) the nose

la boca   11) the mouth

los labios   12) the lips

los dientes   13) the teeth

la lengua   14) the tongue

el cerebro   15) the brain

la garganta   16) the throat

~~los oídos~~   17) the inner ear

los oídos

VOCABULARIO

NOUNS

abogado (a)	-	lawyer
el ataque (m)	-	attack
boca (f)	-	mouth
cabeza (f)	-	head
calor (m)	-	hot, heat
ceja (f)	-	eyebrow
cerebro (m)	-	brain
cuello (m)	-	neck
diente (m)	-	tooth
éxito (m)	-	success
frente (f)	-	forehead
garganta (f)	-	throat
labio (m)	-	lip
laboratorio(m)	-	laboratory
lengua (f)	-	tongue
miedo (m)	-	fear
nariz (f)	-	nose
ocupación (f)	-	occupation
oído (m)	-	inner ear
ojo (m)	-	eye
oreja (f)	-	outer ear
párpado (m)	-	eyelid
pestaña (f)	-	eyelash
prisa (f)	-	the act of being in a hurry
razón (f)	-	reason
recepcionista (m&f)	-	receptionist
secretario (a)	-	secretary
sed (f)	-	thirst
sueño (m)	-	dream, the feeling of being sleepy
suerte (f)	-	luck
veterinario (a)	-	veterinary

maestro (a) — teacher
peluquero (a) — hairdresser

ADJECTIVES

casado	-	married
divorciado	-	divorced
soltero	-	single, unmarried
viudo	-	widower, widow

VERBS

doler	-	to hurt
recomendar	-	to recommend

I have a headache — Me duele la cabeza.

1. Fill in the blanks with the corresponding word from the column at the right.

   a. ¿ _Cuántos_ años tiene?   cuál

   b. ¿Es soltera o _casada_ ?   cuántos

   c. ¿ _Cuál_ es su ocupación?   quién

   d. _Tengo_ 18 años.   tengo

   e. ¿ _Quién_ le recomendó al   casada

   doctor?

2. Write the appropriate answers in complete sentences.

   a. ¿Cuál es su ocupación?   _Mi ocupación es estudiante._

   b. ¿Cuántos años tiene?   _Tengo veinte y tres años._

   c. ¿Es soltera o casada?   _Soy soltera._

   d. ¿Quién le recomendó al doctor?   _La señora de Buehler_

3. Read the following sentences, and decide if the _a_ should be used. Write **Sí** or **No** to answer.

   _No_ a. Veo _____ el libro.

   _Sí_ b. Veo _____ alguien.

   _No_ c. Veo _____ un regalo.

   _No_ d. Veo _____ la puerta.

   _Sí_ e. Veo _____ las maestras.

4. Fill in the blank with _a_ or _al_. When neither one is needed, write an "X".

   Todos los días veo _a_ Carlos en la

   clase de español, y escucho _a_ la

   profesora. Mi amigo Tomás escucha _X_ el

   radio. Veo _al_ hermano de Pedrito. El

   no escucha _a_ las profesoras.

5. Write sentences by substituting the word underlined in the model sentence with the new nouns listed below. Make the necessary changes.

   Llego a la casa.   _Llego a las seis._   _Llego al laboratorio_
   a. seis   b. laboratorio   c. tres   _Llego a las tres_

   Llego de Miami   _Llego del teatro_   _Llego de la tienda_
   a. teatro   b. hospital   c. tienda   _Llego del hospital_

6. Organize the following groups of words into meaningful expressions.

   a. tiene – años – cuántos – ¿ ?
   ¿Cuántos años tiene?

   b. ocupación – su – es – cuál – ¿ ?
   ¿Cuál es su ocupación?

c. -al - recomendó - doctor - quién - le - ¿ ?

¿Quién le recomendó al doctor?

d. 18 - tengo - años

Tengo diez y ocho años.

7. Write the number of the English expression beside the letter of its corresponding Spanish expression.

a. las orejas _17_
b. la garganta _11_
c. la cara _6_
d. la frente _14_
e. la boca _8_
f. los labios _9_
g. la cabeza _15_
h. los ojos _5_
i. los dientes _12_
j. el cuello _7_
k. los párpados _(eyelids)_ _13_
l. la nariz _(eyebrows)_ _10_
m. las cejas _1_
n. la lengua _(eyelashes)_ _2_
o. las pestañas _3_
p. el cerebro _16_
q. los oídos _4_

1. the eyebrows
2. the tongue
3. the eyelashes
4. the inner ears
5. the eyes
6. the face
7. the neck
8. the mouth
9. the lips
10. the nose
11. the throat
12. the teeth
13. the eyelids
14. the forehead
15. the head
16. the brain
17. the outer ears

8. If the human body has two or more of the following, underline the word.

a. el cerebro
b. la boca
c. la nariz
d. el ojo
e. el diente
f. la cara
g. la pestaña
h. la lengua

i. el párpado
j. la oreja
k. la frente
l. la garganta
m. la ceja
n. el cuello
o. la cabeza

9. Write the plural of the words that you have chosen from Exercise 8. Use the proper article.

los ojos

los dientes

las pestañas

los párpados

las orejas

las cejas

10. **Translate into Spanish.**

    a. the head   _la cabeza_

    b. the face   _la cara_

    c. the neck   _el cuello_

    d. the eyes   _los ojos_

    e. the mouth   _la boca_

    f. the nose   _la nariz_

    g. the inner ear   _los oídos_

    h. the tongue   _la lengua_

    i. the throat   _la garganta_

    j. the forehead   _la frente_

11. **Write the preposition a or de to complete the following expressions.**

    a. Los discos son _de_ Miami.

    b. Veo _a_ mi perro.

    c. El vestido _de_ fiesta.

    d. Llamo _a_ alguien.

    e. Rosa es _de_ México.

TOPICS: FORMAL DIRECT COMMANDS OF -AR VERBS, THE VERB VENIR, MORE STEM-CHANGING VERBS, PARTS OF THE BODY – THE TORSO

CONVERSATION XVI

EL SEGURO			INSURANCE	
1.	Recepcionista:	¿Tiene seguro?	–	Receptionist: Do you have insurance?
2.	Paciente:	Sí, tengo.	–	Patient: Yes, I do.
3.	Recepcionista:	Siéntese, por favor, y espere un rato.	–	Receptionist: Sit down, please, and wait a while.

I. Formal Direct Commands of -ar Verbs

While in general, English uses the forms of the indicative to express commands, Spanish uses a different form. In almost all -ar verbs the formal command is formed by adding -e to the stem of the first person singular of the present indicative for Ud., and -en for Uds. The following chart illustrates the forms of the first person present indicative and command forms for Ud. and Uds.

Infinitive	Yo	Ud. Command	Uds. Command
esperar	espero	espere	esperen
pensar	~~piensa~~ ? piens~~o~~	piense	piensen

It is most important when constructing a sentence that you distinguish between making a statement or giving an order, so that you will correctly use the inidicative form for statements, and the command forms for orders or commands.

Examples: (Singular Commands)

Entre, por favor.	Come in, please
Firme aquí.	Sign here.
Hable ahora.	Speak now.
Tome el recibo.	Take the receipt.
Espere un rato.	Wait a while.

(Plural Commands)   ON EXAM

Entren, por favor.	– Come in, please (you plural)
Firmen aquí.	– Sign here. "
Hablen ahora.	– Speak now. "
Tomen el recibo.	– Take the receipt. "
Esperen un rato.	– Wait a while. "

The subject pronouns used with these forms are Ud. for the first group, and Uds. for the second group. It is not necessary to use them because the endings -e and -en indicate the person and number corresponding to the verb form, however, sometimes the pronouns are used, in which case they should follow the verb.

Entre Ud.

Firme Ud.

Hable Ud. ahora.

Tome Ud. el recibo.

Negative commands: To turn a formal command into a negative one, the word <u>no</u> precedes the verb:

No entre.   —   Do not enter.

No cierre la puerta.   —   Don't close the door.

II. The Verb <u>Venir</u>

The verb <u>venir</u>, like <u>tener</u>, introduces a <u>g</u> between the stem and the ending for the first person singular indicative·

(Yo)	vengo
(Tú)	vienes
Ud., él, ella	viene
(Nosotros/as)	venimos
Uds., ellos, ellas	vienen

Examples

¿Vienen por primera vez?	—	Are you here for the first time?
Sí, vengo por primera vez.	—	Yes, I am here for the first time.
¿Vienen hoy?	—	Are you coming today?
No, venimos hoy.	—	No, we are not coming today.
¿Vienes mañana?	—	Are you coming tomorrow?

III. More Stem-Changing Verbs

empezar	—	to begin
comenzar	—	to begin
recomendar	—	to recommend
merendar	—	to have a snack
calentar	—	to heat
perder	—	to lose
encender	—	to light, to turn on

The conjugation of the present indicative of these verbs follows the pattern of the stem-changing verbs·

	empezar	perder
(Yo)	empiezo	pierdo
(Tú)	empiezas	pierdes
Ud., él, ella	empieza	pierde
(Nosotros/as)	empezamos	perdemos
Uds., ellos, ellas	empiezan	pierden

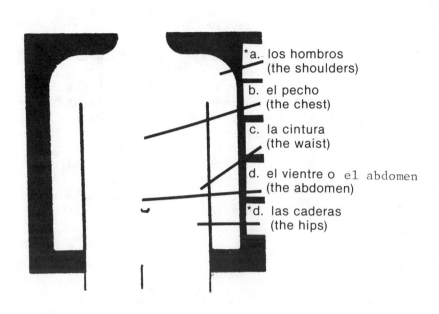

*a. los hombros
(the shoulders)

b. el pecho
(the chest)

c. la cintura
(the waist)

d. el vientre o el abdomen
(the abdomen)

*d. las caderas
(the hips)

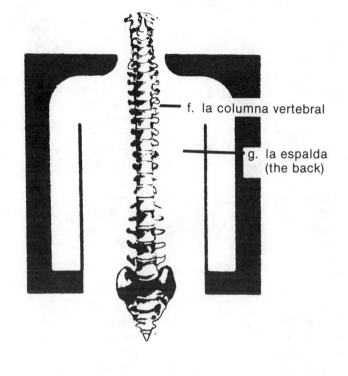

f. la columna vertebral

g. la espalda
(the back)

*Notice that these words are in the plural.

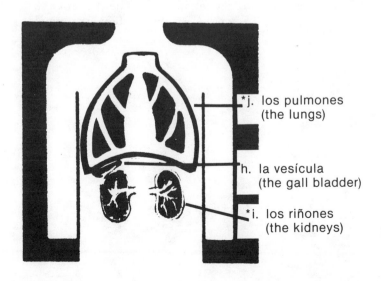

*j. los pulmones
(the lungs)

h. la vesícula
(the gall bladder)

*i. los riñones
(the kidneys)

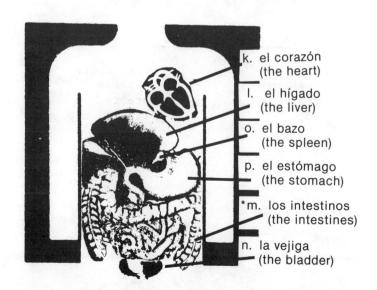

k. el corazón
(the heart)

l. el hígado
(the liver)

o. el bazo
(the spleen)

p. el estómago
(the stomach)

*m. los intestinos
(the intestines)

n. la vejiga
(the bladder)

VOCABULARIO

NOUNS

abdomen (m)	-	abdomen
bazo (m)	-	spleen
cadera (f)	-	hip
cintura (f)	-	waist
columna vertebral(f)	-	spinal column
contador (a)	-	accountant
corazón (m)	-	heart
dolor (m)	-	pain
espalda (f)	-	back (of body)
estómago (m)	-	stomach
habitación (f)	-	room
hígado (m)	-	liver
hombro (m)	-	shoulder
hospital (m)	-	hospital
intestino (m)	-	intestine
país (m)	-	country
pecho (m)	-	chest
peluquero (a)	-	hairdresser
pulmón (m)	-	lung
riñón (m)	-	kidney
seguro (m)	-	insurance
tronco (m)	-	torso
vejiga (f)	-	bladder
vesícula (f)	-	gall bladder
vientre (m) *, el abdomen*	-	abdomen

ADJECTIVES

bajo	-	low, short
italiano	-	Italian
lindo	-	pretty
poco	-	little, not enough

VERBS

calentar	-	to heat
cambiar	-	to change, exchange
cantar	-	to sing
comenzar	-	to begin
cortar	-	to cut
empezar	-	to begin
encender	-	to light
esperar	-	to wait
mirar	-	to look
perder	-	to lose
preparar	-	to prepare
recordar	-	to remember
regresar	-	to go back, to return
respirar	-	to breath

to turn on

ADVERB

cerca	-	near

EXPRESSIONS

ataque al corazón	-	heart attack
¿Cómo le va?	-	How are you?

1. Complete the expressions, choosing from the words at the right.

   a. Sí, _tengo_ .   ~~espere~~

   b. ¿Tiene _seguro_ ?   tengo

   c. _Siéntese_, por favor.   seguro (insurance)

   d. _Espere_ un rato.   siéntese

2. Write the appropriate question for the answer.

   ¿Tiene seguro? . Sí, tengo seguro.

3. Write the Spanish for the following English expressions. This exercise also should be practiced orally.

   a. Wait a while, please. _Espere un rato, por favor_

   b. Do you have insurance? _¿Tiene seguro?_

   c. Sit down, please _Siéntese, por favor_

4. Answer the following questions in Spanish and translate into English.

   a. ¿Vive Ud. cerca de la consulta del doctor?

   Sí, _Vivo cerca._

   Do you live near the doctor's office.

   b. ¿Cuándo vas al hospital?

   Voy al hospital mañana

   When are you going to the hospital

   c. ¿Quién abre la puerta de la consulta?

   La receptionista

   Who opened the doctor office's door?

   d. ¿Comen Uds. con la recepcionista?

   No, _Comemos con la receptionist_

   Do you (all) eat with the receptionist.

   e. ¿La señora de López bebe agua o Coca Cola?

   No bebe agua.

   Mrs Lopez drink water or coca cola

   f. ¿Cuánto dinero debes pagar en la consulta?

   Debo pagar veinte _dolares_

   How much must you pay the doctor?

   g. ¿Viven María y tú en Miami?

   Sí, _Vivimos en Miami._

   They (Maria and you) live in Miami.

5. Change the infinitive in parentheses to the correct verb form in the present tense.

   a. Mamá _Va_ al hospital los lunes.
          (ir)

   b. Yo no _como_ con el médico.
          (comer)

c. La recepcionista y yo **VIVImoS** cerca.
         (vivir)

d. La señorita Pérez y la señora de Martínez
     abren las puertas temprano.
     (abrir)

6. **Read the narrative and the five incomplete sentences which follow. Complete each item by choosing the correct completion from the choices given.**

I'm going to Doctor Perez's office at 3 pm
Voy a la consulta del Dr. Pérez a las tres.
I am sick I don't read because I don't see well
Estoy enfermo; no leo porque no veo bien;
I eat a little and drink a lot of water
como poco y bebo mucha agua.
I live near the doctor. Maria doesn't live
Vivo cerca del médico. María no vive cerca
near but she goes also to the doctors office because
pero ella va también a la consulta porque no
she doesn't feel well.
está bien.

A. Voy al médico porque_____.

    a. veo bien
    b. vivo cerca del Dr. Pérez
    c. María va
    (d.) estoy enfermo

B. A las tres _____.

    a. María está bien
    (b.) voy a la consulta
    c. leo poco
    d. veo bien

C. María _____.

    a. lee mucho
    b. es el Dr. Pérez
    (c.) va también
    d. vive cerca

D. Yo _____.

    (a.) como poco
    b. vivo cerca de María
    c. estoy bien
    d. no vivo cerca del doctor

E. El Dr. Pérez _____.

    a. bebe poca agua
    (b.) trabaja a las tres
    c. lee con María
    d. está enfermo

7. **This conversation is between the receptionist and the patient at the doctor's office. Read the conversation and the four incomplete items which follow. Complete each item by choosing the correct completion from the choices given.**

Recepcionista: ¿Cómo le va, señora?
How are you doing. Mrs.
Paciente: No muy bien, señorita López.
Not well
¿Está el doctor Martínez en la consulta?
Here. This doctor Martinez in the office
Recepcionista: No, pero ahora vive cerca de aquí. Debe llegar a la una. Espere un rato.
But now she lives near here. She must arrive at 1 pm
Paciente: Bien. *OK*

A. El doctor _____.

    a. espera a la señora.
    (b.) vive cerca.
    c. habla con la señorita López.

B. La señorita López _____.

    a. llega a la una
    b. va con la señora
    (c.) es la recepcionista

C. La señora _____.

    (a.) espera al doctor
    b. se llama López
    c. está muy bien

D. La consulta del doctor _____.

    a. no va bien
    b. es ahora
    (c.) es a la una

8. Translate into Spanish.

a. The teacher lives close by — profesor/a
   (near here).

   El profesor vive cerca de aquí.

b. The medical doctor eats — médico/a
   well.

   El médico come bien

c. The waiter open the door. — camarero/a

   El camerero abre la puerta

d. The secretary live in a — secretario/a
   house.

   El secretario vive en la casa

e. The lawyer lives here. — abogado/a

   El abogado vive aquí.

f. The nurse eats with the — enfermero/a
   doctor.

   El enfermo come con el medico

g. The accountant drinks water. — contador/a

   El contador bebe agua

h. The hairdresser drinks — peluquero/a
   Coca-Cola.

   La peluquera bebe Coca-cola

9. Translate the following commands into Spanish.

a. Sign (singular).

   Firme

b. Wait (singular).

   Espere

c. Give (singular).

   Dene

d. Change (all of you).

   Cambien

e. Tomar (all of you).

   Tomen

10. Read the following forms of the verbs tomar
    "to take", and entrar "to come in". Write
    sí if the form can be used as a command,
    otherwise write no.

   Sí a. Entren   *Sí* d. Tome
   No b. Entras   *Sí* e. Tomen
   No c. Entramos   *No* f. Toman

11. **Write the Spanish command for each of the following situations.**

a. Some of your friends knock at your front door. You say:

   Entren

b. You arrive at the doctor's office. The receptionist will tell you:

   Se siente or Sientese

c. A lady is watching TV with you. She wants you to switch to another channel. She says:

   Cambie , por favor.

12. **Write the subject noun corresponding to the following commands.**

a. Dé   _Ud._

b. Calienten   _Vds_

c. Corte   _Ud._

d. Respire   _Ud._

e. Firme   _Ud._

13. **Read the following conversation between two friends, Rosa and Pepe.**

Rosa: Pepe, tome el dinero. Gracias por el disco.
Pepe: Es muy lindo. ¡Escúchelo![1]
Rosa: ¡Una canción italiana! Cante, Pepe.
Pepe: Cante Ud. Yo no recuerdo bien la canción.
Rosa: Bueno, hable bajo y escuche.

Notice that Pepe is used in direct address. The comma indicates that we are speaking directly to him.

a. Make a list of the command forms used in the conversation.

   1. _Tome_   4. _Cante_
   2. _Escúchelo_   5. _hable_
   3. _Cante_   6. _escuche_

b. Change the commands in the conversation to the plural.

   1. _Tomen_
   2. _lo Escuchen_
   3. _Canten_
   4. _Canten_
   5. _hablen_
   6. _escuchen_

14. **Read the following orders given by Mr. Martínez to his employees.**

Señor Martínez: Señores, empiecen a trabajar mañana a las 8. Recuerden todo. Cierren las puertas temprano y preparen las cosas para el martes. Regresen con el Sr. López.

Rewrite this paragraph using the plural commands in the singular (formal).

empiece
recuerde
cierre
prepare
regrese

---

[1]The lo in escúchelo is a direct object pronoun, "it" in English. See Leccións Veintidós.

15. Write the command singular formal form for each of the following infinitives.

a. comprar _Compre_   e. tomar _tome_

b. pensar _piense_   f. ahorrar _ahorre_

c. llamar _llame_   g. contestar _conteste_

d. estudiar _estudie_   h. pronunciar _pronuncie_

16. Turn the following affirmative commands into negative commands.

a. Hable bajo   _No hable bajo_

b. Tome el dinero   _No tome el dinero_

c. Preparen las cosas _No preparen las cosas._

d. Pase, por favor   _No pase,_

e. Firme aquí   _No firme aquí_

17. Fill in the blanks with the correct forms of **venir** in the present tense.

a. (Tú) _Vienes_ a mi casa.

b. (Yo) _Vengo_ de la escuela.

c. María y Juan _vienen_ de México.

d. (Nosotros or Nosotras) _venimos_ en el auto.

e. Papá _viene_ del cine.

f. Los empleados _vienen_ temprano.

g. María _viene_ a esta tienda.

18. Write the number of the English expression beside the letter of its corresponding Spanish expression.

a. el bazo   _5_   1. shoulders
b. la cintura   _6_   2. the back
c. el pecho   _16_   3. the heart
d. el corazón   _3_   4. the stomach
e. la espalda   _2_   5. the spleen
f. los riñones   _11_   6. the waist
g. el vientre   _9_   7. the lungs
h. los intestinos   _13_   8. the liver
i. la columna vertebral _12_   9. the abdomen
j. el hígado   _8_   10. the gall bladder
k. los pulmones   _7_   11. the kidneys
l. la vesícula   _10_   12. the spinal column
m. la vejiga   _14_   13. the intestines
n. el estómago   _4_   14. the bladder
o. los hombros   _1_   15. the hips
p. Las caderas   _15_   16. the chest

19. Translate into English.

a. el corazón _heart_   f. los intestinos _intestine_
b. el pecho _chest_   g. el vientre _abdomen_
c. la cintura _waist_   h. la columna vertebral _Spinal colmn_
d. los pulmones _lungs_ i. los riñones _kidney_
e. la espalda _back_   j. los hombros _shoulder_

-137-

20. **Translate into Spanish.**

a. the back — _la espalda_

b. the chest — _el pecho_

c. the heart — _la corazón_

d. the stomach — _el estómago_

e. the waist — _la cintura_

21. **Translate into Spanish.**

a. My throat hurts. — _Me duele la garganta_

b. My head hurts. — _Me duele la cabeza_

c. My inner ear hurts. — _Me duelen los oídos_

d. My back hurts. — _Me duele la espalda_

e. My stomach hurts. — _Me duele el estómago_

f. My lungs hurt. — _Me duelen los pulmones_

g. My legs hurt. — _Me duelen las piernas_

h. My feet hurt. — _Me duelen los pies_

i. My kidneys hurt. — _Me duelen los riñones_

j. My eyes hurts. — _Me duelen los ojos_

22. **Translate the following sentences into Spanish.**

a. Heat the coffee. — _Caliente el café_

b. Close the door. — _Cierre la puerta_

c. Wait a while. — _Espere un rato_

d. Don't change the channel. — _No cambie el canal_

e. Come in, please. (use pasar) — _Pase, por favor_

f. Call the receptionist. — _Llame el recepcionista_

g. Sign here, please. — _Firme aquí, por favor_

h. Buy the insurance. — _Compre el seguro_

i. Answer the phone. — _Conteste el teléfono_

j. Take the receipt. — _Tome el recibo._

23. **Answer the following questions in Spanish.**

a. ¿A qué hora empiezas a estudiar?
   Empiezo a estudiar _____ ocho

b. ¿Quién calienta el café?
   La camarera _caliente el café_

c. ¿Dónde meriendan Uds.?
   Meriendan en _____ la casa.

d. ¿Recomienda Ud. el pescado al horno?
   Sí, _recomiendo._

3. ¿Vienen ellos el lunes?
   Sí, _vienen._

TOPICS: STEM-CHANGING VERBS (O → UE), SPELLING CHANGE FROM Z TO C. THE EXTREMITIES, REVIEW OF HEALTH SERVICE
CONVERSATIONS, RADICAL CHANGING VERBS

I. Stem-changing verbs (o → ue)

In some Spanish verbs, the vowel o of the stem changes to ue in all forms of the present tense, except for nosotros/as.

Study the following chart·

	Encontrar (to find)	Poder (to be able)	Dormir (to sleep)
Yo	encuentro	puedo	duermo
Tù	encuentras	puedes	duermes
Ud., él, ella	encuentra	puede	duerme
Nosotros/as	encontramos	podemos	dormimos
Uds., ellos, ellas	encuentran	pueden	duermen

In addition to the three verbs presented in the chart, the following verbs will be used in exercises in this lesson, they are also stem-changing o ue verbs.

recordar	-	to remember
almorzar	-	to have lunch
costar	-	to cost
volver	-	to return, to come back
devolver	-	to return, to give back
doler	-	to hurt

Study the following examples:

Almuerzo a las once y media.	- I have lunch at eleven thirty.
El no recuerda el número de teléfono de María.	- He doesn't remember Maria's phone number.
¿Encuentras el abrigo?	- Do you find the overcoat
Las frutas cuestan mucho ahora.	- Fruit cost a lot now.
No podemos ir al cine hoy.	- We are not able (cannot) go to the movies today.
¿Vuelves temprano?	- Are you returning (coming back) early?
Ella nunca devuelve los libros.	- She never returns (gives back) the books.
Me duele la cabeza.	- I have a headache (or my head hurts).
¿Duermes mucho?	- Do you sleep a lot?
Duermo hasta las nueve.	- I sleep until nine.

II. Spelling change from z to c

In Spanish, the combinations ze and zi are considered contrary to the tradition of the language, and only words imported from other languages will show them (even those words are very few). Consequently, in the event that such combinations occur, there is a change in spelling from z to c and the sounds will appear written as ce and ci.

For example, the words that end in z will
change to c in the formation of their plurals·

lápiz	–	lápices
nariz	–	narices
vez	–	veces
luz	–	luces

III The Extremities   –   La Extremidades.

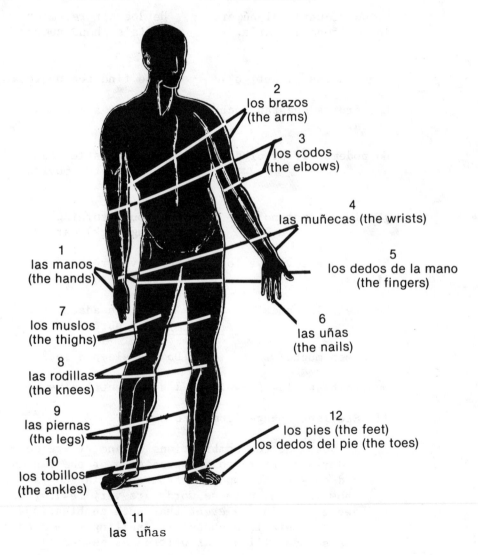

2
los brazos
(the arms)

3
los codos
(the elbows)

4
las muñecas (the wrists)

5
los dedos de la mano
(the fingers)

1
las manos
(the hands)

7
los muslos
(the thighs)

6
las uñas
(the nails)

8
las rodillas
(the knees)

9
las piernas
(the legs)

12
los pies (the feet)
los dedos del pie (the toes)

10
los tobillos
(the ankles)

11
las uñas

III. Radical Changing Verbs

-<u>ir</u> radical changing verbs in the present indicative.
These verbs change <u>e</u> to <u>i</u> in all persons except the
first person plural.

	pedir	repetir	servir	seguir
Yo	pido	repito	sirvo	sigo
Tú	pides	repites	sirves	sigues
Ud., él, ella	pide	repite	sirve	sigue
Nosotros/as	pedimos	repetimos	servimos	seguimos
Uds., ellos, ellas	piden	repiten	sirven	siguen

(Yo) sirvo la cena temprano.   - I serve dinner early.

(Tú) repites la lección   - You repeat the lesson.

Ud. pide un pañuelo   - You ask for a hankerchief.

(Nosotros) servimos el   - We serve breakfast at 8.
desayuno a los 8.

VOCABULARIO

NOUNS

brazo (m)	-	arm
codo (m)	-	elbow
crucero (m)	-	cruise ship
dedo (m)	-	finger, toe
extremidad (f)	-	extremity
lugar (m)	-	place
luz (f)	-	light
mano (f)	-	hand
muñeca (f)	-	wrist, doll
pie (m)	-	foot
pierna (f)	-	leg
rey (m)	-	king
rodilla (f)	-	knee
tobillo (m)	-	ankle
uña (f)	-	fingernail, toenail

VERBS

devolver	-	to return, to give back
dividir	-	to sort to divide
dormir	-	to sleep
encontrar	-	to find
hacer	-	to do, to make
subir	-	to climb to raise
volver	-	to come back, to return

ADVERBS

nunca	-	never

EJERCICIOS

1. **Write each verb in the present tense for the subjects indicated.**

dormir
- a. ella _____
- b. nosotros _____
- c. yo _____
- d. él _____

volver
- e. estedes _____
- f. ellos _____
- g. tú _____
- h. nosotras _____

almorzar
- i. ellos _____
- j. usted _____
- k. tú y yo _____
- l. tú _____

2. **Complete the following sentences with the correct Spanish verb form written in parentheses. Use the verbs in the present tense.**

a. Nosotras no _____ el lugar. (to remember)

b. ¿Ellas _____ la falda? (to give back)

c. La falda no _____ mucho. (to cost)

d. Tú _____ el lugar. (to find)

e. Yo _____ con ella. (to eat lunch)

3. **Organize the following groups of words into meaningful sentences.**

a. el	b. ella	c. no
encuentras	con	la
lugar	almuerzan	devuelvo
¿ ?	ustedes	falda

4. **Write the singular verb forms for the following:**

a. Recordamos _____

b. Duermen _____

c. Cuestan _____

d. Pueden _____

e. Almorzamos _____

5. **Read the following examples.**

How much does it cost? — ¿Cuánto cuesta?

How much do they cost? — ¿Cuánto cuestan?

Complete each of the questions following the examples above.

a. ¿_____ blusas?

b. ¿_____ camisa?

c. ¿_____ falda?

d. ¿_____ zapatos?

e. ¿_____ pantalones?

6. **Complete the narrative with each verb in the present tense.**

Cuando María y yo llegamos _____
                               a. (encontrar)

a la profesora en la clase y los libros en la mesa.

Ella habla con nosotros. María necesita

comprar un libro de español, pero _____ cinco
                                    b. (costar)

dólares. La profesora necesita un libro de francés

también. Los libros de francés _____ más.
                                  c. (costar)

Yo no _____ cuánto _____ pero no tengo
       d. (recordar)   e. (costar)

dinero hoy para comprar libros.

7. **Read the following conversation and answer the questions in complete sentences:**

Ana: ¿Pueden ustedes salir conmigo hoy?

María: Yo puedo pero Roberto no puede.
        ¿Qué podemos hacer?

Ana: Podemos almorzar primero y luego
        visitar la universidad.

María: Recuerda que allí puedes comprar los
        boletos para el fútbol.

a. ¿Quién puede salir con Ana?

_____

b. ¿Qué pueden hacer las chicas primero?

_____

c. ¿Qué pueden hacer ellas luego?

_____

d. ¿Dónde puede Ana comprar los boletos?

_____

8. **Complete the following crossword puzzle by using the correct present tense form of the verb that corresponds to the sentences below.**

Horizontal

3. Tú no (remember) las noticias.

5. El auto (costs) mucho. (familiar)

6. ¿(Do you find) la biblioteca? (familiar)

8. Nosotras (remember) el partido.

Vertical

1. Juan y yo (find) los boletos.

2. ¿Cuánto (cost) las blusas?

4. Infinitive form of (remember).

7. Ustedes no pueden (go out).

9. Change the following words to the plural:

a. mujer _____

b. lapiz _____

c. clase _____

d. nariz _____

e. rey _____

f. luz _____

g. lunes _____

h. vez _____

10. Write the number of the English expression beside the letter of its corresponding Spanish expression.

a. los dedos de la mano   1. the feet

b. los brazos   2. the wrists

c. las rodillas   3. the ankles

d. las piernas   4. the nails

e. las uñas   5. the toes

f. los codos   6. the hands

g. los tobillos   7. the fingers

h. los muslos   8. the legs

i. los dedos del pie   9. the knees

j. las muñecas   10. the thighs

k. las manos   11. the elbows

l. los pies   12. the arms

11. Separate the following parts of the body into two lists: the upper and lower extremities.

a. los muslos   f. las rodillas

b. los pies   g. las piernas

c. los brazos   h. las muñecas

d. los codos   i. las manos

e. los tobillos   j. los dedos del pie

12. Translate into Spanish.

a. the legs _____

b. the arms _____

c. the ankles _____

d. the wrists _____

e. the elbows _____

f. the knees _____

g. the hands _____

h. the feet _____

i. the nails _____

j. the thighs _____

13. **Write in the Spanish names of the parts of the body.**

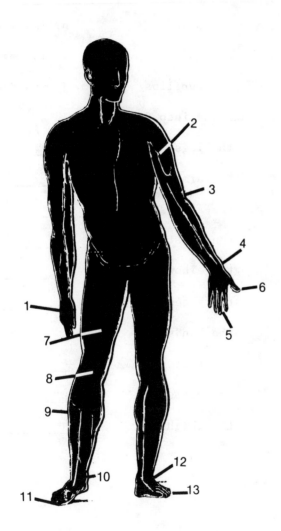

1. _____   8. _____

2. _____   9. _____

3. _____   10. _____

4. _____   11. _____

5. _____   12. _____

6. _____   13. _____

7. _____

14. **Translate into Spanish.**

a. My throat hurts.

_____

b. My head hurts.

_____

c. My inner ears hurt.

_____

d. My back hurts.

_____

e. My stomach hurts.

_____

f. My lungs hurt.

_____

g. My legs hurt.

_____

h. My feet hurt.

_____

i. My kidneys hurt.

_____

j. My eyes hurt.

_____

15. **Read the model sentences, then construct a new expression by substituting the word(s) written below each model. Make any other necessary changes.**

a. Me duele / la cabeza / no puedo almorzar.

   (pecho)   (querer)

   _____

b. José / vuelve / a las doce.

   (José y Ana)   (temprano)

   _____

c. La chica / tiene / las orejas / grandes.

   (El)   (pies)

   _____

d. No pienso / en el doctor Pérez.

   (creer)   (médico)

   _____

e. Me duelen / el cuello y los hombros.

   (estómago)

   _____

16. **Complete the following crossword puzzle by translating the English words into Spanish.**

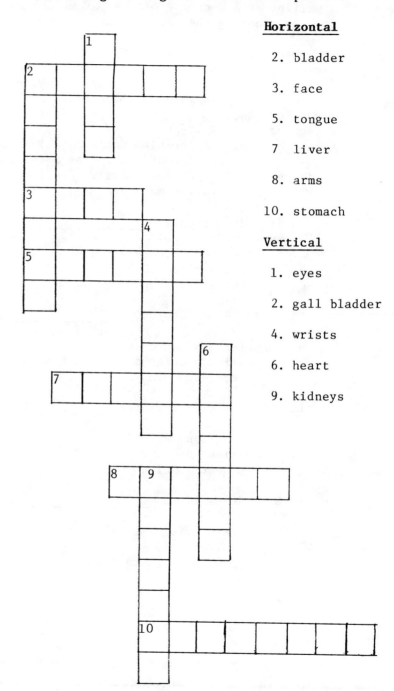

Horizontal

2. bladder

3. face

5. tongue

7. liver

8. arms

10. stomach

Vertical

1. eyes

2. gall bladder

4. wrists

6. heart

9. kidneys

17. This conversation is between a receptionist and a patient at a doctor's office. Complete each item by choosing the correct form.

Recepcionista: ¿Cómo está, Sra. de Martínez?
Paciente: Mal, señorita. Siento frío y me duelen la garganta, el pecho, la espalda y los brazos.
Recepcionista: ¿A qué hora tiene el turno?
Paciente: No recuerdo.
Recepcionista: La consulta comienza a las dos. El turno de usted es a las cuatro.
Paciente: No puedo esperar. Prefiero volver mañana.

A. La Sra. de Martínez _____.

  a. tiene un turno a las dos
  b. espera al doctor
  c. está enferma

B. La consulta del doctor _____.

  a. cierra a las cuatro
  b. comienza antes de las cuatro
  c. tiene dos turnos

C. La señorita y la paciente _____.

  a. conversan
  b. meriendan
  c. encuentran al doctor

D. La Sra. de Martínez _____.

  a. siente frío
  b. recuerda todo
  c. tiene la garganta fría

E. Mañana_____.

  a. comienza la consulta
  b. recuerdo la hora
  c. vuelve la Sra. de Martínez

18. Review of stem-changing verbs. Answer the following questions in Spanish.

a. ¿Duerme Ud. mucho?

    Sí, _____

b. ¿Cuánto cuesta el vestido rojo?

    _____$15.00

c. ¿Recuerdan Uds. la conversación siete?

    Sí, _____

d. ¿No encuentran Uds. los zapatos?

    Sí, _____

e. ¿A qué hora vuelves?

    _____ nueve

f. ¿No devuelves la camisa?

    Sí, _____

g. ¿Duermen Uds. mucho?

    Sí, _____

h. ¿Dónde almuerzas hoy?

    _____ playa

19. **Answer the following questions:**

a. ¿Quién pide un médico?

Nosotros _____.

b. ¿Repiten Uds. la lección?

Sí, _____.

c. ¿No sirves la merienda ahora?

No, _____.

d. ¿Qúe pides?

_____ café con leche.

e. ¿Lo piden Uds. ahora?

Sí, _____.

f. ¿Dónde pides?

_____.

20. **Using the model sentence, replace the verb.**

a. Hago dos ejercicios.
   (repetir   pedir   seguir)

   1. _____

   2. _____

   3. _____

b. Estudiamos dos lecciones.
   (seguir   repetir   pedir)

   1. _____

   2. _____

   3. _____

c. Tú miras dos.
   (seguir   servir   pedir)

   1. _____

   2. _____

   3. _____

d. Ella trae tres.
   (servir   seguir   repetir)

   1. _____

   2. _____

   3. _____

e. Uds. nos dan dos.
   (pedir   servir   repetir)

   1. _____

   2. _____

   3. _____

TOPICS: FORMAL COMMANDS OF -ER AND -IR VERBS, FAMILIAR COMMANDS OF -AR, -ER AND -IR VERBS

CONVERSATION XVII

	EN LA AGENCIA DE PASAJES			AT THE TRAVEL AGENCY
1.	Pasajera:	Quiero una reservación para el vuelo de mañana a Buenos Aires.	- Passenger:	I want a reservation for tomorrow's flight to Buenos Aires.
2.	Empleada:	¿En primera o en turista?	- Employee:	First or economy class?
3.	Pasajera:	En turista.	- Passenger:	Economy class.
4.	Empleada:	¿Directo o con escala?	- Employee:	Non-stop[1] or with a stop?
5.	Pasajera:	Directo.	- Passenger:	Non-stop

I. Formal Commands of -er and -ir Verbs (Imperative Form)

Both the -er and -ir formal commands use the same form.

Infinitive	Present Indicative (yo)	Singular Command (Ud)	Plural Command (Uds.
comer	como	coma	coman
escribir	escribo	escriba	escriban

Examples:

Lea la lista de precios. — Read the price list.

Venda el traje blanco. — Sell the white suit.

No coma aquí. — Don't eat here.

Suba los suéteres viejos. — Take up the old sweaters.

Divida los pantalones por talla. — Sort the pants by size.

Aprenda la nueva lección. — Learn the new lesson.

II. Familiar Affirmative Commands of -ar, -er and -ir Verbs

In almost all verbs, the familiar affirmative command form for tú is the same as the third person singular of the present indicative.

Infinitive	Formal Command	Present Tense 3rd Person Sing.	Affirmative Familiar Command
hablar	hable	habla	habla
comer	coma	come	come
escribir	escriba	escribe	escribe

Examples:

Firma aquí, por favor. — Sign here, please.

Toma los suéteres viejos. — Take the old sweaters.

Come el postre. — Eat your dessert.

Vende el traje blanco. — Sell the white suit.

Escribe la carta ahora. — Write the letter now.

Abre la ventana. — Open the window.

---

[1]A direct flight in English may involve a stop, whereas directo in Spanish implies non-stop.

III. Familiar negative commands of -ar, -er and -ir verbs.

The familiar negative commands are like the Ud. form, but have an s added to them at the end.

The following chart illustrates this point:

Infinitive	Formal (Ud) Command	Negative Familiar (tú) Command
entrar	entre	no entres
comer	coma	no comas
subir	suba	no subas

Examples·

No termines el trabajo todavía. — Don't finish the work yet.

No hables inglés en la clase de español. — Don't speak English in the Spanish class.

No comas ensalada hoy. — Don't eat salad today.

No abras el libro todavía. — Don't open the book yet.

No tomes la medicina. — Don't take the medicine.

When commands were introduced, it was stated that in general, the changes that occur in the stem of the first person indicative, yo would take the place in all the command forms, but so far in this lesson only regular verbs have been used. There are two important verbs, ir and ver, that do not follow this rule. Their command forms are vaya and vea respectively for Ud. and vayan, vean for Uds. The following chart will serve as a review of all command forms studied including some irregular verbs.

Infinitive	Formal (Ud) Aff or Neg	Formal (Uds) Aff or Neg	Familiar (tú) Aff	Familiar (tú) Neg
dar	dé	den	da	no des
terminar	termine	terminen	termina	no termines
leer	lea	lean	lee	no leas
escribir	escriba	escriban	escribe	no escribas
pensar	piense	piensen	piensa	no pienses
volver	vuelva	vuelvan	vuelve	no vuelvas
calentar	caliente	calienten	calienta	no calientes
perder	pierda	pierdan	pierde	no pierdas
encender	encienda	enciendan	enciende	no enciendas
recomendar	recomiende	recomienden	recomienda	no recomiendes
dormir	duerma	duerman	duerme	no duermas
ir	vaya	vayan	ve	no vayas
ver	vea	vean	ve	no veas

VOCABULARIO

NOUNS

aeropuerto (m)	-	airport
Argentina	-	country in South America
Asunción	-	capital of Paraguay
aviso (m)	-	sign, message
Bolívar	-	Venezuelan hero, monetary unit of Venezuela
crucero (m)	-	cruise, monetary unit of Brazil
escala (f)	-	stop over
excusa (f)	-	excuse
extinguidor (m)	-	extinguisher
guaraní (m)	-	monetary unit of Paraguay
La Paz	-	capital city of Bolivia
Lima	-	capital city of Perú
lista (f)	-	list
medicina (f)	-	medicine
Montevideo	-	capital city of Uruguay
Paraguay	-	country in South America
Quito	-	capital city of Ecuador
pasajero (a)	-	passenger
peso (m)	-	weight, monetary unit
policía (m&f)	-	policeman, policewoman
precaución (f)	-	precaution, guard
reservación (f)	-	reservation
salida (f)	-	exit, departure
Santiago	-	capital city of Chile
semáforo (m)	-	traffic light
sucre (m)	-	monetary unit of Ecuador
Uruguay	-	country in South America
vuelo (m)	-	flight

ADJECTIVES

directo	-	direct

VERBS

confirmar	-	to confirm
correr	-	to run
dejar	-	to leave behind
evitar	-	to avoid
manejar	-	to drive

EXPRESSIONS

en primera	-	first class
en seguida	-	right away
en turista	-	tourist
hora de salida	-	departure time

1. Read the following expressions and determine who said each of them first in the Basic Conversation. Write <u>pasajera</u> or <u>empleada</u> beside the corresponding expression.

    a. ¿En primera o en turista? _____

    b. Directo _____

    c. Quiero una reservación para el vuelo de mañana a Buenos Aires. _____

    d. ¿Directo o con escala? _____

2. Match the expressions in Column A with the appropriate ones in Column B.

A	B
a. quiero	1. o en turista?
b. ¿En primera	2. o con escala?
c. ¿Directo	3. una reservación
d. .. para el vuelo	4. de mañana a Buenos Aires.

3. Complete the following line of conversation with the appropriate words. Choose from the words given below.

    Quiero una _____ para el _____ de
                   a   b

    _____ a Buenos Aires.
        c

    mañana   turista   reservación   vuelo   escala

4. Organize the following groups of words into meaningufl expressions.

a. una	b. en	c. con
el	o	directo
reservación	en	escala
quiero	turista	o
vuelo	primera	¿ ?
para	¿ ?	

5. Write a six-line conversation between the passenger and the employee at a travel agency.

    Pasajera:_____

    Empleada:_____

    Pasajera:_____

    Empleada:_____

    Pasajera:_____

    Empleada:_____

6. Notice that the following expressions are commands or requests. Give the Spanish for each one using the formal form.

    a. Enter here. _____

    b. Give me the book. _____

    c. Wait at the house._____

d.   Speak with the employee.

_____

7.   **Make a list of the imperative forms used in this conversation. State if they are formal or familiar commands.**

Sr. Gómez: Cambie las reservaciones para el día 7, por favor.

Empleada: Déme los boletos. Firmen aquí.

Sr. Gómez: Ana, firma tú también y toma los boletos.

a.   _____   c.   _____

b.   _____   d.   _____

e.   _____

Translate the commands into English.

Sr. Gómez: _____

Empleada: _____

Sr. Gómez: _____

8.   **For each of the infinitive verbal forms, write the two singular commands: the formal and the familiar.**

Infinitive	Formal Command	Familiar Command
		(Affirmative)
a. hablar	_____	_____
b. dar	_____	_____
c. tomar	_____	_____
d. entrar	_____	_____
e. cambier	_____	_____

9.   **What subject pronoun can you add for each of the following verb forms?**

a. Firmen   _____   g. Hable   _____

b. No esperes   _____   h. Entra   _____

c. Sube   _____   i. No firmes   _____

d. Coma   _____   j. No suba   _____

e. Lee   _____

f. Suban   _____

10.   **What is the affirmative imperative familiar form of each of the verbs listed?**

a. leer   _____

b. recibir   _____

c. manejar   _____

d. evitar   _____

e. aprender   _____

f. subir   _____

11.   **The following are statements. Change each of to commands.**

a. Ud. espera al policía.

_____

b. (Tú) evitas el semáforo.

_____

c. Ud. mira al policía.

_____

d. Ud. no sube por esa calle.

_____

e. (Tú) no recibes las excusas del policía.

_____

12. **Pick out from each pair sentences the one you think is a command or request.**

a. Rosa aprende a manejar el automóvil de María.

Rosa, aprende a manejar el automóvil de María.

b. Espere al policía.

Esperas al policía.

c. Ellos leen los avisos de la calle.

Lean ustedes los avisos de la calle.

d. Usted pasa por aquí.

Pase usted por aquí, por favor.

13. **Write a negative command for each of the following infinitive forms.**

Negative familiar singular forms:

a. creer   _____

b. vender   _____

c. encender_____

d. perder   _____

Negative plural forms (Uds.)

e. comer   _____

f. correr   _____

g. volver   _____

h. subir   _____

14. **Change the following statements to commands or requests.**

a. Ustedes tienen precaución.

_____

b. Ud. abre la puerta.

_____

c. Usted come después.

_____

d. Ustedes cuentan hasta diez.

_____

e. Ud. llama por teléfono.

_____

15. **What Spanish imperative form can you see in each of the following situations? You may want to use some of the verbs listed below.**

a. Some of your friends are knocking at your front door. You say:

_____

b. You are in the hospital filling out a form. The employee pointing at one of the lines tells you:

_____

c. To enter a road on your right is not permitted. A sign has been placed there saying:

_____

entrar   comer   firmar   pasar   escribir

16. Give two commands and/or requests with the verb _ir_ and two with the verb _ver_.

           Ir

a. _____(ustedes).

b. _____(usted).

           Ver

c. _____(usted).

d. _____(ustedes).

17. Change the affirmative commands listed below to negative commands.

a. Vuelva mañana.

_____

b. Cierra la puerta.

_____

c. Piensen en el peligro.

_____

d. Calienta el café.

_____

e. Deje el extinguidor aquí.

_____

18. Give a formal command to each of the persons written on the left. Use the correct form of each verb written at the right.

a. Señora, _____ (terminar).

b. Rosa, _____ (leer).

c. Daniel, _____ (pensar).

d. María, _____ (volver).

e. Raúl, _____ (dormir).

TOPICS: MONTHS OF THE YEAR, DEFINITION OF OBJECTS OF A VERB (DIRECT AND INDIRECT OBJECTS)

CONVERSATION XVIII

	EN LA AGENCIA DE PASAJES		AT THE TRAVEL AGENCY
6.	Empleada; ¿Boleto de ida y vuelta?[1]	– Employee:	A round trip ticket?
7.	Pasajera: De ida solamente.	– Passenger:	One way only.
8.	Empleada: Está confirmado para el 8 de julio.	– Employee:	It is confirmed for July 8.
9.	Empleada: Vuelo número 42 a las tres de la tarde.	– Employee:	Flight No. 42 at three p.m.
10.	Empleada: No olvide llegar temprano al aeropuerto.	– Employee:	Don't forget to arrive at the airport early.

I. The months of the year are:

enero – January

febrero – February

marzo – March

abril – April

mayo – May

junio – June

julio – July

agosto – August

septiembre – September

octubre – October

noviembre – November

diciembre – December

II. Objects of a verb

In a simple sentence in English, usually there is a subject, a verb, and an object. The object(s) is(are) the receiver(s) of the action of the verb. There are two types of objects. direct objects and indirect objects. It is said that direct objects receive the action of the verb directly, and the indirect objects receive the action of the verb indirectly.

Examples of direct objects·

John brings the girls. - Juan trae a las chicas.

Mary throws the ball. - María tira la pelota.

They cut the meat. - Ellos cortan la carne.

She opens the door. - Ella abre la puerta.

"The girls", "the boys", "the meat", and "the door" are the direct objects of the sentences. They receive the action of the verbs "brings", "throws", "cut" and "open" directly. To find the direct object in a sentence, ask "whom" (for people) or "what" (for things) after the verb. Your answer is the direct object.

[1]Ida and vuelta are forms of the verbs ir, "to go" and volver, "to return". See past partciples, Lección Veintinueve.

The indirect object of the verb in English precedes the direct object and usually tells to whom the action of the verb is done. Therefore, to find the indirect object, ask the question <u>to whom</u> or <u>for whom</u> the action of the verb is done.

The material presented in this lesson concerning direct and indirect objects is of utmost importance. You are urged to learn to spot direct and indirect objects in sentences. It will be impossible to understand direct and indirect object pronouns presented in Lessons 22 and 23 without a thorough understanding of the function of objects in sentences.

Examples of sentences with direct and indirect objects:

He gives the ball to John.

He gives <u>John</u> <u>the ball</u>.
     I.O.   D.O.

El le[1] da la pelota a Juan.

Charles writes a letter to Mary.

Charles writes <u>Mary</u> <u>a letter</u>.

Carlos le escribe una carta a María.

I am telling the truth to Mario.

I am telling <u>Mario</u> <u>the truth</u>
     I.O   D.O.

Le digo la verdad a Mario.

In the above examples, the two forms used in English with the same meaning are stated. The forms "to John", "to Mary", and "to Mario" are not considered indirect objects in English, but prepositional phrases. "John", "Mary", and "Mario" are the objects of the preposition "to." In Spanish, nevertheless, there is only one way to express it, and it is an indirect object, <u>a Juan</u>, <u>a María</u>, <u>a Mario</u>.

---

[1]For the use of <u>le</u>, a redundant pronoun, see <u>Lección Veintitrés</u>.

VOCABULARIO

NOUNS

abril (m)	-	April
agosto (m)	-	August
América Central	-	Central America
América del Norte	-	North America
América del Sur	-	South America
bicicleta	-	bicycle
Centroamérica	-	Central America
diciembre	-	December
enero (m)	-	January
familia (f)	-	family
febrero (m)	-	February
Honduras	-	country in Central America
julio (m)	-	July
junio (m)	-	June
Managua	-	capital city of Nicaragua
marzo (m)	-	March
mayo (m)	-	May
mes (m)	-	month
montuno (m)	-	male costume
muelle (m)	-	pier, whaft
Nicaragua	-	country in Central America
Norte América	-	North America
noviembre (m)	-	November
octubre (m)	-	October
Panamá	-	country in Central America
pelota (f)	-	ball
pollera (f)	-	colorful skirt
reloj (m)	-	clock, watch
septiembre (m)	-	September
Sudamérica	-	South America
tambor (m)	-	drum
tamborito (m)	-	typical dance
verdad (f)	-	truth

ADJECTIVES

confirmado	-	confirmed

VERBS

olvidar	-	to forget
pasar	-	to pass, to enter
tirar	-	to throw

EXPRESSIONS

ida y vuelta	-	round trip

1. **Translate into Spanish.**

August _____

March _____

January _____

April _____

December _____

November _____

May _____

July _____

June _____

September _____

February _____

October _____

2. **Read the Spanish sentences below and decide if the underlined expressions are direct or indirect objects. Write in the space provided D or I.**

a. Alberto mira <u>el reloj</u>. _____

b. Carlos le escribe a <u>la familia</u>. _____

c. Pedro no escribe <u>cartas</u>. _____

d. Agustín tiene el <u>dinero</u>. _____

e. El empleado busca <u>a María</u>. _____

f. La chica le da el dinero a <u>María</u>. _____

g. Uds. le pagan a <u>la cajera</u>. _____

3. **Complete the expressions by writing the dates in Spanish.**

Model· **Está confirmado para el ocho de julio.**

a. Está confirmado para el (Feb. 10). _____

b. Está confirmado para el (Mar. 14). _____

c. Está confirmado para el (June 20). _____

d. Está confirmado para el (May 18). _____

e. Está confirmado para el (Jan. 25). _____

f. Está confirmado para el (Apr. 9). _____

g. Está confirmado para el (Sep. 17). _____

h. Está confirmado para el (July 4). _____

4. **Translate into complete Spanish sentences.**

Model: It's 3:00 P.M.- Son las tres de la mañana.

a. It's 10:00 P.M. _____

b. It's 2:00 A.M. _____

c. It's 5:00 P.M. _____

d. It's 11:00 A.M. _____

e. It's 8:00 P.M. _____

f. It's 1:00 P.M. _____

g. It's 3:00 P.M. _____

5. **Write out the following cardinal numbers.**

a. 321 _____

b. 17 _____

c. 153 _____

d. 68 _____

e. 420 _____

f. 106 _____

g. 97 _____

6. **Write the formal commands of the verbs following the model:**

Model: hablar - hable - no hablen

a. entrar _____ _____

b. pasar _____ _____

c. mirar _____ _____

d. estudiar _____ _____

e. regresar _____ _____

f. tomar _____ _____

g. pronunciar _____ _____

h. respirar _____ _____

i. cortar _____ _____

j. olvidar _____ _____

7. **Write the familiar commands of the verbs following the model.**

Model: hablar - habla - no hables

a. entrar _____ _____

b. pasar _____ _____

c. mirar _____ _____

d. estudiar _____ _____

e. regresar _____ _____

f. tomar _____ _____

g. pronunciar _____ _____

h. respirar _____ _____

i. cortar _____ _____

j. olvidar _____ _____

8. **Give the capitals of the following countries in Central America.**

a. Guatemala _____

b. El Salvador _____

c. Honduras _____

d. Nicaragua _____

e. Costa Rica _____

f. Panamá _____

9. Translate into Spanish.

a. I want a reservation for tomorrow's flight to Buenos Aires.

_____

_____

b. First or economy class?

_____

_____

c. Economy Class.

_____

_____

d. Non-stop or with a stop over?

_____

e. Non-stop.

_____

_____

g. One way only.

_____

_____

h. It is confirmed for July 8.

_____

_____

i. Flight No. 42 at 3 P.M. (write out, do not use numbers.)

_____

_____

j. Don't forget to arrive at the airport early.

_____

_____

TOPICS: DIRECT OBJECT PRONOUNS, DISJUNCTIVE PRONOUNS (OBJECTS OF A PREPOSITION)

I. Direct object pronouns.

me	me
te	you (fam.)
lo	him, it (masc.), you (formal masc.)
la	her, it (fem.), you (formal fem.)
nos	us
los	them (masc. or mixed group), you (masc. plural or mixed group)
las	them (fem.), you (fem., plural)

The study of object pronouns in Spanish first requires a familiarization with the different forms of the pronouns, and second with the position in which they are to be placed with respect to the verb. It is necessary to be able to recognize if the verb is in the indicative or the command form. So far, only the uses of verbs in the indicative and command forms have been studied. If the verb is in the indicative, the pronouns are placed <u>before</u> the conjugated form of the verb. If the verb is in the affirmative command, the pronouns are <u>attached</u> to the end of the verb, but if the command is negative, the pronouns are placed <u>before</u> the verb.

Examples of object pronouns with verbs in the indicative:

Ella me llama los domingos.	– She calls me on Sundays.
María te invita a la fiesta.	– Mary is inviting you to the party.
Ellos no lo ven.	– They don't see him.

En seguida lo traigo todo.	– I'll bring it all right away.
No la veo.	– I don't see her.
Carlos nos llama.	– Carlos is calling us.
Ud. los necesita para hoy.	– You need them for today.
Ella las quiere para mañana.	– She wants them for tomorrow.

Examples of pronouns with affirmative commands:

Aquí está el trabajo; termíne<u>lo</u>.	– Here is the work, finish <u>it</u>.
Estoy en la oficina, lláma<u>me</u>.	– I'm in the office, call <u>me</u>.
La composición es corta, léa<u>la</u>.	– The composition is short, read <u>it</u>.
Necesitamos naranjas, cómpra<u>las</u> hoy.	– We need oranges, buy <u>them</u> today.
El pastel está bueno, cóma<u>lo</u>.	– The pastry is good, eat <u>it</u>.

For examples of pronouns with negative commands, previous sentences are changed to the negative.

Aquí está el trabajo, no <u>lo</u> termine.	– Here is the work, don't finish <u>it</u>.
Estoy en la oficina, no <u>me</u> llame.	– I'm in the office, don't call <u>me</u>.
La composición es corta, no <u>la</u> lea.	– The composition is short, don't read <u>it</u>.

No necesitamos naranjas,   - We don't need oranges,
no las compre.   don't buy them.

El pastel no está bueno,   - The pastry is not good,
no lo coma.   don't eat it.

Sometimes, Spanish uses object pronouns when English
does not. The following examples illustrate the point:

¿Tiene una reservación   - Do you have a reservation
para mañana?   for tomorrow?

Sí, la tengo.   - Yes, I do.

¿Quiere el vuelo número   - Do you want flight No. 42?
42?

Sí, lo quiero.   - Yes, I do.

The verb "to do" is used very often in English when
answering questions, this is an idiomatic usage in
English. In the examples given, Spanish uses the
equivalent of "Yes, I have it", and "Yes, I want it".

II. Disjunctive pronouns (Objects of a preposition)

In English, the pronouns used as objects of preposition have the same form as the direct object
pronouns, but Spanish uses different forms, they
are the same as the subject pronouns, except for
mí and ti.

They are:

mí	usted	ustedes
ti	nosotros/as	
él	ellos	
ella	ellas	

These objects of preposition pronouns are very often
used for clarification or for emphasis.

Examples:

Andrés lo llama a él.   - Andrés is calling him.

Andrés lo llama a Ud.   - Andrés is calling you.

Yo la llamo a ella.   - I am calling her.

Yo la llamo a Ud.   - I am calling you.

María los invita a ellos.- Mary is inviting them.

María los invita a Uds. - Mary is inviting you.

The above examples clearly state the need for clarification since lo can stand for él and for Ud.
(masc. formal), la for ella or for Ud. (feminine),
los for ellos or Uds. and las for ellas or Uds. (fem.)

The following examples illustrate the use of object
of preposition pronouns for emphasis:

María me llama a mí.   - Mary is calling me.

Pepe te llama a ti.   - Pepe is calling you.

Ella nos invita a nosotras. - She is inviting us.

Notice that in English, the progressive tense which
is formed by the verb "to be" plus the -ing form of
the main verb is used (I am calling...I am inviting...
etc.). Spanish also has a progressive tense, Lección
Veintinueve, but the present tense is preferred.

The pronouns mí and ti when used with the preposition
con, "with", become conmigo and contigo.

Ana va conmigo.   - Ana goes with me.

¿Está Pedro contigo?   - Is Peter with you?

VOCABULARIO

NOUNS

composición	– composition
México or Méjico	– Mexico
Navarra	– province in Northern Spain

PRONOUNS

mí	– me
tí	– you (familiar)
la	– you (form., fem., sing.) her, it
las	– you (fem., pl.), them (fem.)
lo	– you (form., masc., sing.) him, it (masc.)
los	– you (masc., pl.) them (masc.)
me	– me
nos	– us
te	– you (fam., sing.)

ADJECTIVES

castellano	– Spanish language, castilian
corto	– short

VERBS

invitar	– to invite

PROPOSITIONS

conmigo	– with me
contigo	– with you

1. **Read each of the following sentences. Write D.O. (direct object) if the underlined pronoun is a direct object.**

    a. <u>Usted</u> ve unos lápices.

    _____

    b. <u>Lo</u> llamas a él.

    _____

    c. María <u>nos</u> invita.

    _____

    d. Las invita <u>a ustedes</u>.

    _____

    e. Juan <u>me</u> ve.

    _____

2. **Organize the following group of words into meaningful sentences.**

a.	la	b.	lápiz	c.	ella	d.	ve
	a		queremos		la		me
	Andrés		un		ve		Juan
	ella				Ana		
	invita				a		

    a. _____

    b. _____

    c. _____

    d. _____

3. **Write the direct object pronoun which stands for each underlined direct object noun in the sentences at the left. Complete the sentences at the right with these pronouns.**

    a. El ve <u>a María</u>.   El _____ ve.

    b. Ella invita <u>a Andrés</u>.   Ella _____ invita.

    c. Usted ve <u>a un amigo</u>.   Usted _____ ve.

4. **Write after each verb the expressions used to clarify the meaning of the underlined object pronoun. There will be two answers for each sentence.**

    a. <u>Las</u> queremos.

    _____

    _____

    b. <u>Lo</u> llaman.

    _____

    _____

    c. <u>La</u> ve.

    _____

    _____

    d. <u>Los</u> invita.

    _____

    _____

5. Write ¿a quién? or ¿a quiénes? to the right of each sentence according to which question phrase is answered by the underlined object pronoun.

   a. Juan nos llama... _____

   b. Ellos la invitan... _____

   c. María la cree... _____

6. Identify the pronoun(s) used as a direct object in each of the following sentences.

   a. Andrés los ve a ustedes.

   _____

   b. Ana nos invita.

   _____

   c. Las queremos.

   _____

   d. Ustedes me invitan.

   _____

7. Give a "no" answer and a "yes" answer to each of the following questions. Use a direct object pronoun in each answer.

   a. ¿Ana me llama?

   No, _____

   Sí, _____

   b. ¿Ustedes buscan las tijeras?

   No, _____

   Sí, _____

   c. ¿Prefieres los guantes?

   No, _____

   Sí, _____

   d. ¿María y Andrés te ven?

   No, _____

   Sí, _____

8. Complete the answer for each question. Use a direct object pronoun in every sentence.

   a. ¿Quién te llama?   El doctor/médico_____.

   b. ¿Quiénes prefieren Nosotros_____.
      estas revistas?

   c. ¿Por qué lo buscas? Porque_____prefiero.

   d. ¿Dónde me ven?   _____en el hospital.

9. Fill in the blanks with the expressions which emphasize or clarify the meaning of the direct object pronoun. (Some sentences have two answers)

   a. No la veo_____

   b. Tú me contestas_____

   c. Los buscamos_____

   d. ¿Dónde te busca?_____

   e. Las llamo_____

-167-

10. Which is the direct object, <u>complemento directo</u> in each of these sentences?

a. ¿Necesitas un regalo para Pepe?

_____

b. No llaman a la cliente.

_____

c. La empleada de la tienda trae una talla pequeña.

_____

d. María busca otra cosa en la tienda.

_____

11. Complete each sentence by adding the direct object noun written at the right to complete the meaning of the verb. Make any other necessary changes.

a. María llama_____.(empleadas)

b. ¿Prefieres_____mejores? (regalos)

c. El empleado me trae_____.(talla)

d. Buscamos_____en la tienda.(padre)

e. Yo compro_____de invierno.(abrigo)

f. ¿Quién invita_____? (jóvenes)

12. Rewrite the sentences used in the previous exercise (11) using direct object pronouns.

a. _____

b. _____

c. _____

d. _____

e. _____

f. _____

13. Read the following conversation and underline the direct object nouns and pronouns.

a. ¿Tiene una reservación para mañana?
b. ¿Sí, la tengo.
c. ¿Va a pagar los boletos de contado?
d. No, los voy a poner en la cuenta.
e. ¿Quién confirma la hora?
f. Yo la confirmo.
g. ¿Quiere Ud. el vuelo No. 42?
h. Sí, lo quiero.

14. Translate into Spanish.

a. The lady calls me.

_____

b. Mr. López invites you (fam.).

_____

c. The employee calls you (fam.).

_____

d. The passenger does not see me.

_____

e. The passenger sees them (masc.)

_____

f. Mr. López buys them (fem.).

_____

g. The lady invites all of you (mixed group).

_____

15. **Fill in the blanks with the proper direct object pronouns:**

a. ¿A quién invita María?

   Ella _____ invita.
         (us)

b. ¿Compra Juan boletos de ida y vuelta?

   Sí, _____ compra.

c. ¿Tiene el turista una reservación?

   Sí, _____ tiene.

d. ¿Cuándo te ve Andrés?

   Andrés _____ ve los sábados.

e. ¿Llama Ud. a las señoras?

   Sí, (yo) _____ llamo por la mañana.

16. **Complete the following sentences in two different ways, using object of preposition pronouns for clarification.**

a. Andrés lo llama.

   _____

   _____

b. María los invita.

   _____

   _____

c. Yo la llamo.

   _____

   _____

d. ¿Quién las ve?

   _____

   _____

17. **Complete the following sentences by using the emphatic pronoun.**

a. Ella nos invita_____.

b. Andrés me ve_____.

c. ¿Cuándo te llaman_____?

18. **Write two sentences using _ti_ and two using _mí_.**

   _____

   _____

   _____

   _____

19. **Do _not_ translate this exercise, interpret in Spanish the English instructions. (Use object pronouns.)**

   Model: Your friends are calling a group of which you are a part.

       Ellos nos llaman

a. María is listening to what you say. You say:

   _____

b. You observe that Pepe is looking at Mary. You tell her:

   _____

c. She makes up her mind not to buy the things (masc.) she is looking at.

_____

d. The Travel Agency employee has Mr. López' tickets. He gives it to him while saying:

_____

20. **Translate into Spanish using formal forms of pronouns.**

a. Take it (masc.), please.

_____

b. You can pay for the tickets now.

_____

c. Pay for them over there.

_____

d. These are the times for the flights.

_____

e. Look at them (fem).

_____

f. The passenger is over there. Call him.

_____

21. **Complete the sentences of the conversation.**

a. Quiero una reservación_____.

b. ¿En primera_____?

c. En_____.

d. ¿Directo_____?

e. _____

f. ¿Boleto de _____?

g. De ida _____.

h. Está _____.

i. Vuelo número cuarenta y dos _____.

22. **Answer the following questions in Spanish.**

a. ¿Vas conmigo a la biblioteca?

Sí, _____

b. ¿Puedo ir contigo al correo?

Sí, _____

c. ¿Van Uds. con él?

Sí, _____

d. ¿Vuelves con nosotros?

Sí, _____

LECCIÓN VEINTITRÉS

TOPICS: THE VERBS <u>PONER</u> AND <u>HACER</u>, THE EXPRESSION <u>VAMOS A</u>, INDIRECT OBJECT PRONOUNS, THE VERB <u>GUSTAR</u> AND SIMILAR VERBS, THE EXPRESSIONS <u>HACE FRÍO</u> AND <u>HACE CALOR</u>, THE FOUR SEASONS.

CONVERSATION XIX

HACIENDO LAS MALETAS		PACKING THE SUITCASES
1. Esposo: Vamos a hacer las maletas.	−	Husband: Let's pack the suitcases.
2. Esposa: ¿Pongo mi abrigo y mi chaqueta?	−	Wife: Shall I put in my overcoat and my jacket?
3. Esposo: Sí, el invierno es frío en la Argentina.	−	Husband: Yes, in winter it is cold in Argentina.
4. Esposo: Voy a poner los guantes y la bufanda.	−	Husband: I'm going to put in the gloves and scarf.

I. The Verbs <u>Poner</u> and <u>Hacer</u>

These verbs are regular in all persons except in the first person of the present indicative:

	Poner (to place, to put)	Hacer (to do, to make)
Yo	pongo	hago
Tú	pones	haces
Ud., él, ella	pone	hace
Nosotros(as)	ponemos	hacemos
Uds., ellos, ellas	ponen	hacen

Examples:

¿(yo) Pongo mi abrigo y mi chaqueta?	−	Shall I put in my overcoat and my jacket?
¿Por qué no lo pones aquí?	−	Why don't you put it here?
Ana no pone los libros ahí.	−	Ana doesn't put the books there.
(Nosotros) No los ponemos aquí.	−	We don't put them here.

Uds. siempre ponen la mesa a las cinco.	−	You always set the table at five.
(Yo) Hago las maletas.	−	I am packing the suitcases.
(Tú) Haces el trabajo bien.	−	You do the work well.
Ella no lo hace ahora.	−	She doesn't do it now.
(Nosotros) Hacemos todo aquí.	−	We do everything here.
Ellas me hacen venir.	−	They make me come.

II.

The most common way to express "let's..." is with the verb <u>ir</u> in the first person plural, <u>nosotros-as</u>, <u>vamos</u> plus the preposition <u>a</u>.

Examples:

Vamos a hacer las maletas.	−	Let's pack the suitcases.
Vamos a comer en el restaurante.	−	Let's eat at the restaurant.
Vamos a la biblioteca.	−	Let's go to the library.
Vamos al cine.	−	Let's go to the movies.

Notice the last two examples, in which "let's go" is simply expressed by <u>vamos a</u>, the meaning of <u>ir</u> is already expressed in the form of <u>vamos</u>.

III. Indirect Object Pronouns

In English direct and indirect object pronouns use the same form: "me", "you", "it", "him", "her", and "them." Spanish uses a different form for the indirect object pronouns that correspond to "you", "him", "her", and "them."

English Direct and Indirect Object Pronouns	Spanish Direct Object Pronouns	Spanish Indirect Object Pronouns
me	me	me
you (fam., sing.)	te	te
you (formal, sing., masc.)	lo	le
you (formal, sing., fem.)	la	le
him	lo	le
her	la	le
us	nos	nos
you (plural, masc.)	los	les
you (plural, fem.)	las	les
them (masc.)	los	les
them (fem.)	las	les

Examples:

¿Quién le recomienda esta consulta?	- Who recommended[1] this office <u>to you</u>?
¿Quién le hace las maletas?	- Who's packing the suitcases <u>for you</u>?
¿Quién le compra los boletos?	- Who is buying the tickets <u>for you</u>?

¿Quién le lleva los guantes?	- Who is taking the gloves for you?
El les da el dinero.	- He gives them the money.

Since <u>le</u> can stand for "to you", "to him", "to her", and <u>les</u> for "to you" (plural), and "to them", in order to avoid confusion, Spanish may add an object of a preposition pronoun that goes along with <u>le</u> and <u>les</u>.

Examples:

¿Quién le recomienda esta consulta <u>a usted</u>?	- Who recommended[1] this office to you?
¿Quién le recomienda esta consulta <u>a él</u>?	- Who recommended[1] this office to him?
¿Quién le recomienda esta consulta <u>a ella</u>?	- Who recommended[1] this office to her?
El les da el dinero a Uds.	- He gives the money to you. (plural)
El les da el dinero a ellos.	- He gives the money to them. (masc.)
El les da el dinero ellas.	- He gives the money to them. (fem.)

The indirect object pronouns are necessary in any sentence that has indirect objects. For instance, it would be incorrect to say <u>El da dinero a Ud.</u>, <u>a Ud.</u> is used for clarification or reinforcement only, and the sentence still needs the indirect object pronoun <u>le</u>. Example: El <u>le</u> da el dinero a Ud.

Remember that although not always needed for clarification, very often even with direct object pronouns, Spanish uses an object-of-a-preposition pronoun for emphasis that goes with <u>me</u>, <u>te</u>, and <u>nos</u>. Examples:

Alberto <u>me</u> llama <u>a mí</u>.	- Albert is calling me.
Laura <u>te</u> paga a <u>ti</u>.	- Laura pays you.
Tú nos llevas a nosotros.	- You are taking us.

---

[1] In English, the past tense of "to recommend" is used while in Spanish, the present tense may be used.

IV. The Verb Gustar and Similar Verbs

The English expressions with the verb "to like," as in: "I like", "you like", "he likes", etc. are not directly translatable, instead, Spanish reverses the subject and object using the verb gustar, to please. Thus, the English expression: "I like the house" must be expressed in Spanish as La casa me gusta or Me gusta la casa. The direct English translation is "the house pleases me."

Indirect Object Pronoun	Verb	Subject
me	gusta	la casa
me	gustan	las casas

The following verbs follow the same pattern as gustar:

Verb Infinitive	Ind. Obj. Pronoun	Verb Forms	Subject	Translation
Parecer	Me	parece	el viaje bueno.	The trip seems good to me.
	Me	parecen	los viajes buenos.	The trips seems good to me.
Encantar	Les	encanta	México.	They love Mexico.
	Les	encantan	México y Caracas.	They love Mexico and Caracas
Faltar	Te	falta	uno.	You lack one.
	Te	faltan	dos.	You lack two.
Doler	Me	duele	la cabeza.	I have a head-ache.
	Me	duelen	los pies.	My feet hurt.

V. The Expressions Hace Frío and Hace Calor.

Spanish uses the verb hacer (to make), when referring cold and hot weather

Examples:

Hace frío.   - It is cold.

Hace calor.   - It is hot.

But if you want to state the intensity of the temperature in a region, you use the verb ser.

Examples:

El invierno es frío en la Argentina.	-	In winter, it's cold in Argentina.
Los veranos son calientes en Puerto Rico.	-	Summers are hot in Puerto Rico.

VI. The Four Seasons.

primavera	-	Spring
verano	-	Summer
otoño	-	Autumn
invierno	-	Winter

The names of the seasons are not capitalized in Spanish unless they begin a sentence.

N O U N S

Bogotá	–	capital city of Colombia
Bolivia	–	country in South America
Colombia	–	country in South America
ecuador (m)	–	Ecuator
garage (m)	–	garage
esposo (a)	–	husband, wife
iglesia (f)	–	church
lana (f)	–	wool
maleta (f)	–	suitcase
mapa (m)	–	map
noticia (f)	–	news
primavera (f)	–	Spring
recado (m)	–	message
vacaciones (f)	–	vacation
verano (m)	–	Summer

P R O N O U N S

le	–	you (sing.), him, her
les	–	them

A D J E C T I V E S

fresco	–	fresh

V E R B S

contar	–	to count, to give an account, to tell
encantar	–	to charm
faltar	–	to lack
hay	–	impersonal form of the verb haber – there is, there are
parecer	–	to seem
poner	–	to put
prestar	–	to lend

1. Use <u>Poner</u> or <u>Hacer</u>.

   a. Yo_____el televisor allí.

   b. Ella_____el trabajo.

   c. Tú_____el libro en la mesa.

   d. Yo_____las maletas.

   e. Nosotros_____el auto en el garaje.

   f. Ellas me_____venir.

   g. Uds._____los ejercicios.

2. Translate into Spanish.

   a. Let's go to the park.

   _____

   b. Let's go to church.

   _____

   c. Let's study Spanish.

   _____

   d. Let's pack the suitcases.

   _____

   e. Let's have breakfast.

   _____

3. Organize the following groups of words into meaningful expressions.

   a. noticias – le – usted – unas – a – dan

   _____

   b. trae – las – cartas – nos – él

   _____

   c. dan – a – mapa – le – un – ella

   _____

   d. el – ellos – les – María – trae – a – álbum

   _____

4. Write the corresponding emphatic form for each of the following indirect pronouns.

   a. te _____   b. me _____   c. nos _____

5. Rewrite the following sentences changing the indirect object pronouns from singular to plural.

   a. Me dan un recado.

   _____

   b. Te dan unas noticias.

   _____

   c. ¿Quién le lleva los guantes?

   _____

6. **Translate into Spanish.**

a. María brings me the books.

_____

b. She brings a present for me.

_____

c. María buys me a map.

_____

d. Does she buy him the album?

_____

e. We tell him the news.

_____

f. María gives her a message.

_____

g. I buy you (fam.) the bicycle.

_____

h. They never tell Pepe the news.

_____

7. **Fill in the blanks with the correct indirect object pronouns.**

a. A las alumnas no_____cuento nada.

b. El cartero _____ trae cartas a María.

c. ¿Por qué_____compra regalos a los chicos?

d. Mañana_____cuentas a Roberto la noticia.

e. _____damos una fiesta a mamá.

f. El_____trae los libros a nosotros.

g. María_____trae el álbum a ellas.

h. _____dan un recado a mí.

i. ¿Quién_____paga los boletos a él?

j. ¿Quién_____lleva los guantes a ellos?

k. La señora_____paga los boletos a mí.

l. ¿Quién_____recomendó el[1] doctor a usted?

m. _____llevo el abrigo a Uds.

n. _____veo bien a ti ahora.

8. **Complete these sentences by using the clarifying or emphazising object pronouns.**

a. Me dan el dinero. _____

b. Te dan los zapatos. _____

c. Le prestan el libro._____

d. Nos invitan. _____

e. Les preguntan la hora._____

---

[1]When the direct and indirect objects are both persons, the personal <u>a</u> of the direct object is dropped in order to make the meaning clear.

9. **Translate into Spanish using the verbs gustar, parecer y encantar.**

a. She loves the Spanish class.

_____

b. What do you think of the weather.

_____

c. I like Lima.

_____

d. The dictionary seems good to us.

_____

e. They like the vacation.

_____

f. I don't like the book.

10. **Answer the following questions in complete Spanish sentences.**

a. ¿Te gusta el álbum?

_____

b. ¿Qué les parece el diccionario a Uds.?

_____

c. ¿Qué les parece la lección a llos?

_____

d. ¿Le gusta París a usted?

_____

e. ¿Qué te falta? (a suitcase)

_____

11. **Look at the pictures. Translate the expressions into Spanish.**

Winter _____

It's cold. _____

Spring _____

It's cool. _____

Summer _____

It's hot. _____

Autumn _____

It's cool. _____

12. **Answer in complete sentences.**

¿Hace calor o frío en verano?

a. Answer:_____

¿Hace fresco en primavera?

b. Answer:_____

¿Hace calor en invierno?

c. Answer:_____

¿Cuántas estaciones hay en el año?

d. Answer:_____

¿Hace fresco en Miami en diciembre?

e. Answer:_____

13. **Complete the sentences.**

En los Estados Unidos:

a. Se llama_____la estación de marzo.
   abril y mayo.

b. Se llama_____la estación de junio,
   julio y agosto.

c. Se llama_____la estación de septiembre, octubre y noviembre.

d. Se llama_____la estación de diciembre, enero y febrero.

14. **Underline the indirect object pronouns in the following sentences. If there is no indirect object, write "none."**

a. La empleada nos trae un vestido.

b. ¿Qué le parecen los zapatos?

c. Yo veo el traje y lo compro.

d. El cartero te trae las cartas.

e. Yo la llamo.

f. Me dan las noticias.

g. Le dan un mapa a él.

h. Me gusta el arroz con pollo.

i. Ellos le traen el recibo.

j. Juan nos da la lista.

15. **Complete the sentences in Spanish with the indirect object pronouns and their clarifying or emphatic form.**

a._____pregunto por su esposa_____.(to you, formal)

b._____doy el libro_____, mamá.

c._____doy las noticias_____.(to the gentlemen)

d._____habla_____.(to me)

e._____da el desayuno_____.(to us)

f._____hablo en español_____.(to them)

TOPICS: OTHER RADICAL-CHANGING O→UE VERBS, REVIEW AND EXPANSION OF THE USES OF DIRECT AND INDIRECT OBJECT PRONOUNS

CONVERSATION XX

HACIENDO LAS MALETAS			PACKING THE SUITCASES
1. Esposa: Recuerda llevar tu traje de lana.	–	Wife:	Remember to take your wool suit.
2. Esposa: También tu sombrero.	–	Wife:	Also your hat.
3. Esposo: ¿Cuántos libras se pueden llevar?	–	Husband:	How many pounds can you take?
4. Esposa: 44 por persona.	–	Wife:	44 per person.

I. Other Radical-Changing o→ue Verbs

The verbs <u>jugar</u>, "to play", <u>probar</u>, "to try" or "to taste."

Subject	jugar	probar
Yo	juego	pruebo
Tú	juegas	pruebas
Ud., él, ella	juega	prueba
Nosotros, -as	jugamos	probamos
Uds., ellos, ellas	juegan	prueban

Examples:

Tú siempre lo pruebas. - You always taste it.

Prueba las manzanas. - Taste the apples.

Juega con él. - Play with him.

Yo juego con el chico. - I play with the boy.

Ellos prueban todos los platos. - They try all the dishes.

Notice that some examples are given in the familiar affirmative commands.

II. Review and Expansion of the Uses of Direct and Indirect Object Pronouns.

Some prepositional phrases in English are expressed by indirect object pronouns in Spanish. The indirect object can stand for the English "for" or even "from" someone. The best way to express this feature of the Spanish language is through examples:

I buy a ticket for you.
I buy a ticket from you.
⎤ Le compro un boleto.

Although with different meanings, both sentences are expressed the same way in Spanish, yet, in context, the meaning becomes clear.

Study the following examples:

Te voy a vender el auto.
⎡ I am going to sell the car to you.
⎣ I am going to sell the car for you.

Nos compran los boletos.
⎡ They buy the tickets for us.
⎣ They buy the tickets from us.

Le compro los discos.
⎡ I'm buying the records for you.
⎣ I'm buying the records from you.

VOCABULARIO

NOUNS

abuelo (a)	-	grandfather
		grandmother
barco (m)	-	boat, ship
cartero (m)	-	mailman
diccionario (m)	-	dictionary
guayabera (f)	-	a loose fitting
		shirt worn in the
		tropics
Hispanoamerica	-	Hispanic America
libra (f)	-	pound
mantilla (f)	-	lace,
música (f)	-	music
nieto (a)	-	grandson, grandaughter
novio (a)	-	fiance, fiancee
nuera (f)	-	daughter-in-law
padres (m)	-	parents
peineta (f)	-	ornamental comb
primo (a)	-	cousin
rebozo (m)	-	shawl
ruana (f)	-	woolen poncho
sarape (m)	-	Mexican heavy shawl,
		small blanket
sobrino (a)	-	nephew, niece
suegro (a)	-	father-in-law
		mother-in-law
yerno (m)	-	son-in-law

VERBS

jugar	-	to play
salir	-	to go out, to leave

ADVERBS

demasiado	-	too much

EXPRESSIONS

¡Caramba!	-	expression of surprise
		dismay, anger, etc.
por teléfono	-	on the phone, by phone

1. Read the following expressions and determine who **said each of** them in the Basic Conversation. Write <u>esposo</u> or <u>esposa</u> beside the corresponding expression.

    a. También tu sombrero.   _____

    b. 44 por persona.   _____

    c. Tu traje de lana.   _____

    d. ¿Cuántos libras se pueden llevar? _____

2. **Fill in the blanks with the proper words.** Choose from the words given below each expression.

    a. Sí, el _____ es frío.

        calor   bufanda   invierno

    b. ¿Cuántas _____ se pueden llevar?

        abrigo   camisas   sombrero

    c. Vamos a llevar los _____.

        chaqueta   maletas   zapatos

    d. Voy a poner la _____ y la bufanda.

        corbata   invierno   maletas

3. **Complete the following line of conversation with the appropriate words.** Choose from the words given below.

    _____ llevar tu _____ de _____.
        a   b   c

    traje   guantes   recuerda   lana

4. **Organize the following groups of words into meaningful expressions.**

    a. se

        llevar

        libras

        pueden   _____

        cuántas

        ¿ ?

    b. y

        mi

        pongo

        mi   _____

        chaqueta

        abrigo

    c. a

        la

        voy

        poner   _____

        bufanda

5. Translate into Spanish.

a. I can have lunch. _____

b. You (fam.) can eat break- _____
fast.

c. You (formal) can go out. _____

d. He can go out. _____

e. She can come early. _____

f. We can eat dinner. _____

g. They can eat a snack. _____

h. Do you (fam.) remember _____
the place?

i. I eat lunch with her. _____

j. The skirt does not cost _____
much.

k. He returns from New York. _____

l. You (formal) give back _____
the pants.

m. All of you sleep too much. _____

n. They do not sleep much. _____

6. First, translate the sentences into Spanish, then
rewrite them using direct object pronouns following
the model:

Model: I buy the pencil.

Yo compro el lápiz.

Yo lo compro.

a. You (fam.) call Andrew. _____

_____

b. You (formal) call Andrew. _____

_____

c. You (fam.) invite the _____
lady.

_____

d. You (formal) invite the _____
lady.

_____

e. All of you invite _____
Andrew and the lady.

_____

7. Complete the answers to the following questions using
direct object pronouns.

a. ¿Buscas los guantes?

Sí, _____

b. ¿Ella prefiere las tijeras?

No, _____

c. ¿Te mira él?

No, _____

d. ¿Ellos los ven a Uds. los domingos?

Sí, _____

8. **Translate into Spanish using indirect object pronouns.**

a. They give you (fam.) some news.

_____

b. They give you (form.) some news.

_____

c. They give him some news.

_____

d. They give her some news.

_____

e. They give us some news.

_____

f. They give me some news.

_____

g. They give them some news.

_____

h. They give John some news.

_____

i. I give María a map.

_____

j. The mailman brings you (pl.) the letters.

_____

k. The mailman brings you (sing.) the letters.

_____

l. I like Lima.

_____

m. The dictionary seems good to us.

_____

n. She loves the class.

_____

9. **Write a Spanish sentence to express each of the following ideas. Use the verbs parecer, encantar, and gustar respectively.**

a. You don't think the map is big.

_____

b. You love the music.

_____

c. They like Lima.

_____

10. **Exercises A and B relate to the following conversation:**

<u>Una visita a Pepe</u>

Esposa: ¿Qué piensas llevarle a Pepe?
Esposo: Le podemos llevar corbatas, camisa y zapatos.
Esposa: Me parece bien, pero a él le encantan las bufandas y los sombreros. ¿Qué tú crees?
Esposo: Me gusta la idea.
Esposa: ¿Vamos en barco, en tren o en avión?
Esposo: Prefiero un vuelo directo.
Esposa: Sí, es mejor.

A. Write **sí** if the statement is true, or **no** if the answer is false.

1. El esposo quiere llevarle zapatos a Pepe. _____

2. La esposa prefiere llevarle camisas. _____

3. A la esposa le parece bien llevarle corbatas a Pepe. _____

4. Los dos van en barco a visitar a Pepe. _____

5. Al esposo le gusta el avión. _____

6. A la esposa también. _____

B. Write a check mark to the right of the sentences when the underlined pronoun stand for the noun **Pepe**.

1. **Le** podemos llevar sombreros. _____

2. **Me** gusta la idea. _____

3. **Le** encantan las bufandas _____

4. ¿Qué **tú** crees? _____

5. ¿Qué piensas lleva**rle** _____

11. Complete the following answers.

a. ¿Les gusta el vuelo directo a ustedes?

   Answer: Sí, _____

b. ¿Qué le parece a Ud. el tren?

   Answer: _____ encanta.

c. ¿Le gusta a Ud. ir en turista?

   Answer: No, _____

12. Translate into Spanish and then change to the negative. Notice that they are commands.

   Model: Give (formal) me. Déme.

   No me dé.

a. Take it (Ud., fem. pronoun).

   _____

   _____

b. Take it (tú, fem. pronoun).

   _____

   _____

c. Take it (tú, masc. pronoun).

   _____

   _____

d. Change it (Ud., fem. pronoun).

   _____

   _____

e. Change it (tú, masc. pronoun).

   _____

   _____

f. Change it (Uds., masc. pronoun).

_____

_____

g. Give me (Uds.)

_____

_____

h. Give (fam.) him the book.

_____

_____

i. Give (formal) him the book.

_____

_____

j. Give (formal) her the book.

_____

_____

k. Give (Us.) John the book.

_____

_____

l. Come in (Uds.)

_____

_____

m. Remember it (Uds. masc. pronouns).

_____

_____

13. Rewrite the following sentences using object pronouns when possible.

a. Pepe, tome el dinero.

_____

b. Gracias por el disco.

_____

c. Dame los zapatos.

_____

d. Yo no recuerdo bien la canción.

_____

e. Cierren las puertas temprano.

_____

f. Preparen las cosas para el martes.

_____

g. Regrese con el Sr. López.

_____

h. Espere, por favor.

_____

i. Compre el mapa.

_____

j. Recuerden la lección.

_____

14. These sentences are taken from Exercise 13. Rewrite them changing the commands to the tú form first and then make the sentences negative. Use object pronouns when possible.

a. Pepe, tome el dinero.

(tú) _____

(neg) _____

b. Cierren las puertas.

(tú) _____

(neg) _____

c. Preparen las cosas para el martes.

(tú) _____

(neg) _____

d. Regrese con el Sr. López.

(tú) _____

(neg) _____

e. Espere, por favor.

(tú) _____

(neg) _____

f. Compre el mapa.

(tú) _____

(neg) _____

g. Recuerden la canción.

(tú) _____

(neg) _____

16. Translate into Spanish.

a. I am giving you the tickets, Mary.

_____

b. Do you write him often?

_____

c. Why don't you write her?

_____

d. He always tells us the truth.

_____

e. Are you going to buy us a book?

_____

TOPICS: DEMONSTRATIVE ADJECTIVES AND PRONOUNS, TWO OBJECT PRONOUNS TOGETHER, POSITION OF OBJECT PRONOUNS WHEN AN INFINITIVE FOLLOWS A CONJUGATED FORM OF A VERB.

CONVERSATION XXI

	EL VIAJE		THE TRIP
1.	Pasajera: Tengo una reservación para el vuelo de las tres de la tarde.	- Passenger:	I have a reservation for the three P.M. flight.
2.	Empleado: Déme su pasaporte y boleto.	- Ticket Agent:	Give me your passport and ticket.
3.	Empleado: ¿Tiene su certificado de vacuna?	- Ticket Agent:	Do yo have your vaccination certificate?
4.	Pasajera: Sí, aquí está.	- Passenger:	Yes, here it is.
5.	Pasajera: Estas son mis maletas.	- Passenger:	These are my suitcases.
6.	Empleado: Muy bien. Todo está en orden.	- Ticket Agent:	Fine. Everything is in order.

I. Demonstrative Adjectives and Pronouns

Demonstrative adjectives point to a noun answering the question "which one?" In English, the demonstrative adjectives are: "this", "these", "that" and "those."

	Masculine	Feminine	
singular	este	esta	this (next to the speaker)
singular	ese	esa	that (next to the person spoken to)
singular	aquel	aquella	That (away from both the speaker and the person spoken to)
plural	estos	estas	these (next to the speaker)
plural	esos	esas	these (next to the person) spoken to
plural	aquellos	aquellas	those (away from both the speaker and the person spoken to)

In general, aquel, aquella, aquellos y aquellas mean "that" or "those over there", in other words, a thing which is away from both the speaker and the person to whom is being spoken.

Singular forms:

Este queso y ese pan son excelentes.	- This cheese and that bread are excellent.
¿Es nuevo aquí aquel camarero?	- Is that waiter new here.
¿Están los postres en aquella mesa?	- Are the desserts on that table?
Dame esa cuchara y toma esta servilleta.	- Give me that spoon and take this napkin.

Plural forms:

¿De quién son estos zapatos?	- Whose shoes are these?
Estas maletas son de Carmen.	- These suitcases are Carmen's.
Necesito esos pantalones.	- I need those pants.
Dame esas camisas.	- Give me those shirts.
Voy a llevar aquellos guantes.	- I'm going to take those gloves.
No necesito aquellas bufandas.	- I don't need those scarves.

Remember, use <u>aquel</u>, <u>aquellas</u>, and <u>aquellos</u> to point to items which are away from both speakers.

II. Demonstrative Pronouns

A demonstrative pronoun, as all pronouns, replaces a noun. When you say in English· "this one", "these", "that one", "those", you are using demonstrative pronouns instead of nouns. In Spanish, you use the same forms as the demonstrative adjectives, but they require an accent mark which indicates that they are being used as pronouns.

éste,	ésta,	éstos,	éstas
ése,	ésa,	ésos,	ésas
aquél,	aquélla,	aquéllas,	aquéllas

¿Está el postre en esa mesa o en aquélla?	–	Is the dessert on that table or on that one over there?
Déme ésos, éstos son muy grandes.	–	Give me those, these are too big.
Necesito estas cajas y aquéllas también.	–	I need these boxes and those over there also.

III. Two Object Pronouns Together

When there are direct and indirect object pronouns in the sentence, the indirect object pronoun is placed first and the direct object pronoun second.

¿Vas a dármelo?	–	Are you going to give it to me?
Traémelas ahora.	–	Bring them to me now.
Sí, te las traigo ahora.	–	Yes, I'm bringing them to you now.

Ellas nos la abren.   –   They open it for us.

When the indirect object pronouns <u>le</u> and <u>les</u> are used together with any of the direct object pronouns, (lo, la, los, las), the form <u>se</u> substitutes <u>le</u> and <u>les</u>.

Study the following chart:

	lo	lo – se lo (It (masc.) to) him, her you (formal) all of you, them
le	la	la – se la (It (fem.) to him, her, you (formal), all of you, them
+	= Se	
les	los	los – se los (them (masc.) to), him, her, you (formal), all of you, them.
	las	las – se las (them (fem.) to)to them, him, here, you (formal), all of you, them.

Se lo llevamos al aeropuerto.	– We are taking it to him at the airport.
El se las trae siempre.	– He always brings them to him.
Quiero llevársela en seguida.	– I want to take it to him.

IV. Position of object pronouns when an infinitive follows the conjugated form of a verb. The object pronouns may be placed before the conjugated form of the verb or attached to the ending of the infinitive form.

¿Vas a dármelo?	or	¿Me lo vas a dar?
Quiero llevársela.	or	Se la quiero llevar.
No puedo verlo.	or	No lo puedo ver.

VOCABULARIO

NOUNS

aceite (m)	-	oil
andén (m)	-	railway platform
asiento (m)	-	seat
certificado (m)	-	certificate
coche-cama (m)	-	pullman car
coche-comedor (m)	-	dining car
muelle (m)	-	pier, dock
muchacho (a)	-	young adult
orden (m)	-	order
pasaporte (m)	-	passport
periódico (m)	-	newspaper
queso (m)	-	cheese
radio-reloj (m)	-	clock radio
vacuna (f)	-	vaccine
ventanilla (f)	-	window in a train, car, plane, box office

ADJECTIVES

algún (o, a, os, as)	-	some
dominicano	-	native of Dominican Republic

VERBS

responder	-	to answer
tratar	-	to try

ADVERBS

antes	-	before

PREPOSITIONS

antes de	-	before

DEMONSTRATIVE ADJECTIVES

este, esta	-	this
estos, estas	-	these
ese, esa	-	that
esos, esas	-	those
aquel, aquella	-	that (over there)
aquellos, aquellas	-	those (over there)

DEMONSTRATIVE PRONOUNS

éste, ésta	-	this one
éstos, éstas,	-	these
ése, ésa	-	that one
ésos, ésas	-	those
aquél, aquélla	-	that one (over there)
aquéllos, aquéllas	-	those (over there)

1. **Read** the expressions and **determine who** said each of them in the Basic Conversation. Write <u>pasajera</u> or <u>empleado</u> beside the corresponding expression.

    a. Déme su pasaporte y boleto. _____

    b. ¿Qué asiento quiere? _____

    c. El número 15, de ventanilla. _____

    d. Tengo una reservación para el vuelo de las tres de la tarde. _____

2. **Write** the appropriate answer for this question.

    ¿Tiene su certificado de vacuna?

    Answer: _____

3. **Complete** the following line of conversation with the appropriate words. Choose from the words given below.

    Muy _____, _____ está en_____.
         (a)   (b)   (c)
    orden   está   mis   bien   todo

4. **Organize** the following groups of words into meaningful expressions.

    a. son

        maletas

        éstas   _____

        mis

    b. tú

        también

        sombrero

        _____

    c. persona

        44

        por

        _____

5. **Read the following narrative and complete the items below it.**

Una narración

La señorita Gómez trabaja en el aeropuerto. Esta muchacha tiene una oficina grande y nueva con fotografías de la Florida, el Perú y la Argentina. Esas fotos son pequeñas, pero muy bonitas. Allí todo está en orden.

a. La señorita Gómez _____.

   1. es nueva en el aeropuerto
   2. tiene una oficina grande
   3. trae el pasaporte

b. En la oficina _____.

   1. la Srta. Gómez tiene fotos del Perú.
   2. las fotografías son muy grandes.
   3. trabaja una muchacha pequeña.

c. Allí está la oficina de la Srta. Gómez_____.

   1. A esa oficina debemos llevar las fotos.
   2. Es pequeña y bonita
   3. Debemos llegar allí antes de la hora del viaje.

d. Con los papeles también llevamos_____.

   1. aquellas maletas
   2. la fotografía nueva
   3. esta narración

e. Esas fotos _____.

   1. están en la Florida
   2. son muy bonitas
   3. me parecen grandes

6. **Translate into Spanish.**

a. I like that bread. _____

b. Those radios are big. _____

c. I need these narratives. _____

d. That meat is excellent. _____

e. May I see those photographs? _____

7. **Read the nouns at the left and the demonstrative adjectives at the right. Choose the appropriate adjective to modify each noun. Write out the complete expression.**

a. radios   aquella   _____

b. pan   este   _____

c. carne   estos   _____

d. narraciones   esas   _____

8. **Read the following expressions and write them in the plural.**

a. Esta ensalada. _____

b. Ese camarero. _____

c. Aquel almuerzo. _____

d. Aquella cena. _____

e. Este comedor. _____

9. Translate the following demonstrative adjectives.

Me gusta_____leche y_____postres.
　　　　　a. (this)　　　b. (these)

¿Es nuevo_____vino? En_____mesa
　　　　　c. (this)　　　　d. (that)

está la carne.

10. Write the appropriate demonstrative adjectives to indicate the distance of these objects to the speaker. Here the photos are next to the person spoken to.

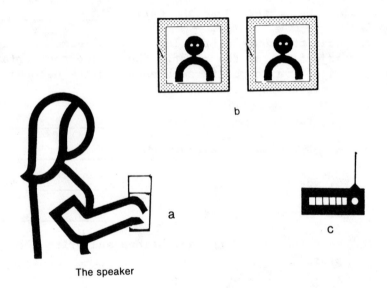

The speaker

a. _____

b. _____

c. _____

11. Find the correct demonstrative adjectives for the nouns listed below each explanation. Write out the complete expression.

a. María is showing her friends some of the things she is holding.

　　1. radio reloj_____

　　2. narraciones_____

b. Roberto is pointing out items at another table.

　　1. periódicos _____

　　2. cosas _____

c. Isabel and her brother are at the table having lunch. Isabel is asking her brother to hand her some items of foods which are on the table.

　　1. pan _____

　　2. ensalada _____

12. Complete the following sentences with the correct demonstrative form. Choose from those written in parentheses.

a. ____reloj es pequeño. (este, esa, esos)

b. ¿Puedo ver____periódicos. (esas, este, aquellos)

c. Están en____biblioteca. (esa, este, aquel)

d. ____camarero es excelente. (aquellos, este, esa)

e. ¿Es nuevo____radio? (aquel, esta, aquellos)

13. **Read the dialogue and write the accent mark on each of the demonstrative forms that require it.**

¿Te gustan estos radios?
     a̲

No, esos no me gustan.
    b̲

¡Qué bonitos son aquellos!
                c̲

Necesito comprar un regalo.
Este radio-reloj es excelente.
d̲

Sí, ese es bueno y barato.
    e̲

14. **Substitute the underlined word with the word in parentheses. Make all necessary changes.**

a. Aquellas cosas (comedor)_____

b. Ese número (leche)_____

c. Esta cena (almuerzo)_____

d. Estos relojes (narración)_____

e. Aquella carne (periódicos)_____

15. **Decide if the underlined object pronouns are direct or indirect.**

a. Les prestamos dinero a ustedes.

b. Los ve.

c. Míranos.

d. Cómpreme la casa.

e. Te invitan.

16. **Place the object pronouns written in parentheses in the correct position, before or after the verb forms.**

a. (lo) ____ mire ____.

b. (las) ____ miran ____.

c. (me) ____ miras ____.

d. (los) ____ mire ____.

e. (nos) ____ miren ____.

17. **Rewrite each of the following sentences by changing the position of the object pronoun.**

a. Puedo dejarlos allí.

_____

b. No quieren contestarles.

_____

c. Podemos darle el recibo.

_____

d. Prefiere vernos el lunes.

_____

e. ¿Quieres mirarla?

_____

f. Pueden traerte la lista.

_____

18. Complete each expression by placing the object
    pronouns written in parentheses in the correct
    sequence. Write out the complete sentence.

a. ¿Quieres prestar? (los-nos)

_____

b. Puedo escribir. (te-la)

_____

c. Prefiere llevar. (las-me)

_____

d. Juan escribe. (nos-la)

_____

e. Ustedes no quieren prestar. (las-me)

_____

f. Da. (los-se)

_____

g. Preste. (se-la)

_____

19. Translate into Spanish.

a. Give me the list. (formal)

_____

b. We lend them some money.

_____

c. I prefer to exchange it.

_____

d. They invite you. (fam.)

_____

e. Look at her. (formal)

_____

20. Complete the following sentences by writing in
    the appropriate Spanish Word.

a. Ellos quieren dejar _____.
                                us

b. Prefiero escribir _____.
                              them (fem.)

c. María quiere hablar _____.
                                her

d. Quiero llevar _____.
                          her

e. Ellos prefieren cambiar _____.
                                    it (masc.)

21. Change the underlined plural pronouns to the
    singular. Write out the complete sentence
    making any other necessary changes.

    a. <u>Nos</u> traen el recibo.

    _____

    b. Cómprale<u>s</u> el auto a ellos.

    _____

    c. Quiero ver<u>las</u>.

    _____

    d. Juan <u>les</u> da el menú a ustedes.

    _____

    e. <u>Los</u> llamamos.

    _____

22. Write the Spanish for the English expressions in
    parentheses. Write out the complete sentence.

    a. Pueden prestar _____.
                       it (masc. thing) to them

    b. ¿Quieres traer _____?
                       them (masc. things) to him

    c. Prefiero comprar _____.
                        it (masc. things) for all of you

d. María no puede dar _____.
                       them (masc. things.) to us

e. Quiere llevar _____.
                  it (masc. thing) to me

TOPICS: THE NEUTER DEMONSTRATIVE PRONOUNS. REVIEW AND EXPANDED USAGE OF DIRECT AND INDIRECT OBJECT PRONOUN THROUGH
EXERCISES.

CONVERSATION XXII

EN EL AEROPUERTO		AT THE AIRPORT
1. Empleado: ¿Qué asiento quiere?	– Ticket Agent:	What seat do you want?
2. Pasajera: El número 15, de ventanilla.	– Passenger:	Number 15, a window seat.
3. Empleado: ¡Buen viaje! El avión sale a su hora.	– Ticket Agent:	Have a good trip! The plane will leave on time.

I. Neuter demonstrative pronouns.

The neuter demonstrative pronouns are esto, eso, aquello. They are only used in the singular and they require

no accent. These pronouns are used when asking or referring to something that is unknown to you.

¿Qué es eso?	– What is that?
¿Es esto un radio?	– Is this a radio?
¿Puedo ver aquello?	– May I see that over there?
Déme eso.	– Give me that.
Necesito todo eso.	– I need all that.

Notice, in the examples given, the speaker does not know the gender of the thing to which he is referring,
consequently, he cannot use a demonstrative pronoun that reflects gender.

VOCABULARIO

NOUNS

águila (f)	-	eagle
antena (f)	-	antenna
camarote (m)	-	cabin, state room
camello (m)	-	camel
capital (f)	-	capital city
capital (m)	-	wealth
conversación (f)	-	conversation
cuento (m)	-	story, tale
departamento (m)	-	department
desfile (m)	-	parade
edad (f)	-	age
enjuague (m)	-	rinse
Estados Unidos	-	United States
Italia	-	Italy
litera (f)	-	berth
mensaje (m)	-	message
partido (m)	-	game
pelota (f)	-	ball
pluma (f)	-	pen
rato (m)	-	while
República Dominicana	-	Dominican Republic
respuesta (f)	-	answer
revista (f)	-	magazine
ropa (f)	-	clothes, clothing
semana (f)	-	week
tenis (m)	-	tennis
vecino (a)	-	neighbor
verbo (m)	-	verb

ADJECTIVES

adelantado	-	early
bondadoso	-	kind
gordo	-	fat
modesto	-	modest
ocupado	-	busy
pobre	-	poor
próximo	-	next
retrasado	-	late
urgente	-	urgent

VERBS

ayudar	-	to help
comprender	-	to understand
defender	-	to defend
descansar	-	to rest
enseñar	-	to teach, to show
explicar	-	to explain
llover	-	to rain
pronunciar	-	to pronounce
pintar	-	to paint
sufrir	-	to suffer

ADVERBS

atentamente	-	attentively
debajo	-	under

PRONOUNS

aquello	-	that (over there)
eso	-	that
esto	-	this

EXPRESSIONS

a su ahora	-	on time
a tiempo	-	on time
como a	-	at about
pasado mañana	-	the day after tomorrow
todas las semanas	-	every week

PREPOSITIONS

debajo de	-	under

EJERCICIOS

1. **Write the Spanish for the English expressions written below. Use the Spanish neuter forms.**

   a. May I see this? _____

   b. Is this a radio? _____

   c. I need all that. _____

   d. This is not easy. _____

   e. I like that. _____

2. **In the following expressions decide which demonstratives should have written accents.**

   a. Me gustan esos radios y aquellos también.

   b. Necesito estos y aquellos.

   c. Aquel reloj es muy bonito.

   d. Este es demasiado grande.

   e. ¿Puedo ver eso?

Some of the following exercises are old, some are new, constant review is essential for learning a language. You will also find quite a few new words, so use your dictionary, this is a good opportunity to increase your vocabulary.

1. **Divide the following words into syllables and place accents, if needed.**

   a. dia _____   k. hermanos _____

   b. pasado _____   l. ingles _____

   c. mañana _____   m. chico _____

   d. miercoles _____   n. cancion _____

   e. Maria _____   o. canciones _____

   f. amigo _____   p. consulta _____

   g. biblioteca _____   q. antena _____

   h. pronuncia _____   r. enjuague _____

   i. español _____   s. imagen _____

   j. Pedrito _____   t. aceite _____

2. **Supply proper question words.**

   a. ¿_____ es él? Who is he?

   b. ¿_____ es él? What is he?

   c. ¿_____ es él? Which one is he?

   d. ¿_____ estudia ella? What does she study?

   e. ¿_____ estudia ella? Where does she study?

   f. ¿_____ estudia ella? Why does she study?

   g. ¿_____ se llama él? What is his name?

   h. ¿_____ años tiene ella? How old is she?

   i. ¿_____ vive él? Where does he live?

   j. ¿_____ hablan español? Who speaks Spanish?

   k. ¿_____ está la biblioteca? Where is the library?

   l. ¿_____ edad tiene él? How old is he?

3. **Use the proper form of estar.**

   a. (Yo)_____ aquí.

   b. (Tú)_____ bien.

   c. (Nosotros)_____ en clase.

   d. ¿Cómo_____ Roberto?

   e. ¿Dónde_____ María?

   f. ¿_____ Elena en la sala?

   g. El y ella_____ allí?

   h. ¿Quién_____ en la clase?

   i. Tú y yo_____ en el portal.

   j. Tú y él_____ en la cocina.

4. Give the definite and indefinite articles for the following·

a. (_____) (_____) amigo.

b. (_____) (_____) mano.

c. (_____) (_____) hermano.

d. (_____) (_____) mapa.

e. (_____) (_____) lunes.

f. (_____) (_____) águila.

g. (_____) (_____) desfile.

h. (_____) (_____) canción.

i. (_____) (_____) agua.

j. (_____) (_____) parque.

5. Conjugate the regular verbs. (Some of them may be new to you, but their conjugation should be no problem.)

a. Yo (estudiar) _____

b. Tú (aprender) _____

c. El (practicar) _____

d. Nosotros (beber) _____

e. Ellos (comer) _____

f. Ella (abrir) _____

g. Ud. (vivir) : _____

h. Tú y yo (pronunciar)_____

i. El y yo (recibir) _____

j. El y ella (responder)_____

k. Yo (correr) _____.

l. Tú (cantar) _____.

m. Ella (leer) _____.

n. Ud. y yo (trabajar)_____.

o. Uds. (mirar) _____.

p. El (sufrir) _____.

q. Tú (creer) _____.

r. Nosotros (usar) _____.

s. Ella (tratar) _____.

t. Yo (pagar) _____.

6. Complete the sentences with the proper form of the adjectives.

a. El chico (good)_____, (modest)_____, (intelligent)_____.

b. La chica (beautiful)_____, (blonde)_____, (tall)_____.

c. La canción (popular)_____, (new)_____, (Spanish)_____.

d. La lección (easy)_____, (difficult)_____, (third)_____.

e. Los autos (big) _____, (blue)_____, (brown)_____.

f. Las sillas (green)_____, (new)_____, (white)_____.

g. La ciudad (old) _____, (big) _____,

(French) _____.

h. Los chicos (small) _____,

(sad) _____, (thin) _____.

i. El hombre (fat) _____, (good) _____,

(tall) _____.

7. Use the proper form of _ser_ or _estar_.

a. Mis amigos _____ bien.

b. Washington _____ la capital de los
Estados Unidos.

c. Ellos _____ franceses.

d. Mi tío _____ médico.

e. La comida _____ caliente.

f. Tú _____ muy ocupado.

g. La mamá _____ generosa.

h. Juan _____ cansado.

i. El perro _____ debajo de la mesa.

j. Ellos no _____ pobres.

k. El camello _____ un animal muy grande

l. Los automóviles nuevos _____ pequeños.

m. ¿_____ Ud. profesor?

n. La casa no _____ limpia.

o. Hoy _____ lunes.

8. Complete the expressions with the proper forms
of prepositions, articles, or both.

a. Es el sombrero _____ Roberto.

b. La carta es _____ mi amigo Luis.

c. La esposa _____ médico es enfermera.

d. Le da el lápiz _____ alumno.

e. Caracas es la capital _____ Venezuela.

f. Son amigos _____ vecina.

g. Son los padres _____ vecino.

h. Una _____ muchachas es muy inteligente.

i. El profesor enseña _____ estudiantes.

j. Abro _____ puertas.

k. Voy _____ parque.

9. Translate into Spanish.

a. Rosa's blouse is white.

_____.

b. Arturo's shirts are also white.

_____.

c. The Spanish teacher is Spanish.

_____.

d. He arrives early from the airport.

_____.

e. Juan is from Argentina.

_____

f. The photo album is green.

_____

g. I see someone now.

_____

h. I call Dad on the phone.

_____

i. I arrive home at four.

_____

j. He studies at eight.

_____

k. The records are from Italy.

_____

l. He doesn't listen to the teachers (fem.)

_____

m. Rosa is from Mexico.

_____

n. I see Pedrito's brother

_____

10. **Fill in the blanks with the proper form of the verb ir.**

a. Yo_____en enero.

b. Tú_____al parque.

c. El_____a su casa.

d. Los estudiantes no_____.

e. Ellos_____a la playa los domingos.

f. Uds._____a España el año próximo.

g. Pedro_____a comer temprano hoy.

h. Tú y él_____a estudiar mañana.

i. ¿_____Ud. al centro a menudo?

j. ¿Quiénes_____a cenar en el restaurante?

11. **Translate into Spanish (irregular e→ir verbs).**

a. I close the windows.

_____

b. I understand the conversation.

_____

c. The lawyer defends him.

_____

d. You (plural) understand Spanish.

_____

e. We always lose.

_____

f. When does the class begin?

_____

g. What do you think?

_____

h. He lights the oven.

_____

i. We prefer wine.

_____

j. We want to eat fish.

_____

k. Do all of you feel the cold?

_____

l. Does she want chicken salad?

_____

m. I want cold beer.

_____

n. But I prefer wine.

_____

o. Do you understand the verbs?

_____

12. **Translate into Spanish (o→ue verbs).**

a. They can go out now.

_____

b. You (formal) give back (return) the pants.

_____

c. The skirt does not cost much.

_____

d. Does it rain now?

_____

e. Do you (fam.) play tennis?

_____

f. Does he remember the place?

_____

g. I cannot see.

_____

h. She eats lunch at twelve.

_____

i. The tickets cost twenty dollars.

_____

j. You show her the book.

_____

k. They do not sleep well.

_____

1. The French books cost more.

_____

m. Who can go out with Ann?

_____

n. Remember to buy tickets for the game.

_____

o. Where can you buy it?

_____

13. **Answer in Spanish.**

a. ¿Prefiere salir ahora?

Sí, _____

b. ¿Duerme Ud. mucho los sábados?

Sí, _____

c. ¿Cuesta mucho el automóvil?

Sí, _____

d. ¿Entiende Ud. la lección?

Sí, _____

e. ¿Recomienda Ud. el curso de español?

Sí, _____

f. ¿A qué hora vuelve Ud. a la casa? (9 PM)

Sí, _____

14. **Complete the crossword puzzle by using the correct present tense form of the verb in parentheses.**

Horizontal

3. Tú no (<u>remember</u>) las noticias.

5. El auto (<u>costs</u>) mucho.

6. ¿(<u>Do you find</u>) la biblioteca (<u>familiar</u>)?

8. Nosotras (<u>remember</u>) el partido.

Vertical

1. Juan y yo (<u>find</u>) los boletos.

2. ¿Cuánto (<u>cost</u>) las blusas?

4. Yo (<u>remember</u>) el número?

7. Ustedes (<u>to be able, can</u>) go out.

15. Using the model sentence, replace the command by the verbs given.

a. Miren Uds. ese libro.

    1. estudiar   2. dar   3. comprar

1. _____

2. _____

3. _____

b. Descanse Ud. un rato.

    1. trabajar   2. entrar 3. esperar

1. _____

2. _____

3. _____

c. Mira tú esa silla.

    1. dar   2. comprar   3. pintar

1. _____

2. _____

3. _____

d. Descansa tú ahora.

    1. trabajar 2. entrar 3. esperar

1. _____

2. _____

3. _____

e. Trae tú la gasolina.

    1. comprar   2. pagar   3. llevar

1. _____

2. _____

3. _____

16. Change to the negative.

a. Empiecen a trabajar.

_____

b. Trae todo.

_____

c. Regresa con María.

_____

d. Escúchalo.

_____

e. Traigan.

_____

f. Firma aquí.

_____

g. Dame el boleto.

_____

h. Espera un momento.

_____

i. Cámbialo hoy.

_____

j. Olvida eso.

_____

17. Translate into Spanish.

a. She doesn't visit him.

_____

b. I see them (masc.).

_____

c. Take it (formal)!

_____

d. Don't take it (familiar)!

_____

e. I do not understand it (masc.).

_____

f. I do not understand him.

_____

g. Do you (formal) want to sell it (fem.)?

_____

h. Do you see them (mixed group) everyday?

_____

i. Yes, I am looking for them (fem.).

_____

j. We want it (fem.) yellow.

_____

18. Answer in Spanish using object pronouns.

a. ¿Quieres las revistas?

_____

b. ¿Ayudas a tus padres?

_____

c. ¿Invitas a tus amigas a menudo?

_____

d. ¿Comprende Ud. muy bien este ejercicio?

_____

e. ¿Escuchan Uds. atentamente al profesor?

_____

f. ¿Desea Ud. vender las camisas?

_____

g. ¿Te ven?

_____

h. ¿Prefieren Uds. estas plumas?

_____

19. **Translate into Spanish.**

a. They give her a map of the U.S.A.

_____

b. He gives me an urgent message.

_____

c. The mailman brings us the letter.

_____

d. The dictionary seems good to us.

_____

e. He talks to us very often.

_____

f. She doesn't write them.

_____

g. Why don't you (fam.) answer me?

_____

h. We like these short lessons.

_____

i. Don't talk to them (formal)!

_____

j. Don't talk to them (fem.)!

_____

k. I write her every week.

_____

l. We send him money.

_____

m. Buy her a gift!

_____

n. She reads them stories.

_____

o. I am talking to her.

_____

20. **Translate into Spanish.**

a. They bring it (masc) to me.

_____

b. We lend it (masc.) to all of you (mixed group).

_____

c. Juan gives it (masc.) to them (mixed group).

_____

d. I am going to sell it (fem.) to him.

_____

e. I am going to sell it (fem.) to her.

_____

f. Do you (fem.) want to lend them (masc.) to us?

_____

g. I write it (fem.) to you (fem.).

_____

h. He teaches it (fem.) to us.

_____

i. I can write it (fem.) to you (fam.).

_____

j. They give them (fem.) to us.

_____

k. Do you lend it (fem.) to your friends? (fam.)

_____

l. Give it (masc.) to me, (fam.)

_____

m. He must explain it (fem.) to us.

_____

n. Buy them (masc.) for her. (formal)

_____

o. Lend it (fem.) to her. (formal)

_____

21. A. **Read the following paragraph carefully and then answer the questions in complete Spanish sentences.**

Pasado mañana, miércoles, voy a la casa de Pedrito. Pedrito es amigo de María y de los hermanos de Arturo. Pedrito habla inglés y pronuncia muy bien. El es un alumno bueno. María no habla inglés, habla español y estudia inglés. El profesor del chico es el Sr. Pérez y el profesor de inglés de la chica es el Sr. López. Veo al Sr. López en la biblioteca de la escuela los martes y al Sr. Pérez los viernes. Ellos no están hoy en la biblioteca.

B. **Write the answers for the questions, basing your responses on the narrative.**

1. ¿Quién es el amigo de María?

_____

2. ¿Qué habla el amigo de María?

_____

3. ¿Cómo es Pedrito?

_____

4. ¿Cómo pronuncia el chico?

_____

5. ¿Quién habla español?

_____

6. ¿Qué estudia María?

_____

7. ¿Es el Sr. López el profesor de la chica o del chico?

_____

8. ¿Es el Sr. López el profesor de español o de inglés?

_____

9. ¿Cuando está el Sr. López en la biblioteca?

_____

10. ¿Cuándo está el Sr. Pérez en la biblioteca?

_____

22. **Read the following paragraph and answer the questions in complete sentences.**

DE VACACIONES (ON VACATION)

Hoy empiezan las vacaciones. Ana y María quieren ir a las tiendas. La mamá prefiere visitar a tía Rosa. Ellas van a casa de la tía. Todas almuerzan temprano y después van al centro.

(En el centro)

Mamá: Estas blusas azules cuestan mucho.

Tía Rosa: Sí, pero la rosada no. Tiene buen precio.

María: ¿Podemos merendar ahora?

Mamá: Esperen un momento. Luego vamos todas.

1. ¿Cuándo empiezan las vacaciones?

_____

2. ¿A dónde quieren ir María y Ana?

_____

3. ¿Qué prefiere la mamá?

_____

4. ¿Es Rosa hermana o tía de María?

_____

5. ¿Dónde almuerza Ana?

_____

6. ¿Cuándo van todas al centro?

_____

7. ¿Cuánto cuestan las blusas azules?

_____

8. ¿Cuesta mucho la blusa rosada?

_____

9. ¿Qué quiere María ahora?

_____

10. ¿Quiénes van a merendar?

_____

TOPIC: **THE PRETERITE INDICATIVE TENSE**

CONVERSATION XXIII

DESPUÉS DE UN VIAJE		AFTER A TRIP
Clara:	Hola, Berta. ¿Cómo estás? ¿Qué hiciste este verano?	- Clara:	Hello, Bertha. How are you? What did you do this summer?
Berta:	Fuí a Sur América.	- Bertha:	I went to South America.
Clara:	¿Qué países visitaste?	- Clara:	What countries did you visit?
Berta:	Estuve en Argentina dos semanas. Me gustó mucho Buenos Aires.	- Bertha:	I spent two weeks in Argentina. I liked Buenos Aires very much.
Clara:	¿No fuiste al Uruguay? Está muy cerca de Buenos Aires.	- Clara:	Didn't you go the Uruguay? It is very close to Buenos Aires.
Berta:	Quise ir, pero no conseguí reservación.	- Bertha:	I tried to go, but I could not get reservations.
Clara:	¡Qué lástima! ¿Compraste muchas cosas en Buenos Aires?	- Clara:	What a pity! Did you buy a lot of things in Buenos Aires?
Berta:	Sí, compré artículos de piel y varios regalos para la familia.	- Bertha:	Yes, I bought leather goods and several presents for the family.
Clara:	¡Fantástico! Perdóname, pero ahí está el autobús y tengo que irme, pero voy a llamarte esta tarde. Hasta luego.	- Clara:	Fantastic! Excuse me, there is the bus and I have to go, but I'll call you this afternoon. See you later.

Spanish has two past tenses: the preterite tense and the imperfect tense. The preterite tense will be presented in this lesson. The imperfect tense will be presented in the following lesson.

I. Preterite Indicative of Regular Verbs:

	gastar	romper	dividir
	(to spend)	(to break)	(to divide)
(Yo)	gast-é	romp-í	divid-í
(Tú)	gast-aste	romp-iste	divid-iste
Ud., él, ella	gast-ó	romp-ió	divid-ió
(Nosotros/as)	gast-amos	romp-imos	divid-imos
Uds., ellos, ellas	gast-aron	romp-ieron	divid-ieron

II. The Preterite Tense Expresses an Action that has been Completed at any Time in the Past.

(Yo) volví pronto. — I returned soon.

(Tú) volviste pronto. - You returned soon. (familiar)

Usted abrió la puerta.- You opened the door. (formal)

El abrió la puerta. - He opened the door.

Ella abrió la puerta. - She opened the door.

(Nosotros or Nosotras)- We lived well.
vivimos bien.

Ustedes vivieron bien.- You lived well.

Ellos vivieron bien. - They lived well. (masc. or mixed group)

Ellas vivieron bien. - They lived well. (feminine)

(Yo) entré allí	- I entered there.
(Tú) entraste allí.	- You entered there. (familiar)
Usted trabajó aquí.	- You worked here. (formal)
El trabajó aquí.	- He worked here.
(Nosotros or Nosotras) ordenamos ya.	- We ordered already.
Ustedes ordenaron ya.	- You ordered already.
Ellos ordenaron ya.	- They already ordered. (masc. or mixed group)
Ellas ordenaron ya.	- They already ordered. (feminine)

III. Irregular Preterite Forms

The followng verbs have irregular preterite tense forms. Each preterite stem is different from the infinitive stem. The first and third person singular ends in an unaccented -e and -o respectively, the ending for the other persons are regular.

Infinitive		Preterite Stem	Preterite Endings	
caber	(to fit in)	cup		
estar	(to be)	estuv-		
hacer	(to do, to make)	hic-[1]	Yo	-e
poder	(to be able)	pud-	Tú	-iste
poner	(to put)	pus-	Ud., él, ella	-o
querer	(to want)	quis-	nosotros	-imos
saber	(to know)	sup-	Uds., ellos, ellas	-ieron
tener	(to have)	tuv-		
venir	(to come)	vin-		
decir	(to say)	dij-[2]		
traer	(to bring)	traj-[2]		

Ella estuvo aquí	- She was here (came here).
(Yo) estuve en el banco.	- I went to the bank.
El hizo todo el trabajo.	- He did all the work.
Ella hizo un vestido.	- She made a dress.
Yo hice la tarea.	- I did the homework.
Ellos pudieron ir.	- They managed to go.
(Tú) no pudiste hacer.	- You failed to do it.
(Nosotros) no lo pusimos aquí.	- We did not put it here.
La mesa no cupo en el cuarto.	- The table did not fit in the room.
Ella lo puso en la mesa.	- She put it on the table.
(Yo) no lo supe a tiempo.	- I did not learn about it (found out) on time.
(Nosotros) lo supimos ayer.	- We found out yesterday.
(Yo) quise ir.	- I tried to go.
Uds. no tuvieron tiempo.	- You didn't have time.
Yo vine temprano.	- I came early.
Uds. vinieron tarde.	- You came late.
(Yo) lo dije.	- I said it.
Ellos dijeron la verdad.	- They told the truth.
(Tú) trajiste demasiado.	- You brought too much.
Ella no trajo el dinero.	- She did not bring the money.

---

[1]There is an orthographic change in hizo, the c of hic changes to z for phonetic reasons.
[2]In the 3rd person plural, drop the i of ie for ending. Thus, dijeron, trajeron.

The verb ir, "to go", ser, "to be."
The verbs ir and ser have the same forms in the preterite tense.

La recepción fue ayer.	— The reception was (took place) yesterday.
Él fue a bailar anoche.	— He went to dance last night.
Dos exámenes finales fueron el lunes.	— Two final exams were on Monday.

The verb dar:

Dar is considered irregular in the preterite because it takes the regular endings for regular -er and -ir verbs, rather than the ending for -ar verbs.

Él me dió un libro.	— He gave me a book.
Les dimos el dinero.	— He gave them the money.
Nos dieron el resto.	— They gave us the rest.

The verbs creer, "to believe", and leer, "to read", oír, "to hear" and caer, "to fall", have irregular forms for the third person singular and plural (Ud., él, ella, Uds., ellos and ellas). They change the i of the stem to a y.

IV. Meaning of Certain Verbs in the Preterite Tense.

It is very important to understand why certain verbs change their meaning in the preterite. Most verbs fall in the category of action verbs, but there are a few that do not. The following verbs are the most common non-action verbs:

saber	to know, to know how
conocer	to know, to be acquainted with
poder	to be able
querer	to want
estar	to be

	creer		leer		oír		caer	
	Present	Preterite	Present	Preterite	Present	Preterite	Present	Preterite
Yo	creo	creí	leo	leí	oigo	oí	caigo	caí
Tú	crees	creíste	lees	leíste	oyes	oíste	caes	caíste
Ud., él ella	cree	creyó	lee	leyó	oye	oyó	cae	cayó
Nosotros	creemos	creímos	leemos	leímos	oímos	oímos	caímos	caímos
Uds., ellos ellas	creen	creyeron	leen	leyeron	oyen	oyeron	caen	cayeron

In Spanish, a verb used in the preterite must represent or carry an action, consequently, when these non-action verbs are used in the preterite, they acquire action, and in doing so their meaning is changed.

Saber in the preterite means "to learn" in the sense of finding out something

Conocer in the preterite means "to meet" in the sense of being introduced to someone.

Poder in the preterite means "to succeed", "to manage", "to accomplish something".

No poder in the preterite means "to fall" in the sense of of not being able to do something after having tried.

Querer in the preterite means "to try".

No querer in the preterite means "to refuse".

Estar in the preterite means "to be in and out of a place", in the sense of having gone to a place.

(Yo) supe la verdad. — I learned (found out) the truth.

Conocí a Roberto. — I met Roberto.

Pude venir. — I managed to come (succeeded after trying).

No pude pasar el examen. — I failed to pass the exam.

Quise ir. — I tried to go.

No quise ir. — I refused to go.

Estuve en la biblioteca. — I went to the library.

Ir[1] radical changing verbs in the preterite. These verbs change e to i or o to u in the third person, the most common are:

Pedir, seguir, conseguir, decir, sentir, repetir, servir, reír(se), vestir(se), dormir, morir

	Pedir	Conseguir	Dormir
Yo	pedí	conseguí	dormí
Tú	pediste	conseguiste	dormiste
Ud., él, ella	pidió	consiguió	durmió
Nosotros(as)	pedimos	conseguimos	dormimos
Uds.,ellos,ella	pidieron	consigueron	durmieron

(Yo) conseguí el dinero. — I obtained (got) the money.

Ella consiguió la reservación. — She obtained (got) the reservation.

(Tú) le pediste un turno. — You asked her for an appointment.

Ud. le pidió el dinero. — You asked her for the money.

(Yo) no dormí bien. — I did not sleep well.

El no durmió mucho . — He didn't sleep much.

---

[1]All -ir verbs which are stem-changing in the present tense also change in the preterite tense, but only in the third person singular and plural.

VOCABULARIO

NOUNS

alcalde(sa)	-	mayor
artículo (m)	-	goods
auditorio (m)	-	auditorium
banco (m)	-	bank, bench
botella (f)	-	bottle
caramelo (m)	-	candy stick (bar)
conferencia (f)	-	lecture
final (m)	-	final, end
lectura (f)	-	reading
mercado (m)	-	market
piel (f)	-	leather, hide, skin
presentación (f)	-	presentation
recepción (f)	-	reception
resto (m)	-	rest
tarea (f)	-	homework

ADJECTIVES

varios	-	various, several

ADVERBS

ahí	-	there
algo	-	something
anoche	-	last night
ayer	-	yesterday
pronto	-	right away, soon
ya	-	already

VERBS

acabar	-	to finish
acabar de + infinitive	-	to have just + past participle
bailar	-	to dance
caer	-	to fall
conocer	-	to know
conseguir	-	to obtain
decir	-	to tell, to say
elegir	-	to select, elect
gastar	-	to spend
mandar	-	to send
oír	-	to listen
prometer	-	to promise
reír(se)	-	to laugh
repetir	-	to repeat
romper	-	to break
saber	-	to know
servir	-	to serve
vestir(se)	-	to dress
viajar	-	to travel
visitar	-	to visit

EXPRESSIONS

poner la mesa	-	to set the table
¡Qué lástima!	-	What a pity!

EJERCICIOS

1. **Write the verb form preterite for the appropriate missing tenses. Notice the infinitive at the top of the frame. Remember that the regular preterite forms for the subject pronouns _yo_, _Ud._, _él_ y _ella_ must have an accent mark on the last vowel.**

	esperar	romper	subir	llamar	querer	escribir
Yo	1.	9.	17.	25.	33.	41.
Tú	2.	10.	18.	26.	34.	42.
Ud.	3.	11.	19.	27.	35.	43.
Él	4.	12.	20.	28.	36.	44.
Clara	5.	13.	21.	29.	37.	45.
Nosotros	6.	14.	22.	30.	38.	46.
Tú y yo	7.	15.	23.	31.	39.	47.
Uds.	8.	16.	24.	32.	40.	48.

2. **Complete the following sentences with the corresponding preterite form of the infinitive written in parentheses.**

   a. El_____la puerta.   (abrir)

   b. Usted_____allí   (entrar)

   c. (Yo)_____aquí.   (trabajar)

   d. Ella_____pronto.   (volver)

   e. (Tú)_____ya.   (ordenar)

3. **Write the singular of the following preterite forms:**

   a. Vivieron_____.

   b. Trabajamos_____.

   c. Volvimos_____.

   d. Ordenaron_____.

4. **Place accent marks, if needed.**

   a. ¿Estudiaste la leccion?

   b. Pepe salio con ellos.

   c. Le escribi a Maria.

   d. ¿Con quien hablo usted?

   e. Mis hermanos no llegaron anoche.

   f. Viaje por varios paises el mes pasado.

5. **Rewrite the following sentences in the preterite.**

   a. Ana acaba de cenar. _____

   b. ¿Aprendes a bailar? _____

   c. Ellos me invitan a comer._____

   d. Te prometo no gastar mucho dinero.

   _____

6. **Answer the following questions affirmatively.**

   a. ¿Pintaste la mesa de Alberto?

   _____

   b. ¿Escribió ella las cartas?

   _____

   c. ¿Recibieron Uds., el dinero?

   _____

   d. ¿Hablaron ellas con Ana?

   _____

   e. ¿Llovió ayer?

   _____

   f. ¿Aprendiste los verbos irregulares?

   _____

   g. ¿Abrió Ud. la botella de vino?

   _____

   h. ¿Prepararon Pepe y tú el desayuno?

   _____

7. **Change each verb from the present to the preterite tense.**

   a. Van al cine.

   _____

   b. Margarita se lo dice todo.

   _____

   c. ¿Me traes los pasteles?

   _____

   d. Traemos algo.

   _____

   e. ¿Quién va al mercado hoy?

   _____

   f. Ellos dicen la verdad.

   _____

   g. La conferencia es en el auditorio.

   _____

   h. Le damos las revistas.

   _____

   i. Ellos nos dan los periódicos.

   _____

   j. Carlos no lo cree.

   _____

   k. Lo creemos.

   _____

1. Ud. lee muy rápido.

    _____

m. Yo también leo rápido.

    _____

n. ¿No oyes la música?

    _____

o. Abuelo no oye bien.

    _____

8. **Answer the following questions negatively, whenever possible, use object pronouns in your answers.**

    a. ¿Viste las frutas que están en la mesa?

        _____

    b. ¿Fué Ud. al hospital hoy?

        _____

    c. ¿Estuvieron Uds. en casa anoche?

        _____

    d. ¿Trajo Ud. los vasos?

        _____

    e. ¿Ud. lo hizo todo?

        _____

    f. ¿Leyeron Uds. el periódico hoy?

        _____

    g. ¿Leyeron ellos las revistas?

        _____

h. ¿La conociste?

    _____

i. ¿Supo Ud. la noticia?

    _____

j. ¿Lo puso en la cocina?

    _____

k. ¿Diste dinero para el regalo?

    _____

l. ¿Vino Ud. anoche?

    _____

m. ¿Lo creyeron Uds.?

    _____

n. ¿Lo creyeron ellos?

    _____

o. ¿Pudiste hacerlo?

    _____

p. ¿Trajeron Uds. los libros?

    _____

9. **Translate into Spanish.**

    a. What did she say?

        _____

    b. They did not believe the story.

        _____

c. We went to the store.

_____

d. I came early.

_____

e. I didn't hear him.

_____

f. What did she bring?

_____

g. Clara made three dresses today.

_____

h. Did she tell the truth?

_____

i. What did all of you do yesterday?

_____

j. Who saw the boys?

_____

k. Did they meet her?

_____

l. Did you learn of the accident?

_____

m. John and Mary did not believe it.

_____

10. **Answer the following questions in Spanish following the content of the conversation.**

a. ¿Qué hizo Berta este verano?

_____

b. ¿Qué país visitó? (use <u>estar</u>)

_____

c. ¿Por qué no pudo ir al Uruguay?

_____

d. ¿Qué ciudad visitó?

_____

e. ¿Cuánto tiempo pasó en Buenos Aires?

_____

f. ¿Qué compró en Buenos Aires?

_____

g. ¿Para quíen compró regalos?

_____

h. ¿Quién va a llamarla?

_____

11. **Answer the following questions in complete sentences.**

a. ¿Durmió Ud. bien anoche?

No, _____

b. ¿A quién eligieron para alcalde?

_____(Domínguez)

c. ¿Sirven Uds. desayuno ahora?

Sí, _____

d. ¿Siguió Ud. la música?

Sí, _____

e. ¿Lo repetió ella?

Sí, _____

12. **Complete the crossword puzzle by using the correct preterite form of the verb in parentheses.**

Horizontal	Vertical
3. El (slept) mucho.	1. Nosotros (asked for) dos.
4. El (repeated) two.	2. ellos (obtained) uno.
5. Yo (obtained) dos.	
6. Ellas (laughed).	
7. Yo lo (obtained).	
8. Ud. no (served) el desayuno hoy.	
9. Ellos (laughed) mucho.	

TOPICS: THE IMPERFECT INDICATIVE TENSE, IMPERFECT VS PRETERITE, SABER VS CONOCER, POSSESSIVE ADJECTIVES (SHORT FORMS), POSSESSIVE ADJECTIVES (LONG FORM), POSSESSIVE PRONOUNS.

CONVERSATION XXIV

EN LA BIBLIOTECA		IN THE LIBRARY
Empleado:	Buenas tardes, ¿En que puedo servirle?	– Employee:	Good afternoon. What can I do for you?
Sra. López:	Buscaba un libro de cocina oriental que ví aquí el mes pasado.	– Mrs. López:	I was looking for a book on oriental cuisine that I saw here last month.
Empleado:	Los teníamos aquí, estaban en ese espacio. Ahora están en el próximo pasillo, a su derecha. Sígame.	– Employee:	We had them here, they were in that space. Now they are in the next aisle, to your right. Follow me.
Sra. López:	Bien, gracias. ¿Sabía Ud. que es muy difícil encontrar buenos libros de cocina?	– Mrs. López:	Fine, thank you. Did you know that it is very difficult to find good cook books?
Empleado:	No, creía que había buenas selecciones en las bibliotecas y en la librerías.	– Employee:	No, I thought that there were good selections in the libraries and in the bookstores
Sra. López:	Además, cuestan mucho. Costaban mucho menos el año pasado.	– Mrs. López:	Besides, they cost a lot now. They used to cost much less last year.
Empleado:	Lo sé. Aquí están. ¿Desea algo más?	– Employee:	I know it. Here they are. Do you want anything else?
Sra. López:	No, gracias.	– Mrs. López:	No, thank you.
Empleado:	Bueno, si me necesita, llámeme.	– Employee:	Good, if you need me, call me.
Sra. López:	Bien, gracias.	– Mrs. López:	Fine, thank you.

I. The Imperfect Indicative Regular Conjugations

	gastar to spend	romper to break	dividir to divide
Yo	gast-aba	romp-ía	divid-ía
tú	gast-abas	romp-ías	divid-ías
Ud., él, ella	gast-aba	romp-ía	divid-ía
Nosotros/as	gast-ábamos	romp-íamos	divid-íamos
Uds., ellos, ellas	gast-aban	romp-ían	divid-ían

Notice the accent on all forms of the -er and -ir verbs.

Irregular Conjugations

There are only 3 irregular verbs in the imperfect. ir, "to go", ser, "to be", and ver, "to see."

Yo	iba	era	veía
Tu	ibas	eras	veías
Ud., él, ella	iba	era	veía
Nosotros/as	íbamos	éramos	veíamos
Uds., ellos, ellas	iban	eran	veían

Uses of The Imperfect

A. To express a continuing action in the past, something that was taking place at a certain time in the past. It is always expressed in English by was/were plus -ing.

Yo hablaba con él.   – I was talking with him.

(Nosotros) estudiábamos   – We were studying with
con ella.   her.

La semana pasada yo   – Last week I was
buscaba un auto.   looking for a car.

B. To express habitual action in the past.

Yo la llamaba a menudo.   – I used to call her
                               often.

Tú siempre venías.   – You always came early.

Él traía cerveza los   – He would bring beer
domingos.   on Sundays.

Observe that one Spanish imperfect form covers the three different forms which can be used in English to express habitual action in the past. The following English sentences illustrate this point:

I delivered the presents.
(habitually)
                              Yo entregaba
I used to deliver the presents. los regalos.

I would deliver the presents.

C. To describe a mental, physical or emotional state in the past.

Yo quería ir.   – I wanted to go.

Carmen conocía a nuestro   – Carmen knew our brother.
hermano.
No sabíamos que había[1] un – We didn't know there was
examen hoy.   an exam today.

Él era una buena persona.   – He was a good person.

Ella tenía miedo del gato.   – She was afraid of the
                               cat.
Había muchos turistas allí. – There were lots of
                               tourists there.
Yo podía ir si quería.   – I could go if I wanted
                               to.
La casa era azul.   – The house was blue.

Notice that all verbs used to describe mental, physical and emotional conditions are non-action verbs, in other words, they describe a state or of condition of a person or thing.

D. For time expressions in the past.

Eran las cinco.   – It was five o'clock.

Era tarde.   – It was late.

Era primavera.   – It was Spring.

E. To set the stage for another action in the past. Notice that this use is the same as **A** (a continuous action in the past).

---

[1]Había, "there was/were" is the imperfect tense form of hay, "there is/are". Like hay it is always used in the singular.

II. Imperfect vs Preterite

The most important difference between the preterite and the imperfect tenses is that the preterite always represents "an action" which the speaker views as a single completed event. A single completed action is not to be confused with a continuing action in the past or with an habitual action in the past which always takes the imperfect.

Yo siempre comía aquí.	- I always ate here.
Yo comí aquí ayer.	- I ate here yesterday.
María venía de la tienda.	- Mary was coming from the store.
María vino de la tienda.	- Mary came from the store.

Also, it is important to remember that if there is no action in the verb, there is no preterite, that is way verbs like querer, poder, saber, conocer, tener, estar, which are non-action verbs, when used in the preterite, always change meaning.

Study the following examples:

Conocíamos a Carlos.	- We knew Carlos.
Conocimos a Carlos.	- We met Carlos.
Yo estaba aquí a las dos.	- I was here at two.
Yo estuve aquí a las dos.	- I came here at two.
Ella podía ir si quería.	- She could go if she wanted.
Ella pudo ir.	- She managed to go.
El sabía que ella venía.	- He knew that she was coming.
El supo que ella venía.	- he learned that she was coming.

III. Saber vs Conocer.

For the two verbs saber and conocer, English has only one verb, "to know." Saber means "to know by heart" and "to know how", and conocer means "to be acquainted with."

Ellos conocían la ciudad.	- They knew (were acquainted) with the city.
Tu sabías su número de teléfono.	- You knew her phone number.
Carlos sabía hacerlo.	- Carlos knew how to do it.
Pedro conocía ese libro.	- Carlos was acquainted with that book.

IV. Possessive Adjectives (short form).

	singular	plural
my	mi	mis
your (fam.)	tu	tus
your (form.)	su	sus
his, her	su	sus
our	nuestro/a	nuestros/as
your (p.), their	su	sus

-222-

In Spanish, possessive adjectives are treated like other adjectives as far as agreement is concerned. They agree with the noun they modify which is the thing possessed. Except for nuestro/a and nuestros/as which requires agreement for gender (masculine or feminine), all forms require only agreement for number (singular and plural). The possessive adjectives (short form) precede the noun they modify.

Mi primo estaba aquí el sábado.   — My cousin was here Saturday.

Tu hermano no lo vio.   — Your brother did not see him.

¿Dónde puso su abrigo, señora?   — Where did you put your coat, madam?

¿Están listos sus pantalones?   — Are your pants ready?

¿Esta es su blusa, señora.   — This is your blouse, madam.

Nuestra casa es muy grande.   — Our house is very big.

Nuestro auto es muy pequeño.   — Our car is very small.

Nuestros hijos quieren un auto nuevo.   — Our children want a new car.

Tus camisas son caras.   — Your shirts are expensive.

V. Possessive Adjectives (long forms)

(of) mine	mío/a/os/as
(of) yours (fam.)	tuyo/a/os/as
(of) yours (form.)	suyo/a/os/as
(of) his, hers	suyo/a/os/as
(of) ours	nuestro/a/os/as
(of) yours (pl.)	suyo/a/os/as
(of) theirs	suyo/a/os/as

The preposition "of" is not translated into Spanish. The long forms of the possessive adjectives in Spanish requires agreement for both gender (masculine and feminine) and number (singular and plural).

Un amigo mío lo hizo.   — A friend of mine did it.

Una prima suya trajo los pasteles.   — A cousin of hers brought the pastries.

Esos amigos tuyos llegaron tarde.   — Those friends of yours arrived late.

Unos amigos suyos los llevaron al aeropuerto.   — Some friends of theirs took them to the airport.

IV. Possessive Pronouns

In combination with definite articles, the long forms of the possessive adjectives may be used as possessive pronouns.

Mi hijo va al cine con el suyo.   — My son is going to the movies with yours.

Aquí está el mío. ¿Dónde está el suyo?	– Here is mine. Where is yours?
Estos vasos no son nuestros ² ¿Son suyos?	– These glasses are not ours, are they yours?
Nuestra oficina estaba aquí, la suya estaba en el centro.	– Our office was here, theirs was downtown.

K. Prepositional phrase with <u>de</u> to express possessions.

<u>Nuestro/a/os/as</u>, and especially <u>suyo/a/os/as</u>, which
can have a variety of meanings, can be expressed
by de <u>nosotros/as</u>, de <u>usted</u>, de <u>ustedes</u>, de <u>él</u>,
de <u>ella</u>, de <u>ustedes</u>, de <u>ellos</u>, de <u>ellas</u>,
respectively.

Mi hijo va al cine con el de Ud.	– My son is going to the movies with yours.
Aquí está el mío. ¿Dónde está el de Ud.?	– Here is mine. Where is yours?
Estos vasos no son nuestros. ¿Son de Ud?	– These glasses are not ours. Are they yours?
Nuestra oficina estaba aquí, la de ellos estaba en el centro.	– Our office was here, theirs was downtown.
¿Son éstas las de nosotros?	– Are these ours?
Una prima de él lo hizo.	– A cousin of his did it.
Unos amigos de ellos los llevaron al aeropuerto.	– Some friends of theirs took them to the airport.

---

²After the verb <u>ser</u> the possessive pronouns may be used without the definite article.

N O U N S

árbol (m)	-	tree
cocina (f)	-	cuisine, kitchen
correo (m)	-	post office
espacio (m)	-	space
estilo (m)	-	style
jardín (m)	-	garden
oscuridad	-	darkness
persona (f)	-	person
seleccion	-	selection

A D J E C T I V E S

derecho	-	right
mi/s	-	my
ninguno/a	-	none
nuestro/a/os/as	-	our
oriental	-	oriental
tu/s	-	your (familiar)

V E R B S

destruir	-	to destroy
entregar	-	to deliver
insistir	-	to insist

P R O N O U N S

mío/a/os/as	-	mine
nuestro/a/os/as	-	ours
suyo/a/os/as	-	yours (formal) his, hers, theirs
tuyo/a/os/as	-	yours (familiar)

A D V E R B S

además	-	besides
a pie	-	walking, on foot
el año pasado	-	last year
la semana pasada	-	last week

P R O N O U N S

todos	-	all of you, all of them, all of us

1. Match the subject pronouns in Group A with the verb forms in Group B to write correct sentences.

	A	B
a.	El	queríamos
b.	Ustedes	viajabas
c.	Tú	salía
d.	Nosotras	entregaban

2. Write the following verb forms in the singular.

a. Hablábamos _____

b. Querían _____

c. Entregaban _____

Write the following verb forms in the plural.

d. Tenías _____

e. Tenía _____

3. Rewrite each sentence by substituting the verb in parentheses. Make any other necessary changes.

a. La señora <u>entregaba</u> los regalos. (querer)

_____

b. La gente <u>hablaba</u> con ella. (llegar)

_____

c. Nosotros <u>estudiábamos</u> temprano. (salir)

_____

4. Arrange the following groups of words into meaningful expressions.

a. la	b. días	c. veían
veía	íbamos	bien
oscuridad	todos	muy
él	los	ellas
en	nosotros	
la		

5. Complete the answers for each of the following questions.

a. ¿Eras mecánico o chofer?

_____

b. ¿Iban ustedes todos los días?

Sí, _____

c. ¿Veía usted bien?

No, _____

6. Select the verb form which correctly completes each sentence.

a. Una vez él _____ la cuenta ayer.
   (pagó-pagaba)

b. Dos años _____ en Londres.
   (vivimos-vivíamos)

c. En aquellos días _____ en Londres.
   (vivimos-vivíamos)

d. A menudo _____ de Ana.
   (habló-hablaba)

e. _____ siempre, de 2 PM a 5 PM.
   (salieron-salían)

7. Study the following examples and determine if they are expressing. (1) habitual action, (2) continuous action or, (3) a state in the past.

Read carefully.

a. There <u>was</u> a big tree in the entrance. – Había un árbol grande en la entrada.

b. He <u>looked</u> very elegant. – Él <u>estaba</u> muy elegante.

c. My parents <u>used to</u> <u>live</u> near my house. – Mis padres <u>vivían</u> cerca de mi casa.

d. The city was destroyed. (appeared to be) – La ciudad <u>estaba</u> destruida.

e. They <u>wanted</u> to go. – Ellos <u>querían</u> ir.

f. It was <u>reaining</u> hard. – <u>Llovía</u> mucho.

8. Read the following paragraph, then write the correct tense forms, imperfect or preterite to complete the sentences. Use the tense form of the verb written below each line.

Entonces yo _____ con mis padres y mis hermanos.
(a) (vivir)

En nuestro jardín _____ muchos árboles.
(b) (haber)

Mis hermanos _____ dos perros y yo, un gato.
(c) (tener)

Nosotros los _____ mucho.
(d) (querer)

Ayer cuando Pepe _____ todos (nosotros)[3] _____ en
(e) (llegar)   (f)(estar)

la sala. Los niños _____ sus libros y nosotras _____
(g) (leer)   (h)(oír)

música cuando llovía. Ayer Pepe no _____ ,
(i) (entrar)

nos _____ desde la puerta.
(j) (saludar)

9. Change the underlined present tense forms in the following paragraph to the imperfect tense.

Desde la ventana de mi hotel <u>veo</u> mucha gente.
a

Quizás <u>van</u> a trabajar. Algunas personas <u>van</u> en
b   c

automóviles o en autobús, otras a pie. <u>Son</u> casi
d

las 8 A.M.

a _____ b _____ c _____ d _____

10. Fill in the blanks spaces with the correct tense choose from the verbs listed below.

Roberto _____ al restaurante. Ya su papá
a

_____ allí. Ellos no _____ a los
c

Martínes. Cuando _____ estos señores _____
d   e

muy tarde.

vieron – fué – era – estaba – vinieron

---
[3]The pronoun <u>nosotros/as</u>, <u>Ustedes</u>, <u>ellos/as</u> may become added to <u>todos/as</u> for clarification.

11. Complete the following sentences choosing from the words written below each one.

a. Siempre_____caminar.

    a. entregaban   b. querían

b. Luis_____los regalos.

    a. tenía   b. estaba

c. Los alumnos_____la lección.

    a. sabían   b. entregabas

d. Ustedes_____una casa azul.

    a. teníamos   b. tenían

e. Yo_____con ella.

    a. sabíamos   b. salía

12. Select the appropriate verb form from the list on the right.

a. Ustedes _____ en la oscuridad.

b. Yo_____mecánico.

c. Nosotros_____todos los días.

d. Tú _____ muy bien.

e. Ellos _____ choferes.

1. veías

2. eran

3. veían

4. era

5. éramos

6. íbamos

13. Complete the following sentences by writing the Spanish imperfect for the English verb form written in parentheses.

a. Yo _____ las lecciones.
   (used to deliver)

b. (Tú)_____ con él.
   (were talking)

c. Nosotros _____ caminar siempre.
   (wanted)

d. Ellos_____temprano a menudo.
   (went out)

e. El _____ dientes.
   (did not have)

15. Write the correct form of the verb.

Entonces usted_____mecánico.
   (a)   (were)

Nosotros _____ choferes y él _____ enfermo.
   (b) (were)   (c) (was)

Tú y yo _____ todos los días.
   (d) (used to go)

Ellas siempre _____ muy bien.
   (e) (saw)

15. Match the English possessive forms with the Spanish forms in the bottom columns. Write only the number or numbers of your choice. Some of the English forms match with more than one of the Spanish forms.

a. their _____   d. our _____

b. her _____   e. his _____

c. your _____   f. my _____

---

1. tu   5. su (de usted)

2. su (de él)   6. su (de ellas)

3. mi   7. su (de ellas)

4. su (de ellos)   8. nuestro/a

16. Write the plural of the following singular expressions.

a. su hijo _____

b. mi fiesta _____

c. nuestro hermano _____

d. tu teléfono _____

e. nuestra hija _____

17. Read the following expressions using possessive adjectives. Write X if the underlined possessive form refers to one possessor. Write XX if it refers to more than one possessor.

a. mis hermanas _____

b. su teléfono _____

c. nuestra dirección _____

d. sus padres (de usted) _____

e. tus fiestas _____

18. Rewrite these expressions using the corresponding long form of the underlined possessive short forms.

a. tú teléfono   d. sus padres (de ellas)

el_____   los_____

b. nuestras hermanas e. su hermano

las_____   el_____ (de ella)

c. mis hijas

las_____

19. Read the following expressions using possession with de. Rewrite these expressions using the short forms of the possessive adjectives. Make the necessary changes.

a. la hermana de nosotros _____

b. el hijo de ella _____

c. las fiestas de ellos _____

d. el teléfono de ustedes _____

e. los padres de él _____

f. la casa de usted _____

20. Rewrite the same expressions again, using the long forms of the possessive adjectives.

a. _____

b. _____

c. _____

d. _____

e. _____

f. _____

21. Underline the possessive forms in the following examples.

a. María va a dar una fiesta. Su fiesta es el viernes. Mi hermana y yo vamos, pero nuestro hermano Luis no quiere ir porque los amigos de él no van. El prefiere ir a tu casa para hablar con tus hijos.

b. María   ¿Tienes mi dirección?

   Ana: No, tengo la dirección de ellos.

   María: Esta es la dirección de nosotros.

   Ana: Gracias. Voy a tu casa mañana con
           nuestros amigos.

22. **Read the following paragraph, and write the Spanish for the possessive forms.**

Ana,_____amigos y_____hermanos tienen
      (a) (her)   (b)(our)

_____ teléfono. Ellos tienen que llamar a
(c)   (your--fam.)

_____ casa porque necesitan _____
(d)(your--fam.)   (e)   (my)

dirección.

23. **Translate into Spanish using (1) short forms of possessives (2) long forms of possessives (3) prepositional phrases whenever possible.**

a. our city

    1. _____ 2. _____ 3. _____

b. your (fam.) door

    1. _____ 2. _____ 3. _____

c. their (masc.) father

    1. _____ 2. _____ 3. _____

d. her cousins (masc.)

    1. _____ 2. _____ 3. _____

e. my car

    1. _____ 2. _____ 3. _____

f. your (form., pl) uncle

   1. _____ 2. _____ 3. _____

g. his house.

   1. _____ 2. _____ 3. _____

h. your (form., sing.) son

   1. _____ 2. _____ 3. _____

24. **Fill in the blank with the proper form of _saber_ or _conocer_.**

a. Nosotros_____que ella estaba aquí.
             knew

b. María lo _____ ayer.
              learned

c. Ella _____ su dirección.
           knew

d. El _____ a Clara.
         knew

e. Yo no _____ la respuesta.
            know

f. Carlos _____ a Alicia ayer.
             met

g. Ellos y yo _____ que él estaba aquí.
                 knew

h. Él y ella _____ que yo estaba aquí.
                learned

25. **Answer the following questions affirmatively.**

a. ¿Estuviste en el banco hoy?

   _____

b. ¿Estabas en la clase cuando el profesor llegó?

_____

c. ¿Pudieron Uds. ir?

_____

d. ¿Podía hablar ella francés?

_____

e. ¿Querías ir?

_____

f. ¿Quisiste venir?

_____

26. **Answer in Spanish following the content of the conversation. Try to answer without looking at the conversation.**

a. ¿Qué buscaba la Sra. López?

_____

b. ¿Por qué no encontró el libro la Sra. López?

_____

c. ¿Es fácil encontrar buenos libros de cocina?

_____

d. ¿Dónde estában los libros de cocina ahora?

_____

e. ¿Sabía el empleado los precios de los libros de cocina?

_____

f. ¿Tenían el libro que buscaba la Sra. López?

_____

27. **Fill in the blanks using possessive pronouns.**

a. Mi hijo va al cine, con_____.
(yours, formal)

b. Este es el mío. ¿Dónde está_____?
(hers)

c. Estos vasos no son_____. ¿Son_____?
(ours)   (theirs)

d. Mi oficina está aquí. ¿Dónde está_____?
(his)

e. Esta no es_____, es_____.
(yours, fam)   (mine)

f. ¿Son estas cartas_____?
(ours)

TOPICS: THE FUTURE AND CONDITIONAL TENSES, THE PRESENT PARTICIPLE, THE PROGRESSIVE TENSES, POSITION OF OBJECT PRONOUNS WITH THE PROGRESSIVE TENSES

CONVERSATION XXV

ESPERANDO A UNA AMIGA			WAITING FOR A FRIEND
María:	¿Vendrá Teresa?	— Maria:	Will Teresa come?
Alberto:	Sí, me dijo que estaría aquí a las once.	— Albert:	Yes, she told me that she would be here at 11 o'clock.
María:	Pero, ya son las once y cuarto.	— Maria:	But it is already eleven fifteen.
Alberto:	No te preocupes, ella dijo que vendría y vendrá.	— Albert:	Don't worry she said that she would come, and she will come.
María:	Bien, esperaremos un rato.	— Maria:	Well, we will wait a while.
Alberto:	No tendrás que esperar, aquí está	— Albert:	You will not have to wait, here she is.
María:	Hola Teresa. Te estábamos esperando. ¿Vas a comer algo?	— Maria:	Hello Teresa. We were waiting for you. Are you going to eat something?
Teresa:	Quiero algo ligero. Una ensalada quizás.	— Teresa:	I want something light. A salad maybe.
Alberto:	Ahora están sirviendo sólo desayuno.	— Albert:	Now they are serving breakfast only.
María:	No sacarán las ensaladas hasta las doce.	— Maria:	They will not bring out the salads until 12 o'clock.
Teresa:	Entonces comeré frutas.	— Teresa:	Then I will eat fruit.
Alberto:	¿Qué clase de frutas tienen?	— Albert:	What kind of fruits do they have?
María:	Mira, están trayendo peras, manzanas y naranjas.	— Maria:	Look. They are bringing pears, apples and oranges.
Alberto:	Yo también comeré frutas.	— Albert:	I will also eat fruit.
María:	Prefiero esperar. Estaré fuera en la terraza, los esperaré allí.	— Maria:	I prefer to wait. I will be outside on the terrace, I'll wait for you there.

I. The Future Tense

A. Regular forms.

There is only one set of endings for all conjugations in the future tense.

1. The future tense in Spanish is formed by adding the following endings to the infinitive form of any regular verb.

	ENDINGS FUTURE
Yo	-é
Tú	-ás
Ud.	-á
él, ella	-á
Nosotros/as	-emos
Uds.	-án
ellos, ellas	-án

Acabaré esta tarde.	- I will finish this afternoon.
¿Irás a la librería?	- Will you go to the bookstore?
Alberto dice que no apoyará al candidato demócrata.	- Albert says he will not support the Democratic candidate.
Empezaremos a trabajar temprano.	- We will begin to work early.
Ellas no lo negarán.	- They will not deny it.
El año que viene compraré un auto nuevo.	- Next year I will buy a new car.

2. Irregular forms.

There are twelve common verbs which are irregular in the future. We will divide them into three groups.

a. Those that change the stem. (Stem changing)

	decir (to say)	hacer (to do, to make)
Yo	diré	haré
Tú	dirás	harás
Ud., él, ella	dirá	hará
Nosotros/as	diremos	haremos
Uds., ellos, ellas	dirán	harán

b. Those that drop the -e- of the infinitive ending.

	poder (to be)	querer (to want)	saber (to know)	caber (to fit in)	haber (to have)
Yo	podré	querré	sabré	cabré	habré
Tú	podrás	querrás	sabrás	cabrás	habrás
Ud., él ella	podrá	querrá	sabrá	cabrá	habrá
Nosotros/as	podremos	querremos	sabremos	cabremos	habremos
Uds., ellos, ellas	podrán	querrán	sabrán	cabrán	habrán

c. Those that insert -d- between the stem and the -r of the infinitive ending.

	poner (to put)	salir (to go out)	tener (to have)	valer (to be worth)	venir (to come)
Yo	pondré	saldré	tendré	valdré	vendré
Tú	pondrás	saldrás	tendrás	valdrás	vendrás
Ud., él ella	pondrá	saldrá	tendrá	valdrá	vendrá
Nosotros/as	podremos	saldremos	tendremos	valdremos	vendremos
Uds., ellos Ellas	pondrán	saldrán	tendrán	valdrán	vendrán

Notice that the same set of endings are used for
-ar, -er and -ir verbs, and that all the forms
except for the first person plural (nosotros/as)
require written accents on the last vowel.

The future tense is seldom used in Spanish to
express future action. In its place the
Spanish-speaking person prefers to use the
verb ir plus the preposition a or the simple
present tense.

¿Vas a ir al museo mañana?	– Are you going to go to the museum tomorrow?
¿Vas al museo mañana?	– Are you going to go to the museum tomorrow?
¿Irás al museo mañana?	– Will you go to the museum tomorrow?

Notice that the three Spanish sentences above have
exactly the same meaning.

3. **The future tense to express probability or conjecture in the present. It is in this instance that the Spanish-speaking person will use the future tense.**

El ya estará listo.	– He is probably ready.
Pablo lo sabrá.	– Paul probably know it.
¿Quién será?	Who can he or she be? – I wonder who he or she is?
Esa gente tendrá mucho dinero.	– Those people probably have lots of money.
¿Dónde estarán ahora?	Where can they be now? – I wonder where they are?

4. **The conditional tense.**

In English, the conditional is formed by the auxiliary
verbs "should" or "would" and the verb forms: "I should
go","he would go", "you would do it."

As in the future, there is only one set of ending
for all conjugations with conditional tense.

Yo	-ía
Tú	-ías
Ud.	-ía
él, ella	-ía
(nosotros/as)	-íamos
Uds.	-ían
ellos, ellas	-ían

The twelve common verbs which are irregular in the
future have the same irregularities in the conditional.

Yo diría que él viene.	– I would say that he is coming.
¿Querrías ir?	– Would you like to go?
Yo no lo haría.	– I would not do it.
Prometió que lo haría.	– He promised that he would do it.

5. **The conditional tense to express probability or conjecture in the past. The future as we just studied is used to express probability or conjecture in the present. The conditional expresses the same idea of probability or conjecture but in the past.**

¿Quién sería?	– I wonder who he or she was?
Ya estarían listos.	– They were probably ready.
¿Dónde estarían anoche?	– I wonder where they were last night?
Alguien llamó. ¿Sería José?	– Someone called. I wonder if it was Jose?

6. The present participle.

a. The present participle (...ing in English) is formed in Spanish by adding -ando to the stem of -ar verbs, and -iendo to the stem of most -er and -ir verbs.

PRESENT PARTICIPLE		
hablar	comer	abrir
habl-ando	com-iendo	abr-iendo

If the stem of an -er or -ir verb ends in a vowel, the -i of -iendo usually changes to y giving -yendo.

oír	oyendo	hearing
creer	creyendo	believing
leer	leyendo	reading

7. The present progressive tense.

The present participle is used with the verb estar in the present to form the present progressive tense.

Ella está estudiando. — She is studying.

Estoy leyendo Don Quijote. — I am reading Don Quixote.

Estamos comiendo ahora. — We are eating now.

Uds. están hablando mucho. — You are talking too much.

8. The past progressive tense.

The past progressive is formed with the imperfect of estar and the present participle.

Ella estaba oyendo un concierto. — She was listening to a concert.

Tú estabas llamando a Víctor. — You were calling Victor.

Estábamos cocinando. — We were cooking.

Ellos estaban corriendo. — They were running.

Uds. estaban caminando. — You were walking.

9. Object pronouns and the progressive tenses.

With the progressive construction, direct, indirect and reflexive pronouns, either precede the conjugated form of estar or are attached to the ending of the present participle.

Estoy esperando a Teresa. — I am waiting for Teresa.

La estoy esperándo.
Estoy esperándola. — I am waiting for her.

Le estoy dando el dinero a Pedro. — I am giving Peter the money.

Se lo estaba dando.
Estaba dándoselo. — I was giving it to him.

VOCABULARIO

NOUNS

butaca (f)	–	armchair
cabaña (f)	–	cabin
frontera (f)	–	border
museo (m)	–	museum
parador (m)	–	inn for travelers
pera (f)	–	pear
siglo (m)	–	century

ADJECTIVES

demócrata (m&f) – democratic

ADVERBS

quizás	–	perhaps

VERBS

añadir	–	to add
apoyar	–	to support
asistir	–	to attend
caber	–	to fit in
negar	–	**to deny**
preocupar	–	to worry
sacar	–	to take out, to extract
valer	–	to be worth

1. **Substitute the new subjects and make other necessary changes.**

   a. (Nosotros) acabaremos la tarea.

   (Yo) _____

   (Tú) _____

   Ud. _____

   Ellas _____

   b. (Yo) lo esperaré en la playa.

   Uds. _____

   (Tú) _____

   Ellas _____

   Ella _____

   c. (Ud.) les dirá que estoy aquí.

   (Tú) _____

   Él _____

   Ellos _____

   Uds. _____

   d. (Nosotros) saldremos para la cabaña el jueves.

   Ella _____

   (Tú) _____

   (Yo) _____

   Ellas _____

   e. El periódico no vendrá temprano el sábado.

   Los mecánicos_____

   Arturo y yo _____

   Javier y tú _____

   Yo _____

2. **Change the verbs to the future and rewrite the sentences.**

   a. Vamos a la frontera mañana.

   _____

   b. Tengo que añadir juguetes a la lista.

   _____

   c. No lo pongo encima de la mesa.

   _____

   d. La butaca cabe en el balcón.

   _____

   e. ¿Cuándo haces la tarea?

   _____

   f. Mañana la hago.

   _____

3. Change the verbal expressions a+ infinitive to the future and rewrite the sentence. Notice that the meaning of the sentence does not change.

a. Van a venir aquí antes.

_____

b. Lo va a saber alrededor de las seis.

_____

c. Vamos a ver un juego de la serie mundial.

_____

d. Les va a decir que no quiere las joyas.

_____

e. Van a destruir ese parador.

_____

f. Van a poner el negocio aquí.

_____

g. No van a querer ir con él.

_____

4. Translate into Spanish in two ways; first, using ir a + infinitive, then with the future.

a. I will do it early.

_____

b. I will know the answer.

_____

c. Carlos will not be able to attend.

_____

d. They will not pay the rent yet.

_____

e. I will not bring the other dog.

_____

f. Will you give her this present?

_____

g. He will buy the magazine.

_____

5. Change the underlined verbs to the past (preterite or imperfect)[1] and make any other necessary change.

a. Juan dice que vendrá.

_____

b. Ella sabe que Josefina hará el viaje.

_____

c. Creo que Alberto no podrá venir.

_____

d. Saben que yo tendré el dinero para el miércoles.

_____

e. Pregunta qué hora será (probability).

_____

[1]If the verb is an action verb, use preterite, otherwise use imperfect.

6. Following the content of the conversation, answer the following questions. Try to answer without looking at the conversation.

a. ¿Qué están sirviendo ahora?

_____

b. ¿A qué hora traen las ensaladas?

_____

c. ¿Qué le dijo María a Alberto?

_____

d. ¿Va a comer algo María?

_____

e. ¿Qué comerá Alberto?

_____

f. ¿A qué hora dijo Teresa que llegaría?

_____

g. ¿A qué hora llegó Teresa?

_____

h. ¿Por qué no puede Teresa comer una ensalada?

_____

7. Substitute the subject and make other necessary changes.

a. Ella está estudiando ahora.

Yo _____

Tú _____

Nosotros _____

Uds. _____

b. Carlos está lavando el auto.

Ella _____

Uds. _____

Yo _____

Él _____

c. Nosotros estábamos leyéndolo.

Ella _____

Juan y yo _____

Uds. _____

Tú _____

8. Answer the following questions affirmatively in Spanish.

a. ¿Están ustedes hablando de política?

_____

b. ¿Estamos haciendo el trabajo bien?

_____

c. ¿Estás buscando el libro?

_____

d. ¿Está Ud. corriendo?

_____

e. ¿Está ella esperándolo?

   _____

f. ¿Se lo estaban diciendo ellos?

   _____

TOPICS: THE PAST PARTICIPLE USED AS AN ADJECTIVE, THE PRESENT PERFECT AND PAST PERFECT (PLUPERFECT) INDICATIVE TENSES

CONVERSATION XXVI

		COMPRANDO UN REGALO DE BODA			BUYING A WEDDING PRESENT
1.	Elena:	¿No has comprado el regalo para la boda de Ana todavía?	–	Helen:	Haven't you bought the present for Ana's wedding yet?
2.	Alina:	No he podido comprarlo, porque no he tenido tiempo.	–	Alina:	I haven't been able to buy it, because I haven't had time.
3.	Elena:	¿Por qué no lo compras hoy?	–	Helen:	Why don't you buy it today?
4.	Alina:	Todo está cerrado. ¿Has olvidado que hoy es domingo?	–	Alina:	Everything is closed. Have you forgotten that today is Sunday?
5.	Elena:	Verdad, no había pensado que las tiendas no estaban abiertas aquí los domingos.	–	Helen:	True, I had not thought that the stores were not open on Sundays here.
6.	Alina:	La verdad es que no sé qué comprarle.	–	Alina:	The truth is that I don't know what to buy her.
7.	Elena:	Hoy el periódico está lleno de anuncios de artículos para el hogar.	–	Helen:	Today the newspaper is full of ads for home furnishings.
8.	Alina:	No he visto el periódico hoy. No había llegado todavía cuando salí de casa.	–	Alina:	I haven't seen the paper today. It had not arrived yet when I left the house.
9.	Elena:	¿Sabes que no van a vivir aquí? Van a vivir en Caracas.	–	Helen:	Do you know that they are not going to live here? They are going to live in Caracas.
10.	Alina:	Entonces tendré que seleccionar algo pequeño.	–	Alina:	Then I'll have to select something small.
11.	Elena:	He decidido mandarle un cheque.	–	Helen:	I have decided to send her a check.
12.	Alina:	Sería más fácil para mí pero nunca me ha gustado dar dinero de regalo.	–	Alina:	It would be easier for me, but I have never liked to give money as a gift.
13.	Elena:	De acuerdo, pero en este caso es mejor ser práctico.	–	Helen:	I agree, but in this case it is better to be practical.
14.	Alina:	Tienes razón. Me has convencido. Le mandaré dinero.	–	Alina:	You are right. You have convinced me. I will send money.

I. The Past Participle.

A. Regular past participles.

Infinitive	Past Participle	
olvidar	olvid-ado	forgotten
convencer	convenc-ido	convinced
decidir	decid-ido	decided

B. Irregular past participle

There are a few important irregular past participles that end in <u>to</u> and two that end in <u>cho</u>. Notice that that they do not follow a set pattern for the stem.

	Infinitive		Past Participle
abrir,	to open		abier-to
cubrir,	to cover		cubier-to
escribir,	to write		escri-to
freír,	to fry		fri-to
morir,	to die		muer-to
poner,	to put		pues-to
romper,	to break		ro-to
ver,	to see		vis-to
volver,	to return		vuel-to
revolver,	to stir, to scramble		revuel-to
decir,	to say, to tell		di-cho
hacer,	to do, to make		he-cho

II. The Past Participle Used as an Adjective

The past participle used as an adjective functions like any descriptive adjective.

un disco roto	a broken record
un asiento ocupado	an occupied seat
los huevos fritos	the fried eggs
los huevos revueltos	the scrambled eggs
las casas vendidas ya	the houses already sold
las blusas terminadas	the finished blouses

Notice that the past participles used as adjectives end in -o, -os, -a or -as according to the gender and numbers of the noun they modify.

The verb estar is often used with a past participle to describe a state or condition. It is used in the same fashion as estar plus a descriptive adjective.

La puerta está abierta.	The door is open.
Rosa estaba cansada.	Rosa was tired.
Ellas están ocupadas.	They are busy.
El trabajo estaba hecho ayer.	The work was done yesterday.
Los vasos están rotos.	The glasses are broken.
Los documentos estaban firmados.	The documents were signed.

III. The Present Perfect and Past Perfect (Indicative) Tenses.

The present perfect indicative tense is formed by the present tense of haber, plus the past participle. Haber is the equivalent of the auxiliary verb to have in English.

	Pretérito Perfecto	Present Perfect[1]
Yo	he hablado	I have spoken
Tú	has comido	You (fam.) have eaten.
Ud., él, ella	ha venido	You (form.) he, she, have (has) come
Nosotros/as	hemos llamado	We have called
Uds., ellos, ellas	han aprendido	you (pl.) they have learned

[1]The Present Perfect is called in Spanish Pretérito Perfecto. It is considered a past tense in Spanish.

The auxiliary verb _haber_, "to have", changes according
to the subject pronouns. The past participle is
invariable, always ending in -_o_.

IV. **The Past Perfect (Pluperfect) Indicative Tense.**

The past perfect indicative tense is formed with
the imperfect of _haber_ plus the past participle.
Haber in the imperfect is a regular verb.

Yo	había ido	I had gone.
Tú	habías hablado	You (fam.) had spoken.
Ud., él, ella	había venido	You (form., sing) he, had come.
Nosotros/as	habíamos terminado	We had finished.
Uds., ellos, ellas	habían vuelto	You (pl.) they, had returned.

VOCABULARIO

NOUNS

anuncio (m)   —   ad
hogar (m)   —   home

ADJECTIVES

práctico (a) —   practical
lleno (a)   —   full

ADVERBS

todavía   —   yet

VERBS

callar   —   to hush, to keep silence
convencer   —   to convince
cubrir   —   to cover
decidir   —   to decide
decorar   —   to decorate
florecer   —   to bloom
freír   —   to fry
haber   —   to have (auxiliary verb)
morir   —   to die
revolver   —   to stir
seleccionar   —   to select

1. **Give the past participle of the following verbs.**

dormir   _____

perder   _____

contar   _____

acabar   _____

comprender   _____

vivir   _____

ser   _____

estar   _____

comer   _____

venir   _____

tratar   _____

gustar   _____

querer   _____

tener   _____

pagar   _____

almorzar   _____

pedir   _____

encender   _____

regresar   _____

salir   _____

morir   _____

hacer   _____

poner   _____

revolver   _____

cubrir   _____

escribir   _____

decir   _____

ver   _____

abrir   _____

2. **Match the expression in column A with the appropriate ones in Column B.**

A	B
a. Dos cajas	1. cansado
b. La puerta	2. cerradas
c. Los televisores	3 rotos
d. Un chico	4. callada
e. Una chica	5. abierta
f. El pasillo	6. florecida
g. La rosa	7. decorado

3. **Answer the following questions affirmatively in Spanish. Use object pronouns whenever possible.**

   a. ¿Has traído las cervezas?

   _____

   b. ¿Han venido Pedro y Luis?

   _____

   c. ¿Los han visto Uds. esta mañana?

   _____

   d. ¿Has desayunado ya?

   _____

   e. ¿Ha llevado Alicia el niño al parque?

   _____

   f. ¿Hemos contestado bien?

   _____

   g. ¿Han terminado Uds.?

   _____

   h. ¿Han encendido Uds. el televisor?

   _____

4. **Translate into Spanish.**

   a. I see a dead dog.

   _____

   b. The dog is dead.

   _____

   c. We saw a broken window.

   _____

   d. The window was broken.

   _____

   e. We have two lessons finished.

   _____

   f. The lessons are finished.

   _____

   g. We have only one well written letter.

   _____

   h. The letters are well written.

   _____

5. **Answer the following questions from the conversation.**

   a. ¿Por qué Alina no ha comprado el regalo todavía?

   _____

   b. ¿Por qué no puedo comprarlo hoy?

   _____

   c. ¿Qué día están cerradas las tiendas?

   _____

   d. ¿De qué están llenos los periódicos hoy?

   _____

   e. ¿Por qué Alina no ha visto el periódico hoy?

   _____

   f. ¿Dónde va a vivir Ana?

   _____

   g. ¿Qué ha decidido hacer Elena?

   _____

   h. ¿Ha decidido Alina qué hacer?

   _____

6. **Change the following sentences (1) to the present perfect indicative and (2) to the past perfect (pluperfect) indicative.**

   a. Lo hago todo en un día.

   1) _____

   2) _____

   b. Les abrimos la puerta.

   1) _____

   2) _____

   c. Ellos viven en Puerto Rico.

   1) _____

   2) _____

   d. Tú eres la primera siempre.

   1) _____

   2) _____

   e. Ud. no comprende.

   1) _____

   2) _____

   f. Ellos lo hacen temprano.

   1) _____

   2) _____

   g. Duermo mucho, pero él no duerme.

   1) _____

   2) _____

   h. Le decimos la verdad.

   1) _____

   2) _____

TOPICS: DEFINITION OF THE SUBJUNCTIVE MOOD, REGULAR FORMS OF THE PRESENT SUBJUNCTIVE, THE DEPENDENT CLAUSES, SUBJUNCTIVE IN NOUN CLAUSES, SUBJUNCTIVE IN IMPERSONAL EXPRESSIONS

CONVERSATION XXVII

	EN EL CORREO			IN THE POST OFFICE
1. Amanda:	Espera un momento, Aurora. ¿A dónde vas tan de prisa?	–	Amanda:	Wait a moment, Aurora. Where are you going in such a hurry?
2. Aurora:	Voy al correo a mandarle el pasaporte a Héctor. Necesito que lo reciba mañana.	–	Aurora:	I'm going to the Post Office to mail Hector his passport. I need for him to receive it by tomorrow.
3. Amanda:	¿Por qué tiene que tenerlo mañana?	–	Amanda:	Why does he have to have it for tomorrow?
4. Aurora:	Su padre quiere que salga para Suiza en seguida.	–	Aurora:	His father wants him to leave for Switzerland right away.
5. Amanda:	Sí, ya veo. Las competencias de esquí empiezan el sábado.	–	Amanda:	Yes, I see. The ski competitions begin this Saturday.
6. Aurora:	Desde luego, y toda la familia espera que Héctor tome parte activa en el evento.	–	Aurora:	Of course, and the whole family hopes that Hector will participate actively in the event.
7. Amanda:	Yo lo vi esquiar en Colorado el año pasado y, créeme, es muy bueno.	–	Amanda:	I saw him ski in Colorado last year and, believe me, he is very good.
8. Aurora:	No creo que esté en forma este año. Ha practicado muy poco.	–	Aurora:	I don't believe he is in shape this year. He has practiced very little.
9. Amanda:	No te preocupes, no será la primera vez que sorprende a todo el mundo.	–	Amanda:	Don't worry, it won't be the first time that he surprises everybody.
10. Aurora:	¿Por qué no vienes conmigo al correo?	–	Aurora:	Why don't you come with me to the Post Office?
11. Amanda:	Buena idea. Vamos.	–	Amanda:	Good idea. Let's go.

I. Definition of the Subjunctive Mood

So far you have studied two moods of the verb, the INDICATIVE and the IMPERATIVE. The INDICATIVE declares or states of something-ideas based on certainty-and the IMPERATIVE is used to give a command or an order. The SUBJUNCTIVE mood expresses ideas based upon unreality, expectation or contingency upon future development.

II. Regular Forms of the Present Subjunctive

You are familiar with some of the forms of the present subjunctive. The commands introduced in lessons 18 and 20 use forms of the subjunctive for Ud., Uds., and negative tú.

The conjugation of the regular verbs in the present subjunctive is arrived at by dropping the -ar, -er and -ir endings of the infinitive and adding (a) for the -ar verbs -e, -es, -e, -emos, -en, and (b) for the -er and -ir verbs -a, -as, -a, -amos, -an.

Regular Present Subjunctive Chart

	Comprar	Vender	Abrir
Yo	compr-e	vend-a	abr-a
Tú	compr-es	vend-as	abr-as
Ud., él, ella	compr-e	vend-a	abr-a
Nosotros/as	compr-emos	vend-amos	abr-amos
Uds., ellos/as	compr-en	vend-an	abr-an

Summarizing: the present subjunctive forms of Spanish -ar verbs have the characteristic vowel e in the ending of each form, and the -er and -ir verbs have the vowel a in the ending.

III. The Dependent Clauses

In order to understand the use of the subjunctive in Spanish, we must first learn to identify dependent clauses.

A dependent clause is one that has no meaning by itself, that is, it depends on another clause, the main or independent clause, to complete its meaning. For example, if I say in English "that they come tomorrow", although this clause has a subject, "they", and a verb "come", it does not carry meaning, but if I say "I hope that they come tomorrow", the sentence has meaning. The dependent clause "that they come tomorrow", in order to have meaning, must be attached to a main or independent clause, in this case "I hope". The subjunctive is only used in the dependent clauses in Spanish, consequently it is of THE UTMOST importance that you learn to identify dependent clauses.

There are three different types of dependent clauses in Spanish: the noun clause, the adjectival clause and the adverbial clause.

IV. Subjunctive in the Noun Clauses

The best way to learn to identify a noun clause is through examples. You are familiar with the following sample sentence which is made up of a subject, a verb and an object.

Subject	Verb	Object
Johnny	prefers	ice cream
Juanito	prefiere	helado

The object of the sentence "ice cream" is a noun, objects of sentences must be either nouns or pronouns. If we replace the noun "ice cream" by a clause and we say "Johnny prefers that I buy him an ice cream cone", Juanito prefiere que yo le compre un helado, the clause "that I buy him an ice cream cone" functions as the object of the sentence, "Johnny prefers", and since objects are nouns and pronouns, the dependent clause functions as a noun. This type of dependent clause is called a noun clause. The following examples will help you to learn how to identify noun clauses.

María desea que yo le compre un gato.	– Maria wished that I buy her a cat.
Dudo que ella lo coma.	– I doubt that she will eat it.
Espero que él lo compre.	– I hope he'll buy it.

Most noun clauses are introduced by the conjunction que when que follows the verb.

Some noun clauses use the verb in the indicative while others use the subjunctive form.

Examples of the uses of indicative in the dependent noun clause:

Sé que ella viene.	– I know she is coming.
Creemos que ella prefiere estudiar.	– We believe that she prefers to study.

Subjunctive is required in the dependent noun clause when the verb in the independent or main clause expresses wish, desire, order, command, prohibition, preference, approval, disapproval, doubt, intention, advise, regret, necessity or fear.

Some important verbs in the main clause that will trigger subjunctive in the dependent noun clause are:

insistir	– to insist	necesitar	– to need
demandar	– to demand	aconsejar	– to advise
aprobar	– to approve	ordenar	– to order
temer	– to fear	pedir	– to ask for
querer	– to want	prohibir	– to prohibit
desear	– to which	preferir	– to prefer
alegrarse de	– to be happy about	sentir	– to feel
decir	– to say		

Notice that in the two examples given in which the indicative was used in the dependent noun clause, the verbs used in the independent clauses were other than those in the list given that trigger subjunctive.

We have selected two groups of sentences with noun clause. Group A requires indicative and Group B requires subjunctive. Notice that Group A expresses factual information, while Group B does not.

Group A

Veo que vives bien.   - I see that you live well.

Juan cree que ella   - John believes that she
fuma.   smokes.

Pensamos que ellos   - We think that they eat
comen bien.   well.

Confirman que el   - They confirm that the
vuelo llega a las   flight arrives at eight.
ocho.

El cree que ella   - He believes that she
lo vende.   will sell it.

Informan que él llama   - They inform that he is
hoy.   calling today.

El está seguro que   - He is sure that I am here.
estoy aquí.

Group B

Espero que vivas   - I hope that you live well.
bien.

Juan prohíbe que   - John prohibits that she
fume.   smoke.[1]

Preferimos que ellos   - We prefer that they eat
coman bien.   well.

Dudan que el vuelo   - They doubt that the flight
llegue a las ocho.   will arrive at eight.

El espera que ella lo   - He hopes that she will sell it.
venda.

Se alegra de que él   - They are happy that he is calling
llame hoy.   today.

Insiste que yo esté   - He insists that I be[1] here.
aquí.

As you can see, the verbs in Group A have been replaced in Group B by verbs that trigger subjunctive in the noun clauses.

The expression ojalá meaning "I hope" is always followed by subjunctive.

Ojalá que él llame.   - I hope he'll call.

Ojalá que ellos no   - I hope they will not eat that
coman ese pescado.   fish.

On very rare occasions, the subjunctive or indicative may be used to convey the same meaning. The expressions quizas, tal vez, and acaso meaning "maybe" can be followed by the subjunctive or the indicative.

Examples:

Quizás ella llama.   - Maybe she'll call.
Quizás ella llame.

Tal vez yo compro uno.   - Maybe I'll buy one.
Tal vez yo compre uno.

Acaso vive aquí.   - Maybe he lives here.
Acaso viva aquí.

---

[1]Note that "She smokes" is actually a subjunctive form in English, ("smokes" is indicative) though it sounds a bit archaic. The English regular subjunctive normally drops the "s" of the third person singular. In the sentence "He insists that I be here tomorrow", "be" is the irregular subjunctive for all persons.

Unlike English, Spanish always requires that the introduction of a dependent clause uses que. Notice that English usually does not use a clause, but the infinitive construction.

Examples:

Quiero que ella coma bien.   - I want her to eat well.

Ella necesita que él la llame.   - She needs him to call her.

Ellos ordenan que escribamos en seguida.   - They order us to write at once.

Nos piden que leamos.   - They ask us to read.

Tú prefieres que yo lo venda.   - They advise me to sell it.

Me aconsejan que lo compre.   - They advise me to buy it.
                  or
          They advise me that I buy it.

Notice that the English sentences usually do not require the use of a dependent clause. Also in Spanish if there is only one subject in the sentence, there is no dependent clause, therefore, no subjunctive. Study the following examples.

Quiero leer ese libro.   - I want to read that book.

Quiero que Ud. lea ese libro.   - I want you to read that book.

Necesitamos comer temprano.   - We need to eat early.

Necesitamos que él coma temprano.   - We need for him to eat early.

Prefiero comprar este vino.   - I prefer to buy this wine.

Prefiero que tú compres este vino.   - I prefer for you to buy this wine.

The verbs creer, decir, and escribir

Forms of the verb creer in the negative (no creer) and interrogative (¿creer?) imply doubt, consequently, they trigger the subjunctive, also the verbs decir and escribir when they imply command.

No creo que él lo lea.   - I don't believe he will read it.

¿Cree Ud. que él lo tome hoy?   - Do you think he'll drink it today?

Le escribiré que esté aquí el lunes.   - I'll write him to be here on Monday.

Le diré que lo compre.   - I'll tell him to buy it.

Verbs that permit "double construction" with subjunctive or infinitive. The most common are aconsejar, obligar, and permitir. Study these examples.

Le aconsejo que llame temprano.
          or
Le aconsejo llamar temprano.

Nos obligan a que estudiemos.
          or
Nos obligan a estudiar.

No les permiten que hablen en clase.
          or
No les permiten hablar en clase.

V. Subjunctive in Impersonal Expression

The subjunctive is used after impersonal expressions
which indicate necesity, possibility or uncertainty.
Study the following examples:

Es necesario que trabajes.   — It's necessary that you work.

Es importante que ella lea   — It's important that she read
este libro.   this book.

Es posible que compremos   — It is possible that we'll buy
un coche nuevo.   a new car.

Es probable que ellos   — They will probably call.
llamen.

Puede ser que no lo crea.   — It may be that he/she may
                                  not believe it.

But if the impersonal expression indicates certainty, the
indicative is used.

Es cierto que los compra.   — It is true that they are
                                  buying them.

Es un hecho que él está   — It is a fact that he is here.
aquí.

Es evidente que ellos no   — It is obvious that they are
mandan el dinero.   not sending the money.

Es claro que Ud. vive aquí.   — It is clear that you live here.

Es verdad que ella estudia   — It is true that she studies a
mucho.   lot.

NOUNS

competencia (f)	–	competition
costa (f)	–	coast
deporte (m)	–	sport
esquí (m)	–	ski
evento (m)	–	event
explicación (f)	–	explanation
farmacéutico (a)	–	pharmacist
forma (f)	–	form, shape
hecho (f)	–	fact
lástima (f)	–	pity
maletín (m)	–	briefcase
receta (f)	–	prescription, recipe
Suiza	–	Switzerland
tarjeta postal	–	post card

ADJECTIVES

activo	–	active
cierto	–	certain
claro	–	clear
importante	–	important
posible	–	possible
seguro	–	sure

ADVERBS

acaso	–	maybe
evidente	–	evident
sólo	–	only
tal vez	–	maybe
de repente	–	suddenly

VERBS

aconsejar	–	to advise, counsel
alegrarse de	–	to be happy about
aprobar	–	to approve
competir	–	to compete
demandar	–	to demand
dudar	–	to doubt
esquiar	–	to ski
fumar	–	to smoke
informar	–	to inform
obligar	–	to oblige, to compel
permitir	–	to permit
prohibir	–	to prohibit
sorprender	–	to surprise
sugerir	–	to suggest
temer	–	to fear

EXPRESSIONS

de prisa	–	in a hurry
desde luego	–	of course
todo el mundo	–	everybody

1. Use the correct form of the verb listed on the right, in the subordinate clauses that complete the idea expressed in the main clause written below.

Los señores López esperan que....

a. (Yo)_____(llevar).

b. (Nosotros)_____(necesitar).

c. (Tú)_____(visitar).

d. Ella_____(dejar).

e. Uds._____(hablar).

f. El_____(mirar).

g. Tú y yo_____(ayudar).

h. Ellos_____(prestar).

i. Ud. y ella_____(tomar).

j. El y yo_____(mandar).

2. A pharmacist is talking to one of his/her employees telling him/her about how he prefers things to be done in the pharmacy.

He states: Prefiero...

You add 4 completions (formal).

a. _____(arrive at eight)

b. _____(call me Sunday)

c. _____(don't talk too much)

d. _____(work Saturdays)

3. Complete the wish expressed by the verb form deseo with subordinate clauses. Use the appropriate forms of the Spanish verbs listed below.

Deseo que....

a. Juan_____(leer).

b. La clienta_____(subir).

c. Mi hermana_____(correr).

d. El empleado_____(vender).

e. El farmacéutico_____(aprender).

f. Tú_____(escribir).

g. La empleada _____(abrir).

h. El enfermo_____(beber).

4. Change the verb of the subordinate clause of each of the following sentences from the present indicative to the present subjunctive:

a. Creo que el cliente habla mucho.

No creo_____

b. Sé que el farmacéutico vende estas medicinas.

Espero_____

c. Veo que la señora no comprende la explicación.

Siento_____

d. El médico piensa que no necesitas la receta.

_____espera_____

e. Ellos saben que esos clientes compran mucho.

_____necesitan_____

5. **Supply the correct form of the verb.**

a. No quiero que nosotros_____nada.
   (olvidar)

b. Ojalá que él no_____los pasaportes.
   (dejar)

c. ¿Qué quiere ella que él_____en el maletín?
   (llevar)

d. Tomás no sabe que el tren_____por la costa.
   (viajar)

e. El chofer piensa que todos los pasajeros

   _____bien.
   (estar)

f. Estoy seguro que Elena nos_____.
   (esperar)

g. No creo que Elena nos_____.
   (esperar).

h. Sólo quiere que José y yo le_____algo.
   (comprar)

i. Prefieren que tú_____los chicos a las
   montañas.   (llevar)

6. **Fill in the blank with the correct form of the indicative or subjunctive.**

a. Es importante que Ud. lo_____.
   (leer)

b. Es claro que Berta_____mucho.
   (gastar)

c. Es lástima que_____poco español.
   (hablar)

d. No es verdad que ella_____13 perros.
   (vender)

e. Es probable que Juan_____este año.
   (terminar)

f. Es verdad que Enrique_____mucho.
   (comer)

g. Es necesario que los chicos_____vitaminas.
   (tomar)

h. Es probable que él me_____el dinero.
   (dar)

i. No es posible que ellas_____tanto.
   (estudiar)

j. Es un hecho que nosotros no_____a tiempo.
   (llegar)

7. **Translate into Spanish.**

   a. I want her to pay.

      _____

   b. They want us to eat now.

      _____

   c. They advise me to eat often.

      _____

   d. She wants him to study.

      _____

   e. I prohibit them to talk in class.

      _____

8. **Change the verb in the model sentence, and rewrite the sentence after each change.**

   Model: Necesito que lo reciba mañana.

   a. Sé_____

   b. Pensamos_____

   c. No creo_____

   d. Estoy seguro_____

   e. Dudamos_____

   f. Espero_____

   g. Creemos_____

9. **Organize the following group of words into meaningful sentences.**

   a. parte tomen activa que ellos toda clase la espera

      _____

   b. es vez primera que no sorprende la todo a mundo el

      _____

   c. correo tarjetas voy sellos al postales a comprar y

      _____

10. **Answer the following questions based on the conversation.**

   a. ¿Qué deporte practica Héctor?

      _____

   b. ¿Por qué Aurora duda que Héctor esté listo para competir?

      _____

   c. ¿A dónde fué Héctor a esquiar el año pasado?

      _____

   d. ¿Qué verbo se usa en español para traducir "to mail"?

      _____

   e. ¿Qué espera la familia?

      _____

f. ¿Por qué Aurora tiene prisa?

_____

g. ¿Quién le ha dicho a Amanda que las
    competencias de esquí empiezan el
    sábado próximo?

_____

TOPICS: IRREGULAR FORMS OF THE PRESENT SUBJUNCTIVE, STEM-CHANGING VERBS, SPELLING-CHANGING VERBS, SUBJUNCTIVE IN THE ADJECTIVAL CLAUSE, REFLEXIVE CONSTRUCTION

CONVERSATION XXVIII

	LA COMPRA DE UN AUTO		BUYING A CAR
1. Esteban:	Oye, Osvaldo. Quiero que vayas conmigo a ver autos. Busco uno que no sea caro.	– Esteban:	Listen, Osvaldo. I want you to go with me to see cars. I am looking for one that is not expensive.
2. Osvaldo:	No vas a encontrar ninguno que cueste menos de $10,000.	– Osvaldo:	You are not going to find any that cost less than $10,000.
3. Esteban:	Pues, no quiero gastar tanto.	– Esteban:	Well, I don't want to spend so much.
4. Osvaldo:	Quizás puedas encontrar un modelo del año pasado que te cueste menos.	– Osvaldo:	Maybe you can find one of last year's models that will cost you less.
5. Esteban:	No me importa que sea de uso.	– Esteban:	It doesn't matter that it is used.
6. Osvaldo:	Mi primo está vendiendo su Corvette, tiene cuatro años.	– Osvaldo:	My cousin is selling his Corvette, it is four years old.
7. Esteban:	¿Cuánto quiere por él? Querrá una fortuna.	– Esteban:	How much does he want for it? He probably wants a fortune.
8. Osvaldo:	Quiere $8,500.	– Osvaldo:	He want $8,500.
9. Esteban:	Por ese dinero trataré de encontrar uno que sea más nuevo.	– Esteban:	For that kind of money, I will try to find one that's newer.
10. Osvaldo:	¿No te das cuenta que los Corvettes mantienen su valor?	– Osvaldo:	Don't you realize that Corvettes maintain their value?
11. Esteban:	Así y todo, prefiero algo que me dé más por mi dinero.	– Esteban:	Even so, I prefer something that gives me more for my money.
12. Osvaldo:	Entonces creo que debes visitar algunas de las agencias de autos.	– Osvaldo:	Then, I think you must visit some of the car dealers.
13. Esteban:	Sí, buena idea. Vamos.	– Esteban:	Yes, good idea. Let's go.

I. Irregular Forms of the Present Subjunctive

Most irregular verbs in the present subjunctive carry the stem of the first person singular present indicative in all the person.

Infinitive	Present Indicative	Present Subjunctive				
	Yo	Yo	Tú	Ud., él, ella	Nosotros/as	Uds., ellos, ellas
caer	caig-o	caig-a	caig-as	caig-a	caig-amos	caig-an
conocer	conozc-o	conozc-a	conozc-as	conozc-a	conozc-amos	conozc-an
decir	dig-o	dig-a	dig-as	dig-a	dig-amos	dig-an
hacer	hag-o	hag-a	hag-as	hag-a	hag-amos	hag-an
oír	oig-o	oig-a	oig-as	oig-a	oig-amos	oig-an
poner	pong-o	pong-a	pong-as	pong-a	pong-amos	pong-an
salir	salg-o	salg-a	salg-as	salg-a	salg-amos	salg-an
tener	teng-o	teng-a	teng-as	teng-a	teng-amos	teng-an
traer	traig-o	traig-a	traig-as	traig-a	traig-amos	traig-an
venir	veng-o	veng-a	veng-as	veng-a	veng-amos	veng-an
ver	ve-o	ve-a	ve-as	ve-a	ve-amos	ve-an

Notice: you should keep in mind that, most verbs that are irregular in the first present singular of the person indicative have the same irregularity in all the present subjunctive forms.

There are six verbs that do not follow the irregularities stated above. They are dar, estar, haber, ir, saber, and ser. Learn the first person subjunctive and use the same stem for all the persons.

Infinitive	Present Indicative	Present Subjunctive				
	Yo	Yo	Tú	Ud., él, ella	Nosotros/as	Uds., ellos, ellas
dar	doy	dé	des	dé	démos	den
estar	estoy	esté	estés	esté	estemos	estén
haber	he	haya	hayas	haya	hayamos	hayan
ir	voy	vaya	vayas	vaya	vayamos	vayan
saber	sé	sepa	sepas	sepa	sepamos	sepan
ser	soy	sea	seas	sea	seamos	sean

Some Irregular -ir verbs in the subjunctive also change the first person plural (nosotros/as) from e to i and o to u.

Examples using the verbs sentir (e→i) and dormir (o→u) in the first person plural.

	Indicative	Subjunctive	Indicative	Subjunctive
Yo	sient-o	sient-a	duerm-o	duerm-a
Tú	sient-es	sient-as	duerm-es	duerm-as
Ud., él, ella	sient-e	sient-a	duerm-e	duerm-as
Nosotros/as	sent-imos	sint-amos	dorm-imos	durm-amos
Uds., ellos, ellas	sient-en	sient-an	duer-men	duerm-an

II. Stem-Changing Verbs

In previous lessons, you have practiced a number of verbs that are stem-changing in the present indicative mood. Some have changes in the stem, such as e→ie, e→i, o→ue and o→u. Others have the addition of a consonant before the ending or the change of one consonant for another, like c→q, etc. Most verbs that change e to ie and o to ue maintain the same form in the stem as the present indicative, i.e., the changes occur in all person except nosotros.

Examples using the verbs pensar (e→ie) and poder (o→ue):

	Indicative	Subjunctive	Indicative	Subjunctive
Yo	piens-o	piens-e	pued-o	pued-a
tú	piens-as	piens-es	pued-es	pued-as
Ud., él, ella	piens-a	piens-e	pued-e	pued-a
Nosotros/as	pens-amos	pens-emos	pod-emos	pod-amos
Uds., ellos, ellas	piens-an	piens-en	pued-en	pued-an

III. Spelling-Changing Verbs

Verbs whose infinitives end in -car, -gar, -ger, -gir, -guir, -zar, need written changes in the present subjunctive to preserve the original sound of the verb.

Infinitive	Present Subjunctive				
	Yo	Tú	Ud., él, ella	Nosotros/as	Uds., ellos, ella
buscar	busque	busques	busque	busquemos	busquen
tocar	toque	toques	toque	toquemos	toquen
llegar	llegue	llegues	llegue	lleguemos	lleguen
pagar	pague	pagues	pague	paguemos	paguen
escoger	escoja	escojas	escoja	escojamos	escojan
dirigir	dirija	dirijas	dirija	dirijamos	dirijan
seguir	siga	sigas	siga	sigamos	sigan
empezar	empiece	empieces	empiece	empecemos	empiecen

IV. Subjunctive in the Adjectival Clause

As we did with the noun clauses, we will explains the adjectival clauses through examples.

Subject	Verb	Direct Object	Adjective Modifying the Direct Object
La oficina	necesita	una secretaria	bilingüe.

If we replace the adjective bilingüe, "bi-lingual", by a clause expressing the same idea, we will have·

La oficina necesita una secretaria que hable inglés y español.

The dependent clause "que hable inglés y español" functions as an adjective modifying the direct object secretaria and it is called an adjectival clause. The object of the main clause is called the antecedent of the adjective clause.

Notice: The antecedent is nothing but the object of the main clause. As in the noun clause, some adjectival clauses use the verb in the indicative while others use the subjunctive form.

The subjunctive is required in the adjectival clause when the antecedent (the object of the main clause) is indefinite or non-existing. If the antecedent is a definite person or thing, the indicative is used.

Examples of adjectival clauses with
definite objects or antecedents.

Conozco a la chica que   - I know the girl that
trabaja aquí.   works here.
Tengo el libro que tiene   - I have the book that
todas las respuestas.   has all the answers.
Siempre tomo el autobús   - I always take the bus
que va al centro.   that goes downtown.

Notice that la chica, el libro, y el autobús
are definite antecedents, the speaker knows
they are available, therefore the subjunctive
is not required.

Examples of adjectival clauses with indefinite
antecedents.

Necesito un vuelo que   - I need a flight that
salga a las 6 de la tarde.   leaves at 6 P.M.
Espérame en un banco que   - Wait for me on a bench
esté cerca de la puerta.   near the door.
Mándame un estudiante   - Send me a student that
que hable francés.   speaks French.
Tráeme unas naranjas que   - Bring me some oranges
sean dulces.   that are sweet.

Notice that un vuelo, un banco y unas naranjas
are indefinite antecedents, the speaker hopes
that they are available. Examples of adjectival
clauses with non-existing (negative) antecedents.

No tenga nada que pueda   - I don't have anything
usar.   I can wear.
No hay persona que crea   - There is no one who
eso.   will believe that.
No tengo ningún[1]   - I don't have a student
estudiante que hable   that speaks French.
francés.

---

[1]When the antecedent is an indefinite or non-existing person the personal a is omitted.

Notice that the antecedents <u>nada</u>, <u>persona</u> and <u>ningún libro</u> are non-existing (negative) in the context of the examples given.

V. Reflexive Construction

Spanish uses reflexive verbs when the sentence has no object, because the action of the verb reflects back on the subject.

Verbs like <u>mudarse</u>, "to move out", <u>irse</u>, "to go away", <u>sentarse</u>, "to sit down", <u>caerse</u>, "to fall down" are used reflexively in Spanish. Notice that when you "move yourself out of the house", when you "sit down" you sit youself down, etc. Notice also the following reflexive construction which is actually a translation from English.

(Yo) me miro en el espejo. - I look at myself in the mirror.

Study the following examples:

El chofer para el autobús. - The driver stops the bus.

(Yo) corro por la calle, y - I run down the street, de repente me paro.   and suddenly I stop.

In the first sentence, the action of the verb lands on the direct object, <u>el autobús</u>. In the second, <u>me paro</u> uses the same concept. What you are really saying is "I stop myself", because in Spanish the action still must land in a direct object - is this case reflexive - or, the direct object is the same person as the subject. The complete conjugation is:

Yo me paro.

Tú te paras.

Ud., él, ella se para.

Nosotros (as) nos paramos.

Uds. ellos (as) se paran.

Other common reflexive verbs are:

acostarse	-	to go to bed
dormirse	-	to fall asleep
lavarse	-	to wash up
levantarse	-	to get up
peinarse	-	to comb one's hair
ponerse	-	to put on
vestirse	-	to dress, to get dressed
quedarse	-	to remain
quitarse	-	to take off (something)
reírse	-	to laugh

Study the following examples[2].

Me acosté temprano anoche. - I went to bed early
last night.

Gloria se puso el vestido - Gloria wore (put on)
rojo. the red dress.

Levántate. Es tarde. - Get up. It is late.

Nos quedamos dos días más. - We remained two more days.

Los chicos se están riendo - The kids are laughing at
del payaso. the clown.

Juanito no quiere lavarse. - Johnny doesn't want to
wash up.

---

[2]The forms of the reflexive pronouns, me, te, se, nos were presented on Lección VII. Notice that the position of the reflexive pronouns are the same as the object pronouns.

VOCABULARIO

NOUNS

compañero (a)	-	companion
compañero de cuarto	-	roommate
condición (f)	-	condition
dilema (m)	-	dilemma
fortuna (f)	-	fortune
guía (m&f)	-	guide
libertad (f)	-	liberty
parador (m)	-	inn for travelers
sueldo (m)	-	salary
valor (m)	-	value

ADJECTIVES

bilingüe	-	bilingual
cómodo	-	comfortable
correcto	-	correct
disponible	-	available
dispuesto	-	willing
dulce	-	sweet
interesante	-	interesting
tanto	-	so much
único	-	only

ADVERBS

al fin	-	finally
de repente	-	suddenly

VERBS

acostarse	-	to go to bed
bajar	-	to go down, to descend
dirigir	-	to direct
dormirse	-	to fall asleep
escoger	-	to select
importar	-	to matter, to import
irse	-	to go away
lavarse	-	to wash up
mantener	-	to keep, to maintain
mirarse	-	to look at oneself
mudarse	-	to move out
ofrecer	-	to offer
peinarse	-	to comb one's hair
ponerse	-	to wear, to put on
quedarse	-	to remain
quitarse	-	to take off
resolver	-	to solve, to resolve
sentarse	-	to sit down
vestirse	-	to get dressed

EXPRESSIONS

así y todo	-	even so
darse cuenta	-	to realize
de uso	-	used

1. Supply the correct form of the present subjunctive.

a.

	ordenar	comer	escribir	llamar	romper	recibir
Yo						
Tú						
él						
Nosotros						
Ellos						

b.

	tener	oír	ver	poder	cerrar	perder
Yo						
Tú						
ella						
Nosotros						
Uds						

2. Supply the subject pronouns which correspond to the following verbs in the present subjunctive.

a. _____ lea

b. _____ escribas

c. _____ pongan

d. _____ vaya

e. _____ pidan

f. _____ sigan

g. _____ vendas

h. _____ vengan

i. _____ oiga

j. _____ demos

k. _____ sean

l. _____ pidas

m. _____ puedan

n. _____ haga

o. _____ tengamos

p. _____ analicen

q. _____ encuentres

r. _____ viva

s. _____ digan

t. _____ pague

u. _____ empiecen

v. _____ busque

3. Change the following verbs from the present indicative to the present subjunctive.

a. toman _____
b. cierro _____
c. sales _____
d. viene _____
e. tenemos _____
f. podemos _____
g. hacen _____
h. traen _____
i. pago _____
j. conocemos _____

k. somos _____
l. estoy _____
m. almuerzo _____
n. explican _____
o. escoge _____
p. busco _____
q. dirige _____
r. va _____
s. doy _____
t. leen _____

4. Change the following verbs from the present subjunctive to the present indicative. (Some have two different answers.)

a. _____ lea
b. _____ escribas
c. _____ pongan
d. _____ vaya
e. _____ pidan
f. _____ sigan
g. _____ vendas
h. _____ venga
i. _____ oiga
j. _____ demos
k. _____ sean

l. _____ durmamos
m. _____ pidamos
n. _____ lleguen
o. _____ paguen
p. _____ pienses
q. _____ pongas
r. _____ jueguen
s. _____ expliquemos
t. _____ entendamos
u. _____ empieces
v. _____ traigan

5. Fill in the blank with the correct form of the indicative or the subjunctive.

a. Prefiero que tú _____ ahora.
   venir

b. Tú sabes que él no _____ dinero.
   tener

c. Creemos que Juan no _____ bien.
   oir

d. Pídele que _____ más.
   estudiar

e. Tú y yo vemos que ella no lo _____.
   necesitar

f. Quiero que tú la _____ hoy.
   ver

g. ¿Crees que ella lo _____?
   hacer

h. Le pediré que la _____ otra vez.
   escribir

i. Espero que ella _____ mejor.
   estar

j. Ricardo quiere que yo le _____ una sorpresa.
   dar

k. El médico insiste en que yo_____de peso.
   bajar

l. Creo que él _____ a empezar una dieta.
   ir

6. Substitute a clause for each adjective or word used as an adjective, written below the line, to describe the noun.

a. Uds. no pueden traer una maleta _____.
   (pequeña)

b. Tráeme una maleta _____.
   (grande)

c. Queremos visitar algún país _____.
   (interesante)

d. Quiero dormir en una litera _____.
   (cómoda)

e. No encontramos hospedaje en el hotel_____.
   preferido

7. Fill in the blanks with the correct forms of the indicative or subjuncitve.

a. Busca un libro que _____ las respuestas.
   (tener)

b. Hay alguien que _____ las respuestas.
   (saber)

c. Cualquier persona que _____ a
   (viajar)
   China necesita pasaporte.

d. El farmacéutico no entiende las recetas que
   _____ el médico.
   (escribir)

e. Aquí no hay nadie que _____ el
   (leer)
   periódico todos los días.

f. Tengo una amiga que _____ en la ópera.
   (cantar)

g. No hay nadie que _____ la respuesta.
   (saber)

h. Hay algunos que _____ dos colores.
   (tener)

i. No hay ninguno que _____ tres colores.
   (tener)

j. Déme cualquiera que _____ cómodo.
   (ser)

k. No hay nada que (nosotros) _____ hacer.
   (poder)

l. Llegan tres que no _____ maletas.
   (traer)

m. Tráigame una manzana que _____ dulce.
   (estar)

n. Necesita la oficina que _____ dos
   (tener)
   teléfonos.

o. Necesita una oficina que _____ dos
   (tener)
   teléfonos.

p. Necesito un vuelo que no _____ escala.
   (hacer)

q. No hay nadie que lo _____.
   (creer)

r. Hay muchos que lo _____.
   (creer)

s. Buscamos un traje que no _____ mucho.
   (costar)

t. Tenemos dos camareras que _____
   (ser)
   muy buenas.

8. **Translate into Spanish the following sentences.**

a. They know a man who speaks five languages.

   _____.

   _____.

b. They prefer a man who speaks five languages.

   _____.

   _____.

c. We want the guide who is bi-lingual.

   _____.

   _____.

d. We want a guide who is bi-lingual.

   _____.

   _____.

e. You have one book that has all the correct answers. (formal)

_____

_____

f. There is no book here that has all the correct answers.

_____

_____

g. Is there any hotel or traveler's inn that has rooms available?

_____

h. He always recommends hotels that have rooms available.

_____

_____

i. I don't have anything that I can wear.

_____

_____

j. I have a red shirt that I can wear.

_____

_____

9. **Read the following narration, and choose the correct statement from the multiple choice questions below it.**

UNA NARRACIÓN

Alberto quiere comprar un coche nuevo y mudarse de casa de sus padres, pero su sueldo no le permite más que una de las dos cosas. Tiene un dilema, si se muda necesita un coche y si se queda en casa no tiene libertad. Al fin, después de pensarlo mucho, decide buscar un compañero de cuarto, y comprar un coche de uso.

a. 1. Alberto es un empleado nuevo.
   2. Su sueldo le permite comprar un coche.
   3. Tiene mucho trabajo.

b. 1. Si no se muda necesita un coche.
   2. En su casa tiene mucha libertad.
   3. Va a comprar un coche de uso.

c. 1. Quiere hacer dos cosas.
   2. No encuentra solución al problema.
   3. No quiere mudarse de casa de sus padres.

d. 1. El padre le ofrece ayuda.
   2. Alberto piensa que un compañero de cuarto es un dolor de cabeza.
   3. Tiene un dilema, pero lo resuelve.

10. **Answer the following sentences in complete sentences based on the conversation.**

a. ¿Quiere Esteban gastar $10,000 en un coche?

_____

b. ¿Cuántos años tiene el Corvette?

_____

c. ¿A dónde quiere Esteban que Osvaldo vaya con él?

_____

d. ¿Es cierto que el Corvette tiene sólo un año?

_____

e. ¿Busca Esteban un coche nuevo que cueste $10,000?

_____

f. ¿Por qué no compra el Corvette?

_____

g. ¿Cuánto cree Esteban que querrá el primo de Osvaldo por el Corvette?

_____

h. ¿Qué deciden hacer al fin Osvaldo y Esteban?

_____

11. **Organize the following groups of words into meaningful expressions.**

a. ninguno que menos cueste vas no a encontrar

_____

b. entonces autos creo de que agencias debes las visítar de algunas

_____

c. el cuenta das mío coche valor su mantiene que te no

_____

12. **Translate into Spanish.**

a. I don't want to spend so much.

_____

b. He probably wants a fortune for it.

_____

c. Maybe you can find one of last year's models that will cost you less.

_____

d. I think you must visit some of the car dealers.

_____

e. For that kind of money I will try to find one that is newer.

_____

f. That is too much money for a car that is four years old.

_____

13. **Answer the following questions:**

a. ¿Se acostó Ud. tarde anoche?

No, _____

b. ¿De quién se ríen ellos?

_____ policía.

c. ¿Te levantas temprano?

Sí, _____

d. ¿Qué se puso Elena para la fiesta?

_____vestido verde.

e. ¿Te lavaste ya?

Sí, _____

14. **Supply the correct form.**

a. _____ ahora. (familiar)
     <u>get up</u>

b. Ella _____.
              <u>is laughing</u>

c. No _____ el suéter todavía. (formal)
        <u>take off</u>

d. Qué _____ para la fiesta. (familiar)
         <u>did you wear</u>

e. _____ en el espejo. (familiar)
        <u>look at yourself</u>

TOPICS: SUBJUNCTIVE IN THE ADVERBIAL CLAUSE, AFFIRMATIVE WORDS AND THEIR CORRESPONDING NEGATIVES, THE NEUTER
ARTICLE LO

CONVERSATION XXIX

	EN LA PISCINA		AT THE SWIMMING POOL
1. Laura:	Hola, Elisa. ¡Qué sorpresa! Nunca te vi aquí antes.	– Laura:	Hello, Elisa. What a surprise! I never saw you here before.
2. Elisa:	Generalmente voy a la playa, pero los domingos vengo aquí con Paco.	– Elisa:	Usually I go to the beach, but on Sundays I come here with Paco.
3. Laura:	¿Dónde está él?	– Laura:	Where is he?
4. Elisa:	Está allí esperando hasta que abran la cantina.	– Elisa:	He is there waiting for them to open the snack bar.
5. Laura:	¿No está abierta todavía?	– Laura:	Isn't it open yet?
6. Elisa:	Hoy abrirán cuando llegue el dueño, los empleados descansan los domingos.	– Elisa:	Today they'll open when the owner arrives, the employees are off on Sunday.
7. Elisa:	Mira. Ahí viene Paco.	– Elisa:	Look. Here comes Paco.
8. Paco:	¿Qué hay de nuevo, Laura? ¿Vienes a nadar aquí a menudo?	– Paco:	What is new, Laura? Do you come to swim here often?
9. Laura:	Algunas veces vengo aquí. Está un poco lejos de casa y el autobús demora mucho.	– Laura:	Sometimes I come here. It is somewhat far from home, and the bus takes too long.
10. Elisa:	¿Y tu coche? ¿Ya no lo tienes?	– Elisa:	What about your car? Don't you have it anymore?
11. Laura:	No, lo vendí el mes pasado, pero voy a comprar otro tan pronto como vengan los modelos nuevos.	– Laura:	No, I sold it last month, but I'm going to buy another one as soon as the new models get here.
12. Paco:	¿Cómo puedes vivir sin coche en esta sociedad tan complicada?	– Paco:	¿How can you live without a car in this complicated society of ours?
13. Laura:	Muy bien, mi trabajo está a dos cuadras de casa, y para emergencias tengo el coche de papá.	– Laura:	Just fine. My work is two blocks from home, and for emergencies I have daddy's car.
14. Paco:	¿Pero es que tu vida no es más que trabajo y emergencias? ¿Y de diversiones qué?	– Paco:	But is your life only work and emergencies? What about having fun?
15. Laura:	No te preocupes. Tengo muy buenas relaciones con el chico que vive al lado, y tiene un coche deportivo Mercedes.	– Laura:	Don't worry. I have a very good relationship with the boy next door, and he has a Mercedes sports car.
16. Elisa:	¡Felicidades! ¿Cuándo es la boda?	– Elisa:	Congratulations! When is the wedding?
17. Laura:	No tengo prisa. Dios dirá.	– Laura:	I am not in a hurry. Time will tell.

I. Subjunctive in the Adverbial Clause

Again, as we did with the noun and adjectival
clauses, we will explain the adverbial clause
through examples.

Subject   Verb   Adverb

Alberto escribirá pronto   - Alberto will write soon.

If we replace the adverb pronto which modifies
the verb escribirá by a clause expressing the
same idea, we will have:

Alberto escribirá en - Albert will write as
cuanto llegue.   soon as he arrives.

The dependent clause "en cuanto llegue" functions
as an adverb modifying the verb escribirá.

Also, as in the noun clauses and the adjectival
clauses, some adverbial clauses require the use
of the subjuntive and others the indicative.

For the adverbial clause to require the subjunctive
there must be a future implication in the verb of the
dependent clause, with respect to the time of the
verb in the independent clause.

In the model sentence, at the time the speaker is
saying Alberto will write (escribirá), Alberto has
not arrived as yet, consequently, the time at
which Alberto is to arrive is in the future with
respect to the time the speaker is saying that
Alberto will write (escribirá).

The following examples will illustrate the use of
the subjuntive or indicative in the adverbial clause.
Group A requires indicative and Group B requires
subjunctive.

Group A

a. María come aquí cuando viene temprano. – Mary eats here whenever she comes early.

b. Pedro empieza a estudiar tan pronto llega. – Peter begins to study as soon as he arrives.

c. Carlos duerme hasta que yo lo despierto. – Charles sleeps until I wake him up.

d. Siempre dejan todo en orden cuando se van. – They always leave everything in order when they leave.

e. Cuando como mucho, engordo. – When I eat a lot, I gain weight.

f. Fuí a ver al jefe en cuanto llegué. – I went to see the boss as soon as I arrived.

g. Pablo nos llamó tan pronto llegó. – Paul called us as soon as he arrived.

Group B

a. Te escribiré cuando llegue a Los Angeles. – I'll write you when I arrive in Los Angeles.

b. Pedro empezará a estudiar tan pronto llegue. – Peter will begin to study as soon as he arrives.

c. Volveré cuando tú regreses. – I'll return when you come back.

d. Le hablaré tan pronto lo vea. – I'll talk to him as soon as I see him.

e. Lo veremos después que termine. – We'll see him after he finishes.

f. Esperaré hasta que Carlos me vea. – I'll wait until Charles sees me.

g. Comprarán el ventilador cuando tengan dinero. – They'll buy the fan when they have money.

Notice that the sentences in Group A denote habitual action or a total lack of future implication as in f. and g.

Also notice that in the sentences in Group B the verbs in the adverbial clauses have future implication. Everything is up in the air, the outcome has not materialized yet. This is precisely what triggers the subjunctive in the adverbial clause.

Going one step further, we are now going to
take the sentences in Group B and change them
to the preterite. You will notice that the
verbs change to the indicative. This is
because by changing them to the past, the
outcome of the dependent clause has materialized.

a. Te escribí cuando   - I wrote you when I got
   llegué a Los Angeles.   to Los Angeles.

b. Pedro empezó a   - Peter began to study
   estudiar tan pronto   as soon as he got here.
   llegó.

c. Volví cuando tú   - I returned when you came
   regresaste.   back.

d. Le hablé tan pronto   - I spoke to him as soon
   lo vi.   as I saw him.

e. Lo vimos después   - We saw him after he
   que terminó.   finished.

f. Esperé hasta que   - I waited until Charles
   Carlos me vió.   saw me.

g. Compraron el   - They bought the fan when
   ventilador cuando   they had the money.
   tenían el dinero.

Conjunctions that trigger subjunctive.·

The following conjunctions always introduce
adverbial clauses and the subjunctive is always
required in these cases even if the sentence
is in the past tense. This point will be
discussed when we present the imperfect subjunctive.

antes (de) que	before
a menos que	unless
para que	in order that, so that
con tal que	provided that
sin que	without
en caso que	in case

The following examples will illustrate this point.

a. Voy a ver a César — I am going to see Cesar
   antes de que   before Mary arrives.
   llegue María.

b. Me prestará el   — He'll lend me the book
   libro a menos   unless he needs it.
   que lo necesite.

c. Se lo daré para   — I will give it to him so
   que lo lea.   that he may read it.

d. Le pagaré el   — I'll pay for the course
   curso con tal   provided that he studies.
   que estudie.

e. Dejaré la llave   — I'll leave the key in case
   en caso que venga.   he comes.

f. Puedo ir a Europa — I can go to Europe without
   sin que mi padre   my father giving me the
   me dé el dinero.   money.

Notice that example (f) in English doesn't take
an independent clause after "without". Notice
also that sentence (f), in Spanish requires a
clause after <u>sin que</u>, (without).

Commands triggering subjunctive in the dependent clause:

Up to now, we have only given verbs in the indicative
in the independent clauses, but if the condition or
conditions for the use of subjunctive are met, the
verb in the independent clause can also be in the
command form.

The following examples will illustrate this point:

Déle la carta   — Give him the letter
cuando llegue.   when he arrives.

Dígale que venga.   — Tell him to come.

Tráiganle un libro — Bring him a book that
que tenga las   has the answers.
respuestas.

Notice that the verbs dé, diga and traigan are command forms for the verbs dar, decir and traer.

Also notice that the first example has an adverbial clause, the second one has a noun clause and the third one an adjectival clause.

II. Affirmative Words and Their Corresponding Negatives

Affirmative Words

algo	-	something
alguien	-	someone, somebody
algún (a,os,as)	-	any
siempre	-	always
alguna vez	-	some time, ever
también	-	also
uno (a,os,as)	-	either...or

Negative Words

nada	-	nothing
nadie	-	none, nobody
ningún (o,as,os)	-	no, none
nunca, jamás	-	never, (not) ever
tampoco	-	not either, neither
ni...ni	-	neither, not

Negatives are used after mejor que, "better than", peor que, "worse than", más que, "more than", sin, "without", to express affirmative idea.

Lo hace mejor que nadie.	He does it better than anyone.
El está peor que nunca.	He is worse than ever.
Como ahora más que nunca.	Now I eat more than ever.
Ella vivió un mes sin comer nada.	She lived for a month without eating anything.

Spanish, unlike English, accepts the double negative. In such case no precedes the verb and any other negative word must follow.

Affirmative Sentences	Negative Sentences
Tengo a alguien.	Nada tengo aquí or No tengo nada aquí.
Veo a alguien.	A nadie veo or No veo a nadie.
Algunos están aquí.	Ninguno está aquí or No está aquí ninguno.
Siempre vienen.	Nunca vienen or No vienen nunca.
El también viene.	El tampoco viene or El no viene tampoco.
Sirve uno u[1] otro.	Ni uno ni otro sirve or No sirve ni uno niotro.

---

[1]Spanish changes o ("or") to u before a word beginning with o. Also, y ("and") changes to e before an i. Remember that h is silent. Both of these changes are for sound.

Negative expressions.

Memorize the following negative expressions, they are widely used in Spanish:

de ninguna manera (forma) de ningún modo	- by no means
ni siquiera	- not even
ni (subject pronoun) tampoco	- nor (subject pronoun) either
No me vió más que[2] una vez.	- He saw me only once.
Ya no nos visitan.	- They no longer visit us.

III. **The Neuter Article Lo**

The neuter article lo is used before adjectives and past participles to form abstract nouns. Notice the English translation which uses "thing" and "part" to express the abstract nouns.

Lo bueno es que es fácil.	- The good thing is that it is easy.
Hizo lo mismo que Juan.	- He did the same (thing) as John.
Quiero lo mejor para tí.	- I want the best thing for you
Lo bello alimenta el alma.	- The beautiful things in life nourish the soul or Beauty nourishes the soul.

Lo que and lo cual

Lo que is the neuter form of el que, it means "what, that which". It is very important to remember that lo que is the only possible translation for "what" when "what" is not an interrogative word.

Eso es lo que yo dije.	- That is what I said.
Lo que pides es demasiado.	- What you are asking for is too much.
Me dió lo que tenía.	- He gave me what he had.
Sé lo que quiero.	- I know what I want.

Lo que and lo cual both mean "which" when referring to an idea.

Pedro no viene, lo cual (lo que) me hace ir solo.	- Peter is not coming, makes me go alone.
No soy soltero, lo cual (lo que) me impide pertenecer al Club de Solteros.	- I am not a bachelor which prevents me from belonging to the Bachelor's Club.

---

[2]No (verb) más que = solamente.

VOCABULARIO

NOUNS

cantina (f)	-	bar, snack bar
comodidad (f)	-	comfort
concierto (m)	-	concert
cuadra (f)	-	street block
Dios	-	God
diversión (f)	-	fun, entertainment
dueño (a)	-	owner
emergencia (f)	-	emergency
felicidades (f)	-	congratulations
nota (f)	-	grade (school work)
lado (m)	-	side
piscina (f)	-	swimming pool
relación (f)	-	relationship
sociedad (f)	-	society, partnership
sorpresa (f)	-	surprise
taza (f)	-	cup
toalla (f)	-	towel
ventilador (m)	-	electric fan
vida (f)	-	life

ADJECTIVES

bello	-	pretty, beautiful
complicado	-	complicated
deportivo	-	sports
mismo	-	some
rasonable	-	reasonable

ADVERBS

alguna vez	-	sometime, ever
lejos	-	far
peor	-	worse
tampoco	-	not either, neither

VERBS

alimentar	-	to feed, to nourish
demorar	-	to delay, to retard
impedir	-	to prevent
limpiar	-	to clean
nadar	-	to swim
prevenir	-	to prevent
pertenecer	-	to belong
prevenir	-	to prevent

CONNECTORS

a menos que	-	unless
antes (de) que	-	before
con tal (de) que	-	provided that
después (de) que	-	after
en caso (de que	-	in case
en cuanto	-	as soon as
hasta que	-	until
ni...ni	-	neither, nor
ni siguiera	-	not even
para que	-	in order that, so that
sin que	-	without
tan pronto como	-	as soon as

EXPRESSIONS

de ninguna manera (forma)	-	by no means
de ningún modo		

PRONOUNS

alguien	-	someone, somebody
nadie	-	no one, nobody

1. **Change the model sentence to agree with cues given.**

   Model: Traeré a Juan cuando Pedro lo vea.

   a. _____nosotros_____

   b. _____tan pronto_____

   c. _____tú_____

   d. Llevaré_____para que ellos_____

   e. _____con tal que_____

   f. No lleves_____sin que yo_____

2. **Answer affirmatively the following questions Spanish.**

   a. ¿Se lo darás cuando venga?

   _____

   b. ¿Se lo das siempre cuando viene? (a habitual action)

   _____

   c. ¿Lo tendrás listo para que él lo pueda ver?

   _____

   d. ¿Me lo dejarás ver antes (de) que ella llegue? (fam)

   _____

   e. ¿Me prestarás el auto sin que papá lo sepa?

   _____

   f. ¿Siempre ves a tu hermano tan pronto llega?

   _____

   g. ¿Lo terminarás después (de) que lo aprueben?

   _____

3. **Rewrite the following sentences using the form of the verb given.**

   a. Tengo que estudiar mucho cuando tengo examen.

   Tendré_____

   b. Le escribo cuando tengo tiempo.

   Le escribiré_____

   c. Le escribí tan pronto supe de él.

   Le voy a escribir_____

   d. Compraron el ventilador cuando tenían el dinero.

   Comprarán_____

   e. Lo vi después que terminó.

   Lo veré_____

4. **Fill in the blank with the correct form of the of the indicative or subjunctive.**

   a. Volveré cuando el médico_____.

                                        regresar

   b. Felipe empieza siempre a estudiar en cuanto él

   _____.
   llegar

c. Pablo me llamará tan pronto _____ .
                                               hablar
   con ellos.

d. La veremos después que él _____ .
                                        terminar

e. Lo haré todo cuando Ud. _____ .
                                      llegar

f. Se lo presto para que lo _____ .
                                      leer

g. Vendremos antes (de) que ellos _____
                                      salir
   para Europa.

h. Voy a trabajar hasta que me _____ .
                                      cansar

i. Mi padre me prestará dinero cuando
   lo _____ .
               necesitar

j. Te escribiré cuando _____ tiempo.
                       tener

5. **Supply the correct translation.**

a. Usa el auto _____
                   so that you may
   _____ .
     travel today

b. Estudie más _____ .
               so that you have a good grade

c. Deje la taza _____ .
               so that Mary can wash it

d. Juan estará contento _____ .
               when he cleans his suit

e. Juan quiere llegar a Machu Pichu _____
                                   before
   _____ .
     it is night time

f. Empieza a hacer las maletas _____ .
                               as soon as
   _____ .
     you get home

g. Repite la lección _____ .
                    until he learns it

h. Llama a la tienda _____
                       so that they send you
   _____ .
     the towels

i. Déjalo aquí _____ .
                       in case he comes

6. **Translate the following sentences into Spanish.**

a. Give these letters to your brother as soon
   as he arrives. (fam.)

   _____

   _____

b. The boys will eat before we leave.

_____

_____

c. I will explain it so that they will understand it.

_____

_____

d. We will study the subjunctive when we are in the Spanish class.

_____

_____

e. Mary wants to pack the suitcases before her husband gets home.

_____

_____

7. **Answer the following questions using (1) simple negative and (2) double negative.**

a. ¿Ves a alguien?

(1) _____

(2) _____

b. ¿Tienes algo que hacer?

(1) _____

(2) _____

c. ¿Tiene Ud. alguno?

(1) _____

(2) _____

d. ¿Compras pan y leche?

(1) _____

(2) _____

e. ¿Viene Pedro algunas veces?

(1) _____

(2) _____

f. ¿Ella también va?

(1) _____

(2) _____

g. ¿Qué tienes en esa caja?

(1) _____

(2) _____

h. ¿Quiere ir alguna de las chicas?

(1) _____

(2) _____

8. **Change the following sentences to the negative.**
   (Use double negatives)

   a. Voy a llevar a alguien al concierto.

   _____

   b. ¿Tienes algún dinero?

   _____

   c. ¿Estudia Ud. francés o aleman?

   _____

   d. Ella tiene siempre frío.

   _____

   e. ¿Quieres algo?

   _____

   f. Ofelia va también.

   _____

9. **Answer the following questions based on the conversation.**

   a. ¿Cuántos días trabajan los empleados de la cantina?

   _____

   b. ¿Nunca viene Elisa a la piscina?

   _____

   c. ¿Conoce Laura a Paco?

   _____

   d. ¿Por qué Laura no tiene coche?

   _____

   e. ¿Por qué Paco no está con Elisa cuando Laura llega?

   _____

   f. ¿Por qué no está abierta la cantina?

   _____

   g. ¿Quién abre la cantina él sábado?

   _____

   h. ¿Cuándo vendió el coche Laura?

   _____

   i. ¿Cuándo va a comprar Laura un coche nuevo?

   _____

10. **Organize the following words into meaningful expressions.**

a.	b.	c.
que	voy	lejos
no	pero	autobús
que	nuevos	un
pero	a	demora
tu	modelos	está
es	otro	mucho
trabajo	comprar	poco
más	los	el
es	tan	y
vida	como	
¿ ?	pronto	
	lleguen	

11. **Translate into Spanish.**

a. The boy next door has a Mercedes.

_____

b. How can you live without a car?

_____

c. What about your car? Don't you have it anymore?

_____

d. He doesn't have a good car either.

_____

e. Don't you ever go to the beach on Sundays?

_____

f. I don't have anything to wear for the party.

g. I never saw you here before.

_____

h. It is somewhat far from home, and the bus takes too long.

_____

12. **Translate the following sentences into English.**

a. Hicieron lo mismo.

_____

b. ¿Ves lo fácil que es la lección.

_____

c. Lo peor es que él llega tarde siempre.

_____

d. Lo hecho, hecho está.

_____

e. Dígale lo importante que es ser una persona responsable.

_____

13. **Translate the following sentences into Spanish.**

a. Give me what you have. (formal)

_____

b. We don't have what she wants.

_____

c. I'm not part of that group which
   prevents me from eating at their table.

_____

d. Charles is not going which make me go alone.

_____

e. The important part (of it) is that he
   knows all of them.

_____

f. He brought me what I asked for.

_____

TOPICS: FORMS OF THE IMPERFECT SUBJUNCTIVE, USES OF THE IMPERFECT SUBJUNCTIVE, <u>POR</u> AND <u>PARA</u>

CONVERSATION XXX

	ENTREVISTA PARA UN EMPLEO			INTERVIEW FOR A JOB
1.	Recepcionista:	Buenos días. ¿En que puedo servirle?	– Receptionist:	Good morning. What can I do for you?
2.	Alejandro:	Tengo una entrevista con el Sr. Duarte para el puesto de jefe de ventas.	– Alejandro:	I have an interview with Mr. Duarte for the sales manager job.
3.	Recepcionista:	Bien. ¿Ha llenado Ud. la solicitud?	– Receptionist:	Fine. Have you filled out the application?
4.	Alejandro:	Sí, el Sr. Duarte me dijo que llenara una planilla.	– Alejandro:	Yes, Mr. Duarte told me to fill out an application.
5.	Recepcionista:	El Sr. Duarte llamó para decir que estaba en una junta, y para pedirle que lo esperara.	– Receptionist:	Mr. Duarte called to say that he was at a meeting, and to ask you to wait for him.
6.	Alejandro:	Está bien. No tengo prisa.	– Alejandro:	It's O.K. I am not in a hurry.
7.	Recepcionista:	No va a tener que esperar. El Sr. Duarte ha llegado.	– Receptionist:	You will not have to wait. Mr. Duarte has arrived.
8.	El Sr. Duarte:	Carmen, haga pasar al solicitante.	– Mr. Duarte:	Carmen, have the applicant come in.
9.	Recepcionista:	Pase. El Sr. Duarte lo espera ahora.	– Receptionist:	Come in. Mr. Duarte expects you now.
10.	El Sr. Duarte:	Buenos días. Siéntese, por favor.	– Mr. Duarte:	Good morning. Sit down, please.
11.	Alejandro:	Gracias.	– Alejandro:	Thank you.
12.	El Sr. Duarte:	Sus credenciales son excelentes, pero falta un requisito importante.	– Mr. Duarte:	Your credentials are excellent, but there is an important requirement missing.
13.	Alejandro:	¿De qué se trata?	– Alejandro:	What is it?
14.	El Sr. Duarte:	La firma necesitaba alguien que supiera francés.	– Mr.Duarte:	The firm needed someone who knew French.
15.	Alejandro:	No creí que fuera importante, por eso no anoté ese dato. Hablo portugués y francés.	– Alejandro:	I didn't think it was important, that is why I did not supply that information. I speak Portuguese and French.
16.	El Sr. Duarte:	Magnífico, ¿y dónde aprendió esos idiomas?	– Mr. Duarte:	Fantastic, and where did you learn those languages?
17.	Alejadro:	Mis padres estaban en el cuerpo diplomático, y siempre insistieron en que yo aprendiera la lengua del país.	– Alejandro:	My parents were in the Foreign Service and always insisted that I learn the language of the country.
18.	El Sr. Duarte:	Sí está de acuerdo con el sueldo y la comisión, el puesto es suyo.	– Mr. Duarte:	I you agree with the salary terms plus commission, the position is yours.
19.	Alejandro:	No podré empezar hasta el día veinte porque tengo que dar aviso a la firma donde trabajo.	– Alejandro:	I will not be able to start until the twentieth, because I have to give notice to the firm where I work.
20.	El Sr. Duarte:	Desde luego. Si necesita alguna otra información, llámeme.	– Mr. Duarte:	Of course. If you need any additional information, call me.
21.	Alejandro:	Muy bien. Adiós, y gracias por todo.	– Alejadro:	Fine. Good-bye and thanks for everything.

I.

A. Forms of the Imperfect Subjunctive

To form the imperfect subjunctive, use the third person plural of the preterite indicative as your cue. Drop the -on, and add the endings -a, -as, -a, -amos, -an.

Thus·

	hablar(on)	comier(on)	vivier(on)
Yo	hablar-a	comier-a	vivier-a
Tú	hablar-as	comier-as	vivier-as
Ud., él, ella	hablar-a	comier-a	vivier-a
Nosotros(as)	hablár-amos	comiér-amos	viviér-amos
Uds. ellos, ellas	hablar-an	comier-an	vivier-an

This formula works with all verbs, regular, irregular and stem-chaning. Study the chart on the following page.

B. Alternative Forms of the Imperfect Subjunctive

The imperfect subjunctive has an alternate form (The -se form) which is seldom used in the Spanish spoken in Spanish America. We will present the forms so that you will be able to identify them in case you hear them or come across them when reading.

Yo	habl-áse	com-iése	viv-íese
Tú	habl-áses	com-iéses	viv-íeses
Ud., él, ella	habl-áse	com-iése	viv-íese
Nosotros/as	habl-ásemos	com-iésemos	viv-iésemos
Uds.. ellos ellas	habl-áses	com-iésen	viv-íesen

	Preterite			Imperfect Subjunctive		
	3rd Plural					
Infinitive	(Uds.)	Yo	Tú	Ud., él, ella	Nosotros/as	Uds., ellos, ellas
andar	anduvier-on	anduvier-a	anduvier-as	anduvier-a	anduviér-amos	anduvier-an
caber	cupier-on	cupier-a	cupier-as	cupier-a	cupiér-amos	cupier-an
caer	cayer-on	cayer-a	cayer-as	cayer-a	cayér-amos	cayer-an
creer	creyer-on	creyer-a	creyer-as	creyer-a	creyér-amos	creyer-an
dar	dier-on	dier-a	dier-as	dier-a	diér-amos	dier-an
decir	dijer-on	dijer-a	dijer-as	dijer-a	dijér-amos	dijer-an
estar	estuvier-on	estuvier-a	estuvier-as	estuvier-a	estuviér-amos	estuvier-an
haber	hubier-on	hubier-a	hubier-as	hubier-a	hubiér-amos	hubier-an
hacer	hicier-on	hicier-a	hicier-as	hicier-a	hiciér-amos	hicier-an
ir	fuer-on	fuer-a	fuer-as	fuer-a	fuér-amos	fuer-an
leer	leyer-on	leyer-a	leyer-as	leyer-a	leyér-amos	leyer-an
oír	oyer-on	oyer-a	oyer-as	oyer-a	oyér-amos	oyer-an
poder	pudier-on	pudier-a	pudier-as	pudier-a	pudiér-amos	pudier-an
poner	pusier-on	pusier-a	pusier-as	pusier-a	pusiér-amos	pusier-an
querer	quisier-on	quisier-a	quisier-as	quisier-a	quisiér-amos	quisier-an
saber	supier-on	supier-a	supier-as	supier-a	supiér-amos	supier-an
ser	fuer-on	fuer-a	fuer-as	fuer-a	fuér-amos	fuer-an
tener	tuvier-on	tuvier-a	tuvier-as	tuvier-a	tuviér-amos	tuvier-an
traer	trajer-on	trajer-a	trajer-as	trajer-a	trajér-amos	trajer-an
traducir	tradujer-on	tradujer-a	tradujer-as	tradujer-a	tradujér-amos	tradujer-an
venir	vinier-on	vinier-a	venier-as	vinier-a	viniér-amos	vinier-an
ver	vier-on	vier-a	vier-as	vier-a	viér-amos	vier-an
dormir[1]	durmier-on	durmier-a	durmier-as	durmier-a	durmiér-amos	durmier-an
pedir[1]	pidier-on	pidier-a	pidier-as	pidier-a	pidiér-amos	pidier-an

[1]Note that dormir and pedir are stem-changing verbs. The system works for all verbs!

II. Uses of the Imperfect Subjunctive

We will illustrate the use of the imperfect subjunctive by means of example.

Noun clauses that require subjunctive in the present tense have to be changed to imperfect subjunctive when the sentence is changed to the past.

Quiero que Pedro venga.

Quería que Pedro viniera.

Ella necesita que él venga.

Ella necesitaba que él viniera.

Nos piden que paguemos.

Nos pidieron que pagáramos.

Adjectival clauses that require subjunctive in the present tense have to be changed to the imperfect subjunctive when the sentence is changed to the past.

Necesita un vuelo que salga a las 6 de la tarde.

Necesitaba un vuelo que saliera a las 6 de la tarde.

No tengo nada que pueda usar.

No tenía nada que pudiera usar.

Buscamos un hombre que quiera trabajar.

Buscábamos un hombre que quisiera trabajar.

Adverbial clauses that take presente subjunctive do not always require subjunctive if the sentence is changed to the past. The condition for subjunctive in the adverbial clause is future implication, that is the outcome of the action or idea expressed in the dependent clause has not yet materialized. If by changing the sentence to the past the outcome has materialized, then the indicative is used. The following examples will illustrate this point.

Group A: Change to indicative: (Preterite)

a. Le escribiré a María cuando (yo) llegue a Caracas.

Le escribí a María cuando (yo) llegué a Caracas.

b. Lo hará tan pronto como pueda.

Lo hizo tan pronto como pudo.

c. Trabajará hasta que el otro empleado llegue.

Trabajó hasta que el otro empleado llegó.

Group B: Change to the imperfect subjunctive.
(The outcome of the verb in the dependent clause has not materialized even though the verb in the independent clause is in the past).

a. Se lo presto para que lo lea.

Se lo presté para que lo leyera.

b. Ud. lo puede usar hasta que yo vuelva.

Ud. lo podía usar hasta que yo volviera.

c. Se lo traigo para que Ud. lo vea.

   Se lo traje para que Ud. lo viera.

Notice that in Group B at the time of the action of the independent clause the outcome of the dependent clause has not yet materialized.

Impersonal expressions that require subjunctive in the present tense have to be changed to imperfect subjunctive when the sentence is changed to the past.

Es importante que lo hagamos.

Era importante que lo hiciéramos.

Es imposible que él nos vea hoy.

Era imposible que él nos viera hoy.

Es natural que ellos no quieran ir.

Era natural que ellos no quisieran ir.

III. Por and Para

Por is used to express the following:

1. Through

Vamos por el jardín.	- We go through the garden.
Pasamos por aquí ayer.	- We passed through here yesterday.
El gato salió por la ventana.	- The cat left through the window.

2. Duration

Pararon allí por una semana.	- They stopped there for a week.
Comí aquí por un mes.	- I ate here for a month.
Vine a verte por un rato.	- I came to see you for a while.

3. In exchange for

Pagué dos dólares por el pan.	- I paid two dollars for the bread.
No me dió nada por el libro.	- He did not give me anything for the book.
Se lo di por un dólar.	- I gave it to him for a dollar.

4. By means of

Lo mandé por correo.	- I sent it by mail.
Voy por avión.	- I am going by plane.
El no quiere ir por tren.	- He doesn't want to go by train.

5. In quest of

Voy por las medicinas.	- I am going for the medicines.
Venimos por el dinero.	- We come for the money.
Volvemos por tí luego.	- We are coming for you later.

6. Agent[2]

Fué escrito por Cervantes.	- It is written by Cervantes.
La puerta fue abierta por Juan.	- The door was opened by John.
Fue hecho por él.	- It was done by him.

7. For the sake of

Ella lo hizo por mí.	- She did it for me.
Compré el juguete por el niño.	- I bought the toy for the baby. (for his sake)
Lo hago por tí.	- I'm doing it for you.

8. Comparison of equality

Por ser tan viejo no tiene dientes.	- Because he is so old he doesn't have teeth.
Está gordo por comer tanto.	- He is fat, because he eats too much.

---

[2]For an explanation of this construction (passive voice) see Lección Treinta y Cinco.

Para is used to express the following:

1. Purpose, intended for

La mesa es para la sala. -The table is for the leaving
                          room.
Compré cereal para el   - I bought cereal for breakfast.
desayuno.
Compré juguetes para el - I bought toys for the baby.
niño.   (intended for him)
¿Para quién son?   - For whom are they?

2. Toward, direction

Fueron para la playa.   - They went to the beach.
Salen para México hoy. - They leave for Mexico today.
Voy para la clase de   - I am going to the Spanish
español.   class.

3. Future time (by)

La composición es para - The composition is for Tuesday.
el martes.
El profesor la necesita - The professor needs it for
para mañana.   (by) tomorrow.
Te lo daré para mañana. - I'll give it to you by tomorrow.

Idioms with por and para

Idioms (expressions) with por and para are used
frequently in Spanish. The most common are:

Estar por   - To be about to

Estar para   - To be ready to

Por la mañana   - In the morning

Por la tarde   - In the afternoon

Por la noche   - At night, in the evening

Por el día   - During the day

Estoy por ir a verlo   - I'm about to go to see him.

Estoy para salir.   - I'm ready to leave.

Estudio por la mañana. - I study in the morning.

Trabajo por la tarde. - I work in the afternoon.

Miro televisión por la - I watch TV in the evening.
noche.

Por el día estoy muy   - During the day I'm very busy.
ocupado.

VOCABULARIO

NOUNS

arquitecto (a)	—	architect
comisión	—	commission
credencial (f)	—	credential
cuerpo (m)	—	body
dato (m)	—	data, information
entrega (f)	—	delivery
entrevista (f)	—	interview
firma (f)	—	firm, business
idioma (m)	—	language
información (f)	—	information
jefe (a)	—	manager, chief
planilla (f)	—	application, form
puesto (m)	—	job, position
remuneración (f)	—	remuneration
requisito (m)	—	requisite, requirement
Roma	—	Rome
solicitante (m&f)	—	applicant
solicitud (f)	—	application, form
venta (f)	—	sale

VERBS

andar	—	to move along
anotar	—	to take notes, to comment
incluir	—	include
llenar	—	to fill
parar	—	to stop
proteger	—	to protect
traducir	—	to translate
tratarse de	—	to deal with
usar	—	to use, to wear

EXPRESSIONS

de acuerdo	—	in agreement
estar por + infinitive	—	to be about to
estar para + infinitive	—	to be ready to

ADJECTIVES

considerable	—	considerable
diplomático	—	diplomatic
magnífico	—	fine, magnificent
probable	—	probable

EJERCICIOS

1. Supply the correct form of the imperfect.

a. Esperaba que yo lo _____ (traer)

   tú lo _____ (ver)

   nosotros lo _____ (hacer)

   Ud. lo _____ (oír)

b. Mandó que yo la _____ (leer)

   él _____ (decir)

   Uds. _____ (parar)

   nosotros _____ (pagar)

c. Temía que tú lo _____ aquí (poner)

   ella lo _____ (dejar)

   nosotros lo _____ (estudiar)

   ellas lo _____ (querer)

d. Buscaba un libro que ____ las respuestas (tener)

   _____ (dar)

   _____ (traer)

   _____ (incluir)

e. No creían que la mesa _____ allí (caber)

   _____ (venir)

   _____ (estar)

   _____ (entrar)

2. Complete the following sentences to agree with the new tense given.

a. Le traeré las fotos para que las vea.

   Le traje _____

b. ¿Cuándo quieres que José venga?

   ¿Cuándo querías _____?

c. Pídale a Carmen que lo traiga.

   Le pidió _____

d. Traigo el disco para que lo oigan.

   Traje _____

e. Esperan que su hermano vea al médico hoy.

   Esperaban _____

f. Buscan una casa que tenga cuatro habitaciones.

   Buscaban _____

g. No hay nadie que pueda ir hoy.

   No había _____

h. No creo que ella lo crea.

   No creía _____

i. Dudo que tengan el trabajo listo.

   Dudaba _____

j. Insiste en que lo lleve al cine.

   Insistió _____

3. **Fill in the blanks with the correct form of the indicative or subjunctive.**

a. El medico quería que yo lo _____ el lunes.
   ver

b. Esperaba que nosotros _____ temprano.
   volver

c. Quiere ver a la secretaria que _____ francés.
   hablar

d. Volvió cuando _____.
   poder

e. Era un hecho que ella _____ ayer.
   venir

f. No creía que Carlos _____ aquí.
   estar

g. Le pedí que _____ la guitarra.
   traer

h. No lo vi hasta que Juana _____.
   llegar

i. Esperaba que Lola _____ venir.
   poder

j. Temíamos que tú _____ enferma.
   estar

k. Preferían que yo lo _____.
   hacer

l. Lo compré cuando ellas me _____.
   pagar

m. Esperábamos que él _____ la casa.
   comprar

n. Me pidió que le_____.
   pagar

o. Era probable que Lucía_____.
   ir

p. Era imposible que tú lo_____.
   oír

4. **Supply the correct form of _por_ and _para_.**

a. Esos quesos son _____ Laura.

b. Las flores llegan _____ mañana.

c. Voy _____ vino _____ la fiesta.

d. Vivieron en Londres _____ un año.

e. Me dio naranjas _____ las fresas.

f. Lo mandé _____ entrega especial.

g. Compré las papas _____ la sopa.

h. ¿Es eso _____ mí o _____ ti?

i. Llegará _____ las cuatro o _____ las cinco.

5. **Translate into Spanish (por and para).**

a. They went to Rome for a month.

   _____

b. She sold it for one hundred dollars.

_____

c. We bought them for the dining room.

_____

d. Carlos sent it by mail

_____

e. Have you (fam.) studied the lesson for today?

_____

f. What is that money for?

_____

g. They had traveled through Spain.

_____

h. Give me milk for the dog.

_____

i. I am about to eat an apple.

_____

j. She always calls him during the day.

_____

6. **Answer the following questions based on the conversation.**

a. ¿Qué hace Alejandro en la oficina del Sr. Duarte?

_____

b. ¿Dónde estaba el Sr. Duarte cuando Alejandro llegó a su oficina?

_____

c. ¿Dónde aprendió Alejandro varios idiomas?

_____

d. ¿Qué falta en la planilla?

_____

e. ¿Qué puesto busca el solicitante?

_____

f. ¿Por qué Alejandro no informó que sabía francés?

_____

g. ¿Por qué Alejandro no puede empezar a trabajar en seguida?

_____

h. ¿Por qué Alejandro llenó la planilla antes de ir a la entrevista?

_____

i. ¿Por qué Alejandro tendrá que esperar?

_____

j. ¿Cree Ud. que Alejandro esté de acuerdo con la remuneración?

Sí, creo_____

No, no creo_____

7. **Organize the following words into meaningful expressions:**

a.
en
puedo
servirle
qué
¿   ?

b.
Sr.
llenara
una
que
el
planilla
Duarte
sugirió

c.
necesitaba
que
francés
alguien
supiera
firma
la

d.
para
que
llamó
decir
estaba
junta
en
y
una
para
que
pedirle
esperara
lo

LECCIÓN TREINTA Y CINCO

TOPICS: PRESENT PERFECT SUBJUNCTIVE, THE TRUE PASSIVE VOICE, THE REFLEXIVE CONSTRUCTION TO EXPRESS PASSIVE VOICE, COMPARISONS OF ADJECTIVES, THE USE OF THAN, IRREGULAR COMPARISONS OF ADJECTIVES AND ADVERBS, THE ABSOLUTE SUPERLATIVE, EQUAL COMPARISONS

CONVERSATION XXXI

	EN LA GALERÍA DE BELLAS ARTES		AT THE FINE ARTS GALLERY
1.	Joaquín: ¿Qué podemos hacer esta tarde? Quiero hacer algo que no haya hecho últimamente.	- Joaquin:	What can we do this afternoon? I want to do something that I haven't done lately.
2.	Hortensia: Tenemos una selección formidable. ¿No has leído el periódico todavía?	- Hortensia:	We have a lot to choose from. Haven't you read the paper yet?
3.	Joaquín: No, se lo di a Guillermo para que lo leyera primero. Espero que lo haya leído.	- Joaquin:	No, I gave it to Guillermo so that he would read it first. I hope he has read it.
4.	Guillermo: Aquí tienes el periódico, Joaquín. Mira la crítica de la exposición de Bellas Artes, es muy buena.	- Guillermo:	Here is the paper, Joaquin. Notice the review of the Fine Arts Exhibition, it is very good.
5.	Hortensia: A propósito, le hablé a Joaquín de ella. ¿Qué te parece si vamos?	- Hortensia:	By the way, I spoke to Joaquin about it. How do you feel about going?
6.	Guillermo: Si Uds. van, me gustaría ir yo también. Ahora tengo que salir.	- Guillermo:	If you are going, I would like to go also. Now I have to go out.
7.	Joaquín: Magnífico. Regresa antes de las tres para que podamos salir temprano.		Joaquin: Great. Come back before three so we can leave early.

	MÁS TARDE EN LA GALERÍA DE BELLAS ARTES		LATER AT THE FINE ARTS GALLERY
8.	Hortensia: Me gustaría que vieran las esculturas de Carbonell. Nunca me imaginé que fueran tan bellas.	- Hortensia:	I would like you to see Carbonell's sculptures. I never imagined they were so beautiful.
9.	Joaquín: Vamos ahora, y después querría que vieran los óleos de Roselló.	- Joaquin:	Let's go now, and later I would like you to see Rosello's oil paintings.
10.	Hortensia: ¿No es ése el joven pintor que expone aquí por primera vez. Están aquí mismo.	- Hortensia:	Isn't he the young painter that is exhibiting here for the first time. They are right here.
11.	Guillermo: Entonces vamos a verlos ahora y después vemos las esculturas.	- Guillermo:	Then let's go to see them now and later we'll see the sculptures.
12.	Joaquín: ¿Ven cómo se destaca el estilo propio del artista?	- Joaquin:	Do you see how the artist projects his very own style.
13.	Hortensia: Es difícil encontrar palabras para describirlo.	- Hortensia:	It is difficult to find words to describe it.
14.	Guillermo: Vamos a las esculturas ahora. ¿Dónde están?	- Guillermo:	Let's see the sculptures now. Where are they?
15.	Hortensia: Al otro lado. Vengan conmigo. Espero que no hayan cerrado esa sección.	- Hortensia:	On the other side. Come with me. I hope they haven't closed that area.

I. The Present Perfect Subjunctive

The present perfect subjunctive is formed by the present subjunctive of the verb <u>haber</u> and the past participle.

Comparison of the present perfect indicative and the present perfect subjunctive forms.

	Llegar Present Perfect Indicative	Present Perfect Subjunctive
Yo	he llegado	haya llegado
Tú	has llegado	hayas llegado
Ud., él, ella	ha llegado	haya llegado
Nosotros/as	hemos llegado	hayamos llegado
Uds., ellos, ellas	han llegado	hayan llegado

If the dependent clause, noun, adjectival or adverbial, calls for the subjunctive, the present perfect subjunctive is required when the verb in the independent clause is in the present tense or command and the verb in the dependent clause represents an action or idea that has taken place already.

Examples:

Espero que hayan venido.   - I hope that they have come.

Busco una secretaria que haya vivido en Francia.   - I'm looking for a secretary who has lived in France.

Mándeme al estudiante después que haya tomado el examen.   - Send me the student after he has taken the exam.

La llamaremos después que ella haya ido al médico.- I'll call her after she has gone to the doctor.

Notice that in the first sentence the speaker hopes that they have already come, in the second sentence the speaker is looking for someone who has lived in France, and in the third one the speaker will not call until she has arrived.

II. The True Passive Voice

The passive voice in Spanish is formed as in English:

Subject + to be + past participle + by + agent

The house was built by James.	La casa fue construída por Jaime.
Quixote was written by Cervantes.	El Quijote fué escrito por Cervantes.
Many have been eaten by the lions.	Muchos han sido comidos por los leones.
The President will be honored by the Senate.	El Presidente será honrado por el Senado.

The true passive voice is used only when the agent or doer is present as in the above sentences, or strongly implied as in the following sentences:

Quixote was written in the 17th Century.	El Quijote fué escrito en el siglo diecisiete.
Your sister will be invited also.	Tu hermana será invitada también.

A word of caution: Spanish seldom uses the true passive voice, it is considered a very weak form of expression. In English, it is more widely used.

III. The Reflexive Construction to Express Passive Voice

Spanish prefers an alternate form to the true passive which is expressed by a reflexive construction when the agent (doer) is not important and the subject is a thing.

Este edificio se construyó año pasado.	This building was built last year.
Se terminó el trabajo ayer.	The work was finished yesterday.
Se dice que él es muy rico.	It is said that he is very rich.

IV. Comparisons of Adjectives

When comparing adjectives in English, we say "tall", "taller", "tallest", "expensive", "more (less) expensive", "most (least) expensive". In Spanish we use más meaning "more", "most" and menos meaning "less", "least."

Alberto es más alto.	Albert is taller.
Alberto es el más alto.	Albert is the tallest.
Laura es más bonita.	Laura is prettier.
Laura es la más bonita.	Laura is the prettiest.
Estos son menos caros.	These are less expensive.
Esta es la menos cara.	This one is the least expensive.
Roberto es el más inteligente de la clase.[1]	Robert is the most intelligent in the class.
Pedro es más listo.	Peter is smarter.

V. The Use of "Than"

"Than" is translated by que before nouns and pronouns, but before numerals it is translated by de.

---

[1]Such expressions as "in the class" in English are translated by de la clase in Spanish after a superlative. Thus, Elena es la más bella de la familia = Elena is the most beautiful in the family.

Pedro es más alto que
Daniel.

- Peter is taller than
Daniel.

No tenemos más de diez
dólares.

- We don't have more than
ten dollars.

Este cuesta menos de
un dólar.

- This one cost less than
one dollar.

Tengo más que tú.

- I have more than you.

Que is used before a number in the following
situation:

No tiene más que diez
dólares.[2]

- He has only ten dollars.

No tiene más de diez
dólares.

- He doesn't have more than
ten dollars.

VI. Irregular Comparisons of Adjectives and Adverbs

Adjectives:

bueno   (el) mejor[3] (los) mejores - good, better, best
grande (el) mayor[4] (el) más grande - large, greater,
                                   greatest, older,
                                   oldest
malo   (el) peor[3] (los) peores - bad, worse, worst
pequeño (el) menor[4] (el) más pequeño - small, younger,
                                   youngest

Adverbs:

bien   mejor - well, better, best
mal   peor - badly, worse, worst
mucho más - much, more, most
poco   menos - little, less, least

Examples of irregular comparisons of adjectives:

Este libro es mejor que
el tuyo.

- This book is better than
yours.

Ella es mayor que él.

- She is older than he.

Éste es el peor.

- This one is the worst.

Éste es peor.

- This one is worse.

Pepe es su hermano
menor.

- Pepe is his younger
brother.

Ésta es la peor clase.

- This is the worst class.

Examples of irregular comparisons of adverbs:

Ella juega mejor que
él.

- She plays better than him.

Hacen menos ahora.

- They do less now.

Quiero el mejor, no
el peor.

- I want the best one not
the worst one.

III. The Absolute Superlative

Spanish has two different forms to express the absolute
superlative. It can be formed by muy before an adjective or an adverb, or by attaching - ísimo (-a, os, as)
to it. If the adjective or adverb ends in a vowel, the
vowel is dropped before adding -isimo.

Una casa muy grande.

A very big house.

Una casa grandísima

---

[2]Note the difference in meaning of the two sentences.
[3]Mejor & peor precede the noun they modify.
[4]Mayor & menor follow the noun they modify.

Una lección muy fácil.
                    -A very easy lesson.
Una lección facilísima.

Un hombre muy rico.[5]
                    -A very rich man.
Un hombre riquísimo.

Una pareja muy feliz.[5]
                    -A very happy couple.
Una pareja felicísima.

Una lección muy larga.
                    -A very long lesson.
Una lección larguísima.

VII. **Equal Comparisons**

Tanto (a, os, as)...como = As much (as many)... as

No tengo tanta suerte como tú. - I don't have as much luck
                                  as you.

Trajo tantas naranjas como Juan. - He brought as many
                                   oranges as John.

Tan + adjective or adverb + como = as ... as

Ella es tan lista como él.   - She is as smart as he.

Estas son tan buenas como ésas. - These are as good as those.

---

[5]Adjectives ending in -co, -go and -z change to qu, gu and c respectively.

VOCABULARIO

NOUNS

artista (m&f)	-	artist
Bellas Artes (f)	-	Fine Arts
caballo (m)	-	horse
carrera (f)	-	race
circo (m)	-	circus
crítica (f)	-	review, critique
escultura (f)	-	sculpture
edificio (m)	-	building
exposición (f)	-	exhibit
galería (f)	-	gallery
gusto (m)	-	taste
león (a)	-	lion
novela (f)	-	novel
óleo (m)	-	canvas, oil painting
paciencia (f)	-	patience
pintor (a)	-	painter
presidente (a)	-	president
pueblo (m)	-	town, people
sección (f)	-	section
senado (m)	-	senate

ADJECTIVES

honrado	-	honored, honest
largo	-	long
menor	-	younger, youngest
propio	-	own
rico	-	rich
tanto (a,os,as) ...como	-	as much (as many)...as
tan + adjective or adverb + como	-	as...as

ADVERBS

lentamente	-	slowly
últimamente	-	lately

VERBS

apreciar	-	to apreciate
construir	-	to build
describir	-	to describe
destacarse	-	to stand out
exhibir	-	to exhibit
exponer	-	to exhibit
imaginarse	-	to imagine

EXPRESSIONS

a propósito	-	by the way
¡Qué lastima!	-	What a shame!
Así es	-	true

1. **Change the following present perfect indicative verbs to present perfect subjunctive.**

    a. hemos oído   _____

    b. has visto   _____

    c. ha escrito   _____

    d. ha vuelto   _____

    e. han roto   _____

2. **Supply the present perfect subjunctive and translate the sentences into English.**

    a. Véalos después que_____al banco.
    　　　　　　　　　　　　　　　ir

    _____

    b. No creo que ellas lo_____ahí.
    　　　　　　　　　　　　　　　poner

    _____

    c. Espero que Isabel me_____.
    　　　　　　　　　　　　　　escribir

    _____

    d. Dáselo a ellas después que él lo_____.
    　　　　　　　　　　　　　　　　　　leer

    _____

    e. No creo que ella se lo_____todavía.
    　　　　　　　　　　　　　　decir

3. **Translate the following sentences.**

    a. I do not believe that she has done it.

    _____

    _____

    b. We hope she has arrived on time for the flight.

    _____

    _____

    c. Send me the book after you have read it. (formal)

    _____

    _____

    d. It is possible that they have seen it.

    _____

    _____

    e. They know that we have brought the medicine.

    _____

    _____

    f. I don't see why they haven't told him the truth.

    _____

    _____

g. It is a fact that he has not returned yet.

_____

_____

h. They believe that Carmen and I have finished.

_____

_____

4. **Fill in the blanks with the correct form of the present perfect indicative or present perfect subjunctive.**

a. Me alegro de que Uds._____al
                                ir

parque.

b. Busco una secretaria que_____
                              trabajar

con médicos.

c. No creemos que ellos_____temprano.
                          llegar

d. No veo por qué ellas no_____todavía.
                         venir

e. Estoy seguro que Carlos no_____el
                        terminar

trabajo.

f. Ella no sabe que yo le_____los discos.
                      traer

g. Mándame las fotos cuando las_____.
                      ver

h. Ellos dicen que no _____la novela.
                     leer

i. Espero que Pedro le_____a su tío.
                     escribir

j. Es posible que Víctor le_____la
                     dar

noticia.

k. No creo que tú_____esa canción.
                     oir

5. **Answer the following questions in complete sentences based on the conversation.**

a. ¿Quién ha leído el periódico temprano?

_____

b. ¿Quién le habló a Joaquín de la exposición?

_____

c. ¿Quién debe regresar temprano?

_____

d. ¿De quién son los óleos?

_____

e. ¿Por qué van a ver primero los óleos?

_____

f. ¿Quiénes leyeron el periódico primero?

_____

g. ¿Cuál de los tres parece apreciar más la exposición?

_____

h. Cómo se dice "Fine Arts" in Spanish?

_____

i. ¿Dónde están las esculturas?

_____

j. ¿Cree Ud. que les haya gustado la exposición?

Sí, _____

6. **Organize the following words into meaningful expressions.**

a.	ver	b.	Si	c.	esculturas	d.	vuelve
	no		me		volver		para
	algo		Uds.		que		que
	haya		gustaría		después		antes
	que		también		visto		vayamos
	visto		vienen		hayamos		de
	antes		ir		las		temprano
	quiero		temprano		podemos		las
							diez

a. _____

b. _____

c. _____

d. _____

7. **Change the following sentences to the passive voice.**

a. Rómulo construyó Roma.

_____

b. El agente firmó la carta.

_____

c. El pueblo quiere al presidente.

_____

d. Cervantes escribió El Quijote.

_____

e. Mi hermano pagó ese libro.

_____

f. El senado honrará al presidente.

_____

g. Los muchachos cortarán el árbol.

_____

8. Answer the following questions.

a. ¿Cuándo se teminaron las clases?

_____ (the fifth)

b. ¿A qué hora se come aquí?

_____ (8 P.M.)

c. ¿A qué hora se abren las tiendas?

_____ (9 A.M.)

d. ¿Qué se necesita para la fiesta?

_____ (money)

9. Translate into Spanish using the reflexive construction.

a. The doors are closed at six.

_____

b. Many tall buildings are seen here.

_____

c. Much patience is needed.

_____

d. When was it written?

_____

e. It is said that she is very rich.

_____

f. The book was written in 1900.

_____

g. This building was sold last year.

_____

10. Supply the correct form.

a. Esta casa es_____
the best

b. Estas son_____que las otras.
worse

c. Este libro es_____que ése.
better

d. Ella está_____hoy.
better

e. Ella es _____.
the best

f. Juegas_____que yo.
better

g. She is the_____.
oldest

h. She is_____.
older

11. **Translate into Spanish.**

   a. She is the youngest of my brother's children.

   _____

   b. I want the best, not the worst. (fem.)

   _____

   c. Which is bigger, Mexico City or Buenos Aires?

   _____

   d. Peter is her younger brother.

   _____

   e. Her brother is older than she.

   _____

   f. His car is better than mine.

   _____

   g. He has more than half.

   _____

   h. That hotel is less expensive than this one.

   _____

   i. I only have three.   (use <u>que</u>)

   _____

   j. This lesson is more difficult.

   _____

12. **Supply the correct form of <u>tanto (a, os, as)...como</u>.**

   a. Terminó_____ejercicios_____yo.

   b. Tenía_____dinero_____ella.

   c. Había_____hombres_____mujeres.

   d. Compré_____peras_____mi hermana.

13. **Supply the correct form of <u>tan ... como</u>.**

   a. Tu padre es_____viejo_____el mío.

   b. Ellas no son_____altas_____Ana.

   c. Mis trajes no son_____caros_____los de Juan.

   d. Esta lección es_____fácil_____aquélla.

14. **Translate the following superlatives two different ways.**

   a. He is very tall.

   _____

   _____

   b. Raquel is very happy.   (Use the adjective contento).

   _____

   _____

   c. Those men are very rich.

   _____

   _____

d. The bread is very expensive.

    _____

    _____

e. Their brother is very intelligent.

    _____

    _____

f. Those lessons are very long.

    _____

    _____

LECCIÓN TREINTA Y SEIS

TOPICS: THE IF-CLAUSES, SUBJUNCTIVE IN THE IF-CLAUSE CONTRARY TO FACT, USES OF THE DEFINITE ARTICLE

CONVERSATION XXXII

	EN UNA FIESTA			AT A PARTY
1. Gloria:	Hola, Mariana. ¿Cómo estás? ¿Viniste sola?	–	Gloria:	Hello, Mariana. How are you? Did you come alone?
2. Mariana:	Sí, quería que Pedro viniera conmigo, pero tuvo que ir a Toronto. Le pidieron que asistiera a una junta.	–	Mariana:	Yes, I wanted Pedro to come with me, but he had to go to Toronto. They asked him to attend a conference.
3. Gloria:	¡Qué pena! Si no hubiera ido, habría podido estar aquí con nosotras. El es tan simpático, siempre es el alma de las fiestas.	–	Gloria:	What a shame! If he hadn't gone, he could have been here with us. He is so nice, he is always the life of the party.
4. Mariana:	Esperaba que no lo mandaran, pero no había nadie más en la oficina que pudiera ir.	–	Mariana:	He hoped that they wouldn't send him, but there was no one else in the office who could go.
5. Gloria:	Pedro es tan complaciente que acepta con una sonrisa cualquier tarea que le asignen. El trabajo para él es un placer.	–	Gloria:	Pedro is so agreeable that he accepts with a smile any task they assign him. For him, work is a pleasure.
6. Mariana:	Así es. Me dijo que si tuvieras otra fiesta pronto, vendría con mucho gusto.	–	Mariana:	True. He told me that if you had another party soon, he'd be glad to come.
7. Gloria:	Creo que conoces a todo el mundo aquí esta noche.	–	Gloria:	I think you know everybody here tonight.
8. Mariana:	Creo que sí, excepto tu prima de Guadalajara. Recuerda que me dijiste que si yo viniera, la conocería.	–	Mariana:	I think so, except for your cousin from Guadalajara. Remember you told me that if I came, I would meet her.
9. Gloria:	Sí, es verdad. Ven conmigo. Te va a agradar mucho, es muy vivaracha.	–	Gloria:	Yes, it is true. Come with me. You'll like her a lot. She is very vivacious.
10. Mariana:	¿Cuánto tiempo va a estar aquí tu prima?	–	Mariana:	How long is your cousin going to stay here?
11. Gloria:	Regresa el lunes. Si se hubiera quedado más tiempo, habría podido conocer a Pedro también.	–	Gloria:	She returns on Monday. If she had stayed longer, she could have met Pedro too.
12. Mariana:	Mira. Allí está ella. Ven.	–	Mariana:	There she is. Come on.

I. The If-Clauses

There are two different types of "if-clauses" (a) the condition of the "if-clause" may actually become a reality, and (b) the condition of the "if clause falls outside the realm of reality.

In any clause with <u>si</u>, "if", the verb is in the indicative if the condition expressed in the <u>si-clause</u> may actually become a reality.

a. Si estudio, paso — If I study, I will pass
   el examen.   the exam.

b. Si tengo el dinero — If I have the money,
   iré a Europe.   I'll go to Europe.

c. Si vuelves temprano,— If you return early,
   puedes terminar el   you will be able to
   trabajo.   finish the work.

d. Si me pagan bien, — If they pay me well,
   acepto el empleo.   I'll accept the job.

e. Si tú vas, yo voy. — If you go, I will go.

II. Subjunctive in the "If-Clause" Contrary to Fact

If the "if-clause" is contrary to fact, it falls outside the realm of reality. If the condition of the "if-clause" is in the present, it requires the use of the imperfect subjunctive in the "if-clause" and the conditional in the result clause.

If we turn the five previous examples of if-clauses into contrary to fact, we will have the following:

a. Si estudiara,   — If I studied, (were to
   pasaría el examen.   study), I would pass
                        the exam.

b. Si tuviera el dinero, — If I had the money, I
   iría a Europa.   would go to Europe.

c. Si volvieras temprano, — If you returned, (were
   podrías terminar el   to return) early, you
   trabajo.   would be able to finish
                            the work.

d. Si me pagaran bien, — If they paid (were to
   aceptaría el empleo.   pay) me well, I would
                          accept the work.

e. Si tú fueras, yo iría. — If you were to go, I
                            would go.

Notice that when the imperfect subjunctive is used in a contrary to fact clause, it indicates present time.

When the condition of the "if-clause" is in the past, it requires the pluperfect subjunctive in the if-clause and the conditional perfect in the independent clause. The forms of the pluperfect subjunctive are formed by the verb <u>haber</u> in the imperfect subjunctive plus the past participle, and the forms of the conditional perfect are formed by the conditional of the verb <u>haber</u>, plus the past participle.

	Pluperfect Subjunctive	Conditional Perfect
Yo	hubiera hablado	habría hablado
Tú	hubieras hablado	habrías hablado
Ud., él, ella	hubiera hablado	habría hablado
Nosotros/as	hubiéramos hablado	habríamos hablado
Uds., ellos ellas,	hubieran hablado	habrían hablado

a. Si hubieran ido,   - If they had gone, they
les habrían pagado.   would have paid them.

b. Si hubieras salido   - If you had left at six,
a las seis, habrías   you would have arrived
llegado a tiempo.   on time.

c. Lo habríamos hecho, - We would have done it, if
si hubiéramos tenido we had had the time.
tiempo.

Notice that with the "if-clause", the pluperfect subjunctive indicates past time.

III. Uses of the Definite Article

We have presented in previous lessons several different
uses of the definite article. This section will serve
as a review of what has already been studied plus new
uses.

I would like to emphasize the following general rule
for the use of the definite article in Spanish: The
definite article is generally used in Spanish before
every noun except when the meaning of "some" or "any"
is implied.

Although we just gave you a general rule, the following
specific rules will help you master the use of the
article in Spanish.

1. **In general, the definite article is used before
languages and other disciplines except after
<u>hablar</u>, <u>en</u> and <u>de</u>.**

El estudia el francés.[1] - He studies French.

Ella habla francés.   - She speaks French.

Lo entiendo mejor en   - I understand it better
portugués.   in Portuguese.

No entiendo la matemá- - I don't understand
tica.   math.

La lección de español - The Spanish lesson is
es fácil.   easy.

2. **With the Parts of the body and personal belong-
ings.**

Se lavó las manos.   - He washed his hands.

¿Dónde pusiste la   - Where did you put your
cartera?   wallet?

Tengo que lavar el   - I have to wash my car.
auto.

Me voy a poner el traje - I am going to wear my
blanco.   white suit.

3. **With abstract nouns and nouns used in a general
sense.**

Así es la vida.   - That's life.

Los hombres luchan por la - Men fight for freedom.
libertad.

El café es negro.   - Coffee is black.

El oro es un metal.   - Gold is a metal.

El invierno es frío aquí. - Winters are cold here.

4. **With titles, except in direct address.**

El Sr. Blanco está aquí. - Mr. Blanco is here.

Sr. Blanco, pase, por   - Mr. Blanco, please,
favor.   come in.

---

[1]With languages the definite article is often omitted.

El capitán Díaz no ha   - Captain Diaz hasn't arrived.
llegado.

5. **With weight and measure.**

Cuesta diez dólares la - It cost ten dollars a yard.
yarda.

Los vende por un dólar - He sells them for one dollar
la docena.   a dozen.

Este pan cuesta dos   - This bread cost two dollars
dólares la libra.   a pound.

VOCABULARIO

N O U N S

alma (f)	-	soul
católico (a)	-	Catholic
dentista (m&f)	-	dentist
dieta (f)	-	diet
docena (f)	-	dozen
empleo (m)	-	job
joya (f)	-	jewel
junta (f0	-	meeting, conference
lavadora (f)	-	washing machine
matemática (f)	-	mathematics
metal (m)	-	metal
placer	-	pleasure
sonrisa (f)	-	smile
yarda (f)	-	yard

A D J E C T I V E S

complaciente	-	pleasing
vivaracha	-	full of life

A D V E R B S

así	-	that way

V E R B S

aceptar	-	to accept
agradar	-	to please
asignar	-	to assign
luchar	-	to fight

E X P R E S S I O N S

bajar de peso	-	to lose weight
por lo menos	-	at least

1. Change the following "if-clause" to contrary to fact. Make other necessary changes. Use both imperfect subjunctive/conditional and pluperfect subjunctive/conditional perfect construction.

   a. Si puedo ir a la fiesta, iré con Teresa.

   _____

   _____

   b. Si el médico me ve hoy, no podré venir a trabajar esta tarde.

   _____

   _____

   c. Si abren la tienda el domingo, iré a ver la lavadora.

   _____

   _____

   d. Si se siente bien, irá al concierto.

   _____

   _____

   e. Si llamas al dentista, te dará un turno.

   _____

   _____

   f. Si quieres bajar de peso, sigue una dieta.

   _____

   _____

   g. Si ellos se van temprano, podrán regresar hoy.

   _____

   _____

2. Translate the following sentences into Spanish.

   a. If I see them today, I'll tell them.

   _____

   _____

   b. If I had the money, I would buy it.

   _____

   _____

   c. If I were he, I would go. (familiar)

   _____

   _____

   d. If I buy it today, they will send it on Monday.

   _____

e. Had I bought it today, they would have sent it on Monday.

_____

_____

f. If I had gone, I would have seen them.

_____

_____

g. If they had not talked to that lady, what would they have done?

_____

_____

h. If he pays me today, I'll pay you. (familiar)

_____

_____

i. Had he paid me today, I'd have paid you. (formal)

_____

_____

j. If he paid me today, I would pay you. (familiar)

_____

_____

k. If I were to sell the car, they would buy it.

_____

_____

l. If he has the car, they will leave at five P.M.

_____

_____

m. If I had seen him before, I would have told him.

_____

_____

n. I would have helped her, if I had known it.

_____

_____

o. We would have paid, if we had had the money.

_____

_____

p. If they had called me, I would have gone to see them.

_____

_____

3. Answer the following questions in Spanish using the cue:

a. ¿Cuánto cuestan los huevos?

_____($1.00 a dozen)

b. ¿Quién es él?

_____(Mr. Toledo)

-318-

c. ¿Qué te lavas?

_____ (face)

d. ¿Qué idiomas hablas?

_____ (French only)

4. **Translate into Spanish.**

   a. Books are necessary.

   _____

   b. Dr. Jaramillo, do you have one?

   _____

   c. Dr. Jaramillo has two.

   _____

   d. Metals are used every day.

   _____

   e. He is going to wash his car.

   _____

   f. Do they speak Spanish?

   _____

   g. Tell Mr. Perez that I am waiting for him.

   _____

h. Jewels are expensive.

_____

i. French is as important as German.

_____

5. **Answer the following questions based on the conversation:**

   a. ¿A quién no conoce Mariana?

   _____

   b. ¿Por qué Pedro tiene que viajar a Toronto?

   _____

   c. ¿Por qué mandaron a Pedro y no a otra persona a Toronto?

   _____

   d. ¿Conoce Gloria a todo el mundo en la fiesta?

   _____

   e. ¿Con quién vino Mariana?

   _____

6. **Choose the correct answer.**

   a. Mariana quería que Pedro viniera con ella a

      1. Toronto

      2. la fiesta

      3. conocer a unas amigas suyas

b. Pedro cree que

    1. las fiestas son más importante que le trabajo.

    2. no va a tener que ir a Toronto.

    3. Debe aceptar cualquier tarea que le asignen.

c. Pedro vendrá

    1. a la fiesta que Mariana dará la semana proxima.

    2. a la fiesta que Mariana dará el mes próximo.

    3. a otra fiesta que Gloria dé.

d. Pedro es

    1. de Guadalajara

    2. primo de Gloria

    3. el alma de las fiestas.

e. Mariana quería que Pedro

    1. fuera a Toronto.

    2. viniera con ella.

    3. fuera a México.

f. Mariana conoce a

    1. la prima de Guadalajara.

    2. Gloria

    3. a todas las personas que están en la fiesta.

7. **Translate the following sentences into Spanish.**

a. There was no one else in the office that could go.

_____

_____

b. Remember that you told me that if he came, I would meet him.

_____

_____

c. I want Pedro to come with me.

_____

d. He is the life of the party.

_____

e. If it had not been for him, nobody would have have gone to Toronto.

_____

_____

f. Had she stayed longer, she would have met Pedro.

_____

_____

g. I believe you know everybody here tonight.

_____

_____

h.   How long is she going to be here?

_____

i.   If he had not gone, he would have been
able to come.

_____

_____

j.   He accepts willingly (with a smile) any
task he might be assigned.

_____

_____

1. 1. f. ¿Dónde está el sombrero?
    2. e. ¿Qué desea (Ud)?
    3. d. ¿Dónde están los cinturones?
    4. b. ¿Cuántas camisas desea (Ud.)?
    5. a. ¿Cómo está (Ud.)?
    6. c. ¿Por qué habla español (Ud.)?

2. a. una bufanda
    b. un empleado
    c. un chico
    d. una corbata
    e. un cinturón
    f. unos empleados
    g. una cartera
    h. unas chicas

3. a. un cinturón
    b. unos chicos
    c. una corbata
    d. una empleada
    e. unos amigos
    f. unos pantalones
    g. unas empleadas
    h. una cartera
    i. unas medias

4. a. blancas
    b. negras
    c. verdes
    d. blancos

5. a. 5 - cinco
    b. 8 - ocho
    c. 4 - cuatro
    d. 3 - tres
    e. 7 - siete
    f. 2 - dos
    g. 6 - seis
    h. 10 - diez
    i. 9 - nueve
    j. 1 - uno

6. a. ¿Por qué habla español ella?
       ¿Qué desea?
    b. ¿Dónde está él?
       ¿Cuántos pañuelos desea?

1. a. el   f. la
    b. el   g. los
    c. la   h. el
    d. la   i. la
    e. los   j. el

2. a. el
    b. la
    c. el
    d. los
    e. Los

3. a. ¿Dónde están los
    b. ¿Cuánto cuesta la
    c. ¿Cómo está
    d. ¿Dónde están los
    e. ¿Cuánto cuestan las

4. a. Las - blancas cuestan ocho dólares
    b. Las blusas - cuestan ocho dólares
    c. Las blusas verdes cuestan - dólares
    d. Los - verdes cuestan siete dólares
    e. Los guantes - cuestan siete dólares
    f. Los guantes azules cuestan - dólares
    g. Las - azules cuestan diez dólares
    h. Las corbatas - cuestan diez dólares
    i. Las corbatas amarillas cuestan - dólares

5. a. ¿Por qué está la empleada aquí?
    b. ¿Dónde están los amigos?
    c. El empleado está en la tienda.
    d. Buenos días. ¿Cómo está él?
    e. Está muy bien, gracias.

6. a. Buenas tardes. ¿Cómo está?
    b. ¿Dónde está el empleado?
    c. ¿Quién es el empleado?
    d. Estoy aquí.
    e. ¿Cómo está Roberto?
    f. Estoy muy bien.

7. a. Aquí está el sombrero.
    b. ¿Qué desea él?
    c. Estoy en la tienda.
    d. Estás muy bien.
    e. ¿Quién es él?
    f. ¿Quiénes son ellos?

1. a. Bien. Aquí está.
      El blanco es muy bonito.
   b. ¿Qué talla usa Ud.?
      La diez.
      Aquí la tiene.
      ¿Dónde está el probador?

2. a. están
   b. está
   c. está
   d. están
   e. estamos
   f. estamos
   g. están

3. a. Ellas - están
   b. Nosotros/as - estamos
   c. Ellos - están
   d. Ellas - están
   e. Nosotros - estamos
   f. Ellos - están
   g. Nosotros/as - estamos
   h. Ellas - están
   i. Ellos - están
   j. Ellos - están

4. a. Estámos aquí
   b. Están bien.
   c. Estoy aquí.
   d. Estoy aquí.
   e. Estamos aquí.

5. a. Aquí no está el precio.
   b. Los trajes no son muy baratos.
   c. No quiero comprar una chaqueta.
   d. No puedo probarme los pantalones.
   e. La cliente no desea seis vestidos.
   f. Ud. no usa la talla doce.
   g. Aquí no están los zapatos.

6. a. diez y seis
   b. veinte y cuatro
   c. doce
   d. veinte y una
   e. catorce
   f. veinte y siete
   g. trece
   h. veinte
   i. quince
   j. diez y ocho

7. a. ¿Dónde está
   b. dónde - las empleadas
   c. están las empleadas?
   d. Cómo está
   e. Cómo-ustedes
   f. están ustedes?
   g. Dónde está
   h. Dónde - los vestidos

8. a. blusa
   b. chaqueta
   c. pantalones
   d. chaquetas
   e. falda
   f. vestido

9. a. Están en el departamento de ropa.
   b. No, ella desea una chaqueta y unos pantalones.
   c. Quiere una blusa.
   d. Sí, es barata. (or) No, no es barata.
   e. El vestido cuesta $18.25.

10. a. ¿Qué desea?
    b. Los rojos son bonitos.
    c. Allí.
    d. ¿Puedo probarme los pantalones?
    e. Aquí está.
    f. ¿Cuántas corbatas quiere?
    g. ¿Cuánto cuesta la billetera?

11. a. Cuánto - suéter
    b. Están allí.
    c. -
    d. cinturón
    e. ¿Cómo estás tú?

12. a. once
    b. trece
    c. doce
    d. diez y ocho
    e. catorce
    f. trece
    g. diez y nueve
    h. diez y siete
    i. veinte
    j. diez y seis

Lección Cuatro

1. a. ¿Dónde se compra?
   b. ¿Dónde se compran los libros?
   c. Se está bien aquí.
   d. Se paga en la caja.
   e. ¿Dónde se paga el impuesto?
   f. ¿Cómo se aprende español?
   g. ¿Cómo se practica español?
   h. Se vende una casa.
   i. Se habla español aquí.

2. a. veinte más diez son treinta
   b. diez más ocho son diez y ocho
   c. treinta más veinte son cincuenta
   d. cuarenta más cincuenta son noventa
   e. treinta y cuatro más treinta son
      sesenta y cuatro
   f. cincuenta más treinta son ochenta
   g. quince más catorce son veinte y nueve
   h. sesenta más diez son setenta
   i. setenta más veinte y uno son noventa y uno
   j. ochenta más trece son noventa y tres

3. a. veinte y cinco menos diez son quince
   b. cincuenta menos ocho son cuarenta y dos
   c. noventa y nueve menos nueve son noventa
   d. quince menos diez son cinco
   e. cuarenta menos veinte son veinte
   f. ochenta y uno menos uno son ochenta
   g. trece menos diez son tres
   h. nueve menos tres son seis
   i. noventa menos cuarenta son cincuenta
   j. noventa y ocho menos sesenta y tres
      son treinta y cinco

4. a. cien
   b. ciento ochenta y cinco
   c. ciento veinte y tres
   d. ciento cinco
   e. ciento nueve
   f. ciento treinta y siete
   g. ciento noventa y dos
   h. ciento uno
   i. ciento cincuenta
   j. ciento ochenta y dos

6. a. el lunes - los lunes
    b. el martes - los martes
    c. el miércoles - los miécoles
    d. el jueves - los jueves
    e. el viernes - los viernes
    f. el sábado - los sábados
    g. el domingo - los domingos

7. a. ¿Dónde está Ud. los domingos?
    b. ¿Cuándo está Ud. en clase?

8. a. Los domingos estoy en...
    b. Estoy en clase...

Lección Cinco

1. a. hablo
    b. practican
    c. llegamos
    d. pagamos
    e. necesitamos
    f. llegan
    g. hablamos
    h. estudio

2. 1. estudias
    2. estudia
    3. estudia
    4. estudiamos
    5. estudiamos
    6. hablo
    7. habla
    8. habla
    9. habla
    10. hablamos
    11. practico
    12. practicas
    13. practica
    14. practicamos
    15. llamas
    16. llama
    17. llama
    18. llamamos

3. a. Ella practica
    b. Ellas hablan
    c. Tú necesitas
    d. Juan y yo llegamos
    e. María y José estudian
    f. Yo no practico
    g. El y yo hablamos
    h. Ellos no contestan

4.

A. 1. Sí, llego ahora.
    2. Sí, hablo con ellas.
    3. Sí, estudio ahora.
    4. Sí, pago hoy.
    5. Sí, practico siempre aquí.

B. 1. Sí, llegamos ahora.
    2. Sí, hablamos con ellas.
    3. Sí, estudiamos ahora.
    4. Sí, pagamos hoy.
    5. Sí, siempre practicamos aquí.

5. A.
1. hablo mucho
2. hablan mucho
3. hablas mucho
4. hablan mucho
5. habla mucho
6. hablan mucho

6. a. llego
   b. llamo
   c. contesta
   d. habla
   e. practicamos
   f. necesito

Lección Seis

1. a. los guantes amarillos
   b. las chaquetas verdes
   c. unos suéteres rojos
   d. los trajes azules
   e. unas bufandas rosadas
   f. las billeteras negras

2. a. blancos – caros
   b. negros – negras
   c. fácil – difíciles
   d. azules – grande
   e. elegantes – caros

3. a. señora inteligente
   b. silla nueva
   c. autos verdes
   d. canción fácil

4. a. nuevos
   b. nueva
   c. nuevas
   d. nuevas

5. a. los exámenes fáciles
   b. las señoras inteligentes
   c. los restaurantes populares
   d. los chicos simpáticos
   e. las carteras naranja

6. a. el teléfono blanco
   b. la mujer grande
   c. la lección fácil
   d. los autos rojos
   e. el capítulo difícil

7. a. rojas – rosadas
   b. café – amarillos
   c. negro – azul
   d. verde – naranja
   e. blanca – lila

8. a. doscientas ochenta y una casas
   b. tres mil novecientos ochenta y tres libros
   c. doscientos cincuenta y siete mil seiscientos nueve dólares
   d. tres mil trescientos treinta y siete pollos
   e. trece mil seiscientos cuarenta y nueve teléfonos

1. a. Me llamo -------.
    b. Ella se llama ------.
    c. Yo me llamo ------.
    d. El se llama -------.

2. a. ¿Cómo te llamas?
    b. ¿Cómo se llama Ud.?
    c. ¿Cómo se llama ella?
    d. ¿Cómo se llama él?
    e. ¿Cómo se llama Ud.?

3. a. un buen chico
    b. un mal día
    c. un mal negocio
    d. un buen estudiante
    e. un buen cinturón

4. a. Los guantes son grises.
    b. La camisa es azul y verde.
    c. Las blusas son blancas.
    d. Los zapatos son grises y negros.
    e. Los trajes son marrón.
    f. El auto es amarillo.

5. a. ¿De qué color es su carro nuevo?
    b. ¿De qué color son los zapatos nuevos?
    c. ¿Qué desea Ud.? or ¿Qué deseas (tú)?
    d. Déme su tarjeta de crédito.
    e. ¿De qué color es la casa?

6. a. aquí
    b. ponerlo en la cuenta
    c. va a pagar?
    d. su tarjeta de crédito

7. a. ponerlo
    b. la
    c. cuenta
    d. aquí

8. 1.
    a. ¿Cómo va a pagar?
    b. Déme su tarjeta de crédito.
    c. Firme aquí por favor, gracias.
    d. Quiero ponerlo en la cuenta.

9. a. ¿Cómo va a pagar?
    b. Quiero ponerlo en la cuenta.
    c. Déme su tarjeta de crédito.
    d. Aquí está.

10. a. Nosotros pagamos de contado.
        We pay cash.
    b. Toma el cambio
        He takes the change.
    c. Uds. necesitan un billete de cinco.
        All of you need a five dollar bill.
    d. Ustedes necesitan dos identificaciones.
        All of you need two identifications.
    e. Firmo aquí.
        I sign here.

11. a. practicamos
     b. hablan
     c. llego
     d. llamas
     e. estudia

12. a. tomamos
     b. paga
     c. necesitan
     d. compramos
     e. pago

13. a. nuevo
     b. vieja
     c. amarillo
     d. buenas
     e. roja
     f. simpática - bonita
     g. alta - rubia

Section A

1. a. Quién
    b. Cuándo or ¿Por qué?
    c. Dónde
    d. ¿Por qué or ¿Cuándo?
    e. Qué
    f. Cómo
    g. Cuántos
    h. Cuánto

2. a. ¿Quién estudia?
    b. ¿Quién es?
    c. ¿Cómo se llama?
    d. ¿Qué practica?

3. a. unas
    b. una
    c. un
    d. unos
    e. unos

14. a. Son unos exámenes muy viejos.
     b. Las cajeras altas hablan.
     c. Las tiendas populares están aquí.
     d. Los abrigos azules están aquí.
     e. Las clientes simpáticas compran.

15. a. bueno - popular
     b. rubias
     c. popular - nueva
     d. bueno - popular
     e. altos

Lección Ocho

4. a. los
    b. los
    c. el
    d. el
    e. el
    f. Las
    g. las
    h. los

5. a. están en la clase
    b. está en la clase
    c. estoy en la clase
    d. están en la clase
    e. estamos en la clase
    f. están en la clase
    g. estás en la clase
    h. están en la clase

6. a. Nosotros estamos aquí.
   b. Ellos están bien.
   c. Nosotros trabajamos aquí.
   d. Uds. no estudian español.
   e. Ellas no necesitan zapatos.
   f. Uds. están en la clase.
   g. Ellas no están en la tienda.

7. a. Cinco más seis son once.
   b. Nueve más tres son doce.
   c. Nueve más cuatro son trece.
   d. Once más ocho son diez y nueve.
   e. Quince más nueve son veinte y cuatro.
   f. Diez más cuatro son catorce.
   g. Veinte menos cuatro son diez y seis.
   h. Veinte y nueve menos cuatro son veinte y cinco.
   i. Veinte y ocho menos ocho son veinte.
   j. Veinte y tres menos seis son diez y siete.

8. a. Elena está.
   b. Están
   c. María está
   d. estoy
   e. estamos

9. a. el lunes
   b. los domingos
   c. los miércoles
   d. el sábado.
   e. los martes

10. a. unos alumnos
    b. las hermanas
    c. un amigo
    d. el compañero
    e. un alumno
    f. una hermana
    g. los amigos
    h. un compañero

11. a. Sí, llego tarde los lunes.
    b. Sí, hablamos español.
    c. Sí, necesito dos identificaciones.
    d. Sí, estudiamos aquí.
    e. Sí, pagan las compras de contado.

12. a. las camisas azules
    b. los trajes grises
    c. las chaquetas café
    d. las blusas blancas
    e. los libros naranja
    f. los cinturones negros

Section B

1. a. ¿Quién es?
   b. ¿Cómo se llama?
   c. ¿Cómo estás?
   d. ¿Dónde están Uds.?
   e. ¿Dónde vive María?

2. a. Bien, aquí están.
   b. Buenos días. ¿Qué desea?
   c. Los blancos son muy bonitos.
   d. Quiero comprar unos pantalones.

3. a. ¿Dónde está la camisa blanca?
   b. ¿Por qué no habla español Ud.?
   c. ¿Cuánto cuestan los cinturones negros?
   d. ¿Qué desea?

4. a. ¿Cuánto cuestan los pantalones?
   b. ¿Dónde está el precio?
   c. Son muy baratos.
   d. Aquí está. Ocho dólares más el impuesto
   e. ¿Dónde está el probador?
   f. ¿Qué talla usa usted?
   g. ¿Puedo probarme los pantalones?

5. a. Buenas tardes - Qué desea
   b. Cuánto cuestan los zapatos negros
   c. Cómo estás, Roberto
   d. Cómo está Roberto
   e. ¡Hola! Cómo estás, Cómo está Ud.

6. a. ¿Por qué no estás en clase?
   b. ¿Dónde está él el jueves?
   c. ¿Dónde se paga?
   d. ¿Cuánto cuestan?

7. a. Allí, cerca de la puerta.
   b. No, en la caja.
   c. ¿Dónde se paga? ¿Aquí?
   d. Tome el cambio. Muchas gracias.
   e. ¿Cómo va a pagar?
   f. Aquí tiene un billete de diez.

8. a. la - compra la camisa
   b. compro-los azules
   c. compramos los pañuelos
   d. compran los- verdes
   e. compra los vestidos

9. a. La blusa es blanca.
   b. Los pantalones son azules.
   c. El traje es gris.
   d. La casa es verde.

10. a. Tome el recibo y gracias, señorita.
    b. Aquí las tiene.
    c. Necesita dos identificaciones.
    d. Con un cheque.
    e. ¿Cómo va a pagar?
    f. Déme su tarjeta de crédito.
    g. Firme aquí, por favor, gracias.
    h. Quiero ponerlo en la cuenta.

11. a. es un buen chico.
    b. estamos bien aquí.
    c. Cuándo está-en la clase.
    d. es blanca y amarilla.
    e. somos franceses.
    f. está en la tienda.

12. a. ¿Cómo va a pagar?
    b. De contado. ¿Cuánto es?
    c. Con un cheque.
    d. Quiero ponerlo en la cuenta.
    e. Firme aquí, por favor. Gracias.
    f. ¿De qué color es el auto?
    g. ¿De qué color son las camisas?
    h. Las camisas son blancas y naranja.
    i. Aquí tiene un billete de diez.
    j. ¿Puedo probarme los pantalones?
    k. ¿Dónde está el probador?
    l. Es muy barato.
    m. Quiero comprar un pañuelo blanco.
    n. Quiero comprar un cinturón negro talla treinta
       y seis.

1. a. soy
    b. eres
    c. son
    d. es
    e. es
    f. son
    g. somos
    h. es
    i. es
    j. son

2. a. Son las tres.
    b. Son las seis.
    c. Son las ocho.
    d. Es la una.
    e. Son las diez.

3. a. Son las cinco.
    b. Son las once.
    c. Son las cuatro.
    d. Son las siete.
    e. Son las doce.

4. a. Es la una y veinte y tres.
    b. Es la una y media.
    c. Es la una menos cuarto.
    d. Son las doce y veinte y nueve.
    e. Son las doce menos cinco.
    f. Son las doce y cinco.
    g. Son las nueve y cuarto.

5. a. La boda es a la una menos cuarto de la tarde.
    b. Llega a las siete menos veinte y cinco de la
        mañana.
    c. A las dos menos cuarto de la tarde.
    d. A las cinco de la tarde.
    e. La llamada cuesta menos.
        Las llamadas son baratas.
    f. El lunes a las nueve menos diez de la tarde.
    g. Cuesta cuatro dólares y noventa y cinco centavos.

6. a. El señor López es de Miami.
    b. María es rubia.
    c. María y Arturo son alumnos.
    d. Es el Sr. López.

7. a. son
    b. somos
    c. eres
    d. es
    e. soy

8. a. ¿Quién es ella?
    b. ¿De dónde es Ud?

9. a. Son las doce.
    b. Es temprano..
    c. Yo soy francés (francesa).
    d. Tú eres inteligente.
    e. Ana es la pianista.

10. a. Las camisas de unos chicos.
    b. La blusa de Rosa.
    c. La camisa del chico.
    d. Las camisas de Arturo.
    e. El vestido de una chica.

11. a. La camisa del amigo.
    b. La blusa de la señora.
    c. Las blusas de una chica.
    d. La camisa de un señor.
    e. La blusa de Ana.
    f. Las camisas de unos tíos.
    g. La camisa del alumno.

1.
bue-nos	Chi-na	ne-gro	tie-nen
com-prar	chi-co	mo-ra-do	u-na
u-nos	o-cho	ro-sa-do	me-sa
bien	a-ma-ri-llo	ro-jo	cua-tro
de-se-a	po-llo	ver-de	pa-ra
que	pe-rro	a-zul	gus-ta
dí-as	a-rroz	za-pa-tos	me-nú
quie-ro	to-rre	guan-tes	mu-cha
a-quí	Ri-car-do	bi-lle-te-ra	ham-bre
los	es-pa-ñol	sué-ter	te-ne-mos
blan-cos	se-ñor	pa-ñue-lo	de-sa-yu-no
muy	ba-ño	tra-je	es-pe-cial
son	cuan-to	us-ted	hue-vos
bo-ni-tos	pan-ta-lo-nes	él	ja-món
nú-me-ro	cues-tan	e-lla	sal-chi-chas
fra-se	don-de	bi-blio-te-ca	pa-pas
ca-ra	pre-cio	gra-cias	ha-ri-na
Jo-sé	dó-la-res	em-ple-a-do	tos-ta-da
Ju-lio	im-pues-to	tien-da	man-te-qui-lla
na-ran-ja	som-bre-ro	clien-te	
	ca-mi-sas	cuán-tos	
		sí-gan-me	

2.
a. estás	m. es		
b. estamos	n. está		
c. es	o. está		
d. somos	p. son		
e. está	q. es		
f. estoy	r. eres		
g. Estamos	s. estás		
h. es	t. está		
i. son	u. son		
j. estás	v. está		
k. están	w. está		
l. es	x. está		
	y. es		

3.
a. Soy...
b. Soy de Miami.
c. Soy estudiante.
d. Estoy en...
e. Estoy en...

4.
a. está	k. jamón
b. síganme	l. salchichas
c. cuatro	m. papas
d. gusta	n. harina
e. tienen	o. tostada
f. menú	p. café
g. desayuno	q. mantequilla
h. hambre	r. comprar
i. especial	s. camisa
j. huevos	t. cheque

5.
a. Estamos listos.
b. Ella es muy bonita.
c. Ellas son listas.
d. Ud. no está enfermo.

6.
a. Estamos en otoño.
b. Ellas son choferes.
c. Estás en la escuela.
d. (Yo) estoy en Francia.
e. El es simpático.

7. a. Soy Pedrito.
   b. Estoy enferma.
   c. Estoy en la biblioteca.
   d. Soy mecánico.
   e. Soy de Francia.

8. a. Hoy es martes.
   b. Hoy es miércoles.
   c. Hoy es jueves.
   d. Hoy es viernes.
   e. Hoy es sábado.
   f. Hoy es domingo.

9. Soy (name) .....
   Soy estudiante.
   Estoy muy bien.
   Soy de Miami.
   Estoy en la escuela.

Lección Once

1. a. Somos inteligentes.
   b. Somos estudiantes.
   c. Las chicas son rubias.
   d. Ellos son americanos.
   e. Ana está triste.
   f. Ud. es alto.
   g. Juan es el profesor.
   h. María está enferma.
   i. El plato está listo.
   j. El camarero es listo.

2. a. A menudo cenamos temprano.
   b. Es hora de desayunar.
   c. Almorzamos a las once y media.
   d. Los domingos cenamos después de
      las seis de la tarde.

   e. El juego es a las diez y cuarto
      de la mañana.
   f. Yo siempre estudio a las seis y media
      de la mañana.
   g. Pedro siempre desayuna jamón y huevos.
   h. Es hora de estudiar.
   i. El tren llega a las diez de la noche.
   j. Son las once menos cuarto de la mañana.

3. a. Café solo o café con crema.
   b. No queremos arroz con pollo hoy.
   c. No es hora de desayunar.
   d. Los viernes cenamos después de las ocho de la noche.

Lección Once
REPASO

1.
a. televisor
b. crédito
c. cuchara
d. idea
e. alguien
f. agüero
g. vaso
h. delgado
i. pantalla
j. ventana
k. otoño

l. caña
m. popular
n. lápiz
o. miércoles
p. narración
q. ahorra
r. nariz
s. tijeras
t. excelente
u. desayuno

2.
a. soy
b. estás
c. son
d. estamos
e. es
f. es
g. está
h. esta
i. estoy
j. está
k. es
l. Estamos
m. son

Lección Doce

1.
a. La ensalada del chico necesita sal.
b. Las mesas del señor están listas.
c. Quiero llevar el pavo al comedor.
d. Queremos llevar los cubiertos a la mesa.
e. Estoy cansado de la comida del restaurante.

2.
a. Queremos cangrejo relleno y sopa de cebolla.
b. Los chicos quieren ensalada mixta.
c. La langosta es muy cara, voy a ordenar pargo asado.
d. Ordenan camarones empanizados y langosta los sábados.
e. La ensalada de lechuga y las habichuelas están aquí.
f. El maíz y el puré de papas no son platos populares.
g. Los postres más caros son las fresas con crema y el flan.
h. Tomamos helados pero no queremos pastel de manzana.

3.
a. Flan y después café.
b. Llevamos arroz con pollo.
c. ¿Qué desean de postre?

4.
a. Queremos arroz con pollo.
b. Solamente agua.
c. Flan, y después café.

5.
a. a la
b. del
c. a los
d. de las
e. al
f. al
g. del
h. de los
i. al
j. del
k. al
l. a la

6.
a. El auto del alumno.
b. La chaqueta del profesor.
c. El amigo del alumno.
d. La blusa de la profesora.
e. Las camisas del chico.

1. a. La camisa del amigo.
   b. La blusa de la señora.
   c. Las blusas de una chica.
   d. La camisa del señor.
   e. La blusa del chico.
   f. Las camisas de unos tíos.
   g. La camisa del alumno.

2. a. Es de la
   b. Es de la
   c. Es del
   d. Son de
   e. Es del
   f. Son de

3. a. del
   b. de la
   c. de
   d. del
   e. de
   f. de

4. a. del
   b. de los
   c. el
   d. de la

5. a. Un pasaje del avión.
   b. El turista habla inglés.
   c. El viaje del chico es el martes.
   d. ¿Está la señora en el cuarto del hotel?
   e. El boleto del ómnibus.

6. a. Las camisas de unos chicos.
   b. La blusa de Rosa.
   c. La camisa del chico.
   d. Las camisas de Arturo.
   e. El pañuelo de una chica.

Lección Trece
REPASO

1. a. Ellos son de los Estados Unidos.
   b. Es de día.
   c. ¿De qué color es el automóvil.
   d. Estamos en Miami.
   e. Llego al baile a las diez.
   f. Es de noche.
   g. El auto del alumno es verde.
   h. El álbum de fotos es gris.
   i. Llegamos del parque.
   j. La chaqueta del profesor es buena.
   k. La blusa de Rosa es rosada.
   l. Juan es de la Florida.
   m. La clase de inglés es a las dos y media
   n. Camino del teatro a la casa.
   o. Somos de Miami.

2. a. de
   b. de
   c. de
   d. de
   e. --
   f. de
   g. --
   h. --
   i. De
   j. --
   k. de
   l. de
   m. de
   n. de
   o. --

3. a. Quiero merendar.
     b. ¿Están listos para ordenar?
     c. Pedro quiere un batido de fresa.
     d. Ella quiere desayunar.
     e. Bien, ¿qué desean?
     f. María quiere pastel de manzana.

     g. ¿Cuál es el especial de hoy?
     h. Queremos cenar.
     i. Juan y María quieren refrescos.
     j. Jorge quiere jugo de tomate.
     k. Quiero costillas de puerco y arroz.
     l. ¿Cuántas medianoches?
     m. Cuatro, por favor.
     n. ¿Quieren Uds. postre?
     o. Sí, cuatro arroz con leche, por favor.

4. a. Hoy es lunes.
     b. Estoy en la playa los domingos.
     c. Hablo con ella los lunes, (los) miércoles y (los) viernes.
     d. Visito a María los jueves.
     e. Sí, los domingos.
     f. El especial es cóctel de frutas, arroz con pollo, ensalada de lechuga y helado.

5. a. jugo de fruta
     b. ensalada de tomate
     c. pavo asado
     d. helado de chocolate
     e. pastel de manzana
     f. papas fritas
     g. agua fría
     h. vino tinto
     i. cerveza fría
     j. vino blanco

6. a. está
     b. está
     c. es
     d. es
     e. están
     f. están
     g. están
     h. es
     i. es
     j. es
     k. es
     l. es
     m. son
     n. es
     o. son

7. a. nuevos
     b. bonitas

8. a. Sí, hablo español.
       No, no hablo español.
     b. Sí, es bueno.
       No, no es bueno

9. a. El
     b. la
     c. El
     d. el/la
     e. La
     f. los
     g. --
     h. la
     i. el
     j. la

1.
   a. Pilar va a las tiendas.
   b. Ana y Juan van con Pilar.
   c. Ana quiere comprar un regalo.
   d. Juan quiere ir con Ana y Pilar.
   e. Tres personas van a las tiendas.

2.
   a. van
   b. va
   c. vamos
   d. voy
   e. vamos
   f. vas
   g. van

3.
   a. Ellas van a la escuela ahora.
   b. Juan va al centro con las chicas.
   c. No voy a la tienda.
   d. Tú y yo vamos a la casa.
   e. ¿Cuándo vas a la tienda?

4.
   a. voy a la escuela.
   b. Las chicas van a la casa ahora.
   c. vamos al cine.
   d. Ella va
   e. ellos no van.

5.
   a. Va a un restaurante
   b. Quieren almorzar.
   c. La cuenta es treinta dólares.
   d. Son diez.
   e. A las doce y media, más o menos.

6.
   a. Es hora de merendar.
   b. Es hora de desayunar.
   c. Es hora de almorzar.
   d. Es hora de cenar.

Lección Catorce
REPASO

1.
   a. un cinturón
   b. un pañuelo
   c. una corbata
   d. una camisa
   e. una bufanda
   f. una cartera
   g. unas medias

2.
   a. días
   b. unos pantalones
   c. desea
   d. son muy bonitos

3.
   a. Bien, aquí están.
   b. Buenos días, ¿qué desea?
   c. Los blancos son muy bonitos.
   d. Quiero comprar unos pantalones.

4.
   a. los pantalones
   b. los guantes
   c. los zapatos
   d. el suéter
   e. el sombrero
   f. el traje de baño
   g. la billetera

5. pantalones
   baratos
   dólares
   impuesto

6.
   a. Aquí está, ocho dólares más el impuesto.
   b. ¿Puedo probarme los pantalones?
   c. ¿Dónde está el probador?

7. a. el abrigo
    b. el vestido
    c. el traje
    d. la falda
    e. la chaqueta
    f. la blusa

8. a. ¿Quién(es)?
    b. ¿Cómo?
    c. ¿Dónde?
    d. ¿Cuándo?
    e. ¿Cuántos?
    f. ¿Cuánto?
    g. ¿Qué?
    h. ¿Por qué?

9. a. están
    b. estamos
    c. estás
    d. estamos
    e. estoy
    f. está

10. a. ¿Dónde se paga?   ¿Aquí?
    b. No, en la caja.
    c. ¿Dónde está?
    d. Allí cerca de la puerta.

11. a. contado
    b. más el impuesto
    c. pagar
    d. el cambio
    e. billete de diez

12. a. ¿Cómo va a pagar?
    b. Con un cheque.
    c. Necesita dos identificaciones.
    d. Aquí las tiene.
    e. Aquí tiene el recibo, y gracias, señorita.
    f. Quiero ponerlo en mi cuenta.
    g. Déme su tarjeta de crédito.
    h. Firme aquí, por favor. Gracias.

13. a. señorita
    b. el recibo
    c. dos identificaciones
    d. un cheque

14. a. ¿Cómo va a pagar?
    b. Déme su tarjeta de crédito.
    c. Firme aquí, por favor, gracias.
    d. Quiero ponerlo en la cuenta.

15. a. Pagamos de contado.
    b. Toma el cambio.
    c. Necesitan un billete de cinco.
    d. Ustedes necesitan un libro.
    e. Firmo aquí.

16. a. Unos exámenes muy fáciles.
    b. Las cajeras altas hablan.
    c. Las tiendas populares.
    d. Los abrigos azules están aquí.
    e. Las clientes simpáticas compran.

17. a. Buenos días. ¿Cuántos son?
    b. Queremos una mesa para cuatro, por favor.
    c. Muy bien. Síganme.
    d. Aquí tiene una mesa para cuatro.
    e. ¿Les gusta?
    f. Sí, está muy bien.
    g. Aquí tienen el menú.
    h. Muchas gracias.
    i. Tenemos mucha hambre.

18. a. desayunar
    b. desean
    c. naranja, jamón, huevos
    d. pan, mantequilla
    e. revueltos, fritos
    f. leche
    g. En seguida

19. a. ¿Desea (quiere) almorzar?
    b. Queremos arroz con pollo.
    c. ¿Qué desean tomar?
    d. Solamente agua.
    e. ¿Qué desean de postre?
    f. Flan y después café.
    g. ¿Café con crema o solo?
    h. Café solo, por favor.

20. a. merendar
    b. desean
    c. batidos, medianoches
    d. fruta, chocolate
    e. mamey

1. a. (I) bebemos
    b. (C)
    c. (I) comes
    d. (C)
    e. (C)
    f. (I) comen
    g. (C)

2. a. bebes
    b. abren
    c. vivo
    d. vivimos
    e. come

3. a. (Yo) como ahora.
    b. Bebemos agua.
    c. Ellas abren la caja.
    d. El vive aquí.
    e. Tú abres la caja.

4. a. bebemos
    b. abren
    c. comen
    d. vivimos

5. a. Cerca de Ana.
    b. Ana abre la puerta.
    c. Rosa entra en la casa.
    d. Meriendan en la casa de Ana.

6. a. conversamos
    b. deben
    c. escriben
    d. leen
    e. cree
    f. vemos

7. a. El tío de Juan escribe una carta.
    b. Las chicas viven en las casa.
    c. Ana y yo conversamos en la casa.
    d. ¿Lees los libros ahora?
    e. Ana y Juan meriendan y conversan.

8. a. No, ellos no viven en la casa de Rosa.
    b. No, no debo mucho.
    c. Juan escribe una carta.
    d. Sí, conversamos mucho.

9. a. ¿Cómo te llamas tú?
    b. ¿Cómo se llama Ud.?
    c. Me llamo Juan.
    d. Se llama María.

Lección Dieciséis

1. a. Ustedes meriendan con ella.
    b. Tú piensas en la fiesta.
    c. Nosotros cerramos la puerta.
    d. ¿Siente usted el frío?
    e. Yo no quiero pescado.

2. a. S
    b. S
    c. P
    d. P
    e. S

3. a. queremos
    b. cierro
    c. meriendo
    d. prefiere
    e. quiere

4. 1. pienso
    2. piensa
    3. piensan
    4. cierras
    5. cerramos
    6. cierran
    7. siento
    8. sientes
    9. siente
    10. sentimos
    11. entiendes
    12. entiende
    13. entendemos
    14. entienden
    15. meriendo
    16. merienda
    17. merendamos
    18. meriendan
    19. prefiero
    20. prefieres
    21. prefiere
    22. prefieren

5.   a. quiere
    b. queremos
    c. quiere
    d. quiero
    e. quieren
    f. quiero
    g. quieres
    h. quiere
    i. quiere
    j. queremos
    k. quieren
    l. quieren

6.   a. (Yo) cierro la puerta.
    b. ¿Piensas en la fiesta?
    c. Usted merienda con ella.
    d. Él entiende el español.
    e. Ella quiere sopa.
    f. ¿Sienten Uds. el frío?
    g. Ellos prefieren café.
    h. Nosotros cerramos la puerta.
    i. Merendamos con ella.
    j. Entendemos el español.

7.   a. (Ella) va a la cafetería.
    b. Porque solamente merienda al mediodía.
    c. Van Pedro, Carlos y Carmen.
    d. Porque quiere algo ligero.
    e. Carmen siente frío.

8. Pedro: We are planning to go to the restaurant.
   Carlos: I am planning to eat well.
   Pedro: Are you planning to go too, María?
   María: No, you are planning to have lunch.
          I only have a snack at noon. I prefer
          to go to the cafeteria because I want
          something light.
   Carlos: They close the cafeteria at two.
   María: I am leaving right away, I don't want to
          arrive late.
   Pedro: Don't you feel cold today, Carmen?
   Carmen: Yes, I feel cold but I prefer winter.
          Why don't we walk to the restaurant?

9.   a. Avenida setenta y nueve del suroeste, número
       doscientos once.
    b. Calle ciento veinte y uno del noreste, número
       diez y nueve.
    c. Calle setenta del noroeste, número quince.
    d. Avenida ciento dos del sureste, número diez
       y nueve.

1. a. Cuántos
    b. casada
    c. Cuál
    d. Tengo
    e. Quién

2. a. Soy...
    b. Tengo...años.
    c. Soy...
    d. La Sra...

3. a. no
    b. sí
    c. no
    d. no
    e. sí

4. a. a
    b. a
    c. X
    d. al
    e. a

5. a. Llego a las seis.
    b. Llego al laboratorio.
    c. Llego a las tres.

    a. Llego del teatro.
    b. Llego del hospital.
    c. Llego de la tienda.

6. a. ¿Cuántos años tiene?
    b. ¿Cuál es su ocupación?
    c. ¿Quién le recomendó al doctor?
    d. Tengo 18 años.

7. a. 17   i. 12
    b. 11   j. 7
    c. 6   k. 13
    d. 14   l. 10
    e. 8   m. 1
    f. 9   n. 2
    g. 15   o. 3
    h. 5   p. 16
                 q. 4

8. d. el ojo
    e. el diente
    g. la pestaña
    i. el párpado
    j. la oreja
    m. la ceja

9. a. los ojos
    b. los dientes
    c. las pestañas
    d. los párpados
    e. las orejas
    f. las cejas

10. a. la cabeza
    b. la cara
    c. el cuello
    d. los ojos
    e. la boca
    f. la nariz
    g. los oídos
    h. la lengua
    i. la garganta
    j. la frente

11. a. de
    b. a
    c. de
    d. a
    e. de

Lección Dieciocho

1. a. tengo
   b. seguro
   c. siéntese
   d. espere

2. ¿Tiene seguro?

3. a. Espere un momento, por favor.
   b. ¿Tiene seguro?
   c. Siéntese, por favor.

4. a. Do you live near the doctor's office?
      Sí, vivo cerca.
   b. When are you going to the hospital?
      Voy al hospital mañana.
   c. Who opens the doctor's office?
      La recepcionista abre la puerta de la consulta.
   d. Do you (all) eat with the receptionist?
      No, no comemos con ella.
   e. Mrs. López, does she drink water or Coca-Cola?
      Ella bebe agua (Coca-Cola).
   f. How much money must you pay in the office?
      Debo pagar veinte dólares.
   g. Do you and María live in Miami?
      Sí, vivimos en Miami.

5. a. va
   b. como
   c. vivimos
   d. abren

6. a. d
   b. b
   c. c
   d. a
   e. b

7. a. b
   b. c
   c. a
   d. c

8. a. El profesor vive cerca de aquí.
   b. El médico come bien.
   c. El camarero abre la puerta.
   d. La secretaria vive en una casa.
   e. El abogado vive aquí.
   f. La enfermera come con los médicos.
   g. El contador bebe agua.
   h. El peluquero bebe Coca-Cola.

9. a. Firme
    b. Espere
    c. Dé
    d. Cambien
    e. Tomen

10. a. sí
    b. No
    c. No
    d. Sí
    e. Sí
    f. No

11. a. Entren
    b. Siéntese
    c. Cambie

12. a. Ud.
    b. Uds.
    c. Ud.
    d. Ud.
    e. Ud.

13. a. 1. tome   b. 1. tomen
       2. Escúchelo   2. Escúchenlo
       3. Cante   3. Canten
       4. Cante   4. Canten
       5. hable   5. Hablen
       6. escuche   6. Escuchen

14. Señor, empiece a trabajar mañana a las ocho.
    Recuerde todo. Cierre las puertas temprano
    y prepare las cosas para el martes. Regrese
    con el Sr. López.

15. a. compre
    b. piense
    c. llame
    d. estudie
    e. tome
    f. ahorre
    g. conteste
    h. pronuncie

16. a. No hable bajo.
    b. No tome el dinero.
    c. No preparen las cosas.
    d. No pase, por favor
    e. No firme aquí.

17. a. vienes
    b. vengo
    c. vienen
    d. venimos
    e. viene
    f. vienen
    g. viene

18. a. 5
    b. 6
    c. 16
    d. 3
    e. 2
    f. 11
    g. 9
    h. 13
    i. 12
    j. 8
    k. 7
    l. 10
    m. 14
    n. 4
    o. 1
    p. 15

19. a. the heart
    b. the chest
    c. the waist
    d. the lungs
    e. the back
    f. the intestines
    g. the abdomen
    h. the spinal column
    i. the kidneys
    j. the shoulders

20. a. la espalda
    b. el pecho
    c. el corazón
    d. el estómago
    e. la cintura

21. a. Me duele la garganta.   f. Me duelen los pulmones.
    b. Me duele la cabeza.   g. Me duelen las piernas.
    c. Me duelen los oídos   h. Me duelen los pies.
    d. Me duele la espalda.   i. Me duelen los riñones.
    e. Me duele el estómago.   j. Me duelen los ojos.

22. a. Caliente el café.
    b. Cierre la puerta.
    c. Espere un rato.
    d. No cambie el canal.
    e. Pase, por favor.
    f. Llame a la recepcionista.
    g. Firme aquí, por favor.
    h. Compre el seguro.
    i. Conteste el teléfono.
    j. Tome el recibo.

23. a. Empiezo a estudiar a las ocho.
    b. La camarera calienta el café.
    c. Meriendo en la casa.
    d. Sí, recomiendo el pescado al horno.
    e. Sí, (ellos) vienen los lunes.

Lección Diecinueve

1. a. duerme
    b. dormimos
    c. duermo
    d. duerme
    e. vuelven
    f. vuelven
    g. vuelves
    h. volvemos
    i. almuerzan
    j. almuerza
    k. almorzamos
    l. almuerzas

2. a. recordamos
    b. devuelven
    c. cuesta
    d. encuentras
    e. almuerzo

3. a. ¿Encuentras el lugar?
    b. Uds. almuerzan con ella.
    c. No devuelvo la falda.

4. a. recuerdo
    b. duerme
    c. cuesta
    d. puede
    e. almuerzo

5. a. ¿Cuánto cuestan las...
    b. ¿Cuánto cuesta la...
    c. ¿Cuánto cuesta la...
    d. ¿Cuánto cuestan los...
    e. ¿Cuánto cuestan los...

6. a. encontramos
    b. cuesta
    c. cuestan
    d. recuerdo
    e. cuestan

7. a. María puede salir con Ana.
    b. Ellas pueden almorzar primero.
    c. Pueden visitar la universidad.
    d. Ana puede comprar los boletos en la
       Universidad.

8. 1. encontramos
    2. cuestan
    3. recuerdas
    4. recordar
    5. cuesta
    6. encuentras
    7. salir
    8. recordamos

9. a. mujeres
    b. lápices
    c. clases
    d. narices
    e. reyes
    f. luces
    g. lunes
    h. veces

10. a. 7
    b. 12
    c. 9
    d. 8
    e. 4
    f. 11
    g. 3
    h. 10
    i. 5
    j. 2
    k. 6
    l. 1

11. a. lower
    b. lower
    c. upper
    d. upper
    e. lower
    f. lower
    g. lower
    h. upper
    i. upper
    j. lower

12. a. las piernas
    b. los brazos
    c. los tobillos
    d. las muñecas
    e. los codos
    f. las rodillas
    g. las manos
    h. los pies
    i. las uñas
    j. los muslos

13. 1. mano
    2. brazo
    3. codo
    4. muñeca
    5. dedos de la mano
    6. uña
    7. muslo
    8. rodilla
    9. pierna
    10. tobillo
    11. uña
    12. pie
    13. dedos del pie

14. a. Me duele la garganta.
    b. Me duele la cabeza.
    c. Me duelen los oídos.
    d. Me duele la espalda.
    e. Me duele el estómago.
    f. Me duelen los pulmones.
    g. Me duelen las piernas.
    h. Me duelen los pies.
    i. Me duelen los riñones.
    j. Me duelen los ojos.

15. a. Me duele el pecho, no quiero almorzar.
    b. José y Ana vuelven temprano.
    c. El tiene los pies grandes.
    d. No creo en el médico.
    e. Me duele el estómago.

16. Horizontal   Vertical
    2. vejiga   1. vesícula
    3. cara   2. ojos
    5. lengua   4. muñecas
    7. hígado   6. corazón
    8. brazos   9. riñones
   10. estómago

17. a. está enferma (c)
    b. comienza antes de las cuatro (b)
    c. conversan (a)
    d. siente frío (a)
    e. vuelve la Sra. de Martínez (c)

18. a. Sí, duermo mucho.
    b. El vestido rojo cuesta...
    c. Sí, recordamos la conversación siete.
    d. Sí, encontramos los zapatos.
    e. Vuelvo a las...
    f. Sí, devuelvo la camisa.
    g. Sí, dormimos mucho.
    h. Hoy almuerzo en la playa.

1. a. empleada
   b. empleada
   c. pasajera
   d. empleada

2. a. 3
   b. 1
   c. 2
   d. 4

3. a. reservación
   b. vuelo
   c. mañana

4. a. Quiero una reservación para el vuelo.
   b. ¿En primera o en turista?
   c. ¿Directo o con escala?

5. Free exercise

19. a. Nosotros pedimos un médico.
    b. Sí, repetimos la leccion.
    c. No, no sirvo la merienda ahora.
    d. Pedimos café con leche.
    e. Sí, lo pedimos ahora.
    f. Pido allí.

20. a. 1. Repito dos ejercicios.
      2. Pido dos ejercicios.
      3. Sigo dos ejercicios.
    b. 1. Seguimos dos lecciones.
      2. Repetimos dos lecciones.
      3. Pedimos dos lecciones.
    c. 1. Sigues dos.
      2. Sirves dos.
      3. Pides dos.
    d. 1. Sirve tres.
      2. Sigue tres.
      3. Repite tres.
    e. 1. Nos piden dos.
      2. Nos sirven dos.
      3. Nos repiten dos.

Lección Veinte

6. a. Entre(n) aquí.
   b. Déme el libro.
   c. Espere(n) en la casa.
   d. Hable(n) con el empleado.

7. a. cambie (formal) – change
   b. Déme (formal) – give me
   c. Firmen (formal) – sign
   d. firma (familiar) – sign
   e. toma (familiar) – take

8.

	Formal Command	Familiar Command
a.	hable	habla
b.	dé	da
c.	tome	toma
d.	entre	entra
e.	cambie	cambia

9. a. Uds.
    b. tú
    c. tú
    d. Ud.
    e. tú
    f. Uds.
    g. Ud.
    h. tú
    i. tú
    j. Ud.

10. a. lee
    b. recibe
    c. maneja
    d. evita
    e. aprende
    f. sube

11. a. Espere Ud. al policía.
    b. Evita (tú) el semáforo.
    c. Mire Ud. al policía.
    d. No suba Ud. por esa calle.
    e. No recibas (tú) las excusas del policía.

12. a. Rosa, aprende a manejar el automovil de María.
    b. Espere al policía.
    c. Lean ustedes los avisos de la calle.
    d. Pase usted por aquí, por favor.

13. a. No creas
    b. No vendas.
    c. No enciendas.
    d. No pierdas.
    e. No coman.
    f. No corran.
    g. No vuelvan.
    h. No suban.

14. a. Tengan Uds. precaución.
    b. Abra Ud. la puerta.
    c. Coma Ud. después.
    d. Cuenten Uds. hasta diez.
    e. Llame Ud. por teléfono.

15. a. Pasen, por favor.
    b. Firme aquí, por favor.
    c. No entre a la derecha.

16. a. Vayan Uds.
    b. Vaya Ud.
    c. Vea Ud.
    d. Vean Uds.

17. a. No vuelva mañana.
    b. No cierres la puerta.
    c. No piensen en el peligro.
    d. No calientes el café.
    e. No deje el extinguidor aquí.

18. a. termine Ud.
    b. lea (la novela)
    c. piense (en el futuro)
    d. vuelva (mañana)
    e. duerma (bien)

1. a. agosto
   b. marzo
   c. enero
   d. abril
   e. diciembre
   f. noviembre
   g. mayo
   h. julio
   i. junio
   j. septiembre
   k. febrero
   l. octubre

2. a. D
   b. I
   c. D
   d. D
   e. D
   f. I
   g. I

3. a. diez de febrero
   b. catorce de marzo
   c. veinte de junio
   d. dieciocho de mayo
   e. veinte y cinco de enero
   f. nueve de abril
   g. diez y siete de septiembre
   h. cuatro de julio

4. a. Son las diez de la noche.
   b. Son las dos de la mañana.
   c. Son las cinco de la tarde.
   d. Son las once de la mañana.
   e. Son las ocho de la noche.
   f. Es la una de la tarde.
   g. Son las tres de la tarde.

5. a. trescientos veinte y uno
   b. diez y siete
   c. ciento cincuenta y tres
   d. sesenta y ocho
   e. cuatrocientos veinte
   f. ciento seis
   g. noventa y siete

6. a. entre, no entren
   b. pase, no pasen
   c. mire, no miren
   d. estudie, no estudien
   e. regrese, no regresen
   f. tome, no tomen
   g. pronuncie, no pronuncien
   h. respiren, no respiren
   i. corte, no corten
   j. olvide, no olviden

7. a. entra, no entres
   b. pasa, no pases
   c. mira, no mires
   d. estudia, no estudies
   e. regresa, no regreses
   f. toma, no tomes
   g. pronuncia, no pronuncies
   h. respira, no respires
   i. corta, no cortes
   j. olvida, no olvides

8. a. Guatemala
   b. San Salvador
   c. Tegucigalpa
   d. Managua
   e. San José
   f. Panamá

9. a. Quiero una reservación para el vuelo
       de mañana a Buenos Aires.
    b. ¿En primera clase o en turista?
    c. En turista.
    d. ¿Vuelo directo o con escala?
    e. Directo.
    f. ¿Boleto de ida y vuelta?
    g. De ida solamente.
    h. Está confirmado para el ocho de julio.
    i. Vuelo número cuarenta y dos a las tres
       de la tarde.
    j. No olvide llegar temprano al aeropuerto.

Lección Veintidós

1. a. No (it's the subject)
    b. D.O.
    c. D.O.
    d. D.O.
    e. D.O.

2. a. Andrés la invita a ella.
    b. Queremos un lápiz.
    c. Ana la ve a ella.
    d. Juan me ve.

3. a. la
    b. lo
    c. lo

4. a. a ellas
       a Uds.
    b. a Ud.
       a él
    c. a ella
       a Ud.
    d. a ellos
       a Uds.

5. a. ¿A quiénes?
    b. ¿A quién?
    c. ¿A quién?

6. a. los - a ustedes (clarifies)
    b. nos
    c. las
    d. me

7. a. no te (lo, la) llama.
       te (lo, la) llama
    b. no las buscamos
       las buscamos
    c. no los prefiero
       los prefiero
    d. no me ven
       me ven

8. a. me llama
    b. las preferimos
    c. lo
    d. Te (lo) ven

9. a. a ella "or" a Ud.
    b. a mí
    c. a ellos "or" a Uds.
    d. a ti
    e. a ellas "or" Uds.

10. a. un regalo
    b. la cliente
    c. una talla
    d. otra cosa

11. a. a las empleadas
    b. regalos
    c. la talla
    d. al padre
    e. un abrigo
    f. a los jóvenes

12. a. María las llama.
    b. ¿Prefieres los mejores?
    c. El empleado me la trae.
    d. Lo buscamos en la tienda.
    e. Yo lo compro de invierno.
    f. ¿Quién los invita?

13. a. una reservación
    b. la
    c. los boletos
    d. los
    e. la hora
    f. la
    g. el vuelo No. 42
    h. lo

14. a. La señora me llama.
    b. El Sr. López te invita.
    c. El empleado te llama.
    d. El pasajero no me ve.
    e. El pasajero los ve.
    f. El Sr. López las compra.
    g. La señora los invita a Uds.

15. a. nos
    b. los
    c. la
    d. me
    e. las

16. a. Andrés lo llama a Ud.
       Andrés lo llama a él.
    b. María los invita a Uds.
       María los invita a ellos.
    c. Yo la llamo a Ud.
       Yo la llamo a ella.
    d. ¿Quién las ve a ellas?
       ¿Quién las ve a Uds.?

17. a. a nosotros
    b. a mí
    c. a ti?

18. Free exercise.

19. a. María me escucha.
    b. Pepe te mira.
    c. No los compra.
    d. Tómelos, Sr. López.

20. a. Tómelo or Tómalo, por favor.
    b. Ud. puede pagar los boletos ahora.
    c. Páguelos allí.
    d. Estas son las horas de los vuelos.
    e. Mírelas.
    f. El pasajero está allí. Llámelo.

21. a. para el vuelo de mañana a Buenos Aires.
    b. o en turista
    c. turista
    d. o con escala
    e. Directo.
    f. ida y vuelta
    g. solamente
    h. confirmado para el ocho de julio.
    i. a las tres de la tarde

22. a. Sí, voy contigo.
    b. Sí, puedes ir conmigo.
    c. Sí, vamos con él.
    d. Sí, vuelvo con Uds.?

Lección Veintitrés

1. a. pongo
   b. hace
   c. pones
   d. hago
   e. ponemos
   f. hacen
   g. hacen

2. a. Vamos al parque.
   b. Vamos a la iglesia.
   c. Vamos a estudiar español.
   d. Vamos a hacer las maletas.
   e. Vamos a desayunar.

3. a. Le dan unas noticias a usted.
   b. El nos trae las cartas.
   c. Le dan un mapa a ella.
   d. María les trae el álbum a ellos.

4. a. a ti
   b. a mí
   c. a nosotros

5. a. Nos dan un recado.
   b. Les dan unas noticias.
   c. ¿Quién les lleva los guantes?

6. a. María me trae los libros.
   b. Ella me trae un regalo.
   c. María me compra un mapa.
   d. ¿Le compra ella el álbum?
   e. Le decimos las noticias.
   f. María le da un recado.
   g. Te compro la bicicleta.
   h. Ellos nunca le dicen las noticias a Pepe.

7. a. les
   b. le
   c. les
   d. le
   e. Le
   f. nos
   g. les
   h. Me
   i. le
   j. les
   k. me
   l. le
   m. Les
   n. Te

8.   a. a mí
     b. a ti
     c. a Ud. (a él, a ella)
     d. a nosotros
     e. a Uds. (a ellos, aellas)

9.   a. A ella le encanta la clase de español.
     b. ¿Qué le parece el tiempo?
     c. Me gusta Lima.
     d. El diccionario nos parece bueno.
     e. Las vacaciones les encantan.
     f. No me gusta el libro.

10. a. Sí, (No) me gusta el álbum.
     b. Nos parece bueno.
     c. Les parece buena.
     d. Sí, me gusta París
     e. Me falta una maleta.

11. a. invierno
       Hace frío.
     b. primavera
       Hace fresco.
     c. verano
       Hace calor.
     d. otoño
       Hace fresco.

12. a. En verano hace calor.
     b. Sí, hace fresco en primavera.
     c. No, no hace calor en invierno.
     d. Hay cuatro estaciones en el año.
     e. Sí, hace fresco en Miami en diciembre.

13. a. primavera
     b. verano
     c. otoño
     d. invierno

14. a. nos
     b. le
     c. None
     d. te
     e. None
     f. Me
     g. Le
     h. Me
     i. le
     j. nos

15. a. Le, a Ud.
     b. Te, a ti
     c. Les, a Uds.
     d. Me, a mí
     e. Nos, a nosotros
     f. Les, a ellos

1. a. esposa
    b. esposa
    c. esposa
    d. esposo

2. a. invierno
    b. camisas
    c. zapatos
    d. corbata

3. a. Recuerda
    b. traje
    c. lana

4. a. ¿Cuántas libras se pueden llevar?
    b. Pongo mi abrigo y mi chaqueta.
    c. Voy a poner la bufanda.

5. a. Puedo almorzar.
    b. Tú puedes desayunar.
    c. Ud. puede salir.
    d. El puede salir
    e. Ella puede venir temprano.
    f. Podemos cenar.
    g. Pueden merendar.
    h. ¿Recuerdas el lugar?
    i. Almuerzo con ella.
    j. La falda no cuesta mucho.
    k. El vuelve de New York.
    l. Ud. devuelve los pantalones.
    m. Uds. duermen demasiado.
    n. Ellos no duermen mucho.

6. a. Tú llamas a Andrés.
       Tú lo llamas.
    b. Ud. llama a Andrés.
       Ud. lo llama.
    c. Tú invitas a la señora.
       Tú la invitas.
    d. Ud. invita a la señora.
       Ud. la invita.
    e. Uds. invitan a Andrés y a la señora.
       Uds. los invitan.

7. a. los busco
    b. ella no las prefiere
    c. no me mira
    d. nos ven los domingos

8. a. Ellos te dan unas noticias.
    b. Ellos le dan unas noticias.
    c. Ellos le dan unas noticias a él.
    d. Ellos le dan unas noticias a ella.
    e. Ellos nos dan unas noticias.
    f. Ellos me dan unas noticias.
    g. Ellos les dan unas noticias.
    h. Ellos le dan unas noticias a Juan.
    i. Yo le doy un mapa a María.
    j. El cartero les trae las cartas.
    k. El cartero le trae unas cartas.
    l. Me gusta Lima.
    m. El diccionario nos parece bueno.
    n. A ella le encanta la clase.

9. a. No me parece grande el mapa.
    b. Me encanta la música.
    c. A ellos les gusta Lima.

10. A. 1. sí
       2. no
       3. no
       4. no
       5. sí
       6. sí
    B. 1. sí
       2. no
       3. sí
       4. no
       5. sí

11. a. nos gusta
    b. me
    c. no me gusta

12. a. Tómela.
       No la tome.
    b. Tómala.
       No la tomes.
    c. Tómalo.
       No lo tomes.
    d. Cámbiela.
       No la cambie.
    e. Cámbialo.
       No lo cambies.
    f. Cámbienlo.
       No lo cambien.
    g. Denme.
       No me den.
    h. Dale el libro.
       No le des el libro.
    i. Déle el libro.
       No le dé el libro.
    j. Déle el libro a ella.
       No le dé el libro a ella.
    k. Déle el libro a Juan.
       No le dé el libro a Juan.

l. Entren.
    No entren.
m. Recuérdenlo.
    No lo recuerden.

13. a. Pepe, tómelo.
    b. Gracias por el disco.
    c. Dámelos.
    d. (Yo) no la recuerdo bien.
    e. Ciérrenlas temprano.
    f. Prepárenlas para el martes.
    g. Regrese con el Sr. López.
    h. Espere, por favor.
    i. Cómprelo.
    j. Recuérdenla.

14. a. Pepe, tómalo.
       Pepe, no lo tomes.
    b. Ciérralas.
       No las cierres.
    c. Prepáralas para el martes.
       No las prepares para el martes.
    d. Regresa con el Sr. López.
       No regreses con el Sr. Lópéz.
    e. Espera, por favor.
       No esperes, por favor.
    f. Cómpralo.
       No lo compres.
    g. Recuérdala.
       No la recuerdes.

16. a. Te doy los boletos, María.
    b. ¿Le escribes a menudo a él?
    c. ¿Por qué no le escribes a ella?
    d. El siempre nos dice la verdad.
    e. ¿Vas a comprarnos un libro?

1. a. empleado
   b. empleado
   c. pasajera
   d. pasajera

2. Sí, aquí está, or aquí lo tiene.

3. a. bien
   b. Todo
   c. orden

4. a. Estas son mis maletas.
   b. También tu sombrero.
   c. 44 por persona.

5. a. tiene una oficina grande. (2)
   b. la Srta. Gómez tiene fotos del Perú. (1)
   c. Debemos llegar allí antes de la hora del viaje. (3)
   d. aquellas maletas. (1)
   e. son muy bonitas. (2)

6. a. Me gusta ese pan.
   b. Aquellos radios son grandes.
   c. Necesito estas narraciones.
   d. Esa carne es excelente.
   e. ¿Puedo ver esas fotografías?

7. a. estos radios.
   b. este pan.
   c. aquella carne.
   d. esas narraciones.

8. a. Estas ensaladas.
   b. Esos camareros.
   c. Aquellos almuerzos.
   d. Aquellas cenas.
   e. Estos comedores.

9. a. esta
   b. estos
   c. este
   d. esa

10. a. Este vaso.
    b. Esas fotografías
    c. Aquel radio.

11. a. Este radio reloj.
    Estas narraciones.
    b. Aquellos periódicos.
    Aquellas cosas.
    c. Ese pan.
    Esa ensalada.

12. a. Este
    b. aquellos
    c. esa
    d. Este
    e. aquel

13. a. No accents
    b. ésos
    c. aquéllos
    d. No accents
    e. ése

14. a. Aquel comedor.
    b. Esa leche.
    c. Este almuerzo.
    d. Esta narración.
    e. Aquellos periódicos.

15. a. I
    b. D
    c. D
    d. I
    e. D

16. a. mírelo
    b. las miran
    c. me miras
    d. mírelos
    e. mírennos

17. a. Los puedo dejar allí.
    b. No les quieren contestar.
    c. Le podemos dar el recibo.
    d. Nos prefiere ver el lunes.
    e. ¿La quieres mirar?
    f. Te pueden traer la lista.

18. a. ¿Quiéres prestárnoslos? or ¿Nos los quieres
       prestar?
    b. Puedo escribírtela. or Te la puedo escribir.
    c. Prefiere llevármelas. or Me las prefiero llevar.
    d. Juan nos la escribe.
    e. Ustedes no quieren prestármelas. or Uds. no me las
       quieren prestar.
    f. Dáselos.
    g. Préstesela.

19. a. Déme la lista.
    b. Les prestamos (algún) dinero.
    c. Yo prefiero cambiarlo (la). or Yo lo (la) prefiero
       cambiar.
    d. Ellos te invitan.
    e. Mírela.

20. a. dejarnos
    b. escribirlas
    c. hablarle
    d. llevarla
    e. cambiarlo

21. a. Me traen el recibo.
    b. Cómprele el auto a él.
    c. Quiero verla.
    d. Juan le da el menú a usted.
    e. Lo llamamos.

22. a. prestárselo "or" Se lo pueden prestar.
    b. traérselos "or" Se lo quieren traer.
    c. comprárselo "or" Se lo prefiero comprar.
    d. dárnoslos "or" María nos lo puede dar.
    e. llevármelo "or" Me lo quiero llevar.

1.
   a. ¿Puedo ver esto?
   b. ¿Es esto un radio?
   c. Necesito todo eso.
   d. Esto no es fácil
   e. Me gusta eso.

2.
   a. aquéllos
   b. aquéllos, éstos
   c. No accents
   d. Éste
   e. No accents.

Ejercicios De Repaso

1.
   a. dí-a
   b. pa-sa-do
   c. ma-ña-na
   d. miér-co-les
   e. Ma-rí-a
   f. a-mi-go
   g. bi-blio-te-ca
   h. pro-nun-cia
   i. es-pa-ñol
   j. Pe-dri-to
   k. her-ma-nos
   l. in-glés
   m. chi-co
   n. can-ción
   o. can-cio-nes
   p. con-sul-ta
   q. an-te-na
   r. en-jua-gue
   s. i-ma-gen
   t. a-cei-te

3.
   a. estoy
   b. estás
   c. estamos
   d. está
   e. está
   f. está
   g. están
   h. está
   i. estamos
   j. están

4.
   a. el, un
   b. la, una
   c. el, un
   d. el, un
   e. el, un
   f. el, un
   g. el, un
   h. la, una
   i. el, un
   j. el, un

2.
   a. Quién
   b. Qué
   c. Cuál
   d. Qué
   e. Dónde
   f. Por qué
   g. Cómo
   h. Cuántos
   i. Dónde
   j. Quiénes
   k. Dónde
   l. Qué

5.
   a. estudio
   b. aprendes
   c. practica
   d. bebemos
   e. comen
   f. abre
   g. vive
   h. pronunciamos
   i. recibimos
   j. responden
   k. corro
   l. cantas
   m. lee
   n. trabajamos
   o. miran
   p. sufre
   q. crees
   r. usamos
   s. trata
   t. pago

6.　a.　bueno
　　　modesto
　　　inteligente
　　b.　bonita
　　　rubia
　　　alta
　　c.　popular
　　　nueva
　　　española
　　d.　fácil
　　　difícil
　　　tercera
　　e.　grandes
　　　azules
　　　café
　　f.　verdes
　　　nuevas
　　　blancas
　　g.　vieja
　　　grande
　　　francesa
　　h.　pequeños
　　　tristes
　　　delgados
　　i.　gordo
　　　bueno
　　　alto

7.　a.　están
　　b.　es
　　c.　son
　　d.　es
　　e.　está
　　f.　estás
　　g.　es
　　h.　está
　　i.　está
　　j.　son
　　k.　es
　　l.　son
　　m.　Es
　　n.　está
　　o.　es

8.　a.　de
　　b.　de
　　c.　del
　　d.　al
　　e.　de
　　f.　de la
　　g.　del
　　h.　de las
　　i.　a los
　　j.　las
　　k.　al

9.　a.　La blusa de Rosa es blanca.
　　b.　Las camisas de Arturo son blancas también
　　c.　El maestro de español es español.
　　d.　El llega temprano del aeropuerto.
　　e.　Juan es de la Argentina.
　　f.　El álbum de fotos es verde.
　　g.　Veo a alguien ahora.
　　h.　Llamo a Papá por teléfono.
　　i.　Llego a (la) casa a las cuatro.
　　j.　El estudia a las ocho.
　　k.　Los discos son de Italia.
　　l.　El no escucha a las profesoras.
　　m.　Rosa es de México.
　　n.　Veo al hermano de Pedrito.

10.　a.　voy
　　b.　vas
　　c.　va
　　d.　van
　　e.　van
　　f.　van
　　g.　va
　　h.　van
　　i.　va
　　j.　van

11. a. Cierro las ventanas.
    b. Entiendo la conversación.
    c. El abogado lo defiende
    d. Uds. entienden español.
    e. Nosotros siempre perdemos.
    f. ¿Cuándo empieza la clase?
    g. Qué cree Ud.?
    h. El enciende el horno.
    i. Preferimos vino.
    j. Queremos comer pescado.
    k. ¿Sienten Uds. el frío?
    l. ¿Quiere ella ensalada de pollo?
    m. Quiero cerveza fría.
    n. Pero prefiero vino.
    o. ¿Entiende Ud. los verbos?

12. a. Ellos pueden salir ahora.
    b. Ud. devuelve los pantalones.
    c. La falda no cuesta mucho.
    d. ¿Llueve ahora?
    e. ¿Juegas tú al tenis?
    f. ¿Recuerda él el lugar?
    g. No puedo ver.
    h. Ella almuerza a las doce.
    i. Los boletos cuestan veinte dólares.
    j. Ud. le enseña el libro a ella.
    k. Ellos no duermen bien.
    l. Los libros de francés cuestan más.
    m. ¿Quién puede salir con Ana?
    n. Recuerde comprar los boletos para el juego.
    o. ¿Dónde puede Ud. comprarlo?

13. a. Sí, prefiero salir ahora.
    b. Sí, duermo mucho los sábados.
    c. Sí, el automóvil cuesta mucho.
    d. Sí, la entiendo.
    e. Sí, lo recomiendo.
    f. Vuelvo a la casa a las nueve de la noche.

14. Horizontal
    3. recuerdas
    5. cuesta
    6. encuentras
    8. recordamos

    Vertical
    1. encontramos
    2. cuestan
    4. recuerdo
    7. pueden

15. a. 1. Estudien Uds...
       2. Den Uds...
       3. Compren Uds...
    b. 1. Trabaje Ud...
       2. Entre Ud...
       3. Espere Ud...
    c. 1. Da tú...
       2. Compra tú...
       3. Pinta tú...
    d. 1. Trabaja tú...
       2. Entra tú...
       3. Espera tú...
    e. 1. Compra tú...
       2. Paga tú...
       3. Lleva tú...

16. a. No empiecen a trabajar.
    b. No traigas todo.
    c. No regreses con María.
    d. No lo escuches.
    e. No traigan agua.
    f. No firmes aquí.
    g. No me des el boleto.
    h. No esperes un momento.
    i. No lo cambies hoy.
    j. No olvides eso.

17. a. Ella no lo visita a él.
    b. Los veo a ellos.
    c. ¡Tómelo!
    d. ¡No lo tomes!
    e. No lo entiendo.
    f. No lo entiendo (a él).
    g. ¿Quiere venderla?
    h. ¿Los ve todos los días?
    i. Sí, las busco (a ellas).
    j. La queremos amarilla.

18. a. Sí, las quiero.
    b. Sí, los ayudo.
    c. Sí, las invito a menudo.
    d. Sí, lo comprendo muy bien.
    e. Sí, lo escuchamos atentamente.
    f. Sí, deseo venderlas.
    g. Sí, me ven.
    h. Sí, prefiero esas plumas or sí, las prefiero.

19. a. Le dan un mapa de los Estados Unidos a ella.
    b. El me da un recado urgente.
    c. El cartero nos trae las cartas.
    d. El diccionario nos parece bueno.
    e. El nos habla muy a menudo.
    f. Ella no les escribe a ellos.
    g. ¿Por qué no me contestas?
    h. Nos gustan estas lecciones cortas.
    i. ¡No les hable a ellos!
    j. ¡No les hables a ellas!
    k. Le escribo a ella todas las semanas.
    l. Le mandamos dinero a él.
    m. ¡Cómprele un regalo a ella!
    n. Ella les lee cuentos a ellos.
    o. Hablo con ella.

20. a. Ellos me lo traen.
    b. Se lo prestamos a Uds.
    c. Juan se lo da a ellos.
    d. Voy a vendérsela a él.

    e. Voy a vendérsela a ella.
    f. ¿Quieres prestárnoslos?
    g. Yo te la escribo.
    h. El nos la enseña.
    i. Puedo escribírtela.
    j. Ellos nos las dan.
    k. ¿Se la prestas a tus amigos?
    l. ¡Dámelo!
    m. El debe explicárnosla.
    n. Cómpreselos para ella. (a ella)
    o. Préstesela a ella.

21. 1. Pedrito es el amigo de María.
    2. El habla inglés.
    3. El es un alumno bueno.
    4. El pronuncia muy bien.
    5. María habla español.
    6. Ella estudia inglés.
    7. El Sr. López es el profesor de la chica.
    8. El es el profesor de inglés.
    9. El está los martes.
    10. El está los viernes.

22. 1. Las vacaciones empiezan hoy.
    2. Ellas quieren ir a las tiendas.
    3. La mamá prefiere visitar a tía Rosa.
    4. Rosa es tía de María.
    5. Ana almuerza en casa de la tía.
    6. Después del almuerzo.
    7. La blusas azules cuestan mucho.
    8. No, tiene buen precio.
    9. María quiere merendar.
    10. todas van a merendar.

1.
1. esperé
2. esperaste
3. esperó
4. esperó
5. esperó
6. esperamos
7. esperamos
8. esperaron
9. rompí
10. rompiste
11. rompió
12. rompió
13. rompió
14. rompimos
15. rompimos
16. rompieron
17. subí
18. subiste
19. subió
20. subió
21. subió
22. subimos
23. subimos
24. subieron
25. llamé
26. llamaste
27. llamó
28. llamó
29. llamó
30. llamamos
31. llamamos
32. llamaron
33. quise
34. quisiste
35. quiso
36. quiso
37. quiso
38. quisimos
39. quisimos
40. quisieron

41. escribí
42. escribiste
43. escribió
44. escribió
45. escribió
46. escribimos
47. escribimos
48. escribieron

2.
a. abrió
b. entro
c. trabajé
d. volvió
e. ordenaste

3.
a. vivió
b. trabajé
c. volví
d. ordenó

4.
a. lección
b. salió
c. escribí, María
d. quién, habló
e. — —
f. viajé

5.
a. acabó
b. aprendiste
c. invitaron
d. prometí

6.
a. Sí, la pinté.
b. Sí, la escribió.
c. Sí, lo recibimos.
d. Sí, hablaron con ella.
e. Sí, llovió ayer.
f. Sí, los aprendí.

g. Sí, la abrí.
h. Sí, lo preparamos.

7.
a. fueron
b. dijo
c. trajiste
d. trajimos
e. fué
f. dijeron
g. fué
h. dimos
i. dieron
j. creyó
k. creímos
l. leyó
m. leí
n. oíste
o. oyó

8.
a. No, no las vi.
b. No, no fuí.
c. No, no estuvimos en casa anoche.
d. No, no los traje.
e. No, no lo hice todo.
f. No, no lo leímos.
g. No, no lo leyeron.
h. No, no la conocí.
i. No, no la supe.
j. No, no lo puse en la cocina.
k. No, no lo dí.
l. No, no vine.
m. No, no lo creímos.
n. No, no lo creyeron.
o. No, no pude hacerlo.
p. No, no los trajimos.

9. a. ¿Qué dijo ella?
    b. No creyeron el cuento.
    c. Fuimos a la tienda.
    d. Vine temprano.
    e. No lo oí.
    f. ¿Qué trajo ella?
    g. Clara hizo tres vestidos hoy.
    h. ¿Dijo ella la verdad.
    i. ¿Qué hicieron Uds. ayer?
    j. ¿Quién vió a los muchachos (chicos)?
    k. ¿La conocieron ellos?
    l. ¿Supiste del accidente?
        ¿Supo Ud. del accidente?
        ¿Supieron Uds. del accidente?
    m. Juan y María no lo creyeron.

10. a. Fué a Sur América.
    b. Estuvo en Argentina.
    c. Porque no consiguió reservación.
    d. Visitó (a) Buenos Aires.
    e. Pasó dos semanas en Buenos Aires.
    f. Compró artículos de piel y varios regalos para la familia.
    g. Compró regalos para la familia.
    h. Clara va a llamarla.

11. a. No, no dormí bien anoche.
    b. Eligieron a Domínguez para alcalde.
    c. Sí, servimos desayuno ahora.
    d. Sí, la seguí.
    e. Sí, lo repitió.

12. 1. Pedimos
    2. Consiguieron
    3. Durmió
    4. Repitió
    5. Conseguí
    6. Rieron
    7. Conseguí
    8. Sirvió
    9. Rieron

Lección Veintiocho

1. a. salía
    b. entregaban
    c. viajabas
    d. queríamos

2. a. hablaba
    b. quería
    c. entregaba
    d. teníamos
    e. tenían

3. a. quería
    b. llegaba
    c. salíamos

4. a. El la veía en la oscuridad
    b. Nosotros íbamos todos los días.
    c. Ellas veían muy bien.

5. a. Era mecánico (chofer).
    b. Sí, íbamos todos los días.
    c. No, no veía bien.

6. a. pagó
    b. vivimos
    c. vivíamos
    d. hablaba
    e. salían

7. a. State in the past.
    b. State in the past.
    c. Habitual action.
    d. State in the past.
    e. State in the past.
    f. Continuous action.

8. a. vivía
    b. había
    c. tenían
    d. queríamos
    e. llegó

    f. estábamos
    g. leían
    h. oíamos
    i. entró
    j. saludó

9. a. veía
    b. iban
    c. iban
    d. eran

10. a fué
    b. estaba
    c. vieron
    d. vinieron
    e. era

11. a. querían
    b. tenía
    c. sabían
    d. tenían
    e. salía

12. a. veían
    b. era
    c. íbamos
    d. veías
    e. eran

13. a. entregaba
    b. hablabas
    c. queríamos
    d. salían
    e. tenía

14. a. era
    b. éramos
    c. estaba
    d. íbamos
    e. veía

15. a. 4 and 6
    b. 7
    c. 1, 5
    d. 8
    e. 2
    f. 3

16. a. sus hijos
    b. mis fiestas
    c. nuestros hermanos
    d. tus teléfonos
    e. nuestras hijas

17. a. X
    b. XX
    c. XX
    d. X
    e. X

18. a. el teléfono tuyo
    b. las hermanas nuestras
    c. las hijas mías
    d. los padres suyos
    e. el hermano suyo

19. a. nuestra hermana
    b. su hijo
    c. sus fiestas
    d. su teléfono
    e. sus padres
    f. su casa

20. a. la hermana nuestra
    b. el hijo suyo
    c. las fiestas suyas
    d. el teléfono suyo
    e. los padres suyos
    f. la casa suya

21. a. su, mi, nuestro, de él, tu, tus
    b. mi, de ellos, de nosotros,
       tu, nuestros

22. a. sus
    b. nuestro
    c. tu
    d. tu
    e. mi

23. a. nuestra ciudad, la ciudad nuestra, la ciudad
       de nosotros
    b. tu puerta, la puerta tuya
    c. su padre, el padre suyo, el padre de ellos (as)
    d. sus primos, los primos suyos, los primos de ella
    e. mi auto, el auto mío
    f. su tío, el tío suyo, el tío de Uds.
    g. su casa, la casa suya, la casa de él
    h. su hijo, el hijo suyo, el hijo de Ud.

24. a. sabíamos
    b. supo
    c. sabía
    d. conocía
    e. sé
    f. conoció
    g. sabíamos
    h. supieron

25. a. Sí, estuve en el banco hoy.
    b. Sí, estaba en la clase.
    c. Sí, pudimos ir.
    d. Sí, podía hablar francés.
    e. Sí, quería ir.
    f. Sí, quise venir.

26. a. Buscaba un libro de cocina oriental.
    b. Porque estaban en otro lugar.
    c. No, no es fácil.
    d. En el próximo pasillo.
    e. Sí, lo sabía.
    f. Sí, lo tenían.

27. a. el suyo
    b. el suyo
    c. nuestro or los nuestros, suyos
    d. la suya
    e. tuya or la tuya, mía o la mía
    f. nuestras or las nuestras

Lección Veintinueve

1. a. acabaré, acabarás, acabará, acabarán
   b. esperarán, esperarás, esperarán, esperará
   c. dirás, dirá, dirán, dirán
   d. saldrá, saldrás, saldré, saldrán
   e. vendrán, vendremos, vendrán, vendré

2. a. Iremos a la frontera mañana.
   b. Tendré que añadir juguetes a la lista.
   c. No lo pondré encima de la mesa.
   d. La butaca cabrá en el balcón.
   e. ¿Cuándo harás la tarea?
   f. Mañana la haré.

3. a. vendrán
   b. sabrán
   c. veremos
   d. dirá
   e. destruirán
   f. pondrán
   g. querrán

4. a. Voy a hacerlo temprano. Lo haré temprano.
   b. Voy a saber la respuesta. Sabré la respuesta.
   c. Carlos no va a poder asistir a la reunión.
      Carlos no podrá asistir a la reunión.

   d. No van a pagar la renta todavía. No pagarán la
      renta todavía.
   e. No voy a traer el otro perro. No traeré el otro
      perro.
   f. ¿Le vas a dar este regalo ? ¿Le darás este regalo?
   g. El va a comprar la revista. El comprará la revista.

5. a. Juan dijo que vendría.
   b. Ella sabía que Josefina haría el viaje.
   c. Creía que Alberto no podría venir.
   d. Sabían que yo tendría el dinero para el miércoles.
   e. Preguntó que hora sería.

6. a. Sólo desayuno.
   b. A las doce.
   c. ¿Vendrá Teresa?
   d. No, prefiere esperar.
   e. Frutas.
   f. A las once.
   g. A las once y cuarto.
   h. Porque están sirviendo sólo desayuno.

7. a. estoy estudiando ahora
      estás estudiando ahora

　　　　estamos estudiando ahora
　　　　están estudiando ahora
　　b. está lavando el auto
　　　　están lavando el auto
　　　　estoy lavando el auto
　　　　está lavando el auto
　　c. estaba leyendo
　　　　estábamos leyendo
　　　　estaban leyendo
　　　　estabas leyendo

8.　a. Sí, estamos hablando de política.
　　b. Sí, están haciendo el trabajo bien.
　　c. Sí, estoy buscando el libro.
　　d. Sí, estoy corriendo.
　　e. Sí, está esperándolo.
　　f. Sí, se lo estaban diciendo.

Lección Treinta

1.　1. dormido
　　2. perdido
　　3. contado
　　4. acabado
　　5. comprendido
　　6. vivido
　　7. sido
　　8. estado
　　9. comido
　　10. venido
　　11. tratado
　　12. gustado
　　13. querido
　　14. tenido
　　15. pagado
　　16. almorzado
　　17. pedido
　　18. encendido
　　19. regresado
　　20. salido
　　21. muerto
　　22. hecho
　　23. puesto
　　24. revuelto
　　25. cubierto
　　26. escrito
　　27. dicho
　　28. visto
　　29. abierto

2.　a. 2
　　b. 5
　　c. 3
　　d. 1
　　e. 4
　　f. 7
　　g. 6

3.　a. Sí, las he traído.
　　b. Sí, han venido.
　　c. Sí, los hemos visto.
　　d. Sí, he desayunado ya.
　　e. Sí, lo ha llevado.
　　f. Sí, has contestado bien.
　　g. Sí, hemos terminado.
　　h. Sí, lo hemos encendido.

4.　a. Veo un perro muerto.
　　b. El perro está muerto.
　　c. Ví una ventana rota.
　　d. La ventana estaba rota.
　　e. Tenemos dos lecciones terminadas.
　　f. Las lecciones están terminadas.

g. Tenemos sólo una carta bien escrita.
h. Las cartas están bien escritas.

5. a. Porque no ha tenido tiempo.
   b. Porque todo está cerrado.
   c. Los domingos.
   d. De anuncios de artículos para el hogar.
   e. Porque no había llegado cuando salió de casa.
   f. En Caracas.
   g. Ha decidido mandarle un cheque.
   h. Ha decidido mandarle dinero.

6. a. Lo he hecho todo en un día.
      Lo había hecho todo en un día.
   b. Les hemos abierto la puerta.
      Les habíamos abierto la puerta.
   c. Ellos han vivido en Puerto Rico.
      Ellos habían vivido en Puerto Rico.
   d. Tú has sido la primera siempre.
      Tú habías sido la primera siempre.
   e. Ud. no ha comprendido.
      Ud. no había comprendido.

f. Ellos lo han hecho temprano.
   Ellos lo habían hecho temprano.
g. He dormido mucho, pero él no ha dormido.
   Había dormido mucho, pero él no había dormido.
h. Le hemos dicho la verdad.
   Le habíamos dicho la verdad.

1. a. lleve
    b. necesitemos
    c. visites
    d. deje
    e. hablen
    f. mire
    g. ayudemos
    h. presten
    i. tomen
    j. mandemos

2. a. que llegue a las ocho
    b. que me llame el domingo
    c. que no hable demasiado
    d. trabaje los sábados.

3. a. lea
    b. suba
    c. corra
    d. venda
    e. aprenda
    f. escribas
    g. abra
    h. beba

4. a. hable
    b. venda
    c. comprenda
    d. necesites
    e. compren

5. a. olvidemos
    b. deje
    c. lleve
    d. viaja
    e. están
    f. espera
    g. espere
    h. compremos
    i. lleves

6. a. lea.
    b. gasta
    c. hable
    d. venda
    e. termine
    f. come
    g. tomen
    h. dé
    i. estudien
    j. llegamos

7. a. Quiero que ella pague.
    b. Ellos quieren que comamos ahora.
    c. Me aconsejan que coma a menudo.
    d. Ella quiere que él estudie.
    e. Les prohíbo que hablen en clase.

8. a. Sé que él lo recibe mañana.
    b. Pensamos que él lo recibe mañana.
    c. No creo que él lo reciba mañana.
    d. Estoy seguro que él lo recibe mañana.
    e. Dudamos que él lo reciba mañana.
    f. Espero que él lo reciba mañana.
    g. Creemos que él lo recibe mañana.

9. a. Toda la clase espera que ellos tomen parte activa.
    b. No es la primera vez que sorprende a todo el mundo.
    c. Voy al correo a comprar sellos y tarjetas postales.

10. a. Héctor practica el deporte de esquí.
    b. Porque él ha practicado muy poco.
    c. Fué a Colorado.
    d. El verbo es mandar.
    e. Espera que Héctor tome parte activa en el evento.
    f. Tiene que mandarle el pasaporte a Héctor en seguida.
    g. No sé "or" no se sabe.

1. a.

ordene	coma	escriba	llame	rompa	reciba
ordenes	comas	escribas	llames	rompas	recibas
ordene	coma	escriba	llame	rompa	reciba
ordenemos	comamos	escribamos	llamemos	rompamos	recibamos
ordenen	coman	escriban	llamen	rompan	reciban

b.

tenga	oiga	vea	pueda	cierre	pierda
tengas	oigas	veas	puedas	cierres	pierdas
tenga	oiga	vea	pueda	cierre	pierdas
tengamos	oigamos	veamos	podamos	cerremos	perdamos
tengan	oigan	vean	puedan	cierren	pierdan

2.
a. Yo, Ud., él, ella
b. Tú
c. Uds., Ell(os,as)
d. Yo, Ud., él, ella
e. Uds., Ell(os,as)
f. Uds., Ell(os,as)
g. Tú
h. Uds., Ell(os,as)
i. Yo, Ud., él, ella
j. Nosotros(as)
k. Uds., ell(os,as)
l. Tú

m. Uds., ell(os,as)
n. Yo, Ud., él, ella
o. Nosotros(as)
p. Uds., ell(os,as)
q. Tú
r. Yo, Ud., él, ella
s. Uds. ell(os,as)
t. Yo, Ud., él, ella
u. Uds., ell(os,as)
v. Yo, Ud., él, ella

3.
a. tomen
b. cierre
c. salgas
d. venga
e. tengamos
f. podamos
g. hagan
h. traigan
i. pague
j. conozcamos
k. seamos
l. esté

m. almuerce
n. expliquen
o. escoja
p. busque
q. dirija
r. vaya
s. dé
t. lean

4. a. leo, lee
    b. escribes
    c. ponen
    d. voy, va
    e. piden
    f. siguen
    g. vendes
    h. vengo, viene
    i. oigo, oye
    j. damos
    k. son
    l. dormimos
    m. pedimos
    n. llegan
    o. pagan
    p. piensas
    q. pones
    r. juegan
    s. explicamos
    t. entendemos
    u. empiezas
    v. traen

5. a. vengas
    b. tiene
    c. oye
    d. estudie
    e. necesita
    f. veas
    g. haga
    h. escriba
    i. esté
    j. dé
    k. baje
    l. va

6. a. que sea pequeña.
    b. que sea grande
    c. que sea interesante.
    d. que sea cómoda
    e. que preferimos.

7. a. tenga
    b. sabe
    c. viaje
    d. escribe
    e. lea
    f. canta
    g. sepa
    h. tienen
    i. tenga
    j. sea
    k. podamos
    l. traen
    m. esté
    n. tiene
    o. tenga
    p. haga
    q. crea
    r. creen
    s. cueste
    t. son

8. a. Conocen a un hombre que habla cinco
       idiomas.
    b. Prefieren un hombre que hable cinco
       idiomas.
    c. Queremos el guía que es bilingüe.
    d. Queremos un guía que sea bilingüe.
    e. Ud. tiene un libro que tiene todas las
       respuestas correctas.
    f. No hay libro aquí que tenga todas las
       respuestas correctas.
    g. ¿Hay algún hotel o parador que tenga cuartos
       (habitaciones) disponibles?
    h. El siempre recomienda hoteles que tienen
       cuartos (habitaciones) disponibles.
    i. No tengo nada que pueda ponerme.
    j. Tengo una camisa roja que puedo ponerme.

9. a. 2
   b. 3
   c. 1
   d. 3

10. a. No, Esteban no quiere gastar más de $10,000 en el coche.
    b. Tiene cuatro años.
    c. Quiere que vaya con él a ver autos.
    d. No, tiene cuatro años.
    e. No, no quiere gastar tanto.
    f. Esteban cree que es muy caro.
    g. Cree que querrá una fortuna.
    h. Deciden visitar algunas agencias de autos.

11. a. No vas a encontrar ninguno que cueste menos.
    b. Entonces creo que debes visitar algunas de las agencias de autos.
    c. No te das cuenta que el coche mío mantiene su valor.

12. a. No quiero gastar tanto.
    b. Querrá una fortuna por él.
    c. Quizás puedas encontrar un modelo del año pasado que te cueste menos.
    d. Creo (pienso) que debes visitar algunas de las agencias de autos.
    e. Por ese dinero, trataré de encontrar algo mejor (que sea más nuevo).
    f. Eso es mucho dinero por un auto de cuatro años.

13. a. No, no me acosté tarde anoche.
    b. Se ríen del policía.
    c. Sí, me levanto temprano.
    d. Se puso el vestido verde
    e. Sí, me lavé ya or sí, ya me lavé.

14. a. Levántate
    b. se ríe or se está riendo.
    c. se quite
    d. te pusiste
    e. mírate.

Lección Treinta Y Trés

1. a. Traeré a Juan cuando (nosotros) lo veamos.
   b. Traeré a Juan tan pronto (nosotors) lo veamos.
   c. Traeré a Juan tan pronto (tú) lo veas.
   d. Llevaré a Juan para que ellos lo vean.
   e. Llevaré a Juan con tal que ellos lo vean.
   f. No lleves a Juan sin que yo lo vea.

2. a. Sí, se lo daré cuando venga.
   b. Sí, se lo doy siempre cuando viene.
   c. Sí, lo tendré listo para que él lo pueda ver.
   d. Sí, te lo dejaré ver antes que ella llegue.
   e. Sí, te lo prestaré sin que papá lo sepa.
   f. Sí, siempre lo veo tan pronto llega.
   g. Sí, lo terminaré después (de) que lo aprueben.

3. a. Tendré que estudiar mucho cuando tenga examen.
   b. Le escribiré cuando tenga tiempo.
   c. Le voy a escribir tan pronto sepa de él.
   d. Comprarán el ventilador cuando tengan el dinero.
   e. Lo veré después que termine.

4. a. regrese
   b. llega
   c. hable
   d. termine
   e. llegue
   f. lea
   g. salgan
   h. canse
   i. necesite
   j. tenga

5. a. para que Ud. pueda viajar hoy
   b. para que tenga mejores notas
   c. para que María la pueda lavar
   d. cuando limpie su traje
   e. antes (de) que sea de noche
   f. tan pronto como llegues a casa
   g. hasta que la aprenda
   h. para que ellos te manden las toallas
   i. en caso que él venga

6. a. Dale estas cartas a tu hermano tan pronto como (él) llegue.
   b. Los chicos comerán antes (de) que salgamos.
   c. Lo explicaré para que ellos lo entiendan.
   d. Estudiaremos el subjuntivo cuando estemos en la clase de español.
   e. María quiere hacer las maletas antes (de) que su esposo llegue a casa.

7. a. (a) A nadie veo.
      (b) No veo a nadie.
   b. (a) Nada tengo que hacer.
      (b) No tengo nada que hacer.
   c. (a) Ninguno tengo.
      (b) No tengo ninguno.
   d. (a) Ni pan ni leche compro.
      (b) No compro ni pan ni leche.
   e. (a) Pedro nunca viene.
      (b) Pedro no viene nunca.
   f. (a) Ella tampoco va.
      (b) Ella no va tampoco.
   g. (a) Nada tengo en esa caja.
      (b) No tengo nada en esa caja.
   h. (a) Ninguna de las chicas quiere ir.
      (b) No quiere ir ninguna de las chicas.

8. a. No voy a llevar a nadie al concierto.
   b. No tengo ningún dinero.
   c. No estudio ni francés ni alemán.
   d. Ella no tiene frío nunca.
   e. No quiero nada.
   f. Ofelia no va tampoco.

9. a. Trabajan seis días.
   b. Sí, ella viene los domingos.
   c. Sí, Laura lo conoce.
   d. No tiene coche porque lo vendió.
   e. Paco está en la cantina cuando Laura llega.
   f. El dueño no ha llegado.
   g. Los empleados la abren el sábado.
   h. Lo vendió el mes pasado.
   i. Tan pronto como lleguen los modelos nuevos.

10. a. ¿Pero es que tu vida no es más que trabajo?
    b. Pero voy a comprar otro tan pronto como lleguen los nuevos modelos.
    c. Está un poco lejos y el autobús demora mucho.

11. a. El chico que vive al lado tiene un Mercedes.
    b. ¿Cómo puedes vivir sin coche?
    c. ¿Y tu coche ya no lo tienes?
    d. El no tiene un buen coche tampoco.
    e. Nunca vas a la playa los domingos.
    f. No tengo nada que ponerme para la fiesta.
    g. Nunca te vi aquí antes.
    h. Está un poco lejos de casa y el autobús demora mucho.

12. a. They did the same thing.
    b. Do you see how easy the lesson is?
    c. The worst part is that he always arrives late.
    d. What's done, is done.
    e. Tell him how important it is to be a responsible person.

13. a. Déme lo que tenga.
    b. No tenemos lo que ella quiere.
    c. No soy parte de ese grupo lo que (lo cual) me impide comer en su mesa.
    d. Carlos no va lo que (lo cual) me hace ir solo.
    e. Lo importante es que él los conoce a todos.
    f. El me trajo lo que le pedí.

1. a. trajera
        vieras
        hiciéramos
        oyeran
    b. leyera
        dijera
        pararan
        pagáramos
    c. pusieras
        dejara
        estudiáramos
        quisieran
    d. tuviera
        diera
        trajera
        incluyera
    e. cupiera
        viniera
        estuviera
        entrara

2. a. las fotos para que las viera
    b. que José viniera
    c. a Carmen que lo trajera
    d. el disco para que lo oyeran
    e. que su hermano viera al médico hoy
    f. una casa que tuviera cuatro habitaciones
    g. nadie que pudiera ir hoy.
    h. que ella lo creyera
    i. que tuviera el trabajo listo
    j. en que lo llevara al cine

3. a. viera
    b. volviéramos
    c. habla
    d. pudo
    e. venía
    f. estuviera
    g. trajera
    h. llegó
    i. pudiera
    j. estuvieras

k. hiciera
l. pagaron
m. comprara
n. pagara
o. fuera
p. oyeras

4. a. para
    b. para
    c. por, para
    d. por
    e. por
    f. por
    g. para
    h. para, para
    i. para, para

5. a. Ellos fueron a Roma por un mes.
    b. Ella lo vendió por cien dólares.
    c. Los compramos para el comedor.
    d. Carlos lo mandó por correo.
    e. ¿Has estudiado la lección para hoy?
    f. ¿Para qué es ese dinero?
    g. Ellos habían viajado por Europa.
    h. Déme leche para el perro.
    i. Estoy por comerme una manzana.
    j. Ella siempre lo llama por el día.

6. a. Está allí para una entrevista.
    b. Estaba en una reunión (junta).
    c. Vivió en varios países, porque sus padres
        estaban en el cuerpo diplomático.
    d. El hecho que Alejandro habla francés.
    e. Busca un puesto de jefe de ventas.
    f. Porque no creyó que fuera importante.
    g. Porque tiene que dar aviso a la firma donde
        trabaja.
    h. Porque el Sr. Duarte le dijo que la llenara.
    i. Porque el Sr. Duarte está en una junta.
    j. Sí, creo que él está de acuerdo.
        No, no creo que él esté de acuerdo.

7. a. En que puedo servirle.
   b. El Sr. Duarte sugirió que llenara una planilla.
   c. La firma necesitaba alguien que supiera francés.
   d. Llamó para decir que estaba en una junta, y para
      pedirle que lo esperara.

Lección Treinta Y Cinco

1. a. hayamos oído
   b. hayas visto
   c. haya escrito
   d. haya vuelto
   e. hayan roto

   f. he traído
   g. hayas visto
   h. han leído
   i. haya escrito
   j. haya dado
   k. hayas oído

2. a. hayan ido
      See them after they have gone to the bank.
   b. hayan puesto
      I don't believe they have put it there.
   c. haya escrito
      I hope Isabel has written me.
   d. haya leído
      Give it to her after he has read it.
   e. haya dicho
      I don't believe she has told him yet.

3. a. No creo que ella lo haya hecho.
   b. Esperamos que ella haya llegado a tiempo
      para el vuelo.
   c. Mándeme el libro después que lo haya leído.
   d. Es posible que (ellos) lo hayan visto.
   e. Ellos saben que hemos traído la medicina.
   f. No veo por qué (ellos) no le han dicho la verdad.
   g. Es un hecho que él no ha vuelto todavía.
   h. Ellos no creen que Carmen y yo hayamos terminado.

4. a. hayan ido
   b. haya trabajado
   c. hayan llegado
   d. han venido
   e. ha terminado

5. a. Hortensia ha leído el periódico temprano.
   b. Guillermo le habló a Joaquín de la exposición.
   c. Guillermo debe regresar temprano.
   d. Son de Roselló.
   e. Porque están aquí mismo.
   f. Hortensia y Guillermo leyeron el periódico
      primero.
   g. Hortensia parece apreciar más la exposición.
   h. Se dice Bellas Artes.
   i. Están al otro lado.
   j. Sí, creo que les ha gustado.

6. a. Quiero ver algo que no haya visto antes.
   b. Si Uds. vienen temprano, me gustaría ir
      también.
   c. Después que hayamos visto las esculturas
      podemos volver.
   d. Vuelve temprano para que vayamos antes de las
      diez.

7. a. Roma fue contruída por Rómulo.
   b. La carta fué firmada por el agente.
   c. El presidente es querido por el pueblo.
   d. El Quijote fué escrito por Cervantes.
   e. Ese libro fué pagado por mi hermano.
   f. El presidente será honrado por el senado.
   g. El árbol será cortado por los muchachos.

8. a. Se terminaron el día cinco.
    b. Se come a las ocho de la noche.
    c. Las tiendas se abren a las nueve de la mañana.
    d. Se necesita dinero para la fiesta.

9. a. Las puertas se cierran a las seis.
    b. Se ven muchos edificios altos.
    c. Se necesita mucha paciencia.
    d. ¿Cuándo se escribió?
    e. Se dice que ella es muy rica.
    f. El libro se escribió en 1900.
    g. Este edificio se vendió el año pasado.

10. a. la mejor
    b. peores
    c. mejor
    d. mejor
    e. la mejor
    f. mejor
    g. la mayor
    h. mayor

11. a. Ella es la menor de los hijos de mi hermano.
    b. Quiero la mejor, no la peor.
    c. ¿Cuál es mayor (más grande) México o Buenos Aires?
    d. Pedro es su hermano menor.
    e. Su hermano es mayor que ella.

    f. Su auto es mejor que el mío.
    g. El tiene más de la mitad.
    h. Ese hotel es menos caro que éste.
    i. No tengo más que tres.
    j. Esta lección es más difícil.

12. a. tantas.....como
    b. tanto.....como
    c. tantos.....como
    d. tantas.....como

13. a. tan.....como
    b. tan.....como
    c. tan.....como
    d. tan.....como

14. a. El es muy alto.
        El es altísimo.
    b. Raquel está muy contenta.
        Raquel está contentísima.
    c. Esos hombres son muy ricos.
        Esos hombres riquísimos.
    d. El pan es muy caro.
        El pan es carísimo.
    e. Su hermano es muy inteligente.
        Su hermano es inteligentísimo.
    f. Esas lecciones son muy largas.
        Esas lecciones son larguísimas.

1. a. Si pudiera ir a la fiesta, iría con Teresa.
   Si hubiera podido ir a la fiesta, habría ido con Teresa.
   b. Si el médico me viera hoy, no podría venir a trabajar esta tarde.
   Si el médico me hubiera visto hoy, no habría podido venir a trabajar esta tarde.
   c. Si abrieran las tiendas, iría a ver la lavadora.
   Si hubieran abierto las tiendas temprano, habría ido a ver la lavadora.
   d. Si se sintiera bien iría al concierto.
   Si se hubiera sentido bien, habría ido al concierto.
   e. Si llamaras al dentista, te daría un turno.
   Si hubieras llamado al dentista, te habría dado un turno.
   f. Si quisiera bajar de peso seguiría una dieta.
   Si hubiera querido bajar de peso, habría seguido una dieta.
   g. Si ellos se fueran temprano, podrían regresar hoy.
   Si ellos se hubieran ido temprano, habrían podido regresar hoy.

2. a. Si los veo hoy se lo digo (diré).
   b. Si tuviera el dinero, lo compraría.
   c. Si yo fuera él, iría.
   d. Si lo compro hoy, ellos lo mandan (mandarán) el lunes.
   e. Si yo lo hubiera comprado hoy, ellos lo habrían mandado el lunes.
   f. Si yo hubiera ido, yo los habría visto.
   g. Si ellos no le hubieran hablado a la señora ¿qué habrían ellos hecho?
   h. Si él me paga hoy, te pago (pagaré).
   i. Si él me hubiera pagado hoy, le habría pagado a Ud.
   j. Si él me pagara hoy, te pagaría.
   k. Si yo vendiera el coche, ellos lo comprarían.
   l. Si él tiene el auto, ellos salen (saldrán) a las cinco de la tarde.

   m. Si yo lo hubiera visto antes, se lo habría dicho.
   n. La habría ayudado, si lo hubiera sabido.
   o. Habríamos pagado, si hubiéramos tenido el dinero.
   p. Si ellos me hubieran llamado, yo habría ido a verlos.

3. a. Cuesta un dólar la docena.
   b. El es el Sr. Toledo.
   c. Me lavo la cara.
   d. Hablo francés solamente.

4. a. Los libros son necesarios.
   b. ¿Dr. Jaramillo, tiene Ud. uno?
   c. El Dr. Jaramillo tiene dos.
   d. Los metales se usan todos los días.
   e. Él va a lavar el auto.
   f. ¿Hablan ellos español?
   g. Dígale al Sr. Pérez que lo espero.
   h. Las joyas son caras.
   i. El francés es tan importante como el alemán.

5. a. No conoce la prima de Guadalajara.
   b. Porque la junta es en Toronto.
   c. No había nadie en la oficina que pudiera ir.
   d. Sí, Gloria conocía a todo el mundo.
   e. Mariana vino sola.

6. a. 2
   b. 3
   c. 3
   d. 3
   e. 2
   f. 2

7. a. No había nadie más en la oficina que pudiera ir.
   b. Recuerda que me dijiste que si él viniera, (yo)
      lo conocería.
   c. (Yo) quería que Pedro viniera conmigo.
   d. El es el alma de la fiesta.
   e. Si no hubiera sido por él, nadie habría ido a Toronto.
   f. Si ella se hubiera quedado más tiempo, (ella) habría conocido a Pedro.
   g. Creo que conoces a todo el mundo aquí esta noche.
   h. ¿Cuánto tiempo va a estar (ella) aquí?
   i. Si (él) no hubiera ido (él) habría podido venir.
   j. El acepta con una sonrisa cualquier tarea que le asignen.

a eso de	—	at about	alcalde (sa)	—	Mayor
a menos que	—	unless	alegrarse	—	to be happy about
a menudo	—	often	algo	—	something
a pie	—	on foot, walking	alguien	—	someone, somebody
a propósito	—	by the way	algún(o)	—	some, any
a su hora	—	on time	alguna vez	—	sometime, ever
a veces	—	at times	alimentar	—	to feed, to nourish
abdomen (m)	—	abdomen	alma (f)	—	soul
abrigo (m)	—	overcoat	almorzar	—	to have lunch
abril	—	April	almuerzo (m)	—	lunch
abrir	—	to open	alquiler (m)	—	rent
abuelo (a)	—	grandfather, grandmother	alto	—	tall
acabar	—	to finish	alumno (a)	—	pupil
acabar de + infinitive	—	to have just + past participle	allí	—	there
acaso	—	maybe	amarillo	—	yellow
aceite (m)	—	oil	América Central	—	Central America
aceptar	—	to accept	América del Norte	—	North America
aconsejar	—	to advise, to counsel	América del Sur	—	South America
acostarse	—	to go to bed	americano	—	American
activo	—	active	amigo(a)	—	friend
adelantar	—	to advance	anaranjado	—	orange colored
además	—	besides	andar	—	to move along
adiós	—	goodbye	andén (m)	—	railroad platform
¿A dónde?	—	where?	animal (m)	—	animal
aeropuerto (m)	—	airport	anoche	—	last night
agencia (f)	—	agency, dealership	anotar	—	to take note, to comment
agosto	—	August	antena (f)	—	antenna
agradar	—	to please	antes	—	before (adverb)
agua (f)	—	water	antes de	—	before (preposition)
agüero (m)	—	omen	antes (de) que	—	before (connector)
águila (f)	—	eagle	anuncio (m)	—	ad
ahí	—	there	añadir	—	to add
ahora	—	now	año (m)	—	year
ahorrar	—	to save	año pasado	—	last year
al	—	to the (a + el)	año que viene	—	next year
al fin	—	finally, at last	aparato (m)	—	appliance, machine
alambre (m)	—	wire	apellido (m)	—	last name, surname
album (m)	—	album	apoyar	—	to support, to back up

aprender	—	to learn	
aprobar	—	to approve	
aquel, aquella	—	that (over there)	
aquél, aquélla	—	that one (over there)	
aquello	—	that (neuter pronoun)	
aquellos, aquellas	—	those (over there)	
aquí	—	here	
árbol (m)	—	tree	
arquitecto (a)	—	architect	
artículo (m)	—	article	
artista (m&f)	—	artist	
arreglar	—	to repair, to fix	
arreglo (m)	—	rule, order	
arroz (m)	—	rice	
arroz con leche (m)	—	rice pudding	
arroz con pollo (m)	—	chicken with yellow rice	
asado	—	baked, roast	
así	—	so, in this manner	
así y todo	—	even so	
asiento (m)	—	seat	
asignar	—	to assign	
asistir	—	to attend	
Asunción	—	capital city of Paraguay	
ataque al corazón (m)	—	heart attack	
atentamente	—	attentively	
auditorio (m)	—	auditorium	
auto (m)	—	car	
autobús (m)	—	bus	
automóvil	—	automobile	
avenida (f)	—	avenue	
avión (m)	—	airplane	
aviso (m)	—	information, notice	
ayer	—	yesterday	
ayudar	—	to help	
azucarera (f)	—	sugar bowl	
azul	—	blue	
bailar	—	to dance	
baile (m)	—	dance	
bajar	—	to go down, to descend	
bajar de peso	—	to lose weight	
bajo	—	low	
balcón (m)	—	balcony	
banco (m)	—	bank, bench	
bandeja (f)	—	tray	
baño (m)	—	bathroom	
barato	—	inexpensive	
barco (m)	—	boat, ship	
batido (m)	—	milkshake	
bazo (m)	—	spleen	
beber (m)	—	to drink	
Bellas Artes (f)	—	Fine Arts	
bello	—	pretty, beautiful	
biblioteca (f)	—	library	
bicicleta (f)	—	bicycle	
bien	—	well	
biftek (m)	—	steak	
bilingüe	—	bilingual	
billete (m)	—	bill (bank note), ticket (bus, theater)	
billetera (f)	—	wallet	
blanco	—	white	
blusa (f)	—	blouse	
boca (f)	—	mouth	
bocina (f)	—	horn, speaker	
Bogotá	—	capital city of Colombia	
boda (f)	—	wedding	
boleto (m)	—	ticket	
Bolívar (m)	—	monetary unit of Venezuela, name of Venezuelan hero	
Bolivia	—	country in South America	
bondadoso	—	kind	
bonito	—	pretty	
botella (f)	—	bottle	
brazo (m)	—	arm	
buen provecho	—	enjoy your meal	
buenas	—	a formal greeting	
buenas noches	—	good night, good evening	
buenas tardes	—	good afternoon	

buen(o)	–	good
buenos días	–	good morning
bufanda (f)	–	scarf
buscar	–	to look for, to search
butaca (f)	–	armchair
caballo	–	horse
cabeza (f)	–	head
caber	–	to fit in
cabaña (f)	–	cabin
cable (m)	–	cable
cadera (f)	–	hip
caer(se)	–	to fall
café (m)	–	coffee, brown
cafetería (f)	–	coffee shop
caja (f)	–	box, cash register
cajero(a)	–	cashier
calentar	–	to heat
caliente	–	hot
calor	–	heat, warmth
callar	–	to hush, to be silent
cama (f)	–	bed
camarero(a)	–	waiter, waitress
camarón (m)	–	shrimp
camarote (m)	–	cabin, birth, stateroom
cambiar	–	to change
cambio (m)	–	change
camello (m)	–	camel
caminar	–	to walk
camisa (f)	–	shirt
canción (f)	–	song
candidato(a)	–	candidate
cangrejo (m)	–	crab
cansado	–	tired
cantar	–	to sing
cantina (f)	–	bar, snack bar
capital (m)	–	wealth, capital
capital (f)	–	capital city
capítulo (m)	–	chapter
cara (f)	–	face
Caracas	–	capital city of Venezuela

¡caramba!	–	expression of surprise, dismay, anger, (like "heck")
caramelo (m)	–	candy stick (bar)
carmelita	–	brown (Cuba)
carne (f)	–	meat, beef, flesh
caro	–	expensive
carpintero(a)	–	carpenter
carta (f)	–	letter
cartera (f)	–	purse, wallet
cartero	–	mailman
carrera (f)	–	race
casa (f)	–	house, home
casado	–	married
castaño	–	brown
castellano	–	Spanish language, native of Castile
caña (f)	–	cane
católico(a)	–	Catholic
catorce	–	fourteen
cebolla (f)	–	onion
ceja (f)	–	eyebrow
cena (f)	–	dinner
cenar	–	to have dinner
centavo (m)	–	cent, penny
cielo (m)	–	sky
cien	–	one hundred
cierto	–	certain
cincuenta	–	fifty
cine (m)	–	movies, movie house
cintura (f)	–	waist
cinturón (m)	–	belt
circulación (f)	–	circulation
ciudad (f)	–	city
claro	–	clear
clase (f)	–	class
claxon (m)	–	auto horn
cliente	–	customer
cocina (f)	–	kitchen
cocinero(a)	–	cook
coctel (m)	–	cocktail (drink)

coche-cama (m)	— pullman car	contado	— cash
coche-comedor (m)	— dining car	contar	— to count
codo (m)	— elbow	contestar	— to answer
colección (f)	— collection	contigo	— with you
colegio (m)	— school	convencer	— to convince
color (m)	— color	conversar	— to converse
columna vertebral (f)	— spine	copa (f)	— goblet, wine glass
comedor (m)	— dining room	corazón (m)	— heart
comenzar	— to begin	corbata (f)	— tie
comer	— to eat	correo (m)	— post office, mail
comida (f)	— food, supper	correr	— to run
comisión (f)	— commission	cortar	— to cut
¿Cómo?	— how?	corte (m)	— cut
como a	— at about	cosa (f)	— thing
comodidad (f)	— comfort	costa (f)	— coast
cómodo	— comfortable	Costa Rica	— country in Central America
compañero (m)	— companion	costar	— to cost
compañero de cuarto	— room-mate	costilla (f)	— rib
competencia (f)	— competition	credencial (f)	— credential
competir	— to compete	crédito (m)	— credit
complaciente	— pleasing, agreeable	creer	— to believe
complicado	— complicated	crema (f)	— cream
composición (f)	— composition	crítica (f)	— review, critique, critic
comprar	— to buy	croqueta (f)	— croquette, fritter
comprender	— to understand	crucero (m)	— cruise, monetary unit of Brazil
comunista	— comunist		
con	— with	cuadra (f)	— street block
con tal que	— provided that	cuando	— when, whenever
concierto (m)	— concert	¿cuándo?	— when
condición (f)	— condition	¿cuánto?	— how much?
conferencia (f)	— conference	¿cuántos	— how many?
confirmado	— confirmed	cuarenta	— forty
confirmar	— to confirm	cuarto (m)	— room, fourth, quarter
conmigo	— with me	cuatro	— four
conocer	— to know	cuatrocientos	— four hundred
conseguir	— to obtain	cubiertos (m)	— room, fourth, quarter
considerable	— considerable	cubrir	— to cover
construir	— to build	cuchara (f)	— spoon
consulta (f)	— doctor's office	cuchillo (m)	— knife
contador(a)	— accountant	cuello (m)	— neck

cuenta (f)	—	check, bill, calculation, account	dentista (m&f)	—	dentist
			departamento (m)	—	department
cuento (m)	—	story, tale	deporte (m)	—	sport
cuerpo (m)	—	body	deportivo	—	sport
curso (m)	—	course	derecho	—	right
chaqueta (f)	—	jacket	desayunar	—	to have breakfast
cheque (m)	—	bank check	desayuno (m)	—	breakfast
chico(a)	—	boy, girl, youngster	descansar	—	to rest
China	—	China	describir	—	to describe
chocolate (m)	—	chocolate, cocoa	desde luego	—	of course
dar	—	to give	desfile (m)	—	parade
dato (m)	—	data, information	desear	—	to wish
de	—	of, from, about	después	—	after (adverb)
de acuerdo	—	in agreement	destacarse	—	to stand out
de contado	—	cash transaction	destruir	—	to destroy
de día	—	daytime, during the day	devolver	—	to return, to give back
de la mañana	—	a.m., in the morning	día (m)	—	day
de la noche	—	p.m., at night	diccionario (m)	—	dictionary
de la tarde	—	p.m., in the afternoon	diciembre	—	December
de ninguna manera (forma)	—	by no means	diente (m)	—	tooth
de ningún modo	—	by no means, in no way	dieta (f)	—	diet
de noche	—	at night, night time	diez	—	ten
de prisa	—	in a hurry	difícil	—	difficult
de repente	—	suddenly	dilema (m)	—	dilemma
de uso	—	used	dinero (m)	—	money
debajo	—	under	Dios	—	God
deber	—	to owe, must	diplomático(a)	—	diplomat, diplomatic
decidir	—	to decide	dirección (f)	—	address, direction
décimo	—	tenth	directo	—	direct
decir	—	to say, to tell	dirigir	—	to direct
decorar	—	to decorate	disco (m)	—	record
dedo (m)	—	finger, toe	disponible	—	available
defender	—	to defend	dispuesto	—	willing
dejar	—	to leave behind, to let	diversión (f)	—	fun, entertainment
del	—	of the, from the (de + el)	dividir	—	to divide
delgado	—	thin	doce	—	twelve
demandar	—	to demand	docena (f)	—	dozen
demasiado	—	too much	dólar (m)	—	dollar
demócrata	—	democratic	doler	—	to hurt
demorar	—	to delay, to retard	dolor (m)	—	pain

domingo	–	Sunday	enfermo	–	sick, ill
dominicano	–	Dominican	enjuague (m)	–	rinse
dormir(se)	–	to sleep	ensalada (f)	–	salad
dormitorio (m)	–	bedroom	ensalada mixta (f)	–	tossed salad
dos	–	two	enseñar	–	to teach, to show
doscientos	–	two hundred	entender	–	to understand
dudar	–	to doubt	entrar	–	to enter
dueño(a)	–	owner	entrega (f)	–	delivery
dulce	–	sweet	entrevista (f)	–	interview
dúo (m)	–	duet	escala (f)	–	scale, stop over
			escoger	–	to select
Ecuador (m)	–	the Ecuator, country in South America	escribir	–	to write
			escuchar	–	to listen
echar	–	to throw away, to pour	escuela (f)	–	school
edad (f)	–	age	escultura (f)	–	sculpture
edificio (m)	–	building	ese(a)	–	that (adj.)
ejercicio (m)	–	exercise |ése(a)	–	that (pron.)
él	–	he	esos(as)	–	those (adj.)
el	–	the (masc. sing.)	espacio (m)	–	space
elegante	–	elegant	espalda (f)	–	back of body
ella	–	she	España	–	Spain
ellas	–	they (fem.)	español	–	Spanish language
ellos	–	they (masc.)	español(a)	–	Spaniard, Spanish
emergencia (f)	–	emergency	espárrago (m)	–	asparagus
empanizado	–	breaded	especial	–	special
empezar	–	to begin	esperar	–	to wait
empleado(a)	–	employee	esposo(a)	–	husband, wife
empleo (m)	–	job	esquí (m)	–	ski
en	–	in, on	esquiar	–	to ski
en caso (de) que	–	in case	estación (f)	–	station (i.e. train station) season of the year
en cuanto	–	as soon as			
en primera	–	first class	Estados Unidos	–	United States
en punto	–	sharp, on the dot	esta	–	this (fem. adj.)
en seguida	–	right away	ésta	–	this (fem. pron.)
en segunda	–	second class	este	–	this (masc. adj.)
encantar	–	to charm	éste	–	this (masc. pron.)
encargado(a)	–	manager	extinguidor (m)	–	extinguisher
encender	–	to light	esto	–	this (neuter pron.)
encima	–	on top	estilo (m)	–	style
encontrar	–	to find	estómago (m)	–	stomach
enfermero(a)	–	nurse	estos	–	these (masc. adj.)

éstos	— these (masc. pron.)	francés(a)	— French
estrecho	— narrow	Francia	— France
estudiar	— to study	frase (f)	— phrase
Europa	— Europe	freír	— to fry
evento (m)	— event	frente (f)	— forehead, front
evidente	— evident	fresa (f)	— strawberry
evitar	— to avoid	fresco	— fresh, cool
examen (m)	— exam	frío (m)	— cold
excelente	— excellent	frito	— fried
exhibir	— to exhibit	frontera (f)	— border
excusa (f)	— excuse	fruta (f)	— fruit
éxito (m)	— success	fumar	— to smoke
explicar	— explain		
explicación	explanation	galería (f)	— gallery
exponer	— to exhibit	galleta (f)	— cracker
exposición	— show, exhibition	garaje (m)	— garage
extinguidor (m)	— extinguisher	garganta (f)	— throat
extremidad (f)	— extremity	gasolina (f)	— gasoline
		gastar	— to spend
fácil	— easy	gato(a)	— cat
falda (f)	— skirt	general	— general
faltar	— to lack, to miss	generalmente	— generally
familia (f)	— family	gente (f)	— people
farmacéutico(a)	— pharmacist	gimnástica (f)	— gymnastic
farmacia (f)	— pharmacy	ginebra (f)	— gin
fascista	— fascist	giro (m)	— money order, turn
favor (m)	— favor	góndola (f)	— gondola
febrero	— February	gordo	— fat
felicidades (f)	— congratulations	gracias	— thanks, thank you
fideo (m)	— noodle	grande	— big, large
fiesta (f)	— party	gris	— grey
final (m)	— end, final	grupo (m)	— group
firma (f)	— firm, business	guante (m)	— glove
firmar	— to sign	guaraní (m)	— monetary unit of Paraguay
flan (m)	— custard	Guatemala	— country in Central America
flor (f)	— flower	guayabera (f)	— a loose fitting shirt worn
florecer	— to bloom		in the tropics
forma (f)	— shape	guerra (f)	— war
fortuna (f)	— fortune	guía (m&f)	— guide
fotografía (f)	— photo	guitarra (f)	— guitar

gustar	–	to like	
gusto (m)	–	taste, pleasure	
haber	–	to have (auxiliary)	
habichuela (f)	–	string bean	
habitación (f)	–	room	
hablar	–	to talk	
hacer	–	to do, to make	
hambre (f)	–	hunger	
harina (f)	–	flour	
hasta	–	until (prep.)	
hasta que	–	until (connector)	
hay	–	there is, there are	
hecho (m)	–	fact	
helado (m)	–	ice cream	
hermano(a)	–	brother, sister	
hervido	–	boiled	
hígado (m)	–	liver	
hijo(a)	–	son, daughter	
Hispanoamérica	–	Spanish America	
hogar (m)	–	home	
hola	–	hello	
hombre	–	man	
hombro	–	shoulder	
Honduras	–	country in Central America	
honrado	–	honored, honest	
hora (f)	–	hour, time	
horno (m)	–	oven	
hospital (m)	–	hospital	
hotel (m)	–	hotel	
hoy	–	today	
huevo (m)	–	egg	
ida	–	one way (ticket)	
ida y vuelta	–	round trip	
idea (f)	–	idea	
identificación (f)	–	I.D., identification	
idioma (m)	–	language	
iglesia (f)	–	church	

imagen (f)	–	picture (TV), image
imaginar(se)	–	to imagine
impedir	–	to prevent
importante	–	important
importar	–	to import
impuesto (m)	–	tax
incluir	–	to include
información (f)	–	information
informar	–	to inform
inglés	–	English, British
insistir	–	to insist
inspector(a)	–	inspector
instante (m)	–	instant
inteligente	–	intelligent
intestino (m)	–	intestine
invierno (m)	–	winter
invitar	–	to invite
ir	–	to go
irse	–	to go away, to leave
Italia	–	Italy
italiano	–	Italian
jamón (m)	–	ham
jardín (m)	–	garden
jarra (f)	–	pitcher
jefe(a)	–	boss, chief
Jorge	–	George
José	–	Joseph
joven (m&f)	–	young adult, young
joya (f)	–	jewel
Juan	–	John
juego (m)	–	game
jueves	–	Thursday
jugar	–	to play (games)
jugo (m)	–	juice
juguete (m)	–	toy
julio	–	July
junio	–	June
la	–	her, you, it (fem. dir. obj. pron.)

la	–	the (fem. sing.)	luchar	–	to fight
La Paz	–	capital city of Bolivia	luego	–	later
labio (m)	–	lip	lugar	–	place
laboratorio (m)	–	laboratory	lunes	–	Monday
lado (m)	–	side	luz (f)	–	light
lana (f)	–	wool			
langosta (f)	–	lobster	llamada (f)	–	call
lápiz (m)	–	pencil	llamar(se)	–	to call
largo	–	long	llegar	–	to arrive
las	–	the (fem.pl.)	llenar	–	to fill
lástima	–	pity	llover	–	to rain
latir	–	to beat, to throb			
lavadora (f)	–	washing machine	madre	–	mother
lavar(se)	–	to wash, to wash up	Madrid	–	capital city of Spain
le	–	him, her, you (ind.obj.pron.)	magnífico	–	fine, magnificent
lección (f)	–	lesson	maíz (m)	–	corn
lectura (f)	–	reading	mal	–	bad, badly
leche (f)	–	milk	maleta (f)	–	suitcase
lechuga (f)	–	lettuce	maletín (m)	–	briefcase
leer	–	to read	malo	–	bad
legumbre (f)	–	vegetable	mamá	–	mother
lejos	–	far	mamey (m)	–	mammee, tropical fruit
lengua (f)	–	tongue, language	Managua	–	capital city of Nicaragua
león(a)	–	lion	mandar	–	to send
les	–	them, you (ind.obj.pron.)	manejar	–	to drive
libertad (f)	–	liberty, freedom	mano (f)	–	hand
libra (f)	–	pound	mantener	–	to keep, to maintain
librería (f)	–	bookstore	mantequilla (f)	–	butter
libro (m)	–	book	mantilla (f)	–	mantilla, veil
ligero	–	light, not heavy	manzana (f)	–	apple
Lima	–	capital city of Peru	mañana	–	tomorrow, morning
limón (m)	–	lime, lemon	mapa (m)	–	map
limpiar	–	to clean	marisco (m)	–	seafood
limpio	–	clean	marrón	–	reddish brown, maroon
lindo	–	pretty	martes	–	Tuesday
listo	–	smart, ready	marzo	–	March
litera (f)	–	berth	más	–	more, else
lo	–	him, you, it (masc.dir.obj. pron.)	matemática (f)	–	mathematics
			mayo	–	May
los		them, you (masc.pl.dir.obj.pron.)			

mayor	–	greater, older	muchacho(a)	–	boy, girl
me	–	me, myself	mucho	–	much
mecánico(a)	–	mechanic	mudarse	–	to move out
medianoche (f)	–	midnight, type of sandwich	muelle (m)	–	pier, wharf
medias (f)	–	stockings, socks	mujer	–	woman
medicina (f)	–	medicine, medication	muñeca (f)	–	wrist, doll
médico(a)	–	medical doctor	museo (m)	–	museum
medio	–	half	música (f)	–	music
mediodía (k)	–	noon, midday	muslo (m)	–	thigh
mejor	–	better, best	muy	–	very
melocotón	–	peach			
menor	–	younger, youngest	nada	–	nothing
menos	–	less, least	nadar	–	to swim
menú (m)	–	menu	nadie	–	noon, nobody
menudo (m)	–	small change, small, little	naranja (f)	–	orange
mercado (m)	–	market	nariz (f)	–	nose
merendar	–	to have a snack	narración (f)	–	narration
merienda	–	snack	natilla (f)	–	custard
mesa (f)	–	table	Navarra	–	province of Spain
metal (m)	–	metal	necesitar	–	to need
México or Méjico	–	Mexico	negar	–	to deny
mi	–	my	negocio (m)	–	business
mí	–	me (obj. of prep.)	negro	–	black
miedo (m)	–	fear	ni....ni	–	neither....nor
mío(a, os, as)	–	mine	ni....siquiera	–	not even
miércoles	–	Wednesday	Nicaragua	–	country in Central America
mil	–	one thousand	nieto(a)	–	grandson, granddaughter
milla (f)	–	mile	ningún (o, a)	–	none
mínimo	–	minimum	niño(a)	–	child
mirar(se)	–	to look, to look at oneself	no	–	no, not
mismo	–	some	noche (f)	–	night
modelo (m&f)	–	model	nombre (m)	–	name, noun
modesto	–	modest	noreste (m)	–	Northeast
momento (m)	–	moment	noroeste (m)	–	Northwest
moneda (f)	–	coin	norte (m)	–	North
montaña (f)	–	mountain	Norte América	–	North America
montuno (m)	–	male costume	nos	–	us, ourselves
morado	–	purple	nosotros(as)	–	we
morir	–	to die	nota (f)	–	grade (school grade)

noticia (f)	- news	padre	- father
novecientos	- nine hundred	padres (m)	- parents
novela (f)	- novel	paella (f)	- a dish of yellow rice,
noveno	- ninth		chicken, pork and seafood
noventa	- ninety	pagar	- to pay
noviembre	- November	país (m)	- country
novio(a)	- fiancé, fiancée	pan (m)	- bread
nuera	- daughter-in-law	Panamá	- country in Central America
nuestro(a, os, as)	- our	pantalla (f)	- screen
nueve	- nine	pantalón (m)	- pant
nuevo	- new	pañuelo (m)	- handkerchief
número (m)	- number	papa (f)	- potato
nunca	- never	papel (m)	- paper
		para	- for
obligar	- to oblige, to compel	para que	- in order that, so that
octavo	- eighth	parador (m)	- inn for travelers
octubre	- October	Paraguay	- country in South America
ocupación (f)	- occupation	parar(se)	- to stop, to stand up
ocupado	- occupied, busy	parecer	- to seem
ochenta	- eighty	pargo (m)	- red snapper
ochocientos	- eight hundred	París	- Paris
oeste	- West	párpado (m)	- eyelid
ofrecer	- offer	parque (m)	- park
oír	- to hear	parte (f)	- part
oficina (f)	- office	partido (m)	- game
oído (m)	- inner ear	pasado mañana	- the day after tomorrow
ojo (m)	- eye	pasar	- to pass
óleo (m)	- canvas, oil painting	pavo(a)	- turkey
olvidar(se)	- to forget	pasajero(a)	- passenger
ómnibus (m)	- bus	pasaporte (m)	- passport
once	- eleven	pasillo (m)	- hall
orden (f)	- order	pastel (m)	- pie, cake, pastry
ordenar	- to order	pecho (m)	- chest
oreja (f)	- external ear	pedir	- to ask for
origen (m)	- origin	Pedro	- Peter
oriental	- oriental	peinarse	- to comb one's hair
oscuridad (f)	- darkness, obscurity	peineta (f)	- ornamental comb
otoño (m)	- autumn, fall	pelado (m)	- haircut
otro	- other, another	pelota (f)	- ball
paciencia (f)	- patience	peluquería (f)	- beauty parlor

peluquero(a)	–	hairdresser	por	–	for, by
peor	–	worse, worst	por aquí	–	this way
pequeño	–	small, little	por favor	–	please
pera (f)	–	pear	por lo menos	–	at least
perder	–	to lose	¿por qué?	–	why?
permitir	–	to permit	portal (m)	–	porch, portal
periódico (m)	–	newspaper	posible	–	possible
pero	–	but	postre (m)	–	dessert
persona (f)	–	person	práctica	–	practical
perro(a)	–	dog	practicar	–	to practice
pertenecer	–	to belong	precaución (f)	–	precaution
pescado (m)	–	fish	precio (m)	–	price
peso (m)	–	weight, monetary unit	preferir	–	to prefer
pestaña (f)	–	eyelid	preguntar	–	to ask
pianista (m&f)	–	pianist	preocupar	–	to worry
pie (m)	–	foot	prepara	–	to prepare
piel (f)	–	skin, leather, hide	presentación (f)	–	presentation
pierna (f)	–	leg	presentar	–	to introduce, to present
pimentero (m)	–	pepper shaker	presidente(a)	–	president
pimienta (f)	–	pepper	prestar	–	to lend
pingüino (m)	–	penguin	prevenir	–	to prevent
pintar	–	to paint	primavera (f)	–	Spring
piscina (f)	–	swimming pool	primero	–	first
placer (m)	–	pleasure	primo(a)	–	cousin
planilla (f)	–	application, form	prisa (f)	–	the act of being in a hurry
plato (m)	–	dish, plate	probable	–	probable
playa (f)	–	beach	probar	–	to taste, to try on, to
plazo (m)	–	term, payment			prove
pluma (f)	–	pen, feather	profesor(a)	–	professor
pobre	–	poor	programa (m)	–	program
poco	–	little, not enough	prohibir	–	to prohibit
policía (m&f)	–	policeman-woman, police force	prometer	–	to promise
política (f)	–	politics	pronto	–	soon, right away
pollera (f)	–	colorful skirt	pronunciar	–	to pronounce
pollo (m)	–	chicken	propio	–	own
poner(se)	–	to put, to place, to put on	proteger	–	to protect
poner la mesa	–	to set the table	provecho (m)	–	benefit profit
popular	–	popular	provincia (f)	–	province

próximo	–	next	
pueblo	–	hamlet, town, people	
puerco (m)	–	pork	
puerta (f)	–	door	
puesto (m)	–	job, position	
pulmón (m)	–	lung	
punto (m)	–	point, dot	
puré (m)	–	puree	
puré de papas (m)	–	mashed potatoes	
¿qué?	–	what?	
que	–	what	
¡qué lástima!	–	what a pity	
quedarse	–	to remain	
querer	–	to want, to love	
queso (m)	–	cheese	
¿quién(es)?	–	who?	
quince	–	fifteen	
quinientos	–	five hundred	
quinto	–	fifth	
quitarse	–	to take off	
Quito	–	capital city of Ecuador	
quizás	–	maybe	
radio (m)	–	radio set	
radio (f)	–	radio transmission	
radio reloj (m)	–	clock radio	
rápido	–	quick, fast	
rato (m)	–	while	
razón (f)	–	reason	
rebozado	–	basted	
recado (m)	–	message	
receta (f)	–	prescription, recipe	
recepción (f)	–	reception	
recepcionista (m&f)	–	receptionist	
recibo (m)	–	receipt	
recomendar	–	to recommend	
recordar	–	to remember	
refresco (m)	–	refreshment	
regalo (m)	–	present	

regresar	–	to return, to go back
reírse	–	to laugh
relación (f)	–	relation
reloj (m)	–	watch, clock
relleno (m)	–	stuffing
remuneración (f)	–	remuneration, pay
renta (f)	–	rent
repetir	–	to repeat
República Dominicana	–	Dominican Republic
requisito (m)	–	requisite, requirement
reservación (f)	–	reservation
resolver	–	to solve
respirar	–	to breathe
responder	–	to answer
responsable	–	responsible
respuesta (f)	–	answer
restaurante (m)	–	restaurant
resto (m)	–	rest
retrasado	–	late
revista (f)	–	magazine
revolver	–	to stir
rey	–	king
rico	–	rich
riñón (m)	–	kidney
rodilla (f)	–	knee
rojo	–	red
Roma	–	Rome
romper	–	to break
ropa (f)	–	clothes, clothing
rosa (f)	–	rose
rosado	–	pink
ruana (f)	–	poncho
rubio	–	blond
sábado	–	Saturday
saber	–	to know
sacar	–	to take out, to extract
sal (f)	–	salt
sala (f)	–	living room
salchicha (f)	–	sausage

salero (m)	– salt shaker	silla (f)	– chair
salida (f)	– exit, departure	simpático	– nice, pleasant, witty
salir	– to leave, to go out	sin que	– without (connector)
salud (f)	– health	sobrino(a)	– nephew (niece)
Santiago	– capital city of Chile	socialista (m&f)	– socialist
sarape (m)	– Mexican heavy shawl	sociedad (f)	– society
saya (f)	– skirt	solamente	– only
se	– reflexive pronoun	solicitante (m&f)	– applicant
sección (f)	– section	solicitud (f)	– application
secretario(a)	– secretary	solo	– alone
sed (f)	– thirst	sólo	– only
seguir	– to follow	soltero(a)	– single person
segundo (m)	– second (part of a minute)	sombrero (m)	– hat
seguro (m)	– insurance, sure	sonrisa (f)	– smile
seis	– six	sopa (f)	– soup
seiscientos	– six hundred	sorpresa (f)	– surprise
selección (f)	– selection	sorprender	– to surprise
seleccionar	– to choose, to select	su(s)	– your (formal), his, her, its
semáforo (m)	– traffic light	sucio	– dirty
semana (f)	– week	sudamérica	– South America
senado (m)	– senate	subir	– to climb, to raise
sentarse	– to sit down	sucre (m)	– monetary unit of Ecuador
sentir	– to feel	sueldo (m)	– salary
señor	– Mr., Sir	sueño (m)	– dream, the feeling of being
señora	– Mrs. lady		sleepy
señorita	– Miss, young lady	suegro(a)	– father in law, mother in law
septiembre	– September	suerte (f)	– luck
séptimo	– seventh	sufrir	– to suffer
ser	– to be	sugerir	– to suggest
servilleta (f)	– napkin	Suiza	– Switzerland
servir	– to serve	sur (m)	– South
sesenta	– sixty	sureste (m)	– southeast
setecientos	– seven hundred	suroeste (m)	– southwest
setenta	– seventy	suyo (a, os, as)	– yours (formal), his, hers,
sexto	– sixty		theirs
si	– it	tal vez	– maybe
sí	– yes	talla (f)	– size
siempre	– always	también	– also
siete	– seven	tambor (m)	– drum
siglo (m)	– century	tamborito (m)	– typical dance

tampoco	–	not either, neither	torre (f)	–	tower
tan + adj. or adv. + como	–	as soon as	tostada (f)	–	toast (bread)
tan pronto (como)	–	as soon as	trabajar	–	to work
tanto	–	as much	trabajo (m)	–	job, work
tanto (a, os, as)...como	–	as much (as many)...as	traducir	–	to translate
tarde (f)	–	afternoon, late	traer	–	to bring
tarea (f)	–	homework	traje (m)	–	suit
tarjeta (f)	–	card	traje de baño (m)	–	bathing suit
taza (f)	–	cup	tratar	–	to try
te	–	you, yourself (fam)	tratarse	–	to deal with
té (m)	–	tea	trece	–	thirteen
teatro (m)	–	theatre	treinta	–	thirty
teléfono (m)	–	telephone	tren (m)	–	train
temer	–	to fear	tres	–	three
tener	–	to have	trescientos	–	three hundred
tenedor (m)	–	fork	triste	–	sad
tenis (m)	–	tennis	tronco (m)	–	trunk
tercero	–	third	tu(s)	–	your (fam.)
terminar	–	to end, to finish	turista (m&f)	–	tourist
terraza (f)	–	terrace	turno (m)	–	appointment, turn
tiempo (m)	–	time	tuyo (a, os, as)	–	yours (fam.)
tienda (f)	–	store			
tierra (f)	–	earth, soil, land	único	–	only, unique
tijeras (f)	–	scissors	un (o, a)	–	one
tío(a)	–	uncle, aunt	un (os, as)	–	some
tinto	–	red, (wine)	Uruguay	–	country in South America
tirar	–	to throw	urgente	–	urgent
toalla (f)	–	towel	usar	–	to use, to wear
tobillo (m)	–	ankle	usted(es)	–	you
tocino (m)	–	bacon	uva (f)	–	grape
tocino del cielo (m)	–	type of custard			
todavía	–	yet	vacaciones (f)	–	vacation
todo	–	all	vacuna (f)	–	vaccine
todo el mundo	–	everybody	vainilla (f)	–	vanilla
todas las semanas	–	every week	valer	–	to be worth
tomar	–	to take	valor	–	value
tomate (m)	–	tomato	varios	–	various, several
toronja (f)	–	grapefruit	vaso (m)	–	glass
tortilla (f)	–	omelet	vecino(a)	–	neighbor

veinte	–	twenty
vejiga (f)	–	bladder
vender	–	to sell
venezolano(a)	–	venezuelan
venir	–	to come
venta (f)	–	sale
ventana (f)	–	window
ventanilla (f)	–	small window (car, train, airplane, etc.)
ventilador (m)	–	electric fan
ver	–	to see
verano	–	summer
verbo (m)	–	verb
verdad (f)	–	truth
verde	–	green
vertical	–	vertical
vesícula (f)	–	gall bladder
veterinario(a)	–	veterinary
vestido (m)	–	dress
vestirse	–	to get dressed
vez (f)	–	turn, time
viajar	–	to travel
viaje (m)	–	trip
vida (f)	–	life
viejo	–	old
vientre (m)	–	abdomen
viernes	–	Friday
vino (m)	–	wine
visitar	–	to visit
viudo(a)	–	widower, widow
vivaracho	–	full of life
vivir	–	to live
volver	–	to return
vuelo (m)	–	flight
ya	–	already
yarda (f)	–	yard
yerno	–	son in law
yo	–	I
zapato (m)	–	shoe